Handbook of Counselling
in Organizations

Handbook of Counselling in Organizations

edited by

Michael Carroll and Michael Walton

SAGE Publications
London • Thousand Oaks • New Delhi

Introduction © Michael Carroll and Michael Walton 1997
Chapters 1 and 9 © Michael Carroll 1997
Chapter 2 © Andrew Bull 1997
Chapter 3 © Noreen Tehrani 1997
Chapter 4 © Geetu Orme 1997
Chapter 5 © Michael Reddy 1997
Chapters 6 and 8 © Michael Walton 1997
Chapter 7 © Michèle Deverall 1997
Chapter 10 © John Towler 1997
Chapter 11 © Catherine Shea and Tim Bond 1997
Chapters 12 and 16 © Carolyn Highley-Marchington and
Cary L. Cooper 1997
Chapter 13 © Catherine Carroll 1997
Chapter 14 © Peter Martin 1997
Chapter 15 © Annette Greenwood 1997
Chapter 17 © Helen Fisher 1997
Chapter 18 © John Nixon 1997
Chapter 19 © Eileen Pickard 1997
Chapter 20 © Brigid Proctor 1997

First published 1997

SAGE Publications Ltd
6 Bonhill Street
London EC2A 4PU

SAGE Publications Inc.
2455 Teller Road
Thousand Oaks, California 91320

SAGE Publications India Pvt Ltd
32, M-Block Market
Greater Kailash – I
New Delhi 110 048

British Library Cataloguing in Publication data

A catalogue record for this book is available
from the British Library.

ISBN 0 7619 5086 9
ISBN 0 7619 5087 7 (pbk)

Library of Congress catalog card number 96-072192

Typeset by Mayhew Typesetting, Rhayader, Powys
Printed in Great Britain by The Cromwell Press Ltd,
Broughton Gifford, Melksham, Wiltshire

Contents

Contributors' Notes

Tim Bond is a Staff Tutor in Counselling at the University of Durham and a former chairperson of the British Association for Counselling (BAC) (1994–96) and Fellow of BAC. His publications include *Standards and Ethics for Counselling in Action* (1993) and other books and articles on professional issues associated with counselling and multidisciplinary work.

Andrew Bull, MSc (Counselling Psychology), was formerly a lecturer in counselling at the University of Birmingham. He has worked in the NHS, and in industry where he set up an Employee Assistance Programme for Lucas Industries. He has published on the subject of counselling in the workplace. Andrew has a private counselling and supervision practice.

Michael Carroll, PhD, is a chartered counselling psychologist and former Director of Studies in Psychology and Counselling at Roehampton Institute London. He is presently Director of Counselling and Training with Cavendish Partners, an outplacement firm in London. His main focus of interest at present is working with organizations to set up effective provision for employee care.

Catherine Carroll is a BAC accredited counsellor who initially trained as a general and community nurse. Subsequently she gained a diploma in counselling and psychotherapy, a certificate in art therapy and an MSc in counselling psychology. Latterly she was the in-house Employee Counsellor for Shell International, developing a comprehensive confidential service for staff and their families, running a range of workshops in related areas, especially stress management. She is now self-employed.

Cary L. Cooper is currently Professor of Organizational Psychology in the Manchester School of Management, and Pro-Vice-Chancellor (External Activities) of the University of Manchester Institute of Science and Technology (UMIST). He is the author of over 70 books (on occupational stress, women at work and industrial and organizational psychology), has written over 250 scholarly articles for academic journals, and is a frequent contributor to national newspapers, television and radio. He is currently Editor-in-Chief of the *Journal of Organizational Behavior*, Co-Editor of the medical journal *Stress Medicine*, and Fellow of the British Psychological Society, the Royal Society of Arts and the Royal Society of Medicine. Professor Cooper was also the Founding President of the British Academy of Management, and is currently Chair of the Higher Education Funding Council's Panel for the Research Assessment Exercise of all UK business and management schools.

Michèle Deverall, BSc (Hons) Sociology, MSc (Econ) Industrial Relations and Personnel Management, MSc Psychological Counselling, developed a career in human resource management, management development and management consultancy in the UK and USA for organizations such as Arthur Andersen, Price Waterhouse and the Swiss Bank Corporation. For the past seven years she has built up her own practice as a psychotherapist/coach operating within the corporate world. Most clients are senior personnel within their own organizations. Her early career experience included the John Lewis Partnership as a management trainee, the Metropolitan Police Force as a police officer (Fraud and Vice Squads among her postings) and a period as a lecturer in Higher Education.

Helen Fisher is a practising Workplace Counsellor and Manager of an NHS Staff Counselling Service. Her chapter represents a summary of the research study presented in her MA in counselling studies at Keele University. Her special interests are in the causes of workplace stress and the provision of appropriate interventions, providing a holistic approach to counselling and welfare services for NHS staff. These include training strategies, debriefing, ono-to-one counselling and peer support networks.

Annette Greenwood is a counselling psychologist and is a senior member of an NHS EAP team providing a staff counselling service to many of the NHS Trusts within the Trent Regional Health Authority. Her research areas include workplace health, post traumatic stress and psychological debriefing. She is currently writing a book, *Workplace Counselling*, to be published by the Open University as part of the Counselling in Context series.

Carolyn Highley-Marchington has a first degree in psychology and a master's degree in occupational psychology and has also worked in personnel management with Marks and Spencer. She conducted the first nationwide independent assessment and evaluation of British Workplace Counselling Programmes, for the Health and Safety Executive, and now runs her own consultancy, the Highley-Marchington Consultancy, providing independent information and advice in the area of work stress and workplace counselling, as well as audit and evaluation services for Employee Assistance Programmes and Workplace Counselling Programmes.

Peter Martin, MA (Ed), MSc (Psychological Counselling), is a freelance management trainer and consultant. He also runs a private counselling practice and contributes to Employee Assistance Programmes. He specializes in training and counselling on stress and performance management and has an interest and expertise in stress audits. He has a wide background in the educational field and in management contexts.

John Nixon works as a consultant, counsellor and facilitator. His consultancy practice, Countdown UK Ltd, provides a range of personal and management development services mainly to commercial and corporate organizations. With extensive experience in advertising and marketing, he specializes in making ethical use of counselling psychology within the sales and marketing functions.

His focus is increasingly with line managers and staff whose employers are looking for major changes in customer facing attitudes, processes and skills.

Geetu Orme is an independent counsellor, trainer and consultant. She manages Forward, a consultancy in Nether Alderley, Cheshire, which specializes in change management, career counselling and a range of tailor-made programmes to help organizations change positively. Geetu is a trained Workplace Counsellor, a Business Practitioner in Neuro Linguistic Programming (NLP) and a registered member of the Institute of Personnel and Development (MIPD). She is currently developing workshop materials in the areas of advanced facilitation skills, group management and encouraging ownership through change, and her specific interest lies in skills transfer.

Eileen Pickard is a chartered counselling psychologist and is Manager of Consultancy and Training at Roehampton Institute London. She is also a consultant to TDA Consulting Ltd. She initiated and developed Roehampton Institute's Psychology and Counselling Department and a range of programmes in counselling, including organizational counselling. She was the British Psychological Society's representative on the Advice, Guidance, Counselling and Psychotherapy Lead Body. Currently, she develops training and organizational development programmes for a range of organizations. Her research and publications are in creativity, training and organizational counselling.

Brigid Proctor, since retiring as Director of Counselling Courses at South West London College in 1987, has worked as a freelance counsellor and supervisor and as consultant to supervisors, trainers and counsellors. She is also a trainer and writer. With Francesca Inskipp she has developed supervisee and supervisor training and training resources, publishing most recently *The Art, Craft and Tasks of Counselling Supervision*, Part 1 (1993) and Part 2 (1995). Together they formed CASCADE Training Associates. Formerly a member of the BAC Executive and first Convenor/Chair of both the Standards and Ethics and Training Sub-Committees, she is now a Fellow of BAC, as well as an Accredited Supervisor. She supervises counsellors working in a variety of statutory, voluntary and business organizations.

Michael Reddy has been a prominent figure in the counselling world for many years, through his writing and through his support for professional standards and institutions. He is particularly influential in the promotion and acceptance of workplace counselling. He is now Chairman of the company he formed in the mid-1980s, ICAS (Independent Counselling and Advisory Services).

Catherine Shea, a lecturer in counselling at the University of Durham, started her professional life in social work, going on to train and work as a counsellor in a variety of contexts – marriage, student and drug/alcohol counselling in particular. She has also pursued further academic study at various levels in the areas of literature and theology. Her current research interests draw on both these elements of her experience. She is currently writing on the use of 'self' in qualitative research and on the interface between theatre and therapy

Noreen Tehrani is a chartered occupational and counselling psychologist working as the head of the Post Office's Employee Support Service. Noreen has had a varied career working as a medical researcher in the NHS, in industry as an operations manager, as a marital counsellor with Relate and as a director of an Employee Assistance Programme. Noreen has combined her commercial, psychological and counselling knowledge and experience to develop services for the Post Office that meet the needs of both the organization and its employees. Noreen's special interests include trauma care, burnout, bullying and harassment and stress auditing.

John Towler, PGCEA, DipHonsPsych, is a freelance counselling therapist, supervisor and trainer, primarily in organizational settings. Trained as a priest, he has worked as director of a counselling service and senior lecturer at a tertiary college. He is a consultant for Humanitas, and an associate lecturer for the Roehampton Institute, London.

Michael Walton, PhD, is Director of People in Organisations Ltd, an organization and management development consultancy practice. Most of his work is focused on personal and organizational change. A chartered occupational and a chartered counselling psychologist, Michael was trained at Birkbeck College, University of London, and at the Regent's College School of Psychotherapy and Counselling. Michael is an Associate of Ashridge Management College.

List of Figures

List of Tables

Acknowledgements

We would like to thank all the people, and the people behind the people, who have contributed to this *Handbook*. Principally our thanks go to those who wrote the chapters and met deadlines and our quest for perfection through rewrites. Susan Worsey was enthusiastic about the book and continued to encourage us throughout its preparation – our thanks to her and the staff at Sage. And finally, we separate to thank and dedicate the book respectively to:

For Michael Carroll: To Phil, Maggie, Mary, Pat, Oliver, Joe, Eugene, Sean, Phyllis and Tony who provided the original 'organization' within which this book was implicitly written. And to Cathy, who inherited the original family, and provided the immediate family.

For Michael Walton: To the boys Chris and Justin, not forgetting Sandy. Most of all to Frances. And for Dinky Payne, a special person from way way back. I owe a special thanks to Cathy Carroll who was the person who first brought us two Michaels together.

Introduction

Michael Carroll and Michael Walton

The vast literature on counselling in general has been overwhelming in its support for the 'relationship' as a crucial ingredient in therapeutic change (Clarkson, 1995; Orlans, 1996). Many training courses in counselling, building on this belief, have structured their curricula accordingly. Trainee counsellors are taught how to set up, maintain and terminate relationships with clients. Much of that training, whether specific or generic skills, theories from counselling and cognate subjects and personal development, revolves around helping future counsellors relate in ways that help their clients change.

While it is right that such relationships be at the heart of both counselling and counselling training, what is often missed are the values of the administrative and organizational dimensions of counselling (Carroll, 1996). Managing the counselling process, setting up a counselling provision, negotiating how to implement counselling in an already existing organization, understanding and working with the organizations that 'house' the counselling services tend to feature little on training courses. These elements, when given importance, are seen as what counsellors learn once they begin their lives as professional counsellors. Unfortunately, by that time, it is too late. They do learn, eventually, but often learn by default, or by mistake. Understanding that there is more to counselling than what happens in the counselling room enables counsellors to have an eye and perspectives on the 'contexts' in which the counselling takes place.

This book is about those contexts. Counselling is never private. Personal, yes, private, no. Even when confidentiality has been negotiated clearly, even when these two individuals (counsellor and client) meet regularly alone, the context in which they meet, and the contexts to which they return once they have met, influences what happens between them. The counselling room is filled with other individuals, and with the systems, groups and organizations that are part of the lives of both participants. It is those influences, listening to them, isolating them, understanding them, managing them, that provide the focus for this book.

The understanding of counselling considered here is not about counselling in a particular context, though the workplace is undoubtedly the environment most considered, but about an awareness that the vigilant counsellor must keep an eye on the various environments in which counselling occurs. Not to recognize and work with the context in which counselling takes place is to ignore the enormous impact that context has on behaviour. One of the signs of mental illness (or eccentricity or rebellion) is to ignore context, and to behave in one setting as if it were similar to another, for example those who see no difference between making love in the privacy of their homes and making love in a busy airport have ignored the significance of context. Context determines what is appropriate, what is acceptable behaviour, how one dresses, what one says, what language is used, and of course, relationships. Even though behaviours may be the same, the individuals may be similar, the context can change what is perfectly acceptable behaviour into a criminal act, an insult, or unprofessional behaviour.

Counselling takes place within a certain environment that influences what happens, both consciously and unconsciously. This book is about one of those contexts: the organizational setting in which counselling takes place. When an organization pays a counsellor to work with its employees, it has already established a context and a relationship that is part of the counselling. The effect of this is to raise questions, doubts and ambiguities such as:

1   How will the organization view those who come for counselling – officially and unofficially?
2   Will involvement in counselling affect career?
3   Who, in the organization, will know what people have been for counselling?
4   Will counselling be used by managers to get rid of people, to give them bad news, punish them or get them to conform?
5   What information about clients will be shared with whom?
6   How will the organization receive feedback from the counselling service?
7   Will the counsellor/s be seen as part of the organization and how will this affect their credibility?
8   What will happen if counsellors have divided loyalties between the client and the organization?

More and more organizations, both private and public, are hosting counselling services: almost all universities and Colleges of Higher Education maintain a counselling service, a number of private companies have introduced counselling for their employees, staff counselling in the National Health Service has increased rapidly over the past five years and the number of Employee Assistance Programmes on offer to interested organizations is still rising. It may well be that more people in Britain are being counselled as a result of counselling schemes set up by an organization of which they are a part (employee, customer, member of the public) than are being counselled because they pay for it in a private counselling setting. While this is admirable – individuals having access to counselling for which an organization pays – what we know little about is the influence which that specific organization has or may have on counselling provision. Furthermore, it is worth considering why organizations wish to set up counselling provision for others.

Counselling within an organization inevitably entails the meeting of two worlds, the world of the organization itself and the world of counselling. Orlans (1996) has pointed out some of the differences between these worlds:

Table 1   *The worlds of organizations and counselling*

World of organizations	World of counselling
controlling	helping
objective experience	subjective experience
thinking (rational)	feeling and thinking
hierarchical	autonomous
political	personal empowerment
competitive	cooperative

the differences may not pertain in all organizations. Table 1 uses her work to summarize some of them.

The possibility of clashes between the values of both systems highlights the need for clear negotiations before counselling is set up in an organization and the ongoing need for continual discussion when issues emerge. Each world, understanding the other, allows for integration rather than separation. However, not many counsellors are trained to understand the world of organizations: some are even ideologically opposed to practices within some organizations, for example profit-making.

Counsellors who work in organizational settings need to understand the dynamics at work within organizations. Egan (1994) has alluded to the 'shadow-side' of organizations and the power it plays in decision-making; Pfeiffer (1994) has pointed out how managing the workforce can be a powerful element in competitive advantage; Harrison (1972) has suggested that different corporate cultures dictate what behaviours take place in organizations; and Kets de Vries and Miller (1984) have shown how pathology can be as much a part of organizational structures as of individual lives. Working with these elements is part-and-parcel of counsellors' lives when they work within an organizational context. It has to be if they are to understand and work with their clients, and those responsible for funding the counselling service.

Alongside these are the professional and ethical aspects of working in organizations. Strawbridge and Woolfe talk about the need to take a sociological perspective on counselling 'locating it within the social, economic and political structure in which it takes place and of which it is a part' (1996: 608). Ethically this means that counsellors have to consider how counselling in organizations is being used by these same organizations to avoid their responsibilities. It is all too easy to individualize problems and make the person responsible for what an organization is doing. Understanding and managing stress is such an example. All too easily counsellors can be seduced into helping individuals manage stress in their lives (as if these individuals were totally responsible for managing stress) while ignoring the impact of the organization which is unreasonably putting extra stress on employees. Indeed, when does the organization need help, rather than the individual (Clarkson, 1990)? When should the counsellors feed back to the organization issues of injustice, unfairness, abuse, poor management that results in personal problems for employees and the need for structures and policies in key areas? These are important matters which demand more consideration and debate.

There is no doubt that there is more awareness of counselling provision within organizational settings. A new series of books is presently being prepared, some already published, entitled 'Counselling in Context'. Each book reviews a particular context in which counselling is used. Some titles have already been published, for example *Counselling in the Voluntary Sector, Counselling in Independent Practice, Counselling for Women, Counselling in Medical Settings* and *Counselling for Young People*. Applied to the workplace, titles have begun to emerge on what this new type of counsellor might be called and several suggestions have been made: 'organizational counselling psychologist' (Gerstein and Shullman, 1992), occupational counsellor, employee counsellors. 'Sociotherapist' (Whiteley et al., 1973: as quoted in Clarkson and Porkorny, 1994) has been coined as a phrase to show the connections between counselling and other social role demands on counsellors in organizations. What these new books and the range of suggested new titles indicate is the growing acknowledgement of the need to consider the role and dynamics of counselling in organizations. It is not the same as transporting one's private counselling practice and relocating it within an organization. It is significantly different as we hope this book will show.

The contents, therefore, are for those who are employed, or hope to be employed, by organizations (private, public or voluntary). These organizations could be educational or medical, religious or civil, private or public, dedicated to making money or charities. Each in its own way will influence the counselling provision differently. The book will also be helpful to managers in organizations who are thinking about introducing counselling for employees or customers.

These are some of the issues that this book hopes to highlight and investigate. The primary aim is to review the interface between the individual client, the counsellor who is employed by an organization and the organization itself. Ignoring the needs of any of these participants can result in a breakdown of the whole system: a key step in averting this is to consider the range and extent of the dimensions covered by the many contributors to the book. Each has something interesting to say.

References

Carroll, M. (1996) *Workplace Counselling: A Systematic Approach to Employee Care*. London: Sage.

Clarkson, P. (1990) 'The scope of stress counselling in organisations', *Employee Counselling Today*, 2 (4): 3–6.

Clarkson, P. (1995) *The Therapeutic Relationship*. London: Whurr.

Clarkson, P. and Pokorny, M. (eds) (1994) *The Handbook of Psychotherapy*. London: Routledge.

Egan, G. (1994) *Working the Shadow-side: A Guide to Positive Behind the Scenes Management*. San Francisco: Jossey-Bass.

Gerstein, L.W. and Shullman, S.L. (1992) 'Counseling psychology and the workplace: the emergence of organizational counseling psychology', in R. Brown and R.W. Lent (eds), *The Handbook of Counseling Psychology*. (2nd Edition). New York: Wiley. pp. 581–625.

Harrison, R. (1972) 'Understanding your organization's character', *Harvard Business Review*, 50 (23): 119–28.

Kets de Vries, F.R. and Miller, D. (1984) *The Neurotic Organization*. San Francisco: Jossey-Bass.

Orlans, V. (1996) 'Counselling psychology in the workplace', in R. Woolfe and W. Dryden (eds), *Handbook of Counselling Psychology*. London: Sage. pp. 485–504.

Pfeiffer, J. (1994) *Competitive Advantage through People*. Boston: Harvard Business Press.

Strawbridge, S. and Woolfe, R. (1996) 'Counselling psychology: a sociological perspective', in R. Woolfe and W. Dryden (eds) *Handbook of Counselling Psychology*. London: Sage. pp. 605–29.

Whiteley, J.S., Briggs, D. and Turner, M. (1973) *Dealing with Deviants*. London: Hogarth.

PART 1

MODELS OF COUNSELLING IN ORGANIZATIONS

The five chapters in Part 1 concentrate on understanding counselling within organizations, particularly the workplace. They present together ways of thinking about and introducing counselling into organizations. Michael Carroll draws together the many strands of counselling in organizations and presents them under 10 headings. Each could be considered on its own and together they present an overview of the 'state of the art' in counselling in organizations. This chapter offers a springboard from which Andrew Bull considers various models of counselling in organizations. He takes two in particular and applies them to employee counselling, and in doing so offers a paradigm not just about how particular counselling orientations can work within an organization, but also how each needs to be adapted to the organization which hosts it. The final three chapters are written by Noreen Tehrani, Geetu Orme and Michael Reddy, all experienced counsellors who have set up and introduced counselling into organizations from different perspectives. Noreen has headed the employee support system within the Post Office and is an expert in understanding and working with an internal counselling provision. Geetu Orme has been a 'freelance workplace counsellor' who reviews the issues involved in working with organizations from an individual perspective and offers a range of hints and suggestions on how to do so effectively. Michael Reddy, on the other hand, has long experience in running one of the major EAP (Employee Assistance Programme) providers in Britain and considers in some detail the issues involved in offering counselling 'from outside' the organization.

1

Counselling in Organizations: An Overview

Michael Carroll

> Of all the things that characterize the organizational and business work of the nineties, change comes first. Counselling theory and practice is based on a model of managing change. It is only a matter of time before counsellors will be acknowledged as offering models not only of individual, but of organizational change. (Reddy, 1993: 99)

A survey of the literature on counselling in organizational settings, whether that setting is industrial, educational, medical, voluntary, public or private, reveals surprisingly few texts that deal with the organizational dimensions of the work, surprisingly, because counselling, in one form or another, has been taking place in various organizations since the early 1900s. While there is an increasing amount of publications dealing with counselling in particular organizations (for example, Summerfield and Van Oudtshoorn, 1995; Carroll, 1996b, on workplace counselling; Cowie and Pecherek, 1994 and Cowie and Sharp, 1996, on counselling in education; Rowland, 1989 and East, 1994, on counselling in medical environments), what seems to be missing from the literature is a concern with how each organization impacts on counselling provision and how counselling services can be 'tailor-made' to fit different organizations.

When particular organizations set up counselling provision, there are four different counselling arrangements:

1   For their employees. Workplace counselling is increasing: more and more companies, both within the private and public sectors, are paying counsellors to work with their employees. Counselling provision can take the form of either in-house counselling, where counsellors are also employees of the organization, or external provision where Employee Assistance Programmes (EAPs) provide counselling.
2   For their consumers. Most Higher Educational establishments, for example, run counselling services for their students.
3   For members of the public. For example, a local authority funds a Youth Counselling Agency. Here, young people up to a certain age can refer themselves, or be referred, for counselling that is paid for by the local authority.
4   Specifically to engage in counselling. As a counselling agency it offers counselling that is either paid for by its private customers or by some other group, for example doctors, local authorities, etc.

While each of these arrangements has its own specific dynamics and relationships, this chapter will concentrate on the first three, and in particular the first, where employers offer a counselling service to employees. In all three instances an organization chooses to arrange a counselling provision and to fund that counselling.

A number of authors have struggled with the issue of whether or not workplace counselling can justifiably be called 'counselling' in the professional sense of the word (Reddy, 1987; Megranahan, 1989a, 1989b; Carroll and Holloway, 1993; Pickard, 1993; Nixon and Carroll, 1994; Nixon, this volume). The Institute of Personnel Management's *Statement on Counselling in the Workplace* begins with 'Much workplace counselling is not counselling in the modern definition of the term but relates to situations which require the use of counselling skills' (1992: 1). Applied to members of the organization such as managers, personnel officers, human resource personnel, it makes sense that they integrate counselling skills into their already established role/s with people in the organization. But there is also a place for the professional employee counsellor whose task is to set up and maintain therapeutic working alliances with members of an organization.

This chapter will offer an overview of counselling in organizations under 10 headings:

1   Literature on counselling in organizations.
2   Understanding counselling in organizations.
3   The strengths and weaknesses of various types of counselling provision in organizations.
4   Conflicts between the values of organizations and those of counselling.
5   The roles and responsibilities of counsellors in organizations.
6   The impact of organizations on counselling provision.
7   Managing counselling in organizations.
8   Ethical issues in counselling in organizations.
9   Research on counselling in organizations.
10   Training for counsellors who work in organizations.

Literature on Counselling in Organizations

There are few literary resources that deal exclusively with counselling in organizations. Those that do so (Lewis and Lewis, 1986; Reddy, 1987; Megranahan, 1989a; Tehrani, 1994, 1995) often dwell on introducing counselling skills, setting up employee support systems in a particular organization or dealing with specific problem areas, but do not cover substantially the issues and demands of introducing counselling provision into an organization. Not only is this the case for introducing counselling, but there is little to be found on assessing organizations for counselling, matching counselling provision to organizational culture, contracting for counselling within an

organization, evaluating counselling, publicizing counselling in an organization, or terminating counselling within an organization. Only recently have
some of these begun to be considered. Deverall (this volume) offers a method
of assessing organizations and Summerfield and Van Oudtshoorn (1995)
suggest a similar methodology. Carroll (1996b) has outlined a six-stage model
of preparing for, assessing, contracting, introducing, terminating and
evaluating counselling with individuals within an organization and applying
a similar model to counselling in organizations. Bull (1995) has published a
short document to give purchasers and providers guidelines on workplace
counselling. Much work still needs to be done on all of these areas.

The aims and objectives of introducing counselling into organizational
settings is still unclear. There seems to be some kind of unwritten agreement
that such counselling is valuable and its objectives obvious. The latter is far
from the case. We are still uncertain about how to relate organizational aims,
policies and procedures to the purposes and objectives of counselling. There is
little material on the actual impact which various organizational cultures have
on counselling provision and there is no agreement on what actually constitutes counselling in organizations. Madonia concludes from his review on
workplace counselling that 'despite a substantial bibliography on the subject,
close analysis shows that the employee assistance and occupational mental
health literature is primarily anecdotal' (1985: 588).

A recent book by Summerfield and Van Oudtshoorn (1995) focuses on
counselling skills in the workplace and is written primarily for personnel and
human resource managers who want to integrate counselling into their already
existing work. Carroll's (1996b) is one of the few British books that looks at
professional counselling in organizations. A new book entitled 'Counselling at
Work' is being written in the forthcoming 'Counselling in Context' series
(Greenwood, forthcoming). These contributions have opened up areas for
discussion about the differences between professional counselling and the use
of counselling skills and the relationship between counselling and the allied
roles of mentoring, appraisal and, indeed, organizational development.

Some attempts have been made to apply particular counselling approaches
to counselling in organizations (Gray, 1984a, 1984b; Gordon and Dryden,
1989; Hay, 1989; Sanders, 1990; Webb, 1990) but these have dwelt mostly
with the values of the counselling approach rather than concentrating on the
interface between the counselling orientation and the workplace itself.
Summerfield and Van Oudtshoorn (1995) have reviewed briefly six counselling theories and looked at their usefulness/non-usefulness in the workplace
(on p. 86, for example, they consider Rogerian counselling is useful in
creating new relationships and promoting respect, empathy and genuineness
but not useful in that it is not focused on short-term problem-solving, is
entirely client-led and uses open-ended contracts). Though too brief to do
full justice to different counselling orientations, their work highlights the
need critically to evaluate counselling models as they adapt to workplace
counselling.

Most counsellors who use particular counselling approaches apply their
counselling theory within organizations in the same way as they do when

practising independently. There is some understanding of how organizations are assessed using a particular counselling model: for example Kets de Vries and Miller (1984) and Hirschhorn and Barnett (1993) have used a psycho-analytic approach to designate different types of organization; Critchley and Casey (1989) have applied the Gestalt model to explain how organizations get stuck at various levels of their development; Stein and Hollwitz (1992) have looked at organizations through a Jungian perspective; and Morris (1993) has adapted Rational Emotive Therapy as a paradigm for organizations. However, most counselling orientations do not have such a typology. Their main interest is still focused almost exclusively on individuals and the organizational dimensions of counselling work are largely ignored.

Understanding Counselling in Organizations

To date there is no theoretical basis to counselling in organizational settings. There is no text that struggles with what types of counselling are best suited to organizational counselling or that evaluates the various counselling models *vis-à-vis* application to particular organizations and settings (Carroll, 1996b). Short-term counselling work is continually suggested as the main focus of workplace counselling (C. Carroll, 1994), but what kind of short-term counselling? Ought it to be psychodynamic (and indeed there is quite a recent literature on the use of short-term psychodynamic counselling/psychotherapy), humanistic, cognitive-behavioural, systemic, or integrative? All of these have much to contribute to counselling at large, but their application to organizations is left to the individual allegiances of particular counsellors rather than to a studied and prepared application of which counselling models are most suited to which organizations – not, indeed, that it is suggested here that there is one model of counselling that exceeds others in effectiveness when applied to organizations.

What is the precise aim of counselling with employees, and how is that aim perhaps different from counsellors working in private practice? Yeager (1983) is very definite that counselling in an organizational setting is different from counselling in other contexts: '. . . for a practitioner to approach an organizational context case from the point of view of traditional therapeutic criteria of wellness is inappropriate' (1983: 133). For him, the criteria of counselling are 'performance and productivity' and the role of the counsellor is to get the client/employee fit and ready for work. This, he suggests rather strongly, is not the place to help clients 'self-actualise', or work on personal problems not related to the workplace but 'the main criteria for therapy in the business context is that the method must fix the performance problem and it must fix it fast' (1983: 137).

Workplace counselling could be viewed as on a continuum with varying opinions on its aims and objectives. At one end of this continuum is the extreme position outlined above by Yeager ('the business alternatives will determine the clinical goals (1983: 133)). At the other end is the totally person-centred position of those who counsel employees as if they were working in private practice, but within the organization. There is a range of positions between the two poles which combine the above with varying emphasis on one position or the other. Some companies predetermine approaches with policies such as the length of time clients can be seen for (for example, four–six sessions), or by insisting that assessments are first made by a psychologist or a psychiatrist before referral to the counsellor. This, again, points out the lack of clarity about the precise aims and objectives of workplace counselling. Sworder has suggested a framework in which problems at work can be assessed:

1 Problems arising within the individual.
2 Problems caused by the work organization acting on the individual.
3 Problems arising outside the individual or the organization:
   either (a) having visible effects on the work of the individual;
   or   (b) not having visible effects on the work of the individual. (1977: 31).

While recognizing that there may well be 'mixtures' of these three problem areas, such a framework, at least, gives the counsellor a model for deciding when workplace counselling is called for and when it is, or may be, outside the domain of the workplace counselling service.

The Strengths and Weaknesses of Various Types of Counselling Provision in Organizations

Counselling in organizations can be set up in two ways: in-house counselling provision and out-house (external) counselling provision. There is a scarcity of material on the advantages and disadvantages of these. There is almost no research on the values of internal (in-house) versus external counselling services, and whether one is better than the other. Which counselling provision, for which company, by which provider, for the best service, are still open questions. Summerfield and Van Oudtshoorn (1995) are clear that in-house counselling services offer more advantages overall, while Hoskinson (1994) argues that it makes no sense to get into the argument of which is better as both have advantages and can be complementary.

Even though EAPs are an essential part of workplace counselling, they are not the only way in which counselling is provided in an organizational setting. In fact there are a number of possible ways and combination of ways in which counselling in organizations takes place: 'The varieties of employee counselling services are virtually infinite' (Hoskinson and Reddy, 1989: 137).

Externally based models of counselling are those brought in from outside the organization. Usually in the form of an EAP, they are administered and organized from outside. Table 1.1 outlines some of the strengths and weaknesses of externally based models of counselling. It must be remembered that these strengths and weaknesses can vary according to the context and

Table 1.1   *The strengths and weaknesses of externally based counselling provision*

Strengths	Weaknesses
• the counselling service is distinct from the politics of the organization • it can challenge what is taken for granted within the company • it can offer training as well as counselling • it can offer clear confidentiality • it can provide a range of services • it can offer a number of counsellors with different skills, backgrounds, etc. • the organization is not responsible for malpractice of counsellors	• the counsellor may not be flexible in what he/she can offer • the counselling service has to make a profit • it may not adapt easily to individual companies • the counsellor can unwittingly get involved in the politics of the organization • the counsellor may not understand the culture of the organization • the counsellor may be seen as an 'outsider' by potential clients • the counsellor may not be able to educate the system to what counselling means • the counsellor may not have experience of workplace counselling • the counsellor may know nothing about the organization from which clients come

that what is a strength for one organization could be a weakness for another. Furthermore, the strengths and weaknesses outlined in Table 1.1 do not apply to all EAPs and many providers have overcome the potential weaknesses that are posited here.

There are a number of formats of external counselling provision used by organizations: some employ established EAPs, others set up an internal EAP, and others opt for employing individuals to work on a sessional basis with employees. Externally based models of workplace counselling have increased in number over the past decade and it is anticipated that they will continue to increase over the next few years.

In-house counselling provision is the norm in a number of companies (see ICAS research, Reddy, 1993). A part-time or full-time counsellor, or in some instances a team of counsellors, is employed to work with employees. The counselling service can be part of an already existing department or an independent unit in its own right. Table 1.2 shows the potential strengths and weaknesses of internally based counselling.

In-house counselling provision can be set up in a variety of ways: with an in-house EAP, with a team of counsellors, with an individual counsellor, within a particular department or outside all departments, with part-time or full-time provision.

Internal and external counselling provision can be combined within the one organization. Summerfield and Van Oudtshoorn (1995), while arguing for the advantages of internally based counselling services in the workplace, present an integrated model combining internal and external provision using the Post Office as an example.

Table 1.2   *The strengths and weaknesses of internally based counselling provision*

Strengths	Weaknesses
• the counsellor is in touch with the culture of the company • the counsellor can make assessments in the light of the various organizational systems • the counsellor has access to the formal and informal structures of the organization • the counsellor can build up greater credibility for the counselling service • the counsellor is able to get feedback into the system from the counselling work • the counselling work can be adapted to the organizational needs • the counsellor has flexibility to adapt to client needs • the counselling service can provide mediation • the counsellor is a visible, human face • the counsellor can provide multiple roles	• the counsellor can be more subjective in his/her assessments • the counselling service can be vulnerable if re-organization takes place • the counsellor can get pulled very easily into identifying with either the organization or the individual • the counsellor can be identified by employees with management and vice versa • the counselling provision can be isolated • the counsellor can be used by management to do its 'dirty work' • the counsellor is involved in the politics of the organization • counselling can be used by individuals against the organization • it is more difficult to maintain confidentiality: employees may be worried about leakage of personal information

Conflicts between the Values of Organizations and Those of Counselling

Oberer and Lee articulate a major concern about counselling in organizations: 'the most obvious one [area of difficulty] involves the primary role of business versus the counselor's professional goals' (1986: 152). Is there an inherent contradiction between the aims and purposes of industry and those of the counselling profession? Are counsellors compromised by working within industry? There is no doubt that the aim of counselling is to promote growth and autonomy, to encourage clients to care for themselves, to be assertive and to develop their potential. These are not always in accord with the aims of particular organizations which perhaps do not wish their employees to be autonomous. Many organizations want team-work rather than a concentration on the individual, many require 'passive employees' rather than active ones, and many growth-orientated employees would clash with 'macho managers' (Dutfield and Eling, 1990). From a social-work perspective but again dealing with the organizational issues, Gitterman and Miller point out that 'executives are concerned with funding, organizational stability, regulatory issues, and external politics. Clinicians are concerned about client problems and available services' (1989: 154). Orlans highlights possible conflicts:

> One difficulty with counselling within the organizational context is that the values and goals implicit in counselling (especially in non-directive approaches) are not easily reconciled with the economic, rationalistic models which underlie organizational procedures and processes. Counselling is generally concerned with providing individuals with a greater sense of freedom, while an important organizational function is the control of its employees. (Orlans, 1986: 19)

Few texts struggle with the particular problems that arise between the underlying values, philosophies and policies of the world of organizations and the world of counselling. It is all too easily assumed that these two domains blend together and that their marriage ought to be one of continual harmony. Warning voices have been raised (Lane, 1990) about introducing counselling into companies without consultation. Some organizations may not be ready for counselling provision. Counselling can be integrated into industry for all sorts of wrong reasons (Lane, 1990; Carroll, 1995), resulting in unclear boundary issues and in some instances, the 'highjacking' of counselling to cover managerial defects.

Nahrwold has traced the history of antagonism between counselling and business, showing how social scientists, especially in the mid-1960s, have

> depicted businesses as amoral, greedy, polluting, exploitive (or even fascist) organizations that sacrifice human values and social responsibilities to increase profit. To counter criticisms portraying them as Dickensian villains, business people in turn have characterised social scientists as naive, bleeding head academics or crypto-Marxist social agitators seeing to overturn capitalism. (1983: 110–11)

Nahrwold proceeds, while acknowledging the strong stereotypes put forward by both camps, to upbraid counsellors for 'an antibusiness attitude' which is sometimes expressed in the way they dress and maintain both hostile attitudes and professional arrogance. He suggests that the two worlds can exist and blend amicably if common sense, getting to know one another and the roles involved, and an awareness of the politics of the organization, are used with good will.

Which comes first: the individual client or the organization as a whole? Counsellors are trained primarily to deal with the individual and to put the welfare of the individual as a priority. This may conflict with company norms and even policies. 'Values' issues arise when there is a clash between the values of the individual and the needs of the company. Oberer and Lee put it slightly differently: 'It is only when a choice must be made that places an employee's well-being either ahead of or after his contribution to profits, that conflicts arise' (1986: 152). However Reddy (1993) makes the point that benefits for the employee do not automatically translate into non-benefits for the organization. The welfare of the employee and the interest of the organization can proceed hand in hand.

Clashes in values among counsellors, clients, organizations and society have to be faced continually by workplace counsellors who are trying 'to integrate outer-directed business values with the more inner-directed humanistic ones' (Puder, 1983: 96).

The Roles and Responsibilities of Counsellors in Organizations

Little consideration has been given to the roles and responsibilities that characterize the counsellor in the workplace. To date, these have not been articulated clearly, and workplace counsellors are asked to fulfil roles that counsellors in other settings find anathema to their work. It is rare that the employee counsellor has one single role with clients. Rather, he/she is asked often to be trainer, welfare-officer, home-visitor, information-giver, advocate, consultant to managers, personnel adviser and organizational change-agent, as well as being counsellor. While many fulfil these myriad roles admirably, there is nothing to help them sort out and decide which roles fit well together and which result in role conflict with their clients. C. Carroll's (1994) research into the roles and responsibilities of employee counsellors in the private sector shows clearly how these counsellors not only manage multiple roles within the organization, but are excited by them. She concludes that employee counsellors have to engage in a variety of roles with clients while maintaining the boundaries and professionalism of counselling.

What seems certain is that the counsellor at work will not be free simply to be a clinician and nothing else. While it is fundamental to make clear the various roles and responsibilities that are part of counsellors' jobs (Crandall and Allen, 1982), there are, unfortunately, few guidelines to indicate what the extent of these roles and responsibilities might be. Interviewing clients for individual counselling is clearly accepted as one. After that there is little agreement.

Osipow sees the 'first and most obvious applications [for the counseling psychologist] are in the career development area' (1982: 20). He moves on to designate other roles within a number of areas, for example retirement preparation, organization development, training, selection of personnel, consultation, not forgetting of course the mental health contribution, and advocates intervention at the 'individual, group, and systems level' (1982: 21) for the counselling psychologist.

Counsellors, by training, can make significant contributions to a number of organizational areas. However, making them consultants to almost every part of the organization may mean overlooking what they do best, that is individual counselling. It may also fail to recognize the 'boundary issues' or role conflicts that could arise when counsellors take part in a number of organizational activities. The counsellor in an organization has to ascertain which roles can exist together without compromise, and which roles, though good in themselves, are incompatible in this context. Gray (1984a) talks about the importance of role definition, role stress, role overlap, and other people's roles. In attempting to work 'with the organization, the counsellor is extending or re-defining his or her role' (Gray, 1984a: 171). He is adamant that time is wasted when spent solely in individual counselling in organizations. He suggests that 'spending all one's time with individual clients can lead to a lack of awareness of the processes of the organization which provide the opportunities for the clients' particular neurotic, existential or psychotic imperatives to emerge' (Gray, 1984a: 178). Prominent again, for the employee counsellor, is the consideration of roles and how best to integrate time with individuals, with groups, in organizational development, in consulting with management and in training.

The Impact of Organizations on Counselling Provision

There is no work that studies the impact of organizations on counselling provision. A recent publication by Obholzer and Roberts (1994) has summarized some research from a psychodynamic perspective. Few doubt that 'organizational culture' influences most of what takes place within companies (Pheysey, 1993; Egan, 1994; Hampton-Turner, 1994), and even though there are suggestions that different types of culture will influence counselling services (Hawkins and Shohet, 1989; Lane, 1990), there is little researched or written up material to help prepare, introduce, maintain and, where necessary, terminate counselling provision in different company cultures.

Egan (1993a, 1993b) has begun to look at the 'shadow side' of organizational culture and the impact it has when not managed effectively. Gitterman and Miller have stated clearly that 'the organization provides the framework for the helping relationship' (1989: 155). And that framework is very powerful. They continue: 'Almost all, if not all clinical decisions, represent agency policy and organizational imperatives in action. The organization influences and shapes services, problem definition, assessment and intervention, and careers of clients. These in turn influence our professional behaviour and view of ourselves' (1989: 151). Crandall and Allen (1982) have introduced the concept of 'parallel process' into organizational contexts. They see the client as mirroring the organization in the counselling situation. The clients not only bring themselves and their personal problems along, but also their experience of the organization, and represent it in counselling. The counsellor meets the organization in the clients.

All organizations have their own ecology, flavour, ethos, and way of working and interacting with employees and other organizations. Lane, using the work of Van Oudtshoorn (1989) and Harrison (1972), points out that 'different organizations will value different types of counselling service' (1990: 542). He then delineates four types of organizational culture – power cultures, role cultures, achievement cultures, and support cultures – indicating how each of these view counselling differently and have different expectations of a counselling service. Other authors have suggested different culture typologies (see Carroll, 1996b: Chapter 4). Understanding the ecology of the organization will help articulate what may be expected and what needs to be done within that particular organization. As a result of such an assessment, a counsellor may decide he/she is not ready or able to work within its ambience. For example if a power culture organization wants to set up a counselling service, it will do so in a way that does not allow for organizational change and it will expect the counsellor to work with clients in such a way that they emerge as more dedicated members of the organization.

Clarkson (1990), in a stress-related understanding of counselling in organizations, asks key questions about working within an organization. Is counselling for the individual who is growing or who is deteriorating? Does the individual need counselling or the organization need change? Is the organization a healthy environment to work in or one that 'sickens' its employees? Counsellors are not, usually, management consultants, and not, usually, in a strong position to assess the well-being of an organization and its effects on its employees. Perhaps an area of training for those who would work as counsellors in organizational settings is precisely in these skills of how to assess the willingness of an organization to introduce counselling and whether it is the answer to their employee problems. Egan and Cowan (1979) have drawn a distinction between 'upstream' and 'downstream' help that is very pertinent to those working within companies. They see little point in hauling out individuals who are drowning, resuscitating them, and sending them back 'upstream' where they once more become casualties of the system. They insist that it is better to go upstream and help the system so that it does not become an agent in the dysfunction of the individual.

Counsellors, by training, think interpersonally. In organizational settings they are asked to think both interpersonally and organizationally. This can be quite a mind-shift. Counsellors are asked to be of benefit to the organization as a whole, not just to individuals within it. They need to widen their perspectives: 'Employee counselling should not be tackled on a piecemeal basis, but should be coherently and effectively integrated with assessment, training and consultancy endeavours to form part of a coherent overall strategy for the whole organization' (Clarkson, 1990: 4). Orlans (1992) has talked about building bridges between the worlds of counselling and business. Gitterman and Miller have used the terms 'sophisticated mediation between the clients' needs, workers' function and organizational requirements' (1989: 159) as the preferred stance of the counsellor. Whatever the terminology, it seems that employee counsellors are asked to straddle two worlds without getting lost in either. McLeod (1993: 273) has formulated a list of challenges faced by counsellors working in non-counselling organizations:

- Being pressured to produce results desired by the agency rather than the client
- Maintaining confidentiality boundaries
- Justifying the cost of the service
- Dealing with isolation
- Educating colleagues about the purpose and value of counselling
- Justifying the cost of supervision
- Avoiding being overwhelmed by numbers of clients, or becoming the conscience of the organization
- Avoiding the threat to reputation caused by 'failure' cases
- Coping with the envy of colleagues who are not able to take an hour for each client interview
- Creating an appropriate office space and reception system.

Such demands from some organizations give a flavour of how influential a setting can be on what happens to a counselling service.

Managing Counselling in Organizations

Few resources for understanding the particular characteristics of workplace counselling services (or indeed counsellors within this area) have emerged. How to manage the process of such provision is still an open question. For example, is the counselling service best served by being within a particular department in the company, such as Personnel, Human Resources, Occupational Health, or best left as a service on its own? What kinds of facility will help confidentiality in a situation where information (and indeed gossip) flows rapidly on the various 'grapevines' and where an individual's life can be open to the scrutiny of all? How can 'leakage' from the counselling service to the company at large be managed? Where should the counselling rooms be situated? Carroll (1995) has a series of questions centred around 'Managing the counselling process in workplace counselling' that require practical answers.

The types of area covered by counselling management are:

- What physical arrangements are needed to provide confidential counselling to clients in this setting? Where will the counselling room be placed? How will it be furnished?
- How will clients contact the counselling service? Can they be referred by others? Will the counsellor accept referrals and appointments from sources other than the client, for example from, colleagues, managers, supervisors, disciplinary boards, personnel departments?
- How will the counselling service be advertised/publicized?
- What are the circumstances in which a counsellor would not accept a referral? For example, when a manager wants to give a formal warning and insists on counselling to help the employee change his/her behaviour.
- What happens when the client contacts the service? Who is the first contact? What information does the first contact require?
- How is the client assessed, and what referral points are appropriate?
- What does the client (and the appropriate manager) need to know about the counselling service?
- What kind of contract is made with the client?
- What notes are kept on the client? Where are they kept? Who else besides the counsellor has access to these notes? How long are notes kept after the counselling has terminated?
- What happens when the client terminates counselling?
- How are statistics kept within the service and how are they publicized?
- How will the counsellor organize his/her time in respect of clients, publicity, training, contacting?
- Will clients be seen for a specific number of sessions? Will some be long-term clients?

- If the counselling provision is within a department (for example, Occupational Health, Personnel), what are the relationships involved? What contact will the department have with clients? What will the department need to know about the clients, if anything?
- What contact will the counsellor have with referral agencies?
- What methods will be used to evaluate the counselling service?
- When will a client be referred for specialized help?
- When will the counsellor contact other professionals (for example, a doctor, psychiatrist, social worker) with or without the client's permission?
- What insurance (indemnity) is appropriate for the counsellor to have (personally and/or organizationally)?
- What supervision arrangements are essential (desirable) for the counsellor to have? What will the counsellor do in the case of an emergency?

Towler (this volume) suggests that there are six areas that require consideration when managing counselling in organizational settings – negotiating and defining services, contracting with the organization and clients, identifying the client group, assessing, using short-term focused counselling, and exploring organizational culture and dynamics – and has reviewed three types of contract that are needed to maintain clear boundaries – the administrative, the professional and the psychological. There is no doubt that these aspects of organizational counselling, over and above the actual work with clients, can be the most difficult for counsellors. Here they have to work with the organization, with bureaucracy, with policies, with departments, with committees and with management. Furthermore, they have to set up a counselling process which protects clients and meets the organizational aims as well as being managers themselves to a service that may involve other counsellors, secretarial staff, and possibly be housed within a particular department.

Ethical Issues in Counselling in Organizations

Pryor (1989) puts forward an ethical dilemma where an accountant is referred for counselling and in the session talks about an embezzlement charge which he has never revealed to the company. What should the counsellor do? Employed by the company and, no doubt, with the company's interest at heart, should a counsellor, knowing there is a risk (minor, intermediate, serious?) that this employee might embezzle again (he is in financial difficulty), relay this information to the relevant management? Pryor is taken to task by Bishop and D'Rozario (1990) for taking too individualistic a stance in assessing clients within an organizational context. They state that 'the concepts of collective ethics, or organizational ethics, are rarely dealt with' (Bishop and D'Rozario, 1990: 215).

Transport counselling into the workplace and not only does one contend with the full range of ethical issues emerging from counselling, but another full set of issues arrive on the scene both from within the organization where counselling takes place and between the organization and the counsellor.

Puder suggests that the counsellor in such circumstances needs 'the rational and intuitive perceptiveness necessary for straddling the worlds of business and mental health' (1983: 96).

A number of ethical dilemmas arising from counselling in organizations have been raised in the literature: confidentiality (Bond, 1992; Salt et al., 1992; Walker, 1992); the incompatibility between the organization's aims and the aims of counselling (Lee and Rosen, 1984; Orlans, 1986; Sugarman, 1992); the loyalty of the counsellor (Carroll, 1995); and managing different roles with the same client (Carroll, 1995). The following list of possible ethical pitfalls/ dilemmas is adapted from Lakin (1991):

- If the management pays, how can the counsellor serve the interests of employees?
- Can the targets of the interactions – the employees – share in designing interventions?
- How can the counsellor honestly describe what is proposed to those who are to be affected by it?
- What can be said regarding confidentiality?
- Can employees refuse to participate in counselling without penalty?
- Dare the employee confront a manager/supervisor when the counsellor and the employee have worked on this together?
- What safeguards are there for participants against retaliation from supervisors or aggrieved co-workers for what may take place as a result of counselling?

Workplace counsellors face not only a barrage of possible ethical dilemmas, but do so without clear and helpful frameworks for ethical decision-making in work contexts (M. Carroll, 1994). Most see supervision as an essential requirement for continued efficacy here (Sugarman, 1992; Carroll, 1995). Sugarman stresses five focal points for the counsellor where ethical concerns need to be tackled:

- Identifying the extent to which the aims of an organization over and above the aims of counselling compromise counselling's ethical foundation.
- Identifying any point at which the counselling provision benefits the organization at the individual's expense.
- Identifying any points at which the organization exceeds its right to control aspects of the employee's behaviour.
- Negotiating what is implied by the term 'confidentiality' and the conditions under which it will and will not be maintained.
- Identifying whether the resources are sufficient and appropriate to doing more good than harm, and in what ways the origins of the resources compromise the aims of the service. (Sugarman, 1992: 28)

It would be extremely difficult to prioritize ethical issues. However, there is some validity in presenting confidentiality as one of the most crucial factors that can determine the credibility of counselling within organizations. Failure in this area will destroy the reputation of a counselling service (Puder, 1983; Megranahan, 1989b; Bond, 1992; Sugarman, 1992). And yet it is not easy to maintain confidentiality when there are a host of factors within industry vying with one another to compromise it – managers wanting information on employees, personnel asking to be involved, individual clients sharing material detrimental to organizational policy, etc. Because of its complexity there have been calls for specific codes of ethics geared to each counselling service within each company (Puder, 1983).

Research on Counselling in Organizations

There is a paucity of research studies on counselling in organizational contexts. Megranahan has pointed out that 'evaluation . . . has been for a long time the stumbling block for progress of counselling services in the workplace' (1989b: 172). Orlans (1991) has reviewed studies of EAPs, in particular those dealing with alcohol-based or stress-related provision. However, she points out that 'results from the counselling literature, for example, are not brought into the arguments, possibly because of the less tangible factors involved, and possibly because of the fact that evaluation studies have not been carried out specifically in work settings' (Orlans, 1991: 10). She refers to one study by Firth and Shapiro (1986) which ascertains the value of brief psychotherapy for job-related distress. Waite (1992), whose dissertation is entitled 'An investigation of the experience of supervision in the context of counselling at work', further attests to the paucity of research studies in counselling at work and in supervising counsellors at work.

In the UK in 1971, the British Institute of Management, from its survey of 200 firms, discovered that five per cent offered some form of personal counselling to employees. Orlans and Shipley (1983) surveyed 35 large UK organizations and discovered that all but three had occupational health facilities, and whereas nurses employed within these departments had undergone short-term counselling training, there was not a single case where extensive counselling training had been provided. They found that often welfare officers were better trained in counselling and had a clearer and more explicit counselling role.

Two later surveys (Hoskinson and Reddy, 1989; Reddy, 1993) indicate that counselling provision in Britain has grown recently. One of the few pieces of research on counselling in industry was conducted within the Post Office (Cooper et al., 1990). Clients accessing the counselling service completed a set of questionnaires at their first interview, and a second set once their case had been concluded by the counsellor. The results are a clear indication of the value of counselling: 'After counselling, significant improvements are shown on all of these dimensions, indicating significant improvements in clients' mental well-being . . . finally, in terms of sickness absence, the average number of days lost decreases after counselling' (Cooper et al., 1990: 10).

Evaluating counselling in organizational settings has tended to focus almost exclusively on individually based work, that is work with individual clients. A number of workplace counsellors have their own evaluation for clients. What is often missing is evaluation of the full counselling service and its impact on the organization, for example, evaluating the consultancy role of the counsellor. Bull (1994) has compiled a short review of literature on evaluating workplace counselling.

There is value in finding out how cost-effective, in financial terms, counselling in organizations can be. Wrich (1985) studied three US EAPs – General Motors, Control Data Corporation and United Airlines – which had statistical data to show their effectiveness in human and financial terms. General Motors, for example, estimates that it makes $67 for every dollar invested in the EAP. Employers, in particular, will be heartened by the financial returns to be gained from the provision of a counselling service and will be eager to have data backing this up. It has been estimated that the US Postal Service saves $2 million per annum through its EAP (Kim, 1988). Highley and Cooper (1994) have reported positive results from three American studies on the cost-effectiveness of EAPs: the McDonnell Douglas company reported an estimated saving of $5.1 million on using its EAP; the US Department of Health and Human Services concluded that there was an approximate $7.1 return per dollar invested in their EAP; and the Edison Company in Detroit realized reductions in lost time and health insurance claims, a 40 per cent improvement in suspensions and a similar improvement in the number of job-related accidents.

Corney (1992) has shown that subjective evaluations on counselling in general health practice is very positive, with counsellors, clients and doctors expressing overall satisfaction with what is offered.

Recent research studies on counselling in organizations have included C. Carroll's work on how employee counsellors in the private sector view their roles and responsibilities (1994: Chapter 12), Fisher's work on EAP managers in health settings (1995: Chapter 15), Greenwood's research on the stress faced by EAP counsellors (1995: Chapter 16) and Martin's work on the effects of counselling training on public sector managers (1994: Chapter 13). They all comprise much needed investigations into counselling in organizations. Hopefully, these are precursors of further research into counselling in organizational settings. In particular, more work is needed on organizational culture and counselling services, and the relationship between counselling outcome and the organizational impact on both clients and the counselling provision.

Training for Counsellors Who Work in Organizations

Pickard found few precedents to help design training courses for counsellors in organizations: 'At present, workplace counselling is in search of a model for its training and while it waits it draws upon the generic training model for its inspiration' (1993: 8). Highley and Cooper (1995), in the summary of their findings into workplace counselling, have pointed out the lack of training in some counsellors who provided workplace counselling. Orlans (1986, 1991, 1992) has pointed out the notable absence of specialized training for counsellors who work within organizational settings. She argues that being a counsellor is not in itself sufficient and proposes a general curriculum to cover other areas such as the following:

A review of the principles and dynamics of organizational behaviour; models and practices in the design and implementation of Employee Assistance Programmes; ethics and responsibilities in employee counselling; organizational health; the role of legislation; stress diagnosis, management and prevention in the work setting, and the understanding of specialist counselling, AIDS, substance abuse, career counselling, with particular emphasis on their application to the workplace. Such a programme would also need to include the provision of supervised practice, relevant tutorial work and appropriate assessment procedures. (Orlans, 1992: 21)

For those who wrestle with the contents of a comprehensive curriculum for training counsellors in organizations (Osipow, 1982; Lewis and Lewis, 1986; Megranahan, 1989a; Gerstein and Shullman, 1992; Orlans, 1992; Carroll, 1996b), there is a tendency for the counsellor to become a jack-of-all-organizational-trades. They are asked to be professional counsellors, organizational consultants, trainers, welfare officers, personnel officers, internal or external change-agents with expertise in individual work, group dynamics and human resources management. The all-inclusiveness of their tasks could be interpreted as a lack of clarity on the particular aims of counselling in organizations. The need to become acceptable to an organization could drive counsellors into roles not appropriate to their profession.

There is almost no training for counsellors who either work or intend to work as counsellors within organizations. In Britain, to date, there are only a few programmes specifically geared to counselling at work: TDA Diploma in Counselling at Work, Roehampton Institute's Diploma in Counselling in Organizations, Birmingham University's Certificate in Counselling at Work, and the Diploma in Counselling at Work at the University of Bristol. What training exists tends to be unsystematic, short, and usually arranged for people who will integrate counselling skills into their existing work roles. Gerstein and Shullman (1992) have summarized the training in counselling psychology related to work in industry in the US and have given outlines of two courses entitled 'Occupational Counselling Psychology' and 'A Seminar in Counselling Psychology in Business and Organizational Settings'. While the second of these concentrates on applied skills, the first covers a range of topics:

- The history of counselling psychology in business and organizational settings.
- The vocational behaviour of adults (career, work).
- Vocational assessment strategies with adults.
- Models and technologies of consultation and programme evaluation.
- Workplace wellness and safety programmes.
- EAPs.
- Research issues and questions of interest.
- Trade publications important to the business community.

The training outline shows some of the areas in which counselling psychologists are expected to have skills and knowledge, and presumably some of the roles they are expected to take on if they are employed as counselling psychologists in organizations.

Pickard (this volume) has reviewed training for counsellors in organizations and has designated three stages in its development:

- Stage 1, which she calls counselling *in* organizations, where counsellors train as counsellors and apply their work to organizational settings.
- Stage 2, counselling *for* organizations, which combines counselling provision and organizational needs, for example through the use of an EAP.
- Stage 3, organizational counselling, which is an attempt to provide an overall philosophy of employee care where counselling is 'integrated both conceptually and theoretically into organizational philosophy and practice'.

This distinction provides a framework for considering training for workplace counsellors; knowing their roles and responsibilities is a foundation for a suitable curriculum. Trainers are attempting to coordinate what is known, at this stage, into workable training packages for potential workplace counsellors.

Conclusion

As counselling services increase within organizations there is a further need to review their aims and objectives as a key focus in the kind of provision needed. A clearer view of these aims and objectives will clarify, in turn, what kind of counselling is best suited to particular organizations, what concepts of change underlie such aims, and what roles and responsibilities characterize the professional counsellor who works in an organizational setting. This, again, will lead to a theory of counselling in organizations which will influence, hopefully, the training of such counsellors. The 10 points in this chapter offer an agenda for future discussion and research in an area of counselling that will undoubtedly be a facet of the future.

References

Bishop, B. and D'Rozario (1990) 'A matter of ethics? A comment on Pryor (1989)', *Australian Psychologist*, 25 (2): 215–19.

Bond, T. (1992) 'Confidentiality: counselling, ethics and the law', *Employee Counselling Today*, 4 (4): 4–9.

Bull, A. (1994) 'How effective is counselling in the workplace?', *Evaluation of Counselling Selected References*. Rugby: British Association for Counselling Publications.

Bull, A. (1995) *Counselling Skills and Counselling at Work: A Guide for Purchasers and Providers.* Rugby: British Association for Counselling Publications.

Carroll, C. (1994) 'Building bridges: a study of employee counsellors in the private sector'. MSc. dissertation, City University, London.

Carroll, M. (1994) 'Making ethical decisions in organizational counselling', *EAP International*, 1 (4): 26–30.

Carroll, M. (1995) 'The counsellor in organizational settings: some reflections', *Employee Counselling Today*, 7 (1): 23–32.

Carroll, M. (1996a) *Counselling Supervision: Theory, Skills and Practice.* London: Cassell.

Carroll, M. (1996b) *Workplace Counselling: A Systematic Approach to Employee Care*. London: Sage.

Carroll, M. and Holloway, E. (1993) 'Redundancy counselling: is it really counselling?', *Employee Counselling Today*, 5 (4): 14–20.

Clarkson, P. (1990) 'The scope of stress counselling in organisations', *Employee Counselling Today*, 2 (4): 3–6.

Cooper, C.L., Sadri, G., Allison, T. and Reynolds, P. (1990) 'Stress counselling in the Post Office', *Counselling Psychology Quarterly*, 3 (1): 3–11.

Corney, R. (1992) *Evaluating Counsellors in Counselling in General Practice*. London: Royal College of General Practitioners, Clinical Series.

Cowie, H. and Pecherek, A. (1994) *Counselling Approaches and Issues in Education*. London: David Fulton.

Cowie, H. and Sharp, S. (1996) *Peer Counselling in Schools*. London: David Fulton.

Crandall, R. and Allen, R.D. (1982) 'The organisational context of helping relationships', in T.A. Will (ed.), *Basic Processes in Helping Relationships*. London: Academic Press.

Critchley, B. and Casey, D. (1989) 'Organizations get stuck too', *Leadership and Organization Development Journal*, 10 (4): 3–12.

Dutfield, M. and Eling, C. (1990) *The Communicating Manager*. Shaftesbury: Element.

East, P. (1994) *Counselling in Medical Settings*. Milton Keynes: Open University Press.

Egan, G. (1993a) 'The shadow side', *Management Today*, September: 33–8.

Egan, G. (1993b) *Adding Value: A Systematic Guide to Business-Driven Management and Leadership*. San Francisco: Jossey-Bass.

Egan, G. (1994) *Working the Shadow-side: A Guide to Positive Behind the Scenes Management*. San Francisco: Jossey-Bass.

Egan, G. and Cowan, M. (1979) *People in Systems*. Monterey, CA: Brooks/Cole.

Firth, J. and Shapiro, D.A. (1986) 'An evaluation of psychotherapy for job related stress', *Journal of Occupational Psychology*, 59: 111–19.

Fisher, H. (1995) 'Plastering over the cracks?: employee counselling in the NHS'. MA dissertation, University of Keele.

Gerstein, L.W. and Shullman, S.L. (1992) 'Counseling psychology and the workplace: the emergence of organizational counseling psychology', in R. Brown and R.W. Lent (eds), *The Handbook of Counseling Psychology* (2nd Edition). New York: Wiley. pp. 581–625.

Gitterman, A. and Miller, I. (1989) 'The influence of the organisation on clinical practice', *Clinical Social Work Journal*, 17 (2): 151–64.

Gordon, J. and Dryden, W. (1989) 'Counselling employees: the rational–emotive approach', *Employee Counselling Today*, 1 (4): 14–20.

Gray, K. (1984a) 'Counsellor interventions in organisations', in W. Dryden and A.G. Watts (eds), *Guidance and Counselling in Britain: A 20-year Perspective*. Cambridge: Hobson.

Gray, K. (1984b) 'Postscript', in W. Dryden and A.G. Watts (eds), *Guidance and Counselling in Britain: A 20-year Perspective*. Cambridge: Hobson.

Greenwood, A. (1995) 'All in a day's work: how EAP/workplace counsellors cope with the stress'. Unpublished MSc dissertation, University of East London.

Greenwood, A. (forthcoming) *Counselling at Work*. Milton Keynes: Open University Press.

Hampton-Turner, C. (1994) *Corporate Culture*. London: Piatkus.

Harrison, R. (1972) 'Understanding your organization's character', *Harvard Business Review*, 50 (23): 119–28.

Hawkins, P. and Shohet, R. (1989) *Supervision in the Helping Professions*. Milton Keynes: Open University Press.

Hay, J. (1989) 'Transactional analysis as a counselling medium in a management development programme', *Employee Counselling Today*, 1 (4): 21–8.

Highley, C. and Cooper, C. (1994) 'Evaluating EAPs', *Personnel Review*, 23 (7): 46–59.

Highley, C. and Cooper, C. (1995) 'An assessment and evaluation of employee assistance and workplace counselling programmes in British Organisations'. Unpublished report for the Health and Safety Executive.

Hirschhorn, L. and Barnett. C.K. (eds) (1993) *The Psychodynamics of Organizations*. Philadelphia: Temple University Press.

Hoskinson, L. (1994) 'EAPs: Internal versus external service structures. The key differences and potential synergies'. Paper presented at the European EAP Conference, Augsburg, Germany, October 1994.

Hoskinson, L. and Reddy, M. (1989) *Counselling Services in UK Organizations: An ICAS Report*. Milton Keynes: Independent Counselling and Advisory Service.

Institute of Personnel Management (1992) *Statement on Counselling in the Workplace*. London: IPM.

Kets de Vries, F.R. and Miller, D. (1984) *The Neurotic Organization*. San Francisco: Jossey-Bass.

Kim, D.S. (1988) 'Assessing employee assistance programs: evaluating typology and models', *The Clinical Supervisor*, 3 (3/4): 169–87.

Lakin, M. (1991) *Coping with Ethical Dilemmas in Psychotherapy*. New York: Pergamon Press.

Lane, D. (1990) 'Counselling psychology in organisations', *The Psychologist, Bulletin of the British Psychological Society*, 12: 540–4.

Lee, S.S. and Rosen, E.A. (1984) 'Employee counselling services: ethical dilemmas', *Personnel and Guidance Journal*, January: 276–80.

Lewis, J. and Lewis, M. (1986) *Counseling Programs for Employees in the Workplace*. Monterey, CA: Brooks/Cole.

Madonia, J.F. (1985) 'Handling emotional problems in business and industry', *Social Casework: The Journal of Contemporary Social Work*, December: 587–93.

Martin, P.A. (1994) 'The effects of counselling training on public sector managers'. MSc dissertation, University of Surrey/Roehampton Institute, London.

McLeod, J. (1993) *The Organisational Context of Counselling*. Centre for Counselling Studies, Keele University.

Megranahan, M. (1989a) *Counselling: A Practical Guide for Managers*. London: Institute for Personnel Management.

Megranahan, M. (1989b) 'Counselling in the workplace', in Windy Dryden, David Charles-Edwards and Ray Woolfe (eds), *Handbook of Counselling in Britain*. London: Tavistock/Routledge.

Morris, G.B. (1993) 'A rational–emotive paradigm for organizations', *Journal of Rational Emotive and Cognitive Behaviour Therapy*, 11 (1): 33–49.

Nahrwold, S.C. (1983) 'Why programs fail', in James Manuso (ed.), *Occupational Clinical Psychology*. New York: Praeger.

Nixon, J. and Carroll, M. (1994) 'Can a line-manager also be a counsellor?', *Employee Counselling Today*, 6 (1): 10–15.

Oberer, D. and Lee, S. (1986) 'The counselling psychologist in business and industry: ethical concerns', *Journal of Business and Psychology*, 1 (2): 148–62.

Obholzer, A. and Roberts, V.Z. (eds) (1994) *The Unconscious at Work: Individual and Organizational Stress in the Human Services*. London: Routledge.

Orlans, V. (1986) 'Counselling services in organizations', *Personnel Review*, 15 (5): 19–23.

Orlans, V. (1991) 'Evaluating the benefits of Employee Assistance Programs'. Paper presented at the first EAP conference, London, April 1991.

Orlans, V. (1992) 'Counselling in the workplace: Part 1 – Counsellor perspectives and training', *EAP International*, 1 (1): 19–21.

Orlans, V. and Shipley, P. (1983) *A Survey of Stress Management and Prevention Facilities in a Sample of UK Organizations*. London: Stress Research and Control Centre, Birkbeck College, University of London.

Osipow, S.H. (1982) 'Counseling psychology: applications in the world of work', *The Counselling Psychologist*, 10 (3): 19–25.

Pheysey, D.C. (1993) *Organizational Culture*. London: Routledge.

Pickard, E. (1993) 'Designing training for counsellors at work', *Counselling at Work*, Autumn: 7–8.

Pryor, R.G.L. (1989) 'Conflicting responsibilities: a case study of an ethical dilemma for psychologists working in organisations', *Australian Psychologist*, 24: 293–305.

Puder, M. (1983) 'Credibility, confidentiality and ethical issues in employee counselling programming', in James Manuso (ed.), *Occupational Clinical Psychology*. New York: Praeger.

Reddy, M. (1987) *The Managers Guide to Counselling at Work*. Leicester: British Psychological Society.

Reddy, M. (ed.) (1993) *EAPs and Counselling Provision in UK Organizations: An ICAS Report and Policy Guide*. Milton Keynes: ICAS.

Rowland, N. (1989) 'Annual review of the CMS sub-committee on counselling in general practice', *Counselling in Medical Settings Newsletter*, 19: 14–16.

Salt, H., Callow, S. and Bor, R. (1992) 'Confidentiality about health problems at work', *Employee Counselling Today*, 4 (4): 10–14.

Sanders, G. (1990) 'Counselling models in the workplace', *Employee Counselling Today*, 2 (2): 25–8.

Stein, M. and Hollwitz, J. (eds), (1992) *Psyche at Work: Workplace Applications of Jungian Analytical Psychology*. Wilmette, IL: Chiron Publications.

Sugarman, L. (1992) 'Ethical issues in counselling at work', *Employee Counselling Today*, 4 (4): 23–30.

Summerfield, J. and Van Oudtshoorn, L. (1995) *Counselling in the Workplace*. London: Institute of Personnel and Development.

Sworder, G. (1977) 'Counselling problems at work: where do we go from here?', in T. Watts (ed.), *Counselling at Work*. Plymouth: Bedford Square Press.

Tehrani, N. (1994) 'Business dimensions to organizational counselling', *Counselling Psychology Quarterly*, 7 (3): 275–85.

Tehrani, N. (1995) 'The development of employee support', *Counselling Psychology Review*, 10 (3): 2–7.

Van Oudtshoorn, L. (1989) *The Organization as a Nurturing Environment*. Oxford: Van Oudtshoorn Associates.

Waite, J. (1992) 'An investigation of the experience of supervision in the context of counselling at work'. MSc dissertation, University of Bristol.

Walker, V. (1992) 'Confidentiality – the personnel dilemma', *Employee Counselling Today*, 4 (4): 15–22.

Webb, W. (1990) 'Cognitive behaviour therapy: applications for employee assistance counselors', *Employee Assistance Quarterly*, 5 (3): 55–65.

Wrich, J.T. (1985) 'Management's role in EAPs', in S.H. Klarreich, J.L. Francek and C.E. Moore (eds), *The Human Resources Management Handbook: Principles and Practice of Employee Assistance Programs*. New York: Praeger.

Yeager, J. (1983) 'A model for executive performance coaching', in James Manuso (ed.), *Occupational Clinical Psychology*. New York: Praeger.

2

Models of Counselling in Organizations

Andrew Bull

Do any of the following responses to requests for help look familiar:

'If you don't get back to work soon, you won't have a job to go back to!'

'I'm very sorry to hear that. Have a couple of days off to sort things out.'

'Your partner's left you, you can't concentrate and you're worried about the effect this is having on your work, in case you get the sack. Is that right?'

All of these responses have been made in the name of workplace counselling but only the last one is that of a counsellor, someone who is actively and empathically listening to what is being said. So, what is workplace counselling? After all, its nature must be understood before a suitable model can be applied to it. This chapter begins with a review of what constitutes workplace counselling, with reference to who or what is the focus or target group of the service provision, before considering two counselling models.

In a survey of EAP and counselling provision in the UK, 85 per cent of the respondents said they provided counselling, but this included activities such as giving factual information, counselling skills training, coaching and mentoring, and covered areas as diverse as retirement, redundancy, career development, mid-life crises and stress (Reddy, 1993). In only three per cent of cases were in-house services provided by a counsellor or EAP, and Wheeler and Lyon (1992) found most managers understood counselling to be something between advice, guidance and giving instructions.

A story from my own experience illustrates the difficulty identifying what constitutes workplace counselling. Some years ago, I was interviewed for a post of work-based counsellor by trades union representatives who were not counsellors. I was asked how I would respond to the following problem:

A female client comes to see you with an unspecified problem, but I knew her colleagues were finding her body odour a problem on the shop floor. What was I going to do about it?

I said I would not do anything about her body odour unless it related to the issue that together we had agreed to work on. I was told this was an inadequate response as I 'knew' this was a problem on the shop floor. What was I going to do to sort it out? An intense discussion followed during which I was put under considerable pressure to arrive at a solution and a plan for its implementation. The union representatives saw counselling as part of the diagnosis–action approach to helping, that is, something derivative of the medical model. The client brings a problem to the counsellor who makes a diagnosis and, as the expert, prescribes strategies to overcome it – preferably making the intervention on the behalf of others! I suspect this sort of model is a common way in which counselling is understood by the lay person.

Theory and Workplace Counselling

A difficulty in understanding workplace counselling is that there is little theory governing its nature (Albert et al., 1985), and this is partly due to the difficulty in defining the construct under consideration. For example, there is a wide range of ways of providing workplace counselling. It can be delivered internally or externally by either counselling services or Employee Assistance Programmes (EAPs). Counsellors may be employed directly by the service or EAP, the client organization or subcontracted on a freelance basis. It is not always clear whether the counsellors' role is to provide treatment, to act as a gatekeeper by assessing and referring on to specialist help (many American services subscribe to this approach), or to act as an alternative to disciplinary procedures for employees whose problems threaten their jobs (Albert et al., 1985). Finally, the issues dealt with vary enormously, some focusing on a particular problem, for example drugs, while others offer a more general or broad-brush service. The reality is that practice, hence the use of a particular theory, is largely governed by conventional wisdom, custom and a fair degree of myth.

In the absence of a theory of workplace counselling, a brief history of the development of employee assistance is provided in an attempt to identify the focus of help, which, in turn, will help determine appropriate models of counselling that could be used. This focus might appear obvious: they are concerned with employee assistance, but is this assistance enhanced by focusing on the individual, the workplace or the organization?

The first documented employee counselling service was at Western Electric, which was used in the Hawthorne studies during the 1920s. It was not until the 1940s and 1950s, however, that counselling services became a feature of the organizational landscape as occupational alcohol treatment programmes. Using the Alcoholics Anonymous (AA) model, problems were medicalized and seen as part of a disease process. The success of EAPs in this field led to them working with the relatives of alcohol-dependent employees, and, in turn, their work was extended to employees with other problems of living. The impetus for this movement was economic rather than humanitarian, that is, swiftly to return the employee to productivity (Battle, 1988), although Soo Kim (1988) alternatively argues that the early motives were humanitarian and, over time, this was reinforced by economic considerations.

A boost to the development of workplace assistance, in America, came after the Hughes Act 1970, which gave public services mandatory responsibilities towards their employees' psychological health. In the 1980s the concept of health promotion began to take ascendancy over treatment, and this marked a transition from cure and palliation to prevention. More recently, there has been a further move to suggest that counselling should be applied to the organization itself (Hawkins and Miller, 1994) on the grounds that without including the organization in the stress equation its very survival could be threatened (Kets de Vries and Miller, 1984). For example, Warr (1996) identifies how low levels of control over work – in terms of autonomy, influence, power and decision-making – can be psychologically harmful to the individual.

This brief overview suggests that workplace counselling has passed through four stages of development (Bull, 1992):

1. The disease stage, where individuals are seen as victims of an illness which they must learn to manage, for example Alcoholics Anonymous.
2. The client-centred stage (a move to a broad-brush approach), where the post-war development of humanistic/existential therapies, in conjunction with more traditional approaches, enabled employee assistance to help individuals identify and meet their own needs.
3. The employee-work stage, where the workplace is acknowledged as influencing individual well-being.
4. The company as client stage, where the organization's policies and philosophy influence the individual, community and the planet.

But, what evidence is there in the literature to support the idea that workplace counselling operates at one of these four levels? Bull (1993) conducted a computerized literature search and found little evidence to support the idea that counselling focuses on stages three and four. The most frequently reported type of service is one that focuses on the individual and their personal problems (Erfurt and Foote, 1977; Cairo, 1983; Jones, 1983; Putnam and Stout, 1985; Maiden, 1988; Megranahan, 1990; Mullady, 1991).

The above review also revealed three core elements to workplace counselling:

1. Workplace counselling is short term in nature, usually three to six sessions, which mirrors the situation with counselling in general (Koss and Shiang, 1994). The idea of counselling being something that evolves over weeks, months and years appears to be largely a myth.
2. Counselling is geared towards problem-solving, for example, seeking to overcome an acute personal difficulty.
3. Counselling is aimed at returning the employee to work.

Therefore, theoretical models that fit workplace counselling should be short-term in nature and focused on a specific client concern. Searching for practical solutions to concrete problems is likely to be paramount.

At this stage a note of caution about theoretical models should be sounded. There is a danger that employing a model of counselling can lead to one of two extreme and opposing positions. At one extreme there is a tendency to underestimate the part they play in practice while at the other extreme, to give them such importance that the practitioner becomes rigid and inflexible in the delivery of counselling (Cunningham, 1994).

Counselling practice that eschews models as being too inflexible or deterministic to meet the subtlety and ever-changing nature of human needs is in danger of relying purely on hunches, intuition and gut feelings. While these have an important place in counselling, without any coherent thoughts about the nature of disturbance, how it is maintained and ways of working with distress, the counsellor is unable to monitor and evaluate the effectiveness of his/her work. In effect, such 'non-models' imply that in order to help people the counsellor has to hope to intuit the right things or have the right hunches.

At the opposite end of the scale is the practitioner who adheres so strictly to a model that the client becomes subordinate to its needs, that is the client and his/her problems are made to fit the theory. Any deficiencies in the theory are explained by shortcomings in the client, and clients with low self-esteem, for example, have their feelings reinforced by the very system or process they have turned to for help. The counsellors must therefore tread a path that includes an ability to respond spontaneously, intuitively and compassionately to another human being in distress, but also one in which they are able to detach themselves from the immediacy of the situation in order to reflect on what is happening and how they might best be of assistance. With these reservations in mind, I would now like to consider two approaches to counselling that may be adapted for use in the workplace.

Two Models of Counselling

I have thought long and hard about what models to present and the ways in which to bring them to the reader's attention. My starting point was that of a scientist: I would search the literature and present the facts, the hard objective evidence. When I thought about this my heart sank, and I delayed setting about my task (as the editors know only too well!). I was also reminded of a paper by Stiles et al. (1986) which discusses the equivalence paradox, which essentially points to the fact that whatever approach is employed there is little to choose between them in terms of effectiveness. My pursuit for an elixir or something to turn my base metal into the gold of the ideal model appeared fruitless.

I have therefore decided to throw-off the pretence of being an objective scientist and, instead, have concentrated on what energizes me. I have read about and experienced a number of approaches to counselling but two have affected me profoundly. The first was my training as a behavioural psychotherapist and the second, and most recent, is my enthusiasm for the Gestalt ways of working. I identify with the latter now, but I know that the spirit of my earlier training pervades my views. The cognitive-behavioural approaches may seem entirely appropriate for focused and short-term work, although such models can themselves exceed the three to six sessions mentioned above (see Rachman and Wilson, 1980, for a discussion of the treatment of obsessive–compulsive disorders, including duration). But what of the second? Surely it is a heresy to think of using a humanistic-existential approach, such as Gestalt theory, which emphasizes the use of a therapeutic process that respects the client's right to determine the speed at which self-awareness and emotional expression are developed? But why? As I said above, any model that is rigid and inflexible is unable to respond to the needs of people, real people, in distress.

I was relieved to find I was not alone in this struggle. Brian Thorne (1994) has taken a step into this unknown, largely due to the pressures of an ever-growing waiting list in his student counselling service. He writes of his apprehension as he took his first tentative steps in applying the person-centred approach in a short-term (three sessions plus the possibility of a follow-up group) and focused manner:

> Person-centred counsellors tend to recoil in horror from the notion of brief coun-selling. Such a concept, with its built-in assumption of a fixed number of sessions, seems to strike at the very heart of the client's right to self-determination. It puts all the power in the hands of the counsellor or allows an impersonal system to decree when counselling shall end irrespective of the actual wishes or needs of the client. (Thorne, 1994: 60–1)

I sensed a relief in his writing at the apparent success of his experiment, but also a great pleasure in finding more flexibility within himself and in the ideas which he holds so dear. Looking outside the counselling literature, there is further support for the idea of humanistic-existential approaches being applied in a focused way (Clark and Fraser, 1987; Nevis, 1987, Daldrup et al., 1988; Clayton, 1995).

It is beyond the scope of this chapter to provide a complete overview of both theories and practice. A full introduction to Gestalt theory and practice can be found in Clarkson and Mackewn (1993), and see Dryden and Golden (1987) for a discussion of cognitive-behavioural approaches. I will outline the principles of the two approaches and give an example of how each could help the same person.

Cognitive Behaviour Therapy

To write of cognitive behavioural therapy (CBT) as a single approach to the treatment of distress is misleading. Cognitive and behavioural therapies (Wolpe, 1958; Ellis, 1962; Meichenbaum, 1977; Beck et al., 1979; Skinner, 1979) developed independently of each other but there are many parallels between them. They aim to treat circumscribed problems that affect clients' current functioning; practical and attainable goals are set during the course of counselling, as are homework assignments; repeated skills practice is essential; and clients learn to monitor and evaluate behaviour (Marzilier, 1980). In both cognitive and behavioural approaches human distress is seen to arise from learning maladaptive behaviours rather than as a result of unconscious pro-cesses arising from early life experiences, intrapsychic conflict, or from blocks in self-awareness or emotional catharsis, as respectively postulated in the psychodynamic and humanistic schools.

Instrumental in the *rapprochement* between the cognitive and behavioural approaches was social learning theory (Bandura, 1977). Bandura argued that the individual is an important factor in the individual–environment equation. The individual is constantly interacting with the environment, both influencing it and being shaped by it, that is people think about themselves and what they are doing. Traditional behaviour therapy, however, asserted that human behaviour was determined by or contingent upon the environment. In the work environment, this means that employees are likely to work harder if the rewards are greater. The mediating role of the employees as people capable of construing and, in part, determining their own world is overlooked. Instead of learning being purely a function of reinforcement, social learning theory states that human behaviour can also be acquired by watching others perform a task or activity (vicarious learning) and by self-regulatory or self-evaluative processes. Thus a new dimension was introduced: a recognition that individuals are capable of mediating on their experiences by cognitive processes.

Two of the most frequently practised CBT approaches in the UK are based on the work of Ellis (1962) and Beck et al. (1979), who believe it is the way an individual thinks that shapes and alters feelings and behaviour (see Zajonc, 1984 for a criticism of this view). This section will focus on the work of Beck because of its familiarity to the author and not because of any assumed supremacy over other methods.

So far it has been suggested that disorder arises from maladaptive ways of thinking. In Beck's theory these thoughts are based upon certain assumptions that the individuals hold about themselves in relation to the world. These assumptions or *schemata* are often hidden from the individuals' awareness but they are acted upon as though they are true. They also result in rigid or absolutist views about the individuals and their world. In relation to depression, for example, Beck has identified a number of maladaptive 'automatic thoughts', such as:

- *Arbitrary inference* – drawing conclusions about an experience without considering alternative explanations. For example, because my boss has asked me to rewrite a discussion document it means he does not like me.
- *Selective abstraction* – basing a conclusion on an event instead of seeing it in a context. For example, my boss wants to get rid of me because she cancelled our last meeting, despite a history of regular meetings.
- *Over-generalization* – making a general rule about oneself from a limited number of experiences. For example, I did not get that promotion therefore I will never be promoted.
- *Minimization* – greatly underestimating one's abilities or achievements. For example, I got that job because I was probably the best of a poor bunch of candidates.
- *Personalization* – attributing blame to oneself for others' behaviour. For example, I must have been the cause of the boss's bad mood today.
- *Dichotomous reasoning* – categorizing behaviour as either extremely positive or negative. For example, if I don't get this work in on time it proves I am no good at my job.

Identifying and changing the sort of maladaptive thoughts outlined above is a key part of CBT, but it also seeks to go further to identify and change the assumptions upon which such thoughts are based. For example, Bill, a 31-year-old shop-floor supervisor, whose brother Mike died 23 years ago, presents for counselling, stating that he is fed-up and has no energy. When discussing his brother he says he has always felt second best to the memory of him. He now sees himself as hopeless and not capable of very much.

The counsellor, having explained the rationale of CBT to Bill, asks him for a current event he feels bad about. He says he panicked when asked earlier in the day to implement a new work rota. He is then asked what sorts of things went through his mind when he panicked. With careful encouragement he remembers saying to himself, 'I'm hopeless, I'll screw-up'. This is just the sort of automatic thought he can change. Together, Bill and the counsellor look at alternative ways of responding. First, they consider the data to see if it supports his hypothesis. It transpires that Bill has undertaken this exercise a number of times before, and although he has approached the task in much the same negative manner, he has always managed it successfully.

Bill agrees to try out a new thought, like 'this might be tough but I have done it before and I can do it again'. He likes the idea but is still wary about putting it into action. They now agree to rehearse the meeting where Bill has to introduce the new rota. Such an activity provides him with the opportunity for behavioural practice and also the chance to elicit further negative automatic thoughts. Bill learns about keeping a diary to capture his thoughts. He also records the situations that lead up to them and a detailed account of competing adaptive responses. He is further asked to rate the strength of his belief in both positive and negative responses and also to rate the level of change in his mood. By reflecting on his own behaviour he is able to give himself feedback rather than being dependent on others for reinforcement or a prisoner to his own negative thoughts. Over time the strength of belief in the negative thoughts should reduce while the adaptive cognitions should increase.

Bill's 'thoughts diary' gets fuller and he becomes more sophisticated at capturing his thoughts. He discerns a pattern to his thinking and so becomes aware of an assumption. He sees that, in the work context, most of his thoughts are concerned with not being capable of doing his job and that this is based on an assumption that if he is not successful in his job he will not be liked. Capturing assumptions is not often easy and may be beyond the scope of short-term counselling.

What CBT may be able to do in a short-term approach for people whose mood is not significantly lowered is to equip them with a set of skills for monitoring and managing their thoughts. If CBT is delivered in consecutive weekly sessions, its utility might be limited. By delivering it, for example, in three blocks of two weekly sessions over a longer period, its suitability for short-term focused work could be enhanced. CBT is an action-orientated therapy that focuses on thoughts and behaviour but does not directly address affect or emotions. I will now consider an approach where feelings and awareness are the central focus.

Gestalt Theory

The word 'gestalt' comes from the Gestalt school of experimental psychology which studied the ways in which we take in and make sense of information about the world around us. Gestalt refers to a process by which we integrate information delivered by our senses into a complete experience that is more than the sum of its parts (Clark and Fraser, 1987). These complete experiences are referred to as gestalts, and it is an assumption of Gestalt theory that all humans have an organismic drive towards completion of a gestalt. For example, if you hear a tune on the radio but cannot quite remember it, its memory often persists until the title or the full melody is recollected.

It is further posited that the meaning given to an object is not dependent upon the structure itself but takes place in relation to the environment in which it is seen (Parlett, 1991). For example, when I work in my garden I do not look at a plant in isolation but I see it in relation to the garden as a whole, that is I see it in its context. The same plant in a pot by a hospital bed will have a completely different meaning.

Linked to the idea of meaning being dependent upon context is the notion that the context is forever changing. In the above example, the garden is shaped by the seasons. My experience of it will partly be determined by this, and my previous experiences of the seasons. Thus, in the summer the garden is a place of great delight and hope, while in the autumn it takes on a sombre mood as plants die off in preparation for winter. No one person or their environment is a fixed entity. By that I mean who and what we are and our environment is forever changing and evolving. The Greek philosopher Heraclitus summed this up, stating you cannot step into the same spot in the same river twice.

Because I do my planting in the spring I cannot immediately see the fruits of my labours so I imagine what it will look like in the summer. I am seeking to bring about closure to an incomplete gestalt or what is called *unfinished business*. My imagination is a temporary way to bring about closure until the summer's rewards enable me to bring about full closure. The key point is that there is a need to bring about closure, it cannot be willed away.

This pattern of changes is known as the formation and destruction of gestalts and can be likened to a cycle in which people become aware of their needs, prepare for and implement a satisfying course of action before withdrawing and resting before the next need emerges. Nevis succinctly sums this up as 'finding out what is needed and going about getting it' (1987: 2). The destruction of gestalts is positive because those that are not destroyed represent trapped energy, or unfinished business. The stages of the cycle are set out below, and I shall illustrate this using an example of Ellen waking up on a work-day morning:

- *Withdrawal* – Ellen is at rest with no needs pressing for her attention. She is not inert but in her rest she is alive to the possibilities for future action.
- *Sensation* – Ellen cannot remain at rest indefinitely, sooner or later a gestalt will begin to form. At this stage she has a sensation that something

needs to be attended to. She hears a noise in the background which is disturbing her early morning doze.

- *Awareness* – the sensation becomes differentiated or clearer and Ellen is able to discern the nature of the need. The alarm is ringing.
- *Mobilization* – with awareness comes the realization of possible courses of action. Ellen weighs up her options: she will either ignore the alarm or turn it off.
- *Action* – Ellen decides to turn off the alarm, and her whole self is organized for action. She remembers where the alarm is, gets a picture of where the off-switch is and organizes her musculo-skeletal and nervous systems to reach out and turn it off.
- *Full contact* – Ellen discharges this energy satisfactorily and the goal is achieved. This information is relayed to her through her senses. She feels the switch move to the 'off' position and hears the noise of the alarm stop. She sinks back into her bed.
- *Satisfaction* – Ellen is able to allow the gestalt that has just been completed to be destroyed and merge into the background. Satisfaction can be likened to the warm after-glow following a good meal. In Ellen's case, she is able to lie back in the bed to enjoy the blissful absence of the alarm.

In time, Ellen will be faced with a new gestalt: whether or not to get up. So, this never-ending cycle of awareness and experience goes on. Gestalts can be completed in seconds but equally may take weeks, months or years.

Awareness is a central concept in Gestalt theory: it is the ability to use our senses – sight, hearing, touch, taste and smell – in an alert and attentive manner in the present moment to become aware of what is happening within ourselves and the world around us (Nevis, 1987). By attending to our senses we become aware of who we are, what we are and what we need. Therefore we can make better choices for ourselves and the environment in which we live. This means that all the information we need about ourselves is stored in the body, not purely in the mind. Therefore, in Gestalt theory it is important to attend to the whole person. In many ways Gestalt theory is concerned with attending to the obvious. Sadly, though, that which is readily available to our senses so often becomes denied or blocked-off, perhaps because it is too painful. When this happens the gestalt is said to be fixed. Gestalt theory is frequently linked with emotional catharsis, but it is wrong to view it as simply being concerned with this. Clients need to find ways of resolving a situation to which the emotion is attached, that is to complete unfinished business. Let's go back to the example of Bill to illustrates this.

While talking to the counsellor in a matter of fact way about his brother Mike, who died 23 years ago, Bill continually rubs his dry eyes. His head is saying one thing but his body appears to be saying something else. The counsellor does not assume a prior knowledge of the meaning of Bill's behaviour, but pays close attention to it. He invites Bill to explain whether his behaviour has any significance or whether there is an everyday explanation, for example, he might simply have an irritant in his eye. By paying attention to what superficially appears to be a random behaviour, perhaps gently repeating it over and over again, Bill is able to make contact with its deeper meaning.

Bill has not become stuck simply by chance; there is a very good, if redundant, reason. When Mike died there was no room for Bill's thoughts and feelings towards his idealized but dead brother. As he was small and needed his family's protection and love, he made an important (and reasonable) life decision – he would deny his feelings – so the gestalt became fixed. Life is different now. Bill is an adult with his own life and support systems. He no longer has to behave as if he is still that little boy. The challenge for Bill is to identify this split-off part of himself and find a satisfying way of saying good-bye to Mike, as opposed to simply having a cathartic experience like crying. Rather than talk about his brother, Bill's counsellor will help him to experience in the present moment of the counselling relationship his thoughts and feelings towards Mike. Bill might choose to continue to suppress his feelings but the urge to complete unfinished business will always be present.

A central aim of Gestalt theory is to help clients move away from an over-reliance on the environment for support towards self-support (see Perls et al., 1951), and at all times the counsellor will monitor the degree of support that is available to a particular client. For example, the counsellor will watch to see that Bill breathes regularly, particularly when he is distressed or struggling with some long-suppressed feelings. This is necessary for adequate oxygenation of the blood, but it is also a very basic form of support from the environment. At a 'higher' level the counsellor will consider factors such as Bill's support networks at home – friends and loved ones – before embarking on counselling. Finally, Bill can learn to support himself in the counselling chair. If he can ground himself by sitting fully in the chair and with his feet in good contact with the ground he literally supports himself well.

Although the goal is self-support, it does not ignore the fact that at times clients have a need for healthy or non-manipulative support from their environment (Higgins, 1996). It is a balancing act to find the line between support that encourages autonomy and that which overwhelms the client. If the client feels unsupported, it is unlikely that he/she will attempt new ways of being.

Applying Theory to Work Groups

In the above outlines of CBT and Gestalt theory I have focused on working with an individual, as this appears to be the dominant focus in workplace counselling, but there are also those who work with organizations, teams and departments. I have not used CBT as an approach with such a group, although it is possible to conceive of a situation where it would be apropriate, perhaps working with 'groupthink' (Janis, 1972), but I will give an example from my own experience of working with a group using Gestalt principles.

I was working with a team responsible for the design of a new product. They had become stuck, unable to move forward in their thinking and creativity. They appeared to go round and round in circles as they tried to break out of the deadlock. I thought they had become bogged down at the stage of mobilization in the cycle of awareness (see page 36 above). They had a clear idea of what they wanted to do but never seemed to be able to get beyond that (see Clarkson and Mackewn, 1993, for a discussion of interruptions in the cycle of experience). I listened to the group talking and I became aware of a consistent obstructing message coming from them. If the project was successful, they would gain a reputation for themselves which would lead to more work, maybe even new premises. Instead of sounding excited, the distress in their voices and the tension in the room was palpable. Whenever they discussed their difficulties with the boss, all they heard from him was that this was an incredibly exciting opportunity.

This was the point of impasse beyond which they would not go. Instead of exhorting them to do better, like the boss, I decided to honour their reality, to stay with what is rather than how it should be. They would not be able to move on until this gestalt, albeit painful, was completed. As they began tentatively to express themselves, it emerged that a significant number of the group had risen quickly from shop-floor manual jobs into well-paid white-collar occupations. The rate of change was almost too fast for them. They felt as though they were having to give up more than they were getting, and this was compounded by a boss who did not seem interested.

There was real pain for some of them. Their jobs and circumstances had changed enormously which meant that they had lost previously important support networks. The community in which they lived had undergone enormous changes as a result of the recession, with old long-established industries dying away, and one man in the group had suffered a recent significant bereavement. They needed to acknowledge the past, even say good-bye to it. This was the first time they had shared their concerns; before they had always been so busy focusing on the task. As they allowed themselves to experience what was happening, they found ways to support each other and to accommodate the past and integrate it into their lives, rather than being trapped by it. As this process continued, they began to move ahead with the project, and they were able to identify systems and structures that were getting in the way of their productivity. By attending to the obvious, the impasse, rather than relying on interpretation and guidance, they were able to find a satisfying way forward.

Conclusion

In the absence of any clear theory of counselling in organizations, or for the efficacy of one approach over another, this chapter has focused on two approaches, CBT and Gestalt, although it remains to be demonstrated whether they can be adapted to the demands of the workplace. After reviewing the literature, a developmental model of counselling in organizations has been suggested. It has been further suggested that counselling focuses on the individual, is short term, and seeks to deal with specific problems. The success of any theory when applied in the workplace will largely be dependent on its ability to meet these criteria.

The illustrations I have used oversimplify what can be an extended process, and they highlight a difficulty in workplace counselling. The difficulty is that there is always a tension between matching the intensity or depth of work to the time available. It is essential that workplace counsellors are aware of this constraint, particularly when a client is extremely distressed. Counselling should not always be considered as a means to 'unstick' people from rigid and over-controlled ways of being. Sometimes it has a very important task to perform in holding people together (see Kepner, 1995, for a discussion of the importance of support in counselling). Counsellors should therefore have knowledge of major mental health problems, plus other resources in the community that clients may subsequently use. Daldrup et al. (1988) and Koss and Shiang (1994), discuss factors in the decision to 'treat' clients.

Adapting counselling models to the workplace is a challenge to theorists to develop ideas on focused ways of working with clients who may not have traditionally seen counselling as part of their natural constituency. Without this, counselling is a luxury for a select few. Furthermore, it is a challenge to provide ways of helping that bring about meaningful changes in people's lives which do not 'scapegoat' them for very real problems in the workplace. In the example of Bill, his distress may have its roots in the problems outlined, but it may be further seated in work practices and organizational values that strip people of their dignity and sap their energy. Counselling in the workplace should not be used as an apology for a climate where labour is subordinated to the needs of capital.

References

Albert, W.C., Smythe, P.C. and Brook, R.C. (1985) 'Promises to keep: an evaluator's perspective on Employee Assistance Programs', *Evaluation and Program Planning*, 8: 175–82.

Bandura, A. (1977) *Social Learning Theory*. Englewood Cliffs, NJ: Prentice-Hall.

Battle, S.F. (1988) 'Issues to consider in planning Employee Assistance Programs', *Employee Assistance Quarterly*, 3 (3/4): 79–83.

Beck, A.T., Rush, A.J., Shaw, B.F. and Emery, G. (1979) *Cognitive Therapy of Depression*. New York: Guilford Press.

Bull, A.D. (1992) 'Confidential counselling service: a new breed of EAP?', *Employee Counselling Today*, 4 (2): 25–8.

Bull, A.D. (1993) 'An exploratory study to measure satisfaction with the Confidential Counselling Service, and to identify factors associated with clients' satisfaction'. Unpublished MSc dissertation, University of East London.

Cairo, P.C. (1983) 'Counselling in industry: a selected review of the literature', *Personnel Psychology*, 36: 1–18.

Clark, N. and Fraser, T. (1987) *The Gestalt Approach*. Horsham: Roffey Park.

Clarkson, P. and Mackewn, J. (1993) *Fritz Perls*. London: Sage.

Clayton, S. (1995) 'Stepping into the wave', *Counselling at Work*, Winter (11): 3–4.

Cunningham, G. (1994) *Effective Employee Assistance Programs: A Guide for EAP Counsellors and Managers*. London: Sage.

Daldrup, R.J., Beutler, L.E., Engle, D. and Greenberg, L.S. (1988) *Focused Expressive Psychotherapy*. London: Cassell.

Dryden, W. and Golden, W.L. (1987) *Cognitive Behavioural Approaches to Psychotherapy.* London: Hemisphere Publishing Corporation.

Ellis, A. (1962) *Reason and Emotion in Psychotherapy.* Secaucus, NY: Lyle Stuart.

Erfurt, J.C. and Foote, A. (1977) 'Occupational Employee Assistance Programs for substance abuse and mental health problems'. MI dissertation, University of Michigan, Ann Arbor.

Hawkins, P. and Miller, E. (1994) 'Psychotherapy in and with organizations', in P. Clarkson and M. Pokorny (eds), *Handbook of Psychotherapy.* London: Routledge.

Higgins, J. (1996) 'In support of rescuing', *The Gestalt South West Newsletter,* 22: 20–1.

Janis, I.L. (1972) *Victims of Groupthink.* Boston, MA: Houghton Mifflin.

Jones, D. (1983) *Performance Benchmarks for the Comprehensive Employee Assistance Program.* Center City, MN: Hazleden Foundation.

Kepner, J.I. (1995) *Healing Tasks: Psychotherapy with Adult Survivors of Childhood Abuse.* San Francisco: Jossey-Bass.

Kets de Vries, F.R. and Miller, D. (1984) *The Neurotic Organization.* San Francisco: Jossey-Bass.

Koss, M.P. and Shiang, J. (1994) 'Research on brief psychotherapy', in S. Garfield and A. Bergin (eds), *Handbook of Psychotherapy and Behavior Change.* New York: John Wiley and Sons.

Maiden, P.R. (1988) 'EAP evaluation in a government agency', *Employee Assistance Quarterly,* 3 (3/4): 191–203.

Marzilier, J. (1980) 'Cognitive therapy and behaviour practice', *Behavioural Research and Therapy,* 18 (4): 249–58.

Megranahan, M. (1990) 'Employee Assistance Programmes – Part 2: Frameworks and guiding principles', *Addiction Counselling World,* 2 (1): 4–8.

Meichenbaum, D. (1977) *Cognitive Behavior Modification.* New York: Plenum.

Mullady, S.F. (1991) 'The Champion Paper Co. EAP, and major issues for EAPs in the 1990s', *Employee Assistance Quarterly,* 6 (3): 37–50.

Nevis, E.C. (1987) *Organizational Consulting: A Gestalt Approach.* New York: Gestalt Institute of Cleveland Press.

Parlett, M. (1991) 'Reflections in field theory', *The British Gestalt Journal,* 1: 69–81.

Perls, F., Hefferline, R.F. and Goodman, P. (1951) *Gestalt Therapy: Excitement and Growth in the Human Personality.* London: Souvenir Press.

Putnam, S.L. and Stout, R.L. (1985) 'Evaluating Employee Assistance Policy in an HMO-based alcoholism project', *Evaluation and Program Planning,* 8 (3): 183–94.

Rachman, S.J. and Wilson, G.T. (1980) *The Effects of Psychological Therapy.* Oxford: Pergamon Press.

Reddy, M. (1993) *EAPs and Counselling Provision in UK Organizations: An ICAS Report and Policy Guide.* Milton Keynes: ICAS.

Skinner, B.F. (1979) *About Behaviorism.* New York: Knopf.

Soo Kim, D.S. (1988) 'Assessing Employee Assistance Programs: evaluation typology and models', *Employee Assistance Quarterly,* 3 (3/4): 169–88.

Stiles, W., Shapiro, D. and Elliott, R. (1986) 'Are all psychotherapies equivalent?' *American Psychologist,* 41: 165–80.

Thorne, B. (1994) 'Brief companionship', in D. Mearns (ed.), *Developing Person-Centred Counselling.* London: Sage.

Warr, P. (1996) *Psychology at Work.* Harmondsworth: Penguin.

Wheeler, S. and Lyon, D. (1992) 'Employee benefits for the employer's benefit: how companies respond to employee stress', *Personnel Review,* 21 (7): 47–65.

Wolpe, J. (1958) *Psychotherapy by Reciprocal Inhibition.* Stanford, CA: Stanford University Press.

Zajonc, R.B. (1984) 'On the primacy of affect', *American Psychologist,* 39: 117–23.

3

Internal Counselling Provision for Organizations

Noreen Tehrani

Organizations have been providing help for employees to solve emotional and social problems for many years. Originally this help was provided by occupational welfare services. Welfare services have a long history in Britain with the first welfare programmes being introduced towards the end of the nineteenth century. The organizations and the social environments in which welfare services operate have, however, changed enormously during the past 50 years and, as a result, the support demanded by organizations and their employees has altered dramatically. Compared to 10 years ago, there are fewer organizations providing a traditional welfare approach to employee care, while more are providing employee counselling services. This chapter looks at the origins and changing role of occupational welfare services and how the service has developed within the Post Office. There is an identification of the strengths and weaknesses of an internal welfare service and how a new service, Employee Support, is integrating the principles of psychology and counselling with those of welfare in order to produce an organizationally aware employee counselling and support service. The First Line Counselling model developed within the Post Office is described, together with the methods by which this model of counselling is to be monitored and evaluated.

The Origins and Changing Role of Welfare Services

Welfare in the workplace was established in nineteenth-century Britain by a body of enlightened industrialists. The principles adopted by these industrialists demonstrated concern for the quality of life and well-being of employees. The first welfare service was created in 1886 when Rowntrees appointed a welfare officer for their York factory. This idea spread and by 1913 there were sufficient welfare officers to form the Welfare Workers Association (Edmonds, 1991).

In the beginning of the twentieth century the state began to assume a greater influence in the area of employee welfare and employment law. In 1911 the National Insurance Act introduced contributory systems for insuring most of the working population against sickness, providing free medical attention and insurance against unemployment. The Beveridge Report, published in 1942, unified the systems of insurance against sickness, disability, unemployment and old age into a national scheme of social security (Thomson, 1960). These changes provided a minimum level of social security for everyone in Britain and, as a result, the responsibility of organizations to provide for the basic welfare needs of their employees was reduced.

At this time, the Post Office Board decided to undertake a benchmarking exercise to compare the employee welfare provisions in the Post Office with those of a number of other large organizations. Among the organizations taking part in this benchmarking exercise were J. Lyons, London Transport, Birmingham Corporation, Boots, Cable and Wireless, Debenhams, Imperial Tobacco, Woolworths, W.H. Smiths and Raleigh Cycles. The benchmarking report indicated that most of the organizations had appointed staff to be responsible exclusively for employee well-being and that these 'welfare officers' were also responsible for certain social conditions in the workplace, such as ensuring that the canteen, coat-drying and rest-room provisions met the needs of the workforce. The welfare officers also provided advice to employees on domestic and other matters (Post Office Welfare Study Group, 1944). With the welfare state taking responsibility for many activities previously dealt with by organizations' welfare services, there was a need for these services to redefine their roles.

In 1946 the Welfare Workers Association, which had already changed its name several times, became known as the Institute of Personnel Management and with this change there was a gradual separation of the welfare professionals into two groups: first, those who were interested in managing people's problems on behalf of the organization, and secondly, those who chose to remain in welfare, providing a supportive and caring approach to employees' personal problems. By 1966 the role of 'welfare' was no longer seen as appropriate for the new 'personnel professionals', who were more interested in developing their role as an arm of management, involved in improving business efficiency and personnel management rather than looking after the social needs of the workforce (Fox, 1966). Meanwhile, the welfare officers who chose to remain within occupational welfare services continued to promote their role, quoting Martin – 'personnel managers are more interested in managing people than in providing them with the help, advice and guidance they needed to solve their personal and work problems' (1967: 270–2).

Today there are still wide variations in the type and level of welfare services available in organizations. In a study into the welfare situation in 100 UK companies, Edmonds (1991) showed that there was no clear definition of what modern company welfare provisions entailed, nor where the responsibility for developing and providing employee welfare services should rest. Organizations faced with such a poorly defined employee welfare service are likely either to look elsewhere for the provision of welfare and counselling services or to forgo the services altogether (Whitfield, 1995).

Welfare Services in the Post Office

A standard textbook for welfare officers, *Welfare at Work*, was written by Alec Martin who had been the Welfare Adviser to the General Post Office (Martin, 1967). The book described the roles, responsibilities, selection and training of welfare officers adopted by the Post Office. Martin's description of the role of welfare officers is very similar to the role a traditional welfare officer fulfils today. Welfare officers are involved in:

- Helping employees solve their own problems.
- Providing private consultation on any type of personal problem.
- Advising the organization on group welfare matters (e.g., accommodation, safety, first aid, sports and social activities).
- Providing assistance with personal skills training courses.
- Advising on staff relations.

Martin described the major areas of the welfare officers' work as being involved in resolving employees' domestic, financial, sickness (mental and physical), bereavement, living accommodation, employment and retirement, or resignation difficulties. The problems faced by Post Office employees today are very similar to those in 1967 with the exception, in common with most other organizations, of an increase in the number of stress and trauma-related problems. It is important to note that as a result of the Post Office's caring culture and the support provided to employees the levels of stress experienced by Post Office employees are generally less than those found in other organizations.

Martin recognized the value of counselling as an important skill for welfare officers, however his description of counselling as a 'special kind of interviewing' is more appropriate for counselling skills than counselling itself. In the early 1990s the Post Office Welfare Service had, in response to an increasing need to provide emotional and psychological support, initiated training courses for all welfare officers in counselling and trauma care (Conlon, 1991).

The Post Office was one of the first organizations to introduce and evaluate an organizational counselling programme in the UK. The evaluation study, which was set up to investigate the benefits of an in-house specialist counselling service (Cooper et al., 1990), was designed to augment the First Line Counselling support provided for Post Office employees by the welfare officers and occupational health nurses. The specialist counselling role was to deal with the more complex and deep-seated psychological problems which would previously have been referred to external counselling agencies. The researchers predicted that, unlike external specialists, the internal counsellors would have the advantage of a broad knowledge of the organization and its culture, and be better able to help employees, particularly with work-related problems. The study, which lasted four years and involved approximately 250 employees, provided some evidence to support the notion that employee counselling could bring about direct savings due to a reduction in stress-related sickness absence. In this study the savings were estimated to be in the region of £102,000 over a six-month period. Although the specialist counselling study was regarded as a success, the Post Office did not choose to introduce the nation-wide network of internal specialist counsellors, as had been recommended by the study, but decided to focus its attention on developing and strengthening the First Line Counselling and other services provided by its welfare and occupational health services (Welch and Tehrani, 1992).

The Strengths and Weaknesses of the Post Office Welfare Service

A fundamental review of the welfare service was undertaken between 1993 and 1994, the objective of the review being to prepare the service to meet the challenges of the next five years. The review was in three parts. First, there was a need to establish what the users of the service wanted from the service. Secondly, there was an assessment of what the customers of the service (that is the Post Office businesses who were paying for the service) wanted from a welfare service. Finally, the views of the welfare practitioners themselves were sought on how the service could be improved to meet the needs of users, customers and the welfare officers themselves.

One of the main sources of information on user needs came from an independent attitude survey which had been undertaken by Royal Mail in 1993 as part of a larger review of the occupational health and welfare services. This survey looked at the attitudes of managers who had used the service either as a client or as a place to refer an employee with personal problem. Managers who had never used the services were also interviewed in order to establish any reasons for not having done so. The attitude survey showed that there were high levels of satisfaction with the services by managers (Table 3.1).

Although the satisfaction rates were high, welfare officers were concerned to discover that over a quarter of managers did not find the service effective and over 10 per cent did not see it as confidential, professional or satisfying their needs. Of the 322 managers who took part in the survey, only 67 per cent had actually used the service. The reasons given by managers for not using the service were either that they had never had a need (72 per cent) or that no one had ever asked to be referred (15 per cent).

When managers were asked to identify what the welfare service provided, they identified the range of services listed in Table 3.2. Counselling was shown to have the highest level of awareness (60 per cent), with legal advice, sickness absence advice, and debt and bereavement counselling following closely behind.

Over 75 per cent of the managers said that they thought that 'Welfare', as a title of the service, was old-fashioned and gave the wrong impression of what the service offered. However, there was little agreement on what the service should be called.

The attitude survey highlighted the weakness in the area of user or potential user awareness; most of the services had a less than 50 per cent awareness level among managers. The implication of this finding to the service was that if employees do not know what is on offer they are unlikely to take advantage of the help which is available to them. The conclusion from the survey's

Table 3.1   *Satisfaction levels of managers who have used welfare services*

Attribute	Level of satisfaction (%)
Effective	72
Confidential	89
Professional	89
Satisfied	87

Table 3.2   *Manager awareness of services offered by Welfare*

Service	Awareness of service (%)
Counselling	60
Legal advice	52
Advice on sickness absence	52
Debt counselling	49
Bereavement counselling	49
DSS advice	44
Pension advice	41
Assault on duty	39
Medical retirement	38
Stress seminars	33
Retirement seminars	32

researchers was that the general awareness of welfare provision needed to be raised, in particular the knowledge of the actual products and services which were on offer.

In the early 1990s the Post Office businesses began to look at their internal suppliers and to demand the same levels of service as they would expect from external suppliers. A supplier review was carried out on welfare services by Royal Mail (the largest Post Office business) that raised a number of questions which challenged the way that Welfare supplied its services to its business customers. The most important questions were:

- Why should we have a welfare service?
- What are the benefits of providing welfare services to the business?
- What kinds of service do welfare offer?
- How do we know that we are getting value for money?

Trying to answer these questions forced Welfare to look at the strengths and weaknesses of the service in meeting the needs of the business. Managers recognized that welfare interventions could not only help to reduce the levels of sickness absence and attendance problems, but also demonstrate the caring approach of the Post Office to employees. Also, managers were generally satisfied with the level and quality of advice they received. The main weakness identified was the lack of information for management on the benefits of the service to the organization. As a result of the Welfare Services 'open door' policy, where employees had open access to a welfare officer, the costs of the service were driven more by user demand than by business needs, thus resulting in a reactive rather than a proactive approach to employee social and psychological well-being. The lack of a clearly defined portfolio of services and products had led to the businesses being unaware of what was on offer, or the cost of individual products and services. Finally, the charging mechanism, which invoiced the businesses on a time basis rather than on the number of cases handled, gave no incentive to the service to improve levels of productivity as the longer it took for a welfare officer to complete a case, the more the service was paid regardless of the effectiveness of spending the extra time. In summary, the businesses found that although the service was valued, it lacked a business focus which was vital to the development of an effective customer–supplier relationship.

In order to gather the responses of the welfare officers to the attitude survey and the business review, three divisional meetings were held in 1994, at which welfare officers were encouraged to look at the needs of the service as well as their own needs. They recognized the need to address the weaknesses that had been identified and expressed a wish to develop a service which matched more closely the needs of the users and the customers. With respect to their own roles, they said that they found working with employees rewarding, particularly as there was immediate feedback from their clients and customers on the value of their services in helping employees and in reducing the levels of sickness absence and attendance problems, and they believed that the business benefited from an improvement in the work performance of the employees. The welfare officers did not, however, believe that their skills were always valued by the business and they recognized that it was important to develop a more professional image.

Employee Support – the New Concept

In October 1994 there was a change of leadership in Welfare. The new Head of Service was a qualified chartered counselling and occupational psychologist with experience in operational management within a commercial organization.

The work which had been undertaken to identify the strengths and weaknesses of the service was used as the starting point for developing a service which met the needs of customers, users and practitioners. Although the service had been involved in some important work on improving its provisions using the principles of total quality, this work had concentrated on improvements to the existing service rather than taking the more 'blue skies' approach of looking at the kind of service which was required to meet the needs of the customer. The outcome of this process was to develop a service which maximized the strengths of the existing welfare service and which added to its utility by introducing the professionalisms of psychology and counselling. It was clear that in order to help the organization meet its moral and legal obligations to employees, Welfare had to be a more broadly based and professionally qualified service.

The first task was to agree the organization's responsibility for providing care. Essentially, organizational care is of three types. First, employers have a legal 'duty of care' for their employees and this duty is set out in statute and common law. Employees are entitled to expect their employer to fulfil their legal responsibility to provide a reasonable level of care for their physical, psychological and social well-being and if these expectations are not met the employee may claim compensation for any damages which may have resulted from the employer's negligence (Cooke, 1995). There are some areas where the organization's legal duties of care have been specified under statute and these include caring for the victims of violence, preventing and dealing with sexual or racial harassment and the assessment of workplace environments for physical and psychosocial environmental hazards.

Secondly, organizations may take on a role for caring for employees by building the concept of employee care into the organization's mission or business values (Deal and Kennedy, 1982). Marks and Spencer, for example, believe that the organization can assist in preventing mental ill-health by giving people good working environments, clearly defined jobs, regular and honest appraisals and counselling facilities (Miller, 1992). Where organizations have developed a culture of caring, these values become part of the way that the organization operates and as such may form part of the legal or moral contract between the organization and its workforce.

Finally, some organizations take a more active role in promoting the well-being of their workforce, by providing help for individuals with personal problems, particularly where the problem has a negative impact on the employee's performance at work. Organizations which choose to help employees to identify the cause of their problems provide accurate and appropriate information and guidance, short-term counselling and support, and believe that this support will bring about financial and other advantages to the organization (Berridge, 1990). Support for employees which is not provided as a legal duty is seen as an employee benefit rather than an organizational responsibility. However, there is an increasing body of evidence (Cooper et al., 1990) which shows that where organizations accept a role for counselling and supporting employees with personal problems, there are benefits for both the organization and the employee. The three levels of organizational responsibility (Table 3.3) provide a basis for developing a service which is designed to give an appropriate level and range of supports to the organization.

Clearly it was important for the service to help the organization meet its legal obligation (Level 1). This required the practitioners to be competent in the delivery of advice guidance, assessment, counselling, education and training in each of the areas described as any failure to provide an appropriate level of help could be seen as a failure of the organization to meet its duty of care, resulting in being sued by the employee. At Level 2 the Post Office has developed a culture which values the contribution of each member of the workforce. The development of policies which recognize the needs of the employees is therefore an important part of maintaining that culture. The role of the service at Level 2 is to support the business managers to fulfil their roles by providing them with accurate and appropriate advice on handling employees with social or psychological problems, to train managers to deal with incidents in the workplace, to handle difficult or distressed employees, and to make appropriate

Table 3.3 *Levels of organizational responsibility for the psychosocial well-being of employees*

Levels of organizational responsibility	Examples of responsibility
Level 1 – Duty Legal requirement	Violence in the workplace Organizational stress Harassment Risk assessment
Level 2 – Need Organizational mission and values	Policy development Advice to management Manager training Organizational well-being programmes
Level 3 – Benefit Individual effectiveness	Problem assessment Information/guidance Advice Counselling and support

and timely referrals for expert help. In the area of management information the service has a role in providing managers with information which will help them to make decisions on how to handle employees and areas of concern in the workplace. At Level 3 the service provides support for the individual employee. This support needs to be appropriate, competent and relevant to the organization with the focus of helping employees to resolve difficulties which have an impact on their performance in the workplace.

Competency

Whenever an organization provides information, advice or interventions which are designed to meet the requirements of the Health and Safety legislation, it is incumbent on the organization to ensure that the person delivering the advice or support is competent to do so. Many of the areas which are illustrated in the levels of organizational responsibility require a trained and experienced person to provide the advice and guidance, to undertake assessments and to develop interventions and training. There is the additional need for the organization to ensure that the service is professionally managed and monitored. With the increasing need for organizations to address the psychological and social areas of employee well-being within existing Health and Safety policies, it is important that the organization recognizes the need to seek specialist psychological and social advice. The counselling and related psychological interventions which are provided in the areas of stress, trauma and burnout need to be delivered by qualified, professionally trained staff who are monitored by a competent chartered psychologist. As a result of the changing needs of the organization for support in the psychosocial area of employee well-being, there had to be a change in the emphasis of the welfare service from one which had its main focus on social issues to one which also embraced psychological aspects of employee well-being.

Users had already expressed the view that Welfare was not an appropriate title for the service so it became even more important to launch the new-style service with a name which more accurately reflected its actual scope of provision. In order to choose a name which was acceptable to the customers and users, focus groups were set up to look at a range of possible names, from which the name Employee Support emerged as the title. This described most accurately the work which was to be undertaken within the service.

The next stage of the process of establishing Employee Support as a reality was to develop a business plan which was designed to set the course for the development of a new Employee Support service. Some of the key elements of the Employee Support business plan were:

- To introduce a more effective method of service delivery.
- To develop products and services which meet the needs of the organization and employees.
- To assess the levels of competence of all practitioners.
- To work with customers to establish service level agreements.
- To develop tools for monitoring and evaluating the service.

In May 1995 Welfare Services celebrated its 50th birthday with a national conference, at which it launched its new identity 'Employee Support' and approved the new service's mission statement and code of practice, which had been designed to provide the service with a clear statement of its business philosophy (Table 3.4).

Delivering Employee Support

Employee Support delivers seven services:

- Information
- Assessment
- Short-term intervention
- Employee education
- Manager information
- Manager training
- Special services

Each service is broken down into products. For example, in the service of assessment the products delivered by Employee Support include social well-being assessments, individual stress assessments, substance abuse assessments and debt management assessments. Each of the assessment products is defined by a product specification, has a training programme, has practitioner competency requirements and service delivery standards.

Employee Support provides services to around 16 per cent of Post Office employees each year and this volume of work required an efficient and customer-focused process for delivering its services. The service delivery process, which was launched in October 1995 following consultation with customers and clients, uses a network of staff telephones as an intake point and allows a trained Employee Support Adviser (ESA) to assess the needs of the employee and, where there is a need for legal, financial or social information, to provide help on the helpline. Where the employee requires more

Table 3.4   *Employee Support's Mission and Code of Practice*

Employee Support Mission Statement

We will maintain and promote the well-being of individuals and the organization by providing the highest quality Employee Support services. We will anticipate and meet the changing needs of our customers by combining professionalism, objectivity and care with value for money, in an atmosphere of trust and enthusiasm.

Employee Support Code of Practice

We will:

- Provide a nation-wide service to the highest professional standards, both ethically and in terms of delivery for all our customers, businesses, individuals and their representatives alike, enabling them to act with confidence on all Employee Support related issues.
- Work in close partnership with the businesses, and using our knowledge and experience, identify Employee Support related needs and advise on appropriate solutions.
- Undertake research to provide new products and services to benefit the well-being of all our customers, and so maintain our lead in Employee Support practice and contribute positively to the specialism.
- Provide Employee Support staff with the technical resources and skills to carry out our mission and to create an atmosphere of trust and enthusiasm in which they can flourish.

Values:

- Continual improvement
- Customer focus
- Professionalism
- Objectivity
- Care

- Value for money
- Proactive approach
- Responsiveness
- Trust
- Enthusiasm

help, the ESA arranges an appointment with a local ESA for an assessment or other service. The service delivery process has a number of advantages. First, it gives ready access for employees and other users to an information database and expert Employee Support advice and guidance. Secondly, it allows the ESA to undertake an initial assessment of need and to make an appointment for a specific Employee Support service. The process also allows the work of the field ESAs to be planned and appointments to be scheduled.

Where employees' needs are not appropriate for Employee Support, the caller is redirected to the appropriate internal or external resource. For the business, the service delivery process addresses the problem of welfare 'open door' by providing an open access to the telephone network for advice and information and then a sifting process which can take account of the level and types of service the businesses wish to fund. Employees with needs outside the range of services for which the organization is willing to pay, will be referred to external community resources where their needs can be met.

Counselling Defined

Counselling as a profession is a relatively new activity. However, the skills of counselling, which are more accurately described as communication skills, are as old as humankind itself. As a high level of counselling skills are essential to all aspects of Employee Support work, training in counselling skills is included in the training modules for all the Employee Support products. Where an ESA is unable to demonstrate the required level of competence in counselling skills during training for product delivery, the ESA would not be allowed to deliver the product until they had received further training in the counselling skill and been assessed as competent.

There are many different definitions of counselling. The one which is used by the British Association for Counselling (BAC) in their Code of Ethics is: 'Counselling includes work with individuals and with relationships which may be developmental, crisis support, psychotherapeutic, guiding or problem solving. . . . The task of counselling is to give the "client" an opportunity to explore, discover and clarify ways of living more satisfyingly and resource-fully' (BAC, 1984). The BAC emphasis is on counselling facilitating the process of change by allowing the clients the space to explore and discover ways to resolve their difficulties.

A rather different definition is provided by Burkes and Stefflre:

> Counselling denotes a professional relationship between a trained counsellor and a client. This relationship is usually person to person, although it may sometimes involve more than two people. It is designed to help clients to understand and clarify their views on their life space, and to learn to reach their self-determined goals through meaningful, well-informed choices and through resolution of problems of an emotional or interpersonal nature. (1979)

For Burkes and Stefflre, the emphasis is on the professional relationship and the actions which come out of the counselling process. In organizations where the counselling is short term, the Burkes and Stefflre approach to counselling is perhaps the most relevant.

In the field of organizational counselling there has been little research to identify what kind of counselling is most appropriate. Many organizations have set parameters which affect the type of counselling which can be offered to their employees. In the Post Office the organization wanted a model of counselling which was short term (a maximum of four counselling sessions), focused on helping the employee to be more effective and productive at work. This approach looks at problem resolution rather than at deep-seated personal issues. The model of counselling which has been developed to meet the needs of Post Office employees is First Line Counselling. This model of counselling has been developed over a number of years and has recently been revisited to bring it in line with the needs of the Post Office for an integrated approach to Employee Support, ranging from advice to specialist counselling.

First Line Counselling

The emergence of Employee Support as a service which has been able to integrate the professional skills of the welfare officer, counsellor and psychologist challenged the traditional views of counselling. If organizations needed an integrated system for dealing with organizational problems related to the psychological and social well-being of employees, then this suggested that there is also a need to develop an integrated counselling model which combines the tools, techniques and knowledge of welfare, counselling and psychology. The problem which faced the author when attempting to develop this integrated form of counselling was that most other researchers in the field of organizational counselling had focused on the identification or modification of existing models of counselling rather than establishing the needs of organizations and employees from which an organizational model of counselling could be developed.

Employees enter the First Line Counselling programme via Employee Support's service delivery process. The assessing Employee Support Advisers (ESAs) will ask the employee the outline of his/her problem and if they are unable to meet the need of the employee an appointment will be made for a field ESA to undertake an in-depth assessment, the nature of the assessment being determined by the type of problem presented (i.e. individual stress, social well-being, debt or substance abuse). During this second assessment, the employee will become more aware of the full nature of his/her problems and the actions which he/she will need to take to address those problems. If, following this assessment, the employee is unable to resolve these difficulties on his/her own, the ESA will consider the possibility of referring the employee for First Line Counselling. There is a strict selection criteria for employees wishing to enter First Line Counselling and all the ESAs who are trained in assessments will look for the positive and negative indicators for selecting clients for the programme. Among the positive indicators are:

- A strong motivation for change.
- A clearly defined problem.
- The employee's acceptance that change is possible.
- A facility to think objectively.
- An ability to make a working relationship with the counsellor.
- Reasonably good listening skills.

There are a number of clients who are unsuitable for First Line Counselling, including clients who are experiencing the following:

- Overwhelming anger, grief, guilt, sorrow, etc.
- Psychiatric problems.
- Extreme violence.
- Alcohol or drug addiction.
- An inability to recognize the client's own responsibility for his/her situation.
- Sexual problems.

The First Line Counselling model involves four session of counselling which are focused on helping employees develop solutions to their problems. The sessions all last one hour and are spread over a period of six to eight weeks. Each of the four sessions is defined with clear objectives and outputs. Briefly, the content of the four sessions is as follows.

Session One

There are five stages to session one. First, an introduction which sets the scene and states the 'rules' of counselling, including confidentiality, the time available and the type of counselling which is to be provided. The aim of the introduction is to allow the employee an informed choice on whether he/she wishes to enter the counselling contract or would prefer to opt for an alternative way of resolving the difficulty. The introduction links back to the assessment and seeks confirmation of the problem which the employee wishes to address during the counselling. The second stage is a period of 'problem free talk', during which time the counsellor is able to build a relationship with the employee by looking at his/her life and family in order to identify the employee's strengths and successes in handling his/her life to date. The third stage is a period during which the employee defines his/her problem and identifies the times and situations where the problem troubles him/her. In stage four the counsellor identifies, with the employee, the strengths and support network that the employee has at his/her disposal to help him/her address the problem. Finally, in stage five the counsellor summarizes the session and, where appropriate, agrees homework. The session is then closed.

Sessions Two and Three

The second and third sessions have an identical format in that the counsellor's role is to help the employee bring about the changes agreed in the first session. Sessions two and three are made up of four stages. The first stage is to introduce the session and to review what has happened since the last session, including a review of homework. The second stage involves an identification of the areas of change which are required at this stage of the counselling. In stage three the employee looks at the times when he/she has coped well with his/her problem – this may be at different times with different people or in different circumstances. In stage four the counsellor identifies the best of sources of support available to the employee from a portfolio of psychological, counselling, training, information and other interventions which are available to the counsellor as part of the First Line Counselling support material. The session closes with a summary of what happened during the session and an agreement of homework.

Session Four

The most important aspect of the fourth session is to make a good and positive close to the counselling process. The first stage is an introduction to the session and a review of progress. There follows an acknowledgement of any loose ends, which may include unmet expectations. The third stage is focused on self-empowerment and a recognition of the changes that the employee has made during the period of the counselling. Stage four is a summary of the whole counselling process. Stage five allows the counsellor and employee time to say good-bye and close the counselling formally.

Monitoring and Evaluating Employee Support

The Post Office expects its suppliers to monitor and evaluate the standards and quality of its services. This is particularly important for Employee Support where traditionally there has been very little monitoring of service quality and standards. The objectives set by the Post Office for Employee Support in the area of monitoring and standards are as follows:

- Establish an effective method of service delivery which maximizes the productivity of the Employee Support staff and resources.
- Develop and evaluate products which meet the social and personal needs of employees and the organization.
- Deliver tailored services which meet the needs of each of the Post Office business customers.
- Review the cost of the service to ensure an appropriate balance between cost and quality of service.
- Develop data on service delivery, customer and client satisfaction and effectiveness of service which provides the basis for service improvement targets.

Employee Support has begun to provide a clear specification for all of its services; it is agreeing standards of delivery with all its customers and has defined the roles, responsibilities and levels of competency required to deliver specified products and services. Employee Support's services are monitored by the business using agreed quantitative and qualitative measurements, including sickness absence levels, medical retirements and employee satisfaction, which is measured by the use of employee satisfaction questionnaires. In the area of evaluation Employee Support is involved in a number of evaluation studies which are looking at the effectiveness of the model of trauma debriefing developed in the Post Office (Tehrani, 1995) and will be evaluating the First Line Counselling model in the near future.

Conclusion

This chapter has been written from the perspective of one of the largest internal counselling services in the country, meeting the needs of around 200,000 Post Office employees. Employee Support is proud to be part of the Post Office and has valued the support the organization has given it over its 50-year history.

The future of internal counselling services is uncertain, with the need for organizations to focus even more keenly on their core business rather than on the provision of internal services. There are a number of important advantages to organizations in maintaining an internal employee counselling and support service, but perhaps the most obvious from the Post Office's experience has been the way that Employee Support has been able to develop services and products which have been designed to meet the precise needs of the individual

Post Office businesses. It would be difficult to see how an external counselling organization could have developed an employee programme with the range of services and flexibility of Employee Support for an organization of the size and complexity of the Post Office. The organizational benefit of using advisers, counsellors and psychologists, who are employees of the organization, is enormous. Their awareness of the business and its culture gives them an insight into the problems which are presented by managers and employees.

Although there is little research available which compares internal with external counselling provisions, where it has been undertaken it has shown that internal services have been more successful in meeting the needs of the business than their external competitors (Highley and Cooper, 1996). The Post Office is an employer with a genuine wish to provide employees with a support service as a means of demonstrating care and this has provided a rare opportunity for Employee Support to develop exciting and important projects which meet the shared needs of the organization and its employees.

References

British Association for Counselling (1984) *Code of Ethics and Practice for Counsellors*. Rugby: BAC.

Berridge, J. (1990) 'The EAP – employee counselling comes of age', *Employee Counselling Today*, 2 (4): 14–17.

Burkes, H.M. and Steffire, B. (1979) *Theories of Counselling* (3rd Edition). New York: McGraw-Hill.

Conlon, P.G. (1991) 'The Post Office welfare service', *Employee Counselling Today*, 3 (5): 21–2.

Cooke, J. (1995) *Law of Tort* (2nd Edition). London: Pitman Publishing.

Cooper, C.L., Sadri, G., Allison, T. and Reynolds, P. (1990) 'Stress counselling in the Post Office', *Counselling Psychology Review*, 3 (1): 3–11.

Deal, T. and Kennedy, A. (1982) *Corporate Cultures*. Reading, MA: Addison-Wesley. Chapter 2.

Edmonds, M. (1991) 'Exploring company welfare', *Employee Counselling Today*, 3 (3): 26–31.

Fox, A. (1966) 'From welfare to organisation', *New Society*, 9 June.

Highley, J.C. and Cooper, C.L. (1996) 'An evaluation of employee assistance and workplace counselling programmes in British organisations'. Paper delivered at the 1996 Occupational Psychology Conference.

Martin, A.O. (1967) *Welfare at Work*. London: B.T. Batsford. pp. 270–2.

Miller, D. (1992) 'Work problems caused by mental ill health and their management', in R. Jenkins and N. Coney (eds), *Prevention of Mental Ill Health at Work*. London: HMSO/CBI Publications. pp. 59–66.

Post Office Welfare Study Group (1944) Post 64. Mount Pleasant, London: Post Office Archives.

Post Office Records (1855–1938) Post 64. Mount Pleasant, London: Post Office Archives.

Tehrani, N. (1995) 'An integrated response to trauma in three Post Office businesses', *Work and Stress*, 9 (4): 380–93.

Thomson, D. (ed.) (1960) *The Era of Violence 1898–1945*. The New Cambridge Modern History. Cambridge: Cambridge University Press.

Welch, R. and Tehrani, N. (1992) 'Counselling in the Post Office', in R. Jenkins and N. Coney (eds), *Prevention of Mental Ill Health at Work*. London: HMSO/CBI Publications. pp. 67–82.

Whitfield, M. (1995) 'Employers recognise value of counselling', *People Management*, 21 December: 6.

4

On Being a Chameleon – A Freelance Workplace Counsellor's Perspective

Geetu Orme

When asked to write a chapter on a freelance workplace counsellor's perspective of his/her work, my creativity and imagination ran wild and a number of possible titles came to mind: 'Workplace Counselling – How *Not* To Do It', 'So You Think You're *Ready* To Offer Workplace Counselling?', and even 'If Only I Knew *Then* What I Know Now'. These alternative chapter titles capture something of my journey as a workplace counsellor: I learned how not to do it before discovering how best to do it; I was not quite ready to start when I did; and of course, in hindsight, I have gained so much from workplace counselling that I would never begin where I did, if I had my time again. In opting for the title above I hope to capture all of these elements and indicate how the 'chameleon' image reflects the many 'colours' of the freelance workplace counsellor, and the varied roles and the multiple relationships involved. Just as chameleons change colour to blend into their environment, so freelance workplace counsellors take on the colour and hue of the context in which they work. For workplace counsellors, this demands an adaptability and versatility characteristic of chameleons.

This chapter is practical by nature and outlines the perspective of the hands-on freelance practitioner. It contains a collection of hints and tips, some ideas on what to build into the training of workplace counsellors, and examples of challenges, as well as those 'aha!' or BFO (blinding flashes of the obvious) moments which landed on me as if from nowhere. But first, a few words about me and my journey to becoming a freelance workplace counsellor.

Over the last six years I have worked in a range of counselling settings. In 1990, I began working as a consultant in a human resources consultancy, providing training and counselling services to well-known public and private sector organizations. Unusually for consultancies, I was recruited as a trainee Counsellor/Trainer and I learned my job uniquely through 'doing', rather than with limited instruction or training. I now know this to be the stage of 'unconscious incompetence' in Maslow's learning model, where 'I didn't know what I didn't know' (or blissful ignorance). So I found myself providing outplacement counselling before I understood how different 'outplacement' was from 'placement'. It was easy to confuse the two as I was at times working as part of a counselling team in an in-house support centre, where a company (of up to 2,000 employees) was closing a site. The counsellors' task was to help individuals develop CVs and 'market' themselves. Sometimes, this involved direct contact with potential employers, hence the confusion at times with 'placement'. In our spare time on site, we were also helping individuals to deal with any emotions that they were experiencing as they looked for other jobs. Bear in mind that many companies fail to recognize both the personal upheaval and the strong feelings of loss that redundancy can bring on.

As well as providing counselling support for groups of people, I was also working one-on-one with individual clients on short-term career counselling (four to six sessions). The focus of this work was assisting individuals to consider their personal goals and values and to take the first steps towards living their values within their careers. For some clients, this involved a complete re-definition of what was important to them, for others it represented a radical shift in career and work focus. Fortunately, my stage of 'unconscious incompetence' soon came to an end as my enlightened employer recognized that high-quality counselling services could only be provided by trained and qualified counsellors. So I, along with several other counsellors, participated in and completed a diploma course in Counselling at Work, in association with Roehampton Institute.

It was during my training four years ago that I started to move to the stage of 'conscious incompetence', where I started to realize what I didn't know. With each topic covered on the course, from ethics to confidentiality to boundary issues to supervision, I became more and more aware of the limitations of my counselling involvement. At the same time, I started working with my local branch of CRUSE Bereavement Care, a national network of voluntary bereavement counsellors who visit bereaved clients in their own homes. My supervision group included a counsellor who provided long-term personal counselling both within and outside workplace settings. During this time, I was able to compare workplace counselling to counselling in other settings and the differences became strikingly apparent. In 1993 I completed my training and decided to practise as an independent consultant, within the areas of training, counselling and communications. For the last two years, I have provided counselling services for client organizations. Sometimes this is *adhoc* support, though in other instances the counselling is part of a wider, integrated programme of counselling support. I am now consciously and unconsciously using counselling skills in my training and facilitating work. Recently, I have been able to extend my interpersonal ability further with a Business Practitioner qualification in NLP (Neuro Linguistic Programming).

In using the term 'freelance', I am defining a particular type of workplace counselling. This is counselling for individuals within a client organization, where a self-employed counsellor works independently and is contracted directly with the client organization. Since writing this chapter, I have in fact moved from being strictly 'freelance' to collaborating with and managing other counsellors on counselling projects. So while I am taking a freelancer's perspective, my own transition from being strictly 'freelance' to becoming a provider of counselling services means that the messages contained within this chapter have a wider application to counsellors who work full-time within organizations that provide counselling – for example, human resource consultancies, EAP providers and counselling groups within large organizations like the National Health Service. What makes freelance workplace counsellors unique is that they do not tend to have the infrastructure and support of larger organizations (for example, EAP providers), so they are potentially a more vulnerable kind of counsellor. Consequently, they need to give particular care and attention to how they market, set up and monitor their counselling provision.

Having set the scene, the next step is to define some of the things that make workplace counselling different from other forms of counselling, proceeding then to some ideas for moving forwards – my collection of things to do, things to think about, and things to include in checklists for freelance workplace counsellors.

Workplace Counselling is Unpredictable

In other therapeutic settings clients are usually either self-referred or referred by other counsellors. This means that they come to counselling with a maximum of two different perspectives – their own perspective (in cases of self-referral) and/or the perspective of another counsellor (in cases of referred work). The situation is quite different in workplace counselling. Information on workplace clients is normally received through the referral routes of either the personnel department, a line manager of the individual client, an assistant of the line manager of the individual client or the client manager within a consultancy (who has taken notes during a telephone call or meeting with any of the persons previously mentioned). I once received a request for counselling support via a telephone call from a 'temp' who read out some written instructions left for her by a senior manager in the company. At best, the information received from such referrals is second-hand and patchy; at worst, it includes a myriad of perspectives, bias and hidden agendas which the workplace counsellor is called to act upon.

In referral situations, the reason for counselling support can often be expressed by the catch-all banner of 'stress' (see Appendix 1 on p. 71 for a list of situations, issues and behaviours that can give rise to a need for counselling). In the instances where information on the individual client is available, this may be at variance with what the individual client chooses to communicate during the first session. Some examples will illustrate this:

- According to the Personnel Officer who telephoned me, a particular local authority wants to provide career counselling for a group of middle managers. When I meet each of the managers who are offered support, I find out that the counselling is in fact part of their 'exit' or redundancy support package.
- The Operations Director of a subsidiary of a petroleum company telephoned to indicate how strongly his company feels about providing trauma counselling to the families of two employees who recently died in a

tragic company accident. On meeting the family members in question, I discover that both families demanded that support be provided for them, given the circumstances.

The impact of these blatant differences in perception is that workplace counsellors cannot take anything for granted in the initial sessions. They need to exercise great care in the information communicated to a client in the first session (even information on the reasons for the counselling support), otherwise the individual client may find it hard to trust the counselling process.

In addition to the blatant differences in perception between client organization and individual client, there are also the more subtle differences which can be a reflection of poor human resource practice. In situations where the client organization has used a punitive method of dealing with 'difficult' employees – or people of less-than-average work performance – the person who is asked to confront this situation, and sometimes even to communicate this information to the individual client, is the workplace counsellor. I have come across the following examples given by client organizations for severing certain employees, which serve to reinforce the punitive situations in which counselling support is sometimes offered:

- Poor relations with colleagues – the individual was seen to be 'aggressive' and not 'customer friendly', and therefore had appeared on the target list for redundancy.
- Sick parent at home, therefore with unacceptably high level of absenteeism.
- Slow to develop new skills, therefore not 'needed' in the future.
- Poor relations with boss, therefore identified as a 'problem' person.

The above examples serve to reinforce Lane's view that sometimes counselling is 'seen as a method which picks up people who are problems rather than as a framework of psychology which can enhance potential and ensure performance' (Lane, 1990: 542). Even where organizations are committed to counselling on paper, they may not be committed to it in a wider sense. As a freelancer, I have felt the commitment wane when I state my need for hiring a counselling room, off-site, in order to provide neutral ground for the individual client, away from his/her normal working environment. This can be viewed as outside the budget even though the cost implication may be minimal. A client organization's commitment to counselling has to be questioned if the only option available to the counsellor providing a professional and confidential counselling service is an office with a glass-panelled door (so that 'observers' can look through to watch their unsuspecting colleagues who have been 'sent' for counselling), which is close to the individual's work space (where they are unhappy and unfulfilled).

In summary, I would liken workplace counselling to a public WC (it is ironic that they have the same initials): you're never really sure what you're going to find until you're in there. Sometimes it's clean and straightforward – you do what you need to do and get out. At other times, it can be pretty messy and you want to wash your hands of it and go!

The Goal of Workplace Counselling

Another key difference between counselling and workplace counselling is your fundamental goal as a counsellor. Fisher et al. (1991), in their work on negotiation, refer to 'win/win' negotiations. Other writers in the field of self-development refer to techniques for achieving win/win in relationships or conflict situations. Stephen Covey (1989) refers to 'synergy' in one of the Seven Habits of Highly Effective People.

In workplace counselling, however, win/win is not sufficient. The real goal of workplace counselling is in fact 'win/win/win' – *win* for the individual client, *win* for the workplace counsellor and *win* for the client organization. This third aspect adds important dimensions that the counsellor cannot ignore – the counsellor has not *one* but *two* clients (at least), and each of them has different expectations, measures, goals and success criteria; each has different needs for information, confidentiality and results. In turn, the counsellor's needs for information, confidentiality and results will be different. The list below identifies the needs of the three different parties.

The Organization's Needs

- *Expectations* – low-cost counselling for high return.
- *Measures* – the individual client is feeling better and improving performance at work, or 'no news is good news' if individual client is leaving the company.
- *Goals for counselling* – to enhance the company as a good employer, to put the individual 'right', to correct a problem.
- *Success criteria for counselling* – on budget, on time.
- *Information required* – estimate of duration, cost and likely impact of counselling.
- *Confidentiality* – the organization is paying so the organization has a 'right' to know the content of the counselling sessions and to receive an update on progress.
- *Results* – much of the benefit of counselling cannot be measured in tangible terms: 'the concept of counselling in the workplace is not regarded as a benefit that can be quantified' (Megranahan, 1990b: 7), particularly for the organization.

The Individual Client's Needs

- *Expectations* – no or low expectations, wondering if the client organization has an ulterior motive.
- *Measures* – feeling comfortable and 'safe' with the counsellor.
- *Goals for counselling* – to get some personal benefit.
- *Success criteria for counselling* – 'how I felt at the beginning' versus 'how I feel at the end', or success at interview or promotion in case of outplacement or career counselling.

- *Information required* – what will the client organization need to know?
- *Confidentiality* – total confidentiality with counsellor.
- *Results* – seeing something change, feeling different.

The Counsellor's Needs

- *Expectations* – client organization is committed to counselling and has best interests of individual at heart.
- *Measures* – quality of relationship with client, level of 'confrontation' and safety provided for the individual client.
- *Goals for counselling* – to help the individual to improve his/her functioning.
- *Success criteria for counselling* – degree of change in relationship, degree of 'movement' of client.
- *Information required* – very little about the individual client.
- *Confidentiality* – total confidentiality with breaches of confidentiality uniquely in situations where the individual client is in danger of hurting others or him/herself.
- *Results* – benefits for the individual client translated into a more fulfilled and happy life. Repeat business with the same client organization.

The challenge for the workplace counsellor is how to balance these differing needs and how to manage the issues that arise where there is a clash of needs or where the needs are not congruent. For instance, the client organization wants to know in detail the content of the counselling sessions yet this is in conflict with the confidentiality contract agreed at the beginning of the counselling by counsellor and individual client. The individual client is having a tough time and has postponed a number of counselling sessions in view of current work priorities that are getting in the way. The counsellor agrees that this is in the best interest of the counselling relationship and the individual client yet the client organization is wondering what is going on and why the sessions are taking longer than expected. Is the counsellor doing his/her job properly? The key issue is in being aware of what constitutes win/win/win and building a counselling support programme that helps all parties in the relationships to have their needs answered. The workplace counsellor, as chameleon, amends his/her colour and texture based on the environment and context in which he/she is working.

Managing Workplace Counselling

There are a number of areas where the freelance workplace counsellor needs to be alert. These relate to the development stages of setting up a freelance practice. Some of these are:

- Marketing 'know-how'.
- Pre-counselling publicity.
- Strategies and techniques.

Marketing 'Know-how'

There are some key choices for freelance counsellors in how they market their service. First, the 'infrastructure' that they present. Are they offering services as an independent provider or as a collection of freelancers, loosely connected? This makes a difference to both the marketing literature that counsellors create and therefore how the service is perceived by client organizations. Linking up with other counsellors certainly has its benefits in terms of supervision, shared work and ideas and trouble-shooting. By working with other counsellors, larger counselling projects can be supported.

A second key decision is the choice of words to describe the workplace counselling service. There are subtle differences in how clients choose to refer to workplace counselling – is it 'employee support', 'counselling' or 'stress management'? Two client organizations that I have worked with this year have specifically requested that the word 'counselling' is not used on invoices and that the words 'one-to-one coaching' are used instead. Whatever the semantics, the support provided is counselling. While client organizations get more used to the idea of 'counselling', the beginning workplace counsellor is advised to use the term that is most appropriate for the client organization and at the same time to be very clear about what the service involves. A suggestion for counsellors is to include a whole variety of terms in their marketing literature so that any client organization will see a match between its perception of counselling and what is being offered.

Once the counselling service has been accepted in outline, it is vital for freelancers to be clear at the outset about what they are providing. Bear in mind the aspects below when putting together a proposal (or an outline of services and fees). The required skills and qualities of a workplace counsellor are extensive, as working as a freelancer means a professional service has to be provided. It is useful to include the following information in both the written information that the workplace counsellor provides to client organizations and in the verbal conversations before counselling support is initiated:

Credentials
- Counselling qualification(s).
- Experience of providing counselling to other organizations. Given the very wide frame of reference of workplace counselling, Orlans (1992) includes the following on a list of topics appropriate for workplace counselling – experience of any of these can therefore be considered as appropriate 'credentials' in marketing a counselling service to potential clients:
  - the principles and dynamics of organization behaviour;
  - models and practices in the design and implementation of EAPs;
  - ethics and responsibilities in employee counselling;
  - organizational health;
  - the role of legislation;
  - stress diagnosis, management and prevention;
  - AIDS;

- substance abuse;
- career counselling.

A further list of skills and qualities to include in your marketing information from Megranahan (1989) is included in Appendix 2 on p. 72.

- Experience of working in business or in other related fields/sectors. As a provider of workplace counselling, it is vital to describe the experiences you have had working in organizations. Client organizations are particularly interested to know about work that the counsellor has done in similar organizations (for instance, in the same sector).
- Results of previous counselling services provided. As mentioned earlier, it is difficult to articulate the tangible benefits of counselling. In the absence of statistics to demonstrate a direct link between counselling support offered and the benefits to be gained, I find that listing a number of outline case histories is helpful. For example, I often describe the trauma counselling support provided for a site manager of a textile company who was assaulted as part of a 'revenge attack' by a former employee who had been dismissed for gross misconduct. The result of five counselling sessions was that the manager had developed some coping strategies for dealing with chance meetings with his attacker in the future (thus helping him to go about his daily work) and that he had taken ownership of the need to defend himself in the future (by taking up some self-defence lessons). Both these actions would not necessarily have been taken by the individual concerned through the normal support processes after a violent attack (conversations with colleagues and family).

Outline of counselling service

- Number and length of sessions proposed. In my experience in workplace counselling, the therapeutic '50 minute' session is not entirely appropriate to workplace settings, particularly where an individual is already taking time away from work and the counsellor has travelling time and distance involved. For short-term programmes (four to eight sessions), the free-lancer may wish to work on the basis of one and a half hours per session. It is also useful to include in the initial proposal a further phase of sessions (in case more sessions are required at a future date). Some client organizations will indicate up front that the number of sessions agreed is 'cast in stone'. Other client organizations are happy to wait and assess at a later date whether further support is needed. In workplace counselling situations, it is recommended that the workplace counsellor contracts for a minimum of four sessions.
- Arrangements for publicizing the service – see next section. It is useful to articulate that the counsellor's responsibility is to select the appropriate information to communicate to individual clients and that the client organization's responsibility is to check with the counsellor *before* communicating any aspects of the services offered (see next section on 'publicizing the service').
- Back-up of other counsellors in busy times. It is important to include names or sources of other freelancers should the need arise to either refer

clients to another counsellor or to share the counselling workload with other counsellor colleagues.

Quality assurance

- Code of conduct. It is important to mention the British Association for Counselling (BAC) or the Institute of Personnel and Development (IPD) code of conduct that defines the professional standards that you adopt. It is useful to include a copy of the code of conduct where possible.
- Supervision. What it is, how it works and its importance for the effectiveness of the counselling.
- Professional indemnity insurance. This is available through the IPD for members and is in fact a requirement for consultants and counsellors registered with the IPD consultancy service. Other schemes are available from other professional bodies. Insurance is relatively inexpensive and provides the counsellor with legal cover should any client or member of a client's family try to bring a case of professional negligence. Some client organizations insist that all contractors have this cover. Even where this is not required, it helps to give the freelancer peace of mind when negotiating and providing counselling services for organizations. It also helps in presenting a professional image for the counselling service.

Feedback and information flow

- Confidentiality. What it is, how important it is for the effectiveness of the counselling offered and details of the 'confidentiality contract' that will be agreed between counsellor and individual client at the beginning of the relationship.
- Ongoing evaluation and reporting arrangements. Client companies may expect the counsellor to provide detailed reports (as is the norm for other forms of external support, for example consultancy work). It is important for the workplace counsellor to differentiate between the information that the client organization needs to know (dates of sessions, length of sessions) and information that the client organization does not need to know (content of sessions, personal information). The only exception to this is where the individual client chooses to feed back certain information to the client organization.

An example of this is a career development programme that I provided counselling on for middle managers in a well-known public sector organization. It was agreed, at the outset, that the final session would be a three-way meeting between individual client, counsellor and a representative of the paying client organization so that the individual could talk through the key actions that he or she was planning to take. If this is built in from the outset, this is more likely to be an acceptable form of feedback for all three parties and a truly win/win/win situation. Where this is not agreed at the outset, problems can arise later. For instance, if the client organization is not satisfied with the service being provided, an individual client may be 'put on the spot' and asked a number of questions about the content of the counselling sessions. Or, the counsellor may receive telephone calls from a line manager demanding to know why the counselling is taking up so much of his subordinate's time. All of these situations can be managed by having clear agreements at the outset about what information needs to be communicated and to whom.

In summary, the four areas of credentials, outline of counselling service, quality assurance, and feedback and information flow can be used as focus points in both the formal 'proposal' information that the counsellor communicates to clients and the informal discussions with client organizations in setting up a counselling service.

Pre-counselling Publicity

Pre-counselling publicity is the information that the individual client receives before the first session. Two scenarios are worth exploring.

The first scenario is where counselling support is being offered to a group of employees and all employees are aware that the support is being provided. In this instance, it is useful to arrange an informal briefing session where the workplace counsellor comes to the client organization to meet the individuals and to give a brief introduction to the service being provided. This does two things: first, it helps to allay any individual fears about the counsellor ('yes, they are a real person after all!') and second, it clarifies the confidentiality of the service ('it is now very clear what happens – particularly that everything I say will not go straight back to the personnel department'). Points worth covering include:

- What is counselling? (it can be useful to ask the group to answer and then to allay any fears or misconceptions).
- The scope of counselling (what is included, what is outside the support that can be provided).
- Logistics (where the sessions will take place, timing, the number of sessions, how the sessions are triggered, does the individual client decide when to start the counselling or is this pre-determined?).
- Confidentiality.
- Feedback to client organization.
- The accessibility of counsellor (how to contact, where and when).
- Any questions and answers.

A useful tip is to prepare a one-page summary of the above information for individuals to take away with them at the end of the session, including a contact telephone number. Allowing 45 minutes or so for this briefing session is usually sufficient. Think carefully in advance about the room layout and the importance of having a conversation with your group, rather than making a formal presentation.

The second scenario is where the client organization has offered the service to selected individuals and there is no supposed 'peer group' of individual clients. In this instance, it is more effective for the counsellor to arrange to telephone each individual client to make contact, to introduce him/herself and to make arrangements for the first meeting. This again helps to break the ice and reduce the number of 'unknowns' for the individual client. The other items on the previous list for the first scenario can then be discussed at the beginning of the first session.

For wider scale EAPs, it may not be possible to publicize the service through briefing sessions or telephone conversations. However, it is important that this aspect of the counselling service is not left to chance or to the personnel department to organize as this will shape expectations and concerns early on, particularly where representatives of the client organization are describing the counselling service to their 'internal customers' in terms that have not been agreed with the external counsellor. In situations where this is beyond the influence of the workplace counsellor, it is vital to cover the above information at the beginning of the first counselling session. This is more important in workplace settings, where individual clients may not be self-referred, than in therapeutic settings.

Strategies and Techniques

When a workplace counsellor completes his/her training, a toolkit of skills can be used on day one of future counselling projects. For instance, empathy, active listening, paraphrasing and summarizing. While not wanting to down-grade the importance of any of these core skills, the following additional strategies and techniques may assist the workplace counsellor to achieve new levels of rapport and effectiveness in their helping role.

Many of the techniques covered here have their origins in NLP (neuro linguistic programming) and these are particularly appropriate for use in counselling situations in workplace settings. In contrast to the rather poor press given to NLP in a recent counselling work (Summerfield and Van Oudtshoorn, 1995: 87), specific approaches founded in NLP can lead to 'breakthroughs' for the workplace counsellor. A fuller discussion of the approaches listed below can be found in Knight (1995).

Well-formed outcomes.   At the beginning of a counselling relationship, it is useful to encourage clients to articulate their goals for the counselling. Rather than articulate these in vague terms, it is helpful to lead the client through a number of specific questions, the use of which makes the outcome compelling and real for the individual client and therefore easier for the workplace counsellor to review at the end of the counselling. This is at variance with traditional goal-setting (for example, having SMART objectives that are specific, measurable, achievable, relevant and time-scaled).

Outcomes that are well formed involve the use of specific questions detailed here. In counselling, the more compelling the outcomes set by clients, the more likely they are to achieve them. The questions detailed below can be applied to any workplace counselling situation to encourage clients to think through what they are trying to achieve. People say that there are two creations – one in the mind, one in reality. If clients do not create their objectives in their minds, they are probably less likely to achieve them in practice.

- *What do you really want?* The answer should be stated in the positive. The client specifies what he/she really wants, not what he/she doesn't want.
- *How will you know that you have got it? What will you see, hear, feel and what might others see, hear, feel as evidence of success?* Ensure that there is sensory-specific evidence for the outcome.
- *Where, when and with whom do you want it? What will happen when you get it?* Ensure that the outcome is contextualized with details of when, where and with whom the outcome is desired.
- *On whom does it depend? What resources do you need to get it?* Ensure that the outcome is self-maintained, that is, something that the client can initiate and maintain independently.
- *How will getting it benefit you? Is it worth the effort/cost? How will this outcome affect other aspects of your life?* This is to check if the outcome is ecologically sound, that it fits in with other areas of the client's life and provides a win/win situation.
- *What is the first step to achieving your outcome? What is the time scale?* This identifies a first step with a time scale to ensure commitment.

Matching and leading on Non-verbal communication. Given Albert Mehrabian's work, which demonstrated that 55 per cent of the impact our communication is through our body language, insufficient time is dedicated to this aspect in the training of workplace counsellors. With the three different parties involved in counselling (individual client, client organization and counsellor), it is vital for the counsellor to be able to build rapport within the first few seconds.

This can be achieved by matching the non-verbal communication of clients – gestures, sitting position and breathing pace. Giving attention to these finer details and observing very carefully the shifts that clients make in their non-verbal communication, and then matching these, can make a difference to the degree to which clients feel comfortable and 'safe' at the outset. When counsellors have established a degree of rapport, they are then able to lead with body language and non-verbal communication and if the clients are in rapport, they will follow the counsellor.

I have experimented with this at the beginning of two role-play counselling sessions where I have deliberately mismatched the non-verbal communication of my client while listening actively and using core counselling skills at the same time. The difference is astonishing – the two clients in question were visibly uncomfortable and it took much longer to establish a level of empathy.

Another area of non-verbal communication is in dress code. It is important for the counsellor to match the dress code of the client organization (particularly in the initial sessions where an individual client may be assessing the counsellor's 'fit' with the organization). This is where the skill of the chameleon starts to become apparent – how to match the expectations of the client organization and at the same time to be credible in the counselling role.

It is important to notice the dress norms of a particular client organization as these will vary from organization to organization. I remember interviewing a number of counsellors to work with me on a counselling project in French with a North African client. One workplace counsellor indicated her preference to cover her head as a sign of respect when meeting Arab managers. For the client organization, this was considered to be false, unacceptable and a sign of disrespect, hence the necessity for the 'chameleon' to be sensitive to the needs of the environment and to put his/her own preconceptions on hold.

Representation systems. Representation systems are the preferred senses that individual clients use to relate to their internal world – clients may be thinking in pictures (visual), sounds (auditory) or sensations (kinaesthetic) and this is reflected in the words they choose to use in conversations with the counsellor. As individual clients start to express feelings and emotion, it is very powerful for the counsellor to be able to identify the representation system used and then to reflect, paraphrase or summarize using the same representation system. By giving attention to the representation system of the client the counsellor can build rapport, demonstrate a high level of active listening and thus heighten the impact of his/her paraphrase, summary or reflection. An example will serve to illustrate:

> Client: I *hear* all these voices in my head *telling* me that I'm in the wrong job but I can't *bear* the thought of doing something else.
> (*hear, telling = auditory; bear = kinaesthetic*)
> Counsellor: It *sounds* like on the one hand you're *saying* to yourself that you could be doing something else but on the other, you don't *feel* able to change.
> (*sounds, saying = auditory; feel = kinaesthetic*)

In the example above, the client is using auditory and kinaesthetic language so the counsellor uses similar representation systems to reflect back. A fuller description of representation systems can be found in Knight (1995).

Perceptual positions. A range of workplace situations involve clients needing to consider the impact of their situation on others around them. A useful technique for workplace counsellors is the use of perceptual positions to create more choices in a given situation. This is a version of the 'empty chair technique' that some therapists use but with the addition of sensory-specific questions which enable the client to experience more fully each of the different perceptual positions.

It comprises a four-step process. The first step involves asking clients to experience the situation as if in their own shoes – what are they seeing, hearing and feeling in this situation? When clients are sufficiently associated into this 'first position' (which the counsellor can assess from their skin tone, breathing, etc.), the counsellor then asks them to take a second position (of the other person involved in the situation) and experience the situation from their perspective – what are they seeing, hearing and feeling in this second position? Once the clients are fully associated into this position, the counsellor can then ask them to take a third (outsider's) position which is a position of objectivity and detachment. This third step involves asking clients what they are seeing, hearing and feeling in this situation as the third person, what needs each of the people have in the situation and what gifts of insight they can offer from an objective standpoint? Once all positions have been experienced, the fourth and final step involves the counsellor asking the individuals to return to their original position (as themselves) to describe what new choices they may have in the situation to achieve win/win and meet the needs of all the people involved.

In summary, the four NLP strategies of well-formed outcomes, matching and leading on non-verbal communication, representation systems and perceptual positions have much to recommend them to the beginning workplace counsellor or experienced counsellors used to working in settings outside the workplace.

Conclusion

Finally, I come full circle to the title of this chapter – 'on being a chameleon'. For counsellors in other settings who decide to offer their services in workplace settings, imagine yourself as a chameleon needing to alter your shape and colour, to adapt to your individual client and client organization to achieve *win/win/win*. For the beginning workplace counsellor, think about the flexibility that you will need to adapt to situations and try to pre-empt the needs of the environment or situation that you are entering.

For all workplace counsellors, there is much to be learned from chameleons, yet how do we ensure that we don't lose sight of who we are and what we stand for, if we always have to fit into the needs of our clients? The key is to alter and change, like a chameleon, yet to maintain our identity as workplace counsellors with our values and beliefs intact, in all contexts and cultures in which we work. There lies the challenge, and the benefits to be gained are enormous:

> If counselling is to be seen to be a major strategic tool, those practising it must appreciate early on that small matters as seen by an outsider can, and do, assume enormous dimensions in the world of a troubled individual and counselling in the workplace goes far beyond counselling to put the troubled person right; it can be as profound as putting a troubled company right. (Interview with Cary Cooper, 1990: 8)

Appendix 1: Situations/Issues/Behaviours that may Signal a Need for Counselling

What situations might prompt a need to counsel staff?

- People not performing to their usual standard.
- Persistent lateness.
- Inability to communicate clearly.
- Inability to act as part of a team.
- Unusual, or changed behaviours.
- Inability to take or make decisions.
- Change in personal circumstances.
- Change in work circumstances.

What sort of issues might they bring?

- Marital problems.
- Bereavement.
- Drinking.
- Drugs.
- Health.
- Emotional adjustment.
- Inability to cope.
- Lack of skill/activity.
- Career crisis.
- Personality problem.

So what kinds of behaviour might signal a need for counselling?

- Eager to please, wants to help rather than do, looking for a friend, cannot accept success, constantly worries about failure, dependent on others, indecisive, avoid responsibility, always taking on new work, never completes to deadlines, constantly at meetings.
- Aggressive, talks to you, does not listen, bosses others, obstinate, fixed views and opinions, autocratic, unwilling to delegate, critical and contemptuous of others, unreasoned, envious, cannot take criticism.
- Cannot organize own work properly, blames others constantly, finds it difficult to finish jobs, defensive, secretive, has few friends, irrational, prone to panic, avoids personal contact, uncooperative, sometimes deprecating about the organization, uses memos, puts off work, anxious.

Extracted from Sidney and Phillips (1991: 56).

Appendix 2:   Qualities and Skills of an Effective Counsellor

Ability to:

- Conduct short-term counselling (six interviews or less).
- Conduct crisis counselling.
- Assess mental health or coping skills.
- Assess drug/alcohol dependency and make appropriate interventions.
- Carry out promotion of counselling within the organization.
- Develop company and programme policies.
- Conduct programme evaluation.

Familiarity with:

- Organizational structure, job descriptions, job performance expectations and the disciplinary process.
- Industrial relations and union representation.
- The benefits package for the employees.
- Social service agencies and health care systems.

Additional skills including:

- Knowledge of professional ethics and legal liabilities.
- Financial counselling skills.
- Knowledge of legal and illegal drugs.
- Training and public-speaking ability.
- Writing skills.
- Consultative skills.
- Personal time management and organizational skills.

Extracted from Megranahan (1989: 259).

References

'Counselling in the workplace – is UK management ready?' (1990), interview with Cary L. Cooper, *Employee Counselling Today*, 2 (1): 5–8.

British Association for Counselling (1985) *Code of Ethics and Practice for Trainers*. Rugby: BAC.

British Association for Counselling (1989) *Code of Ethics and Practice for Counselling Skills*. Rugby: BAC.

British Association for Counselling (1992) *Code of Ethics and Practice for Counsellors*. Rugby: BAC.

Carroll, M. (1993a) 'Making ethical decisions in organisational counselling', unpublished paper.

Carroll, M. (1993b) 'The counsellor in organisational settings: some reflections', unpublished paper.

Carroll, M. and Holloway, E. (1993) 'Outplacement/redundancy counselling: is it really counselling?', unpublished paper.

Covey, S. (1989) *The 7 Habits of Highly Effective People*. New York: Simon and Schuster.

Crandall, R. and Allen, R.D. (1982) 'The organisational context of helping relationships', in T.A. Will (ed.), *Basic Processes in Helping Relationships*. London: Academic Press.

Egan, G. (1990) *The Skilled Helper*. Belmont, CA: Brooks/Cole.

Fisher, R., Ury, W. and Patton, B. (1991) *Gettting to Yes: Negotiating an Agreement Without Giving In*. Kent: Century Business.

Gitterman, A. and Miller, I. (1989) 'The influence of the organisation on clinical practice', *Clinical Social Work Journal*, 17 (2): 151–64.

Knight, S. (1995) *NLP at Work*. London: Nicholas Brealey Publishing.

Lane, D.A. (1990) 'Counselling psychology in organisations', *The Psychologist, Bulletin of the British Psychological Society*, 12: 540–4.

Megranahan, M. (1989) *Counselling: A Practical Guide for Employers*. London: Institute of Personnel Management.

Megranahan, M. (1990a) 'Employee Assistance Programmes: frameworks and guiding principles', *Employee Counselling Today*, 2 (3): 28–32.

Megranahan, M. (1990b) 'The organisational value of employee assistance', *Journal of Managerial Psychology*, 5 (2): 3–8.

Orlans, V. (1992) 'Counselling in the workplace: Part I – Counsellor perspectives and training', *EAP International*, 1 (1): 19–21.

Sanders, G. (1991) 'Counselling models in the workplace – taking NLP into counselling', *Employee Counselling Today*, 3 (1): 13–20.

Shaw, G.H. and Sugarman, L. (1990) Can people be sent for counselling?', *Employee Counselling Today*, 2 (1): 9–13.

Sidney, E. and Phillips, N. (1991) *One-to-one Management: Counselling to Improve Job Performance*. London: Pitman Publishing.

Summerfield, J. and Van Oudtshoorn, L. (1995) *Counselling in the Workplace*. London: Institute of Personnel and Development.

5

External Counselling Provision for Organizations

Michael Reddy

Employee Assistance Programmes (EAPs) are a mixed bag. Externally or internally provided, they can take on many forms. In Chapter 3 Noreen Tehrani details the philosophy and practice of an internally provided service which is quite specific to the Post Office. It reflects the history of the Post Office and in particular the influence of occupational health specialists. It would have been a different chapter if it had been written by British Telecom, Shell International, Motorola, The Inland Revenue or Polygram, all of whom, incidentally, also have internal EAP-type services. And, of course, it will look very different from an external EAP.

This chapter examines the way ICAS (Independent Counselling & Advisory Services) offers a wide range of other counselling, training and employee support services, as well as EAPs, and might in other circumstances be classified as a counselling 'firm'. It is the EAP provider best known to the writer and the chapter describes its infrastructure, the breadth of its services, its professional values and the way it supports the employ*er* as well as the employ*ee*.

Just as internal providers vary in shape and style among themselves, so there are notable differences between ICAS and other external EAP providers. In parallel with internal providers, these contrasts have much to do with each one's original professional roots, and these in turn are reflected in their personnel, in the way they are structured and managed, and in the type of service options – and end results – for their customer organizations. Some of what follows will be characteristic of other EAP providers and some of it is particular to ICAS. It would be impossible to write it otherwise, given that differences between external providers (as with internal ones) are often more significant than apparent commonalities.

EAP Design

The Cultural Context

Not only do EAP providers, whether internal or external, vary widely among themselves, but they also show marked differences in the UK from those that exist elsewhere. EAPs are very much a product of their environment. In Australia, for example, the employer's contribution is subsidized by the State, a fact that has had a tremendous influence on the popularity of the EAP.

EAPs have had a chequered career, and it is helpful to recognize that there is no single model – that far from being inherited lock, stock and barrel from the USA, the Employee Assistance Programme in Britain is very much a child of our own tradition.

The Background

The 'prehistoric' EAP prototype was focused on alcohol abuse, on the employee whose drinking habits were affecting performance. It is common knowledge that such narrowly defined EAPs, whether they start out in drug and alcohol abuse or as financial cooperatives, as some did in Australia, sooner or later blossom into broadbrush services. Most peoples' problems have a number of causes or a variety of spin-offs, so that services with a single focus rarely meet the true level of need. EAPs typically attract high usage because of their breadth and the way they are introduced. Average uptake is more than 20 per cent of the workforce. But it is doubtful if a prototype EAP, based on alcohol abuse alone, in the present UK cultural climate, would reach even 1 per cent.

The reason is that such an EAP in the UK is designed for a different epoch and for vastly changed needs. For example, the original EAP appeared at a time when the USA was emerging from Prohibition and in the same circumstances that gave birth to Alcoholics Anonymous. It grew in stature when performance management was at a low ebb, if for no other reason than that the USA was at that time sending the cream of its workforce into the Second World War. Later, certainly from the 1960s, the growth of the EAP was consistently fostered by Congress's willingness to enact robust legislation, first in the alcohol, and later in the drug control, arena. None of this has been relevant to the UK during the same half century.

EAP for the UK in the Late 1990s

In Britain we are responding to a period of exceptional cultural and organizational change, to the entirely new challenges of a global economy, and to employees' needs to deal with the impact of all this on their working and personal lives. These new circumstances are reflected in the familiar catalogue of job insecurity, longer hours, a shaky balance at the work–home interface, continuing technological developments, endless change in structure and practices, all at a time when life in general has become more complex and support systems have tended to weaken. In the meantime, we have seen the telephone become part of daily life, and an explosion in the sheer volume of readily available information. Hence the 1990s UK version of an external EAP has the telephone at its heart. Indeed, more than one EAP provider has grown from its origins in a legal helpline.

By contrast, the American EAP has traditionally used the telephone more as a switchboard and clearing-house than as a source of direct help. This, as much as any other single factor, illustrates the extent to which differences are as important as similarities in comparing the UK EAP with its American counterpart. The ICAS Telephone Helpdesk, for example, is staffed by teams of qualified counsellors, by its own case managers and by a wide range of experienced specialists in psychology, nursing, social work, information research, money management, trauma counselling, childcare and eldercare, consumer services, careers, and human resources. It may be anticipated that with this infrastructure and these operational processes in place, the resources accessible through the Helpdesk will continually broaden as client needs are identified and the 'one-stop shop' concept increases its domination.

The UK Welfare Tradition

A second major difference in emphasis between the conventional model and the ICAS (UK) version is that in the UK *every* EAP provider, whether internal or external, builds on a tradition and wealth of employee support largely unknown elsewhere. With many of our largest organizations, especially in the public sector and in the massive family-owned retail businesses, a range of welfare-based services have been available for decades, some of which have transformed themselves today into what is easily recognized as an EAP. Many of the new generation of welfare officers have been trained in the newer counselling skills, and some welfare services, like British Telecom, have changed their name to 'Employee Counselling Services'. What is typical of all of them is that for decades they have given high-quality assistance to individual employees while at the same time taking advantage of their position within the organization *to make things happen*, whether it is a word in the ear of a manager who is taking too severe a view of a particular employee's needs or an attempt to change policy and practice across the whole organization.

Some of ICAS's own personnel have been drawn from this tradition. Hence it is equally a part of ICAS philosophy to mirror this twin service to the organization as a whole, alongside the direct help to individuals. One of the mechanisms through which it does this is an internal EAP Liaison Group within the customer organization (see below).

External EAP Provision

Structure

ICAS professional operations are grouped under Clinical Services and Corporate Services. This division of the core activity into an individually focused and an organizationally focused service, run by separate teams with quite different professional backgrounds, is a key element of the way ICAS construes its mission and objectives.

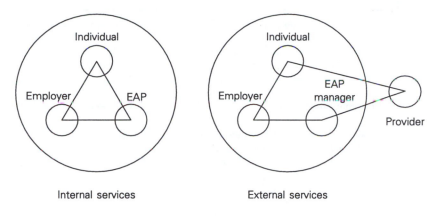

Figure 5.1 *Internal and external services*

As an external EAP provider, of course, there will be differences compared with the service structure of an internal EAP. It can be seen immediately from Figure 5.1 that the external service finds it easier to avoid suspicion of collusion and breach of confidentiality, while the internal service finds it easier to place an employee's problems in context and, when appropriate, deal with the context.

The challenge for the external EAP provider is precisely the latter. A good EAP service will have its ear to the ground through multiple contacts within the organization, will pass on to its counsellors what they need to know about the current context, while simultaneously supporting the organization in relevant policy development, partly by sharing its own professional experience and partly through the volume of rich and usable management information it is collating all the time.

An effective structure for the external EAP provider thus makes for a square rather than triangular set of relationships, as in Figure 5.2.

Clinical Services

Resources

It will already be evident that the resources deployed by a national EAP provider are likely to be considerable, given that to the multiple teams of telephone counsellors, information specialists and other professionals on tap 24 hours a day, every day of the year, must be added an exceptionally broad national network, in the case of ICAS, of over 700 generalist and specialist counsellors. These counsellors have been recruited slowly and carefully over a period of ten years. They will have had to demonstrate:

• their professionalism
• their ability to use a brief problem-solving approach to their work

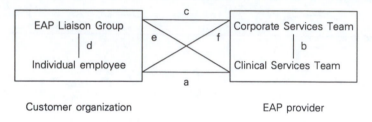

Customer organization   EAP provider

a. The confidential relationship between individual and counsellor.
b. The protected relationship between two parts of the service, allowing appropriate filters to be used on rare occasions when information has to be divulged because of a threat to life, public safety or law and order.
c. Two-way channel of communication between the EAP provider and the customer organization as a whole.
d. Normal channels of communication between the employer and the individual employee.
e. and f. The diagonal channels remain closed in order to protect confidentiality.

Figure 5.2   *Structure of an external EAP*

- their ability to relate readily to different organizational contexts
- their ability to carry out an early assessment of likely need
- their commitment to their own on-going professional development and supervision
- their adherence to recognized codes of ethics and practice
- satisfactory references
- the suitability of their practice premises
- their willingness to accept the protocols and the necessary degree of case management on which a good EAP provider will want to insist.

Additionally, some counsellors will have their own areas of specialization, such as bereavement, relationships, drugs and alcohol, trauma and money management. This depth of resource in the area of employee support is entirely new to the UK, and to it still have to be added the training and consulting capacity which a complete provider will have developed.

Ten years ago, when EAPs were virtually unknown, it was said that the British were unlikely to take to counselling. The fact, however, is that a 'satellite' picture of the UK in the late 1990s would show between forty and fifty counselling sessions per day, every day of the year, conducted by ICAS counsellors alone, alongside three times as many contacts with the Telephone Helpdesk. We are looking today at a vastly changed scene, and what must be considered a revolution in attitudes and in service provision.

Services

Two of the four main delivery systems of a complete EAP provider are its telephone helpdesk and its network of affiliate counsellors. These resources can be, and often are, additionally deployed outside the EAP format.

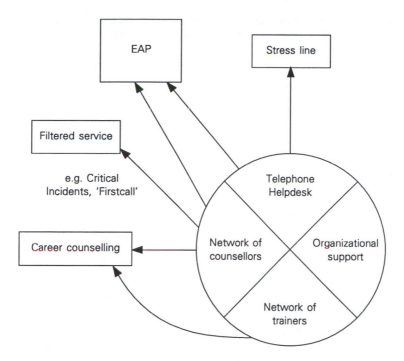

Figure 5.3 *Clinically based services of an EAP provider*

One customer organization wants only a telephone counselling service, perhaps for purely budgetary reasons, or only an emergency service. Another needs only face-to-face counselling, as a referral resource for line managers or to complement existing internal services. Another may wish simply to draw on the specialist expertise of ICAS psychologists and case managers as professional 'supervisors', for a second opinion on difficult cases or of our (HR) managers in their own domain. Other customer organizations want stress management training for managers, assistance with implementing a newly developed harassment policy, and so on, themes which are picked up below. Figure 5.3 shows how the Clinical Services take different forms.

ICAS came into being as a counselling services provider, and has always counted itself as a precursor perhaps of what may eventually come to be known as counselling 'firms', along the lines of other professional joint practices such as law and accountancy. Its early founders were also well aware of Employee Assistance Programmes and of the likelihood that they would cross the Atlantic in due course. Indeed, ICAS was singularly active in promoting this transition and today EAPs form the single most substantial part of its business. It has, however, always considered its total business to be wider than any single service model and Figure 5.3 illustrates the wider range of services which are already implicit in its EAP capacity, such as the personal support line, its 'Firstcall' emergency response, its filtered counselling services (through an internal gatekeeper), and so on.

Less self-evident is the fact that over the course of several years a number of specialist groups have been formed within the extensive ICAS national affiliate counsellor network, such as its specially trained Critical Incident teams, its sub-networks of career counsellors, of money advisers, psychiatric and alcohol/drug assessors, and a specialist team which operates only at Board level.

Corporate Services

There will have been little to surprise in the services mentioned so far, except perhaps the extent of an EAP provider's operation. In the case of ICAS, however, its counselling capacity is still only one main aspect of the whole.

The inspiration behind the birth of ICAS was the observation that the benefits of supporting individual employees in appropriate ways were often magnified in the returns to the organization. The original mission statement did not in fact mention the individual but said simply that the company had been formed to 'make the benefits, values and techniques of counselling more widely available to organizations'. Counselling was used as shorthand for a range of related services. Its original title was intended as Occupational Counselling, Consulting and Information Services, but this was too much of a mouthful. Hence ICAS has always had HR specialists at its core, considerably adding to its impact and broadening both the scope and depth of its services accordingly. It is evident, for example, that while the clinical focus has the individual mostly in view, the HR thrust will be to support *managers* in their own particular tasks, line managers at every level, top management, and managers in HR and occupational health functions.

This specialist contribution is evident in a number of areas.

Programme Integration

The internal EAP, having grown from a long-standing welfare tradition, has much opportunity and experience in integrating its activities with those of other management, HR and occupational health initiatives. The external EAP provider has to work harder to do this and in many cases does not do so, not because incapable, but because the typical UK EAP is sold too cheaply to maintain the links, support, training and consultancy components which a fully resourced EAP would possess.

In the UK the EAP almost immediately became a 'commodity', a little piece of the Benefits package, which is unfortunate, not simply because it devalues EAPs but because, as with any other commodity, price becomes the sole differentiator. In that context buyers can see few differences between providers.

Hence, in the last year or two, purchasers, unaware that they are looking at minimal service levels, unsurprisingly see no difference between providers and are influenced largely by cost, thus continually driving it down and losing quality in the process. The average cost of an EAP is one tenth of 1 per cent of total employment costs and ranks lower than the coffee machine, thus making it increasingly more likely that the potential of the fully resourced EAP is not realized.

Meanwhile, various providers have learned the language of 'case management', 'account management' and 'benefits' to the point where even a relatively sophisticated buyer, to say nothing of the general procurement specialist, will be faced with a similar sounding collection of nuts and bolts, all presented in roughly the same way at slightly (or wildly) different prices.

In practice, the introduction of an EAP is an important and integral addition to the way in which an organization works and to the way it describes itself to its public – including to itself. The implementation of a new EAP is a once-off opportunity to get it right, to have it seen by managers as a significant support to them in their own role, and by employees as saying something important and new about how the organization construes its relationship with them. Getting it wrong at this point will make it harder to retrace steps later, and if dismay and distrust is a prevailing mood, a poorly positioned EAP will not help.

On the other hand, there will normally be considerable scope for an upbeat introduction. Almost certainly, other things of real importance will be happening at the same time, whether this be the introduction of other new – and highly relevant – policies on diversity, equal opportunities, no smoking, harassment, health education, and so on. There may well be a major restructuring in progress which imposes massive change on most of the workforce. It will make a difference if an EAP is introduced at this point as part of a planned and systematic response to employee needs, rather than as an afterthought, or one needing little in the way of explanation. ICAS Corporate Services specialists make sure that appreciation and 'ownership' of the service is spread as widely as possible, that the service is therefore used to maximum advantage.

Reviews

One of the most valued aspects of an ICAS EAP has been identified by customer organizations as its data capture processes and the way highly relevant management information is analysed and presented in usable form. 'If we had had this', said one personnel manager, scanning the first year's full review of the service, 'we would have had no difficulty in making the case – its worth the cost just by itself'.

The reviews are partly statistically based and derived from customized software, often designed to meet the quite unique needs of a particular customer organization; and partly the product of collaboration between the Clinical and Corporate sides of ICAS operation to extract the trends and the qualitative data which the organization needs, to shape its continuing response.

The essence of these reviews depends equally on the continuing contact, throughout the year, between ICAS HR specialists and their opposite numbers in the internal liaison group, contacts which will have issued from the resolution of numerous situations where the interests of the organization and the individual needed to be taken into account at one and the same time. The same continuing contacts will also have alerted both parties to emerging circumstances, trends and events which might impinge on the way an individual would best be helped through his or her contact with the EAP – without ever compromising confidentiality.

Training

ICAS came into being from the very beginning as both a counselling service and a training organization. It was always part of the vision that its mission would be fulfilled as much by helping a customer organization raise the baseline of its own in-house skills as by buying them in. The fundamental philosophy of counselling itself is to do only as much as the client cannot do for him/herself.

Hence, in all the areas in which ICAS deploys its own counsellors – basic counselling skills, redundancy, trauma and Post Traumatic Stress Disorder, money management, career development, harassment, psychiatric assessment, drug and alcohol treatment, stress management, bereavement, relationships, and the rest – it has likewise provided training for in-company specialists to do the same.

Performance Management

From the 1970s at least, EAPs in the USA were adopted, some would say taken over, by healthcare professionals and providers, and in the last ten years have been almost swamped by the Managed Care movement. It is no surprise therefore that to British eyes, EAPs so evidently 'belong' to the health and welfare function, especially in the light of our own strong personnel traditions. In the process, few people in the UK are aware of their original role in performance management. EAPs were a grassroots movement in the 1940s and 1950s, stemming from the discovery that poorly performing employees ('troubled' was the usual term) could be helped by a process of rehabilitation which first assessed the need and most appropriate treatment, then saw the employee into an appropriate form of help and finally helped him or her to be gradually eased back into work.

Supervisors, as the Americans tend to call all first-line and middle managers, were integral to this whole process. Training for supervisors to understand and discharge their role in this process was a core aspect of an Employee Assistance Programme.

In Britain we have lost – or hardly ever had – sight of this original key function of an EAP. In the larger UK organizations at least, managers are used to having a personnel and/or welfare and/or occupational health service, not to mention a National Health Service, to support employees in what relates to personal and emotional well-being. The creation, via an EAP, of a similar mechanism in the USA, some fifty years ago, was akin to a revolution.

It is a revolution which has new relevance in the UK, where support services are being slimmed down, and the line manager is ever more insistently reminded that he/she has the ultimate responsibility for employees' physical and mental health and safety. It is, of course, an aspect of their job for which some managers have no stomach, time or talent. The introduction of an EAP is an opportunity to remind them again of the techniques of good performance management, while demonstrating how an EAP supports them in that role, and how they should regard and use it to their own advantage.

ICAS provides such training as a natural extension of its EAP programmes, and even without such training, will respond to individual managers' requests for guidance in handling particular cases. This kind of assistance, known from its American origins as 'supervisory consultancy', is a natural part of the EAP. It is offered also to internal HR specialists, and is the complement on the part of ICAS Corporate Services to the clinical supervision offered by its Clinical Services team.

Consultancy

Such consultancy to individuals is matched by a growing corporate assistance in the formation of new policies and strategies, as customer organizations wrestle with major change programmes. Over the ten years of its existence, ICAS has necessarily been at the birth of many new systems of employee support, of emerging policy and practice in equal opportunity and harassment, and so on. Its involvement in career counselling and redundancy training has meant the formation of specialist outplacement teams. All of this experience is proving to be invaluable to new customers entering the same arenas. This experience is disseminated further through seminars and briefings, through its commissioning of research reports and through its published *Best Practice and Policy Guides*. Figure 5.4 shows how the clinical-based services take different forms.

EAPs and . . .

. . . Healthcare

It will be self evident that EAPs play a central role in healthcare and it will be no surprise that major healthcare providers in the UK have already formed alliances of one kind or another with EAP providers, as they have in the USA for many years.

A few years ago it was possible to regard the American experience of healthcare as peculiar to the USA; no longer, however, as our traditional, unique reliance on the National Health Service gives way to the realization that a twin-track health service is already here and that we will continue to move further in that direction. The simple fact is that the government (the

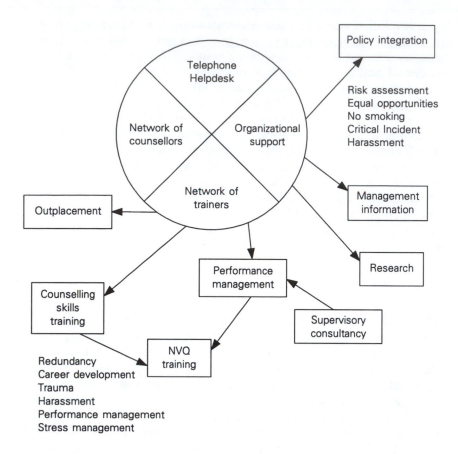

Figure 5.4 *The corporate services of an EAP provider*

taxpayer) will increasingly be unable to foot the bill for an ever-expanding medical technology, available to an ever-growing population, especially needed at the beginning and end of life – that is, by non-wage earners.

One consequence is that healthcare will increasingly be rationed, however distasteful that may appear, and all the more that this means it will be more available to those who can pay more for it. Certain types of healthcare may even be denied to some – liver transplants for drinkers, heart operations for smokers – or a lower priority assigned to them on waiting lists, as a way of emphasizing that the individual has a primary responsibility for his/her own health. But the biggest shift in funding for healthcare will undoubtedly be in the direction of the employer, who is already facing a growing chorus that protecting the health (including the mental health) of the workforce makes good business sense too.

The government (and governments of any hue will continue to do something of the same kind) is adding pressure of its own in the shape of the latest Statutory Sickpay legislation, or the recent Health and Safety Executive Guidelines on assessment of risk to mental as well as physical health – not to mention a rising tax on insurance, including health insurance. Corporate health insurance providers are consequently and understandably busy fine-tuning their products into all sorts of tempting shapes. American templates for 'Managed Care' are crossing the Atlantic at an increasing pace.

Managed Care   The process of Managed Care has fallen into a recognizable set of components, all of which are designed to provide healthcare at the lowest possible cost consistent with maintaining and enhancing standards of treatment. Whether it has always succeeded with both sides of the equation is a question which has been a matter for scrutiny. The best that can be said perhaps is that Managed Care has been around for some time now and has learned some lessons.

The component elements of a full Managed Care programme, omitting the sheer mechanics of claims handling, are four in number. These are, in no particular order of priority:

- The accumulation and analysis of data to pin-point areas of greater (financial) risk to a client organization, allowing continuing modification of the organization's total healthcare strategy.
- A system of gatekeeping all forms of treatment, usually called 'pre-authorization', and staffed by a mixture of administrative and nursing personnel.
- The development of networks of 'preferred providers' and the negotiating of consolidated rates with them for a range of predicted treatments.
- Case management of treatment in progress to ensure that this is delivered to agreed quality standards at most economical cost. In the case of psychiatric treatment this might mean influencing the choice between, say, day and in-patient care.

EAPs are a central factor at virtually every point in this process. First, the relative ease of access and the anonymity of the telephone mean that more people ask for help sooner, and thus pre-empt the need for more serious and costly psychiatric treatment at a later date.

There is enough evidence of the way EAPs fulfil this role that some group insurance schemes in the USA will reduce corporate premiums where an EAP is in place. It is only one step further for a Managed Care scheme to incorporate explicitly an EAP Helpdesk at the front end of its gatekeeping processes.

Secondly, a clinically staffed EAP provider can not only play a key part in the pre-authorization of psychiatric treatment, but can monitor such treatment throughout its course for effectiveness and cost containment. It can also offer further assistance after treatment has been terminated and when the primary need is to reintegrate the individual back into work. At that point the clinical arm of the EAP will hand over to its corporate colleagues who can connect with the individual's manager who is putting together a staged programme for return.

Thirdly, an EAP with good data-capture systems will be awash with valuable information, not only for the attention of top management in developing its broad strategy, but also as a complement to the more medically based statistics which are central to Managed Care's predictive and targeting processes. Finally, EAPs, in any case, are likely to pick up problems at an earlier stage than the GP, and thus reduce the burden on NHS medical staff. Doctors themselves are wont to say that many of the problems they deal with are more apt for counselling than medicine. Counselling, at least in the compact form which is provided by a good EAP with good case management, is an economical response to part of the healthcare conundrum.

. . . Stress Management

There has been a change of emphasis in the way that some corporate customers are now framing their approach to EAPs. The key words tend to be stress management rather than employee support; the enquirer is more likely to wear a health and safety hat than a mainstream HR role; and the point of the enquiry may revolve round the latest Health and Safety Executive (HSE) guidelines, making it incumbent on employers to carry out a mental as well as physical risk assessment of the workplace. The interest therefore is on 'organizational stress management' and the broader remit immediately meets the criticism of some stress management programmes that they put responsibility on the individual (to cope better) while ignoring those aspects of stress which are built into the systems and practices of the organization.

The question is often twofold: can we train managers to identify stress symptoms more quickly and handle them appropriately? And are there ways of measuring stress at the organizational level and developing proactive strategies to pre-empt it? This is a very different mental set from what has typically prevailed until now, although it must be said that it is still characterized by more than a little caution. Few organizations are prepared to take a deep breath and embark on a full stress audit, which they see as telling them little they didn't already know, and at the risk of highlighting aspects of their operation which they feel helpless to redress, given the nature of market pressures over which they have no control. It has been helpful to a number of organizations, however, while remaining wary of unduly raising expectations, to distinguish between three possible levels of intervention – primary, secondary and tertiary – before embarking on an initial strategy. Table 5.1 outlines these.

This matrix allows a much more satisfactory overview of the EAPs' potential role. Too often EAPs are treated as tertiary interventions, as remedial *re*actions to be invoked after something has happened, as simply and solely a safety net. It is clear, however, that this has always devalued the part EAPs play in preventing the escalation of problems at an early stage (a secondary level intervention) when judicious practical guidance and brief counselling is all that is needed. The same process also discounts the proactive role which EAPs have traditionally played in supporting line and HR managers in performance management, through training courses and through assistance

Table 5.1   *Three levels of intervention in organizational stress management*

Primary	Secondary	Tertiary
Systems	**Preventive**	**Remedial**
• Policy development	• Health and wellness – education for all, e.g. smoking, alcohol, stress, etc.	• Occupational health services
• Mental health assessment		• EAPs and counselling via manager and HR referral
• Systems analysis – culture, structure and processes	• Availability of health and fitness facilities	• Grievance and disciplinary procedures
	• EAP and counselling services	• Response to litigation
	• Training for managers	

with individual cases. The matrix also underlines the role of the EAP at primary levels of intervention in supporting strategic organizational changes, not only through the continual stream of management information which customer organizations need in order to modify such developments in policy and strategy, but also, in the light of this close knowledge of their customers, the ability to conduct a flexible, tailored and economical stress audit when this becomes a prime requirement.

The final shape and scope of a complete EAP provider therefore looks like the illustration in Figure 5.5.

Internal versus External Provision of EAPs: A Footnote

This is a theme that has been useful throughout the chapter, mainly by way of illustration. A good deal of sterile debate about pros and cons of internal and external services has overshadowed the very real contributions of both, in this country and elsewhere. Quite simply, the dynamics of each are different. Both internal and external services have almost always emerged from quite unique historical contexts and cultures, and their relative strengths and weaknesses are a matter of counterbalance rather than competition.

The differences in dynamic have sometimes centred on the question of confidentiality and it is easy to see the relative ease with which an external provider may secure it. But confidentiality is a distraction from the main picture. Confidentiality is, in any case, as much a matter of perception as of reality, and the confidentiality of some internal services is beyond reproach. Indeed, there is an irony in the fact that some internal services have gone so far in the direction of confidentiality that even they are accused of failing to respond to the employer's need for non-specific data.

The essence of the debate is not about confidentiality at all, but about the legitimate rights, interests and expectations of employee and employer along a much broader continuum. That spectrum includes policy and practice in grievance and disciplinary procedures (where the conflict is conventionally insti-tutionalized) and, with the ever-shifting boundary between the commercially,

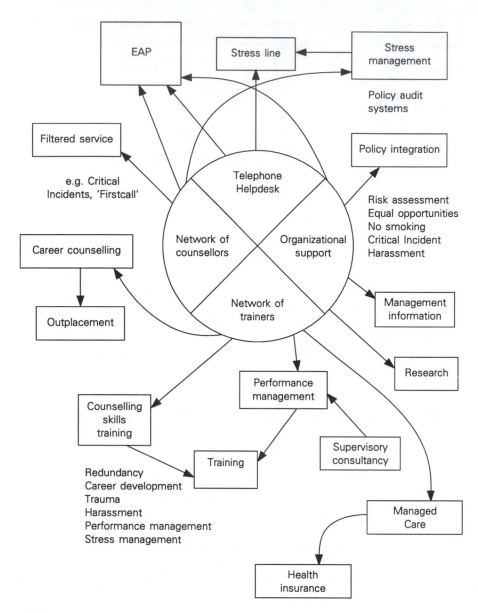

Figure 5.5 *A complete EAP provider*

politically or ideologically inspired 'realities' of the right to employment, of diversity and equal opportunity in employment as opposed to the right to manage and to satisfy institutional shareholders.

As a group of EAP professionals committed to the employer as well as the employee, ICAS expects to have to walk the tightrope no less than an internal service. What it can do is to maximize the advantages it has as an external provider, able on the one side to resist challenges to confidentiality and on the other the expectation of some employees that it will represent them in their disputes with the organization. Meantime, it continues with its core tasks of giving completely confidential support to distressed and perplexed individuals, providing expert guidance to line and staff managers, supplying high quality management information and, wherever possible, influencing the development of corporate strategy.

Conclusion

It will be evident from the foregoing that Employee Assistance Programmes, to the extent that they are regarded simply as an employee benefit, will remain precisely that, and that much of their potential will remain unexploited. It seems more likely, however, that a tried and tested, systematic array of resources and mechanisms, which can simultaneously respond to the challenges of *health* management, *performance* management and *risk* management, has a promising future, to match its past.

PART 2

UNDERSTANDING ORGANIZATIONS AND COUNSELLING PROVISION

Part 2 concentrates on the organizational issues that are important in understanding how counselling and counsellors work within their organizations. Understanding organizations and organizational culture is vital if counsellors are to work effectively, not just *within* the organization but *with* the organization. This is the theme of Chapter 6: Michael Walton reviews organizational culture in depth and shows how an awareness of the culture and an ability to work with it are essential skills for counsellors in organizations to master. Michèle Deverall moves to the perspective of the counsellor and coins a new phrase, 'the counselling consultant', to capture the need for counsellors to work in close harmony with organizations if real assessment is to precede the introduction of counselling. Michael Walton concludes Part 2 by focusing on counselling as a form of organizational change. This, too, is a concept long overdue for consideration by the counselling profession. Using counselling theories, concepts and intervention strategies as ways of helping organizations, as well as individuals within them, to change will become a theme of the future if counselling is to realize its full potential.

6

Organization Culture and Its Impact on Counselling

Michael Walton

Counselling is nearly always viewed as a private, enclosed space between individuals. But that is an illusion. The counselling setting exercises a powerful influence on what happens and when one or other participant in a counselling relationship belongs to an organization – where that organization pays for the counselling – then the organization too becomes an influential part of the counselling dynamic. In workplace counselling, the client, the counsellor and the organization itself comprise the core components of that counselling 'system'. These three entities mutually interact and create a dynamic that is different from that of counsellors working in their own private practice. The culture of the funding host organization pervades workplace counselling because, whether we like it or not, the impact of that organization's culture *will* intrude imperceptibly, and perceptibly, into the counselling room.

When clients come to see the counsellor in the workplace they mirror – in some way or another – their experience of what it means to them to work in that organization. These affects will play themselves out when they interface with the workplace counsellor (see Crandall and Allen, 1982). The notion of organization culture is often used to describe the ways in which an organization works and influences the behaviour of its employees. Paying explicit attention to this culture-of-the-organization is necessary if workplace counsellors are to engage to the full with the material brought to them during the counselling hour.

This chapter sets out some perspectives about this elusive concept 'organization culture' so that workplace counsellors can use these ideas in their counselling practice.

The Notion of an Organization's Culture

In an effort to come to terms with the complexity of organizational life, by business educators, management thinkers and training institutions, a variety of ways of describing organizational life have been developed over the past 20 years. One of the most illuminative and stimulating of these has come from applying sociological perspectives and looking at each organization as a unique living entity in itself, one that has its own history, traditions, character and patterns of internal dynamics; one that has a 'culture' of its own.

The notion 'organizational culture' draws attention not only to what is observed in the way an organization formally goes about its business, but also to the less obvious and more implicit informal characteristics that influence how decisions are made in practice and how people actually treat each other at work. It is these informal, latent and implicit aspects of organizational life which are increasingly being acknowledged as important facets of an organization's make-up and which profoundly influence its behaviour and the well-being of its staff.

However, as well as its ability to offer additional frames of reference, through which we can more rigorously look at what we see and experience in an organization, the notion of 'organizational culture' can also disguise and hide many of the subtleties and deeper meanings of work behaviour. McLean and Marshall refer to Hall in noting how

> Culture hides much more than it reveals and, strangely enough, what it hides, it hides most effectively from its own participants. Years of study have convinced me that the real job is not to understand foreign culture but to understand our own. Organizational culture is something which profoundly affects our action and yet is largely hidden from us – attending to this gives us the chance to stand back and re-appraise aspects of our working world which we have become so used to that we take for granted. . . . In looking at culture it is vital to consider what is happening now before concentrating on what should happen in the future. (Hall, 1959)

Gitterman and Miller echo this theme and describe it in these terms: 'What is "well known" is often least known' and '. . . we often discover that what "goes without saying", the received truths about organizational life, are often myths' (1989: 162). These are valuable insights for workplace counsellors to consider as they need to be informed about, and be aware of, the culture of the organization within which they are providing a counselling service. Without such awareness workplace counsellors may miss the significance of some of the material brought to them by their clients and/or misunderstand its meaning.

Organizations can often be discussed as if they are static and unchanging, whereas they change all the time. Applying the concept of culture invites the observer to look more closely at what the organization actually does and to examine the meanings and importance of the processes and practices enacted. The last 20 years have seen an increasing amount written about organizational cultures and this way of thinking about organizations has been variously described, some examples of which are set out below:

> A culture proves that no group, corporation, tribe or nation can start from nothing. Their members need to be imbued with beliefs and assertions. (Hampden-Turner, 1994: 13)

> . . . the essence of culture is not what is visible on the surface. It is the shared ways groups of people understand and interpret the world. . . . If business people want to gain understanding of and allegiance to their corporate goals, policies, products or services wherever they are doing business, they must understand what those and other aspects of management mean in different cultures. (Trompenaars, 1993: 3)

> The power of the concept of culture comes from its ability to reflect the multiple layers of organizational life and particularly to go below the surface, to illuminate factors which underpin and shape everyday behaviour. (McLean and Marshall, 1988: 2)

A strong culture is a system of informal rules that spells out how people are to behave most of the time. By knowing what exactly is expected of them, employees will waste little time in deciding how to act in a given situation. (Deal and Kennedy, 1982: 15)

. . . the taken for granted and shared meanings that people assign to their social surroundings. (Wilkins, 1989, cited in McLean and Marshall, 1988: 2)

Looking at an organization as a 'culture' encourages workplace counsellors to look beyond the face value of the actions and behaviours that they see and are brought to them by clients. Workplace counsellors can use this notion of organization culture to *re*view the taken-for-granted protocols, rules, ways of behaving and values which they hear talked about in that organization.

The Relevance of Organizational Culture for the Counselling Psychologist

Working in any organization is not a neutral activity. One does not start from zero and the opportunity to influence an organization is affected by that organization's history, its current issues and dilemmas, and the mix of people and personalities currently working there. One's role, job title, professional 'status' (in that organization), who one has contacts with, etc., will all combine – conspire perhaps! – to *position* oneself within that organization's culture.

Workplace counsellors, to function with insight, appropriateness of behaviour, and care for the client, need to have a sufficient awareness and understanding of the traditions, the heritage, the current preoccupations of their host organization. In addition, workplace counsellors need some awareness of the opportunities and constraints on those whom they counsel (and those with whom they interact administratively) in their work. Workplace counsellors need to be able to diagnose the organization's culture if they are to do the best for the client, for the organization and for themselves. One could say that ethically workplace counsellors who do not tune in and consider as fully as they need to the dynamics of the organizational settings in which they work, are failing at a fundamental level in the work they are there to do.

Figure 6.1 shows some of the defining characteristics of a company's corporate culture as viewed by Hampden-Turner (1994). In discussions about organizations these are not the normal features generally discussed. Far more often discussions will focus upon goals, targets, job grades, work-flow problems, and the behaviour of management. However, if the culture determines much of what goes on within an organization, it is to be expected that it will be the culture that will exert an impact on the workplace counsellors' clients and the issues they bring. These can be expected to reflect the types of consideration noted in Figure 6.1.

What counsellors will experience from their clients will, to varying degrees, be a reflection of the wider issues and conditions with which they are living within that organization. Consequently, workplace counsellors need to be as

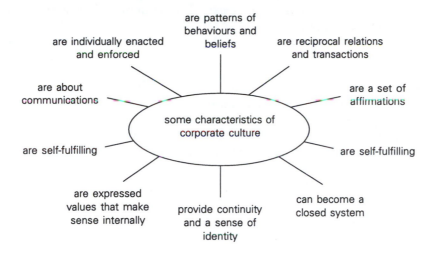

Figure 6.1 *Characteristics of corporate culture*

aware as they can be of what it is they may be picking up from the client and which could be reflections of wider organizational issues. Workplace counsellors must be alert to the wider organizational constraints, opportunities, peculiarities and dilemmas that they *may* be being shown at second hand – through their clients. However, workplace counsellors must take into account that the clients' representations of their experiences will be biased and influenced by the interpretations and meanings attributed to events by their clients.

In addition, workplace counsellors will have their own experiences and views of what it means to work in that organization, which they can use in comparison with the reported work experiences of their clients. These personal experiences and 'sense' of what it may be like to work there as an employee are important for workplace counsellors to acknowledge, identify and draw upon for their own use when in the organization. They enable the counsellors to build a more complete picture of how the organization operates in practice, as opposed to what it says it does or wants to believe it does (see Argyris and Schon, 1974).

This scanning and interpretation of the organization's culture positions the counsellors as integrators of insights and information about that organization. Unless workplace counsellors can utilize such perspectives, they are likely to be less able to understand what may be impacting on their clients and may be less effective in their professional function as workplace counsellors. I am suggesting that some of the essential facets of effective workplace counselling involve the counsellor being able:

- To attend to the primary characteristics of the host organization.
- To describe the organization's culture.
- To consider the likely implications of this for the provision of workplace counselling.

- To anticipate and consider the personal implications of these matters on their counselling practice.
- To see and understand the impact of that culture on particular individuals.

To do this requires:

- Frameworks and ways of describing, understanding and appreciating the organization's culture and traditions.
- Clarity of the counsellors about their role and responsibilities.
- Frameworks for thinking about and describing organizations.
- An explicit contract which recognizes the interplay between the organization, workplace counsellors and clients.
- Awareness of organizational processes within organizations.

A Model of Organization Culture

To meet these challenges workplace counsellors need to have some frameworks which they can use and against which to compare their experiences when working in different organizations. The next two sections offer some frameworks which workplace counsellors can·use as an aid in their organizational work.

One model of organizational culture that has remained in use over the years is one proposed by Roger Harrison (1993), initially with Charles Handy, who views an organization in respect of its emphasis towards one of four basic cultural types (Figure 6.2). Harrison (1972, 1993) suggests that each organization can be viewed as a mix of four orientations – towards *power, role, achievement* and *support* – and that recognizing the underlying preference of an organization for these will then help build understandings about what is going on and what is seen as important in that organization at that time. So in a *power* culture the exercise and productive management of influence are likely to be especially important, whereas in a *role* culture more importance will be given to clarity of role and the need to follow the rule book. In an *achievement* culture getting the job completed will take precedence over everything else – people's feelings, the formal hierarchy, fatigue, etc.

Harrison's framework is a way of getting an idea of the relative weighting an organization gives to these four different orientations. Each of the four cultural types has its positive and negative sides and it is unlikely that any organization will exclusively show the characteristics of just one of these orientations. For example, while it may be productive to have an organization which is characterized by firm and powerful leadership, this advantage can lead to a culture of fear, where almost anything is done to appease those in charge, if power and personal influence become the overriding considerations! Being committed to high levels of achievement in an organization – a sales organization for example – is constructive in focusing one's action towards a clearly specified end-result. However, here too there is a down side when that achievement orientation starts to take over a person's life, or where anything becomes acceptable to justify the end goal.

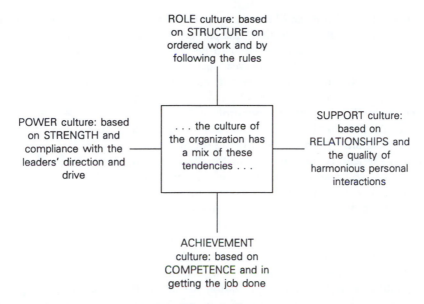

Figure 6.2 *Harrison's model of organization change*

What is more often the case is that there is a mix of Harrison's styles in an organization and this will vary from organization to organization (and possibly from department to department within the same organization). Workplace counsellors can use these descriptions as a basis from which to reflect about some of the ways people behave in the organization, and about the types of interaction that go on between them when at work. It is important to remember that the notion of an organization having a culture is a hypothetical one – a means that can be used to help workplace counsellors to understand more about the organization where they are working and can throw more light and add more meaning to some of the client's material.

Cummins and Hoggett (1995) consider the politics of workplace counselling and note how counsellors can become engaged – knowingly or otherwise – in sustaining, or at least ameliorating, the negative consequences of dysfunctional organizational cultures. In his work, Harrison (1972, 1993) has also drawn attention to both the constructive and destructive facets of each orientation and has alerted us – more than many of his contemporaries – to the shadow, dysfunctional and irrational aspects of organizations (see Kets de Vries, 1991; Egan, 1994; Walton, 1994a).

For Hampden-Turner (1990), an organization's culture is seen to emerge as a result of how it manages its business *dilemmas*, a process he sees as less likely to be determined by the rationality of business organization and practice and more from the *embedded patterns of belief* held by the most influential members of the organization such as the management board (Walton, 1994b).

Noticing what is emphasized – and what is seen as problematic and critical in an organization – gives workplace counsellors a clue as to the underlying priorities of that organization. These can be quite different from what is stated in the annual report or emblazoned upon the mission statement. For example, the authenticity of saying that 'people are our greatest asset' is blunted somewhat, and could be considered to be false, by examples of cavalier and uncaring decisions in how employees are actually treated and managed (see Argyris and Schon, 1974). In one firm, a conference was told 'no more redundancies' by the Personnel Director only to find that three weeks later further redundancies were announced!

Workplace counsellors are bombarded by information about the culture of an organization – from the positioning (or absence) of notices and directional signs, to the feel, smell and state of the place – irrespective of all the formal information you may have received beforehand. It is what it is like to be there that is a key to working with clients in an organization, and workplace counsellors must look around and consciously note the information that is there for them to see. To make sense of all this information workplace counsellors need to develop their own ways of ordering and using such data to elicit additional perspectives and dimensions that will enable them to appreciate the issues and concerns of their clients, relate more sensitively and in an informed way to the organization *per se*, and test the accuracy of the workplace counsellors' own ways of working. The challenge for counsellors is not to seek to change company policy *per se*, but to be clear about what policies are in force, how they are applied, and what they mean within that firm – and then to work with the realities of that local situation. While workplace counsellors may discern a need for change, unless the workplace counsellors' remit and contract allows for such an intervention (see Chapter 7), this is likely to generate tensions and confusions about the role and positioning of workplace counsellors within the organization.

The significance of attending to an organization's culture is that it enables counsellors to adopt a more holistic approach to organizational work and encourages them to consider the effects of tradition, values and taboos on current business practice, personal well-being in that organization and the issues brought to them by clients. Applying the notion of culture to organizations offers an extremely fertile basis from which more understanding, more knowledge and more questions can be raised about what goes on in organizations.

The internal culture of the organization is embodied, and generally guarded over, by those in the formal and informal positions of power and influence who determine much of what goes on, and what can and cannot be altered. They exercise a significant influence on attempts to alter the *status quo*. They function as custodians of the past, which is just one of the reasons why importing new 'blood' is often deemed as the way to change organizations that are viewed as not performing.

As the management of organizational change (see Chapter 7) remains a major organizational preoccupation and occupies much of the literature on organizational development, it would seem important – logical even – that attempts to change organizations should draw carefully from a study of that organization's culture. This is less often the case than might be expected, however, as a review of the published material on organizational change will show. Management theory generally continues to emphasize rational and cognitive strategies to initiate and facilitate change even though these approaches appear to have limited success on their own as effective bases for facilitating organization change. The emergence of the notion of 'organization culture' is one way in which the sophistication, and multi-layered nature, of organizational life is being recognized more fully. It can help workplace counsellors to consider the explicit and implicit influences on the organization in which they are working.

Thinking about Organizations

Counselling within organizations is a complicated matter because attention must be given to the counsellor–client dynamics and tensions, *and* to those that arise within a work setting that is full of meaning, importance and sensitivity for the client. Unless counsellors keep in mind these additional dynamics and perspectives they are less likely to relate most effectively to their client. Nor will they be able to relate with credibility within that organization.

This is quite different from counselling in private practice where the additional organization dimension does not exist. In workplace counselling, counsellors who choose to operate 'as if' they are functioning within their private practice are unlikely to appreciate the full range of pressures and vulnerabilities affecting the client and they run the risk of not being perceived as practical, credible professionals both by their clients and by others with whom they interact within the funding organization. It is in the interests of the counsellor and client alike, therefore, that the counsellors in the workplace can draw to mind, and use, different ways of thinking about organizations and about the nature of organizational life. Three such frameworks are introduced below to outline different ways of thinking about organizations which can be adapted and used by workplace counsellors.

One key point to make, however, is that any model of an organization is just that, a model – a way of representing different aspects of organizations. The value of such models and frameworks is that they draw attention to dimensions and processes that are likely to be present where work takes place. However, no model can adequately capture all that goes on or the complexity of the issues involved. So the best that the following models can give is an approximation of what we are dealing with and a means through which we may be able to understand more fully what might be going on. They are frameworks for workplace counsellors to use and adapt, and on which to position the workplace material that emerges. With this caveat in mind, the three models will give outline frameworks for:

1. Tuning into and ordering workplace counselling experience.
2. Relating counselling perspectives within a wider organizational context.
3. Integrating the three perspectives of client, counsellor and organization.

As a result of your reading, your experiences and your own thoughts, you may want to construct your own organizational model and we would encourage you to do just that, drawing on the material that follows, both in this chapter and elsewhere in the book. A first step would be to use the three frameworks that follow and to see what insights they give to your workplace counselling in practice. They may then form the basis for a framework of your own to guide and inform your workplace counselling.

Three Organization Models

To look at your organization you need to have some sort of conceptual framework that you can use to think about the core functions that will guide that organization's activities. I have selected three different models, each of which offers a different way of looking at organizations. You can decide which makes most sense to you in helping you to look more closely – from the position of a workplace counsellor – at the organization and to speculate about how it is functioning and how your clients' issues may relate to that organization.

At the heart of any organization should be clarity about the reason that it was put together in the first place, that is the *work* it is there to do. Problems usually arise when this focus gets lost or when what began as ways of helping the work get done, over time, become more important than the work itself! An example of this, using Harrison's model, could arise when doing things the 'right' way (role culture) becomes more important than effective or efficient working, where following the set-down procedure and the detail of doing the job may have become more important than completing the actual task that needs to be done.

When I become confused about what I am being told about an organization's behaviour I try to relate the material back – in my mind – to the stated core purpose of the department or section I am being told about. Sometimes it will be about a manager and then I try to relate what they are doing to the purpose of their department or their role as a manager. Doing this helps to ground the material I am hearing. It gives me a starting point from which to consider more deeply (i) the presented problems of my client; (ii) what the underlying problems and issues may be; and (iii) how severe – how ill perhaps – that organization may be showing itself to be.

Workplace counsellors need to keep such organizational considerations in mind as these will add even more depth of awareness and understanding to their work with clients. The three models outlined below can be used as templates against which to view and compare how the organizations in which you work are structured. Through using these models you may identify why some of the organizational matters that arise from your clients are occurring. If so, this will give you more insight into the internal structural dynamics that may be affecting the well-being of your clients.

Galbraith's Organization 'Fit' Model (1977)

An 'organization' means many things to many people. It can be an elusive notion. It can be used to describe a multi-million pound operation or a small

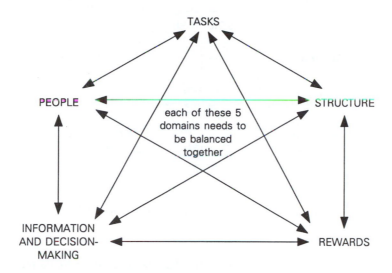

Figure 6.3   *Galbraith's model of organization 'fit'*

one-person business. Whatever the scale, there are a number of dimensions that are common. Figure 6.3 highlights five such areas, each of which is important in its own right but which, when integrated together, will enable an 'organization' to function with internal cohesion and success.

The interesting aspect of Galbraith's model of organizations is that he emphasizes the inter-relationships between the five key areas of organizational functioning. He suggests that to be successful each of these areas needs to be compatible with the others, because if they do not 'fit' together, the organization will not be in balance with itself and problems will arise.

At the heart of the effective organization is clarity about the *work* (the tasks) to be done and this should be the starting point for everything else in the organization. Once the type of work has been clearly established, the discussion can naturally move on to the type of organizational *structure* that will be needed to achieve the desired results. Next come decisions about the *people* who will be needed to make up the organization and the benefits and *rewards* (financial and non-financial) that will be appropriate to secure their commitment. To enable the organization to function effectively and efficiently, attention also must be given to specifying the *information and decision-making* arrangements that will keep the business viable and productive.

Each of these major organizational dimensions impacts on each of the others and, consequently, when any one of them is changed there will be a knock-on effect on some, or perhaps all, of the others. This model suggests that a well-ordered and performing organization has each of these dimensions functioning in an inter-dependent and mutually reinforcing manner, and that if you decide to change one of them (for example, changing the structure or a key person), you should anticipate what the wider effects of this will be within that organization.

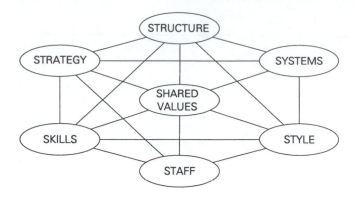

Figure 6.4   *The McKinsey 7-S Model (Peters and Waterman, 1982)*

With Galbraith's model in mind, workplace counsellors may be more able to understand some of the underlying organizational concerns, and the issues relating to them, in the consulting room by their clients.

The McKinsey 7-S Model

In *In Search of Excellence*, Peters and Waterman (1982) highlighted a number of ideas and perspectives which they linked to successful business practice, and to effective organizations. Their research suggested to them that 'any intelligent approach to organizing had to encompass, and treat as interdependent, at least seven variables: structure, strategy, people, management style, systems and procedures, guiding concepts and shared values (i.e. culture), and the present and hoped-for corporate strengths or skills' (Peters and Waterman, 1982: 9). They developed these factors more fully and it became known as the McKinsey 7-S Model (Figure 6.4).

A major emphasis of the model is its emphasis on the softer aspects of management, such as Shared Values and Style, and the culture of the organization as a whole. The message once again is that to be effective each of these different aspects of an organization need to be compatible with each of the others and that if one is altered there will be a knock-on effect on some – perhaps all – of the others.

So far as culture is concerned, this will show itself primarily through the 'Shared Values' and in the 'Style' dimension, whereas in the Galbraith model the culture is determined as a result of the interplay of all the various domains.

Weisbord's Six-Box Model

This framework was developed by Weisbord (1978) because he did not find any other framework which adequately covered all the functions in organiza-

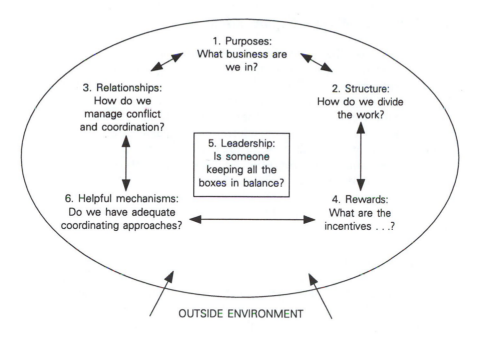

Figure 6.5   *A Six-Box Model*

tions that he wished to show. He saw much of the theory about organizations as being either too narrow to encompass all the things he saw going on, or being too abstract and conceptual. Figure 6.5 shows his Six-Box Model which he uses to consider both the formal and the informal functions of organizations.

It is an uncomplicated framework and the analogy he uses to describe its use is that of a radar screen on which to track and define the organization you are working in. For workplace counsellors the model suggests that they should be alert to issues showing in any of the six 'boxes' because each of them provides valuable information and insight into the organization. Weisbord suggests that you keep alert in your work because you will not know from which of these dimensions information about the organization, relevant to your workplace counselling, will emerge. No single aspect of the organization is seen in isolation and, like the radar screen analogy, each of the six boxes gives you a different type of read-out, each of which is needed to build up an accurate perspective of what you are dealing with.

Use the ideas in these models to frame and order the workplace issues and concerns that are presented because they will provide you with more perspectives about the life in organizations of your clients and allow you to develop even more understanding about some of the material they present to you.

Formal Aspects of your Organization

When asked to describe an organization employees often describe the formal aspects such as the management structure, job titles, reporting relationships, job grades and levels of staff. These are important facets of an organization as they often provide the infrastructure which then enables work to be undertaken. Within the consulting room these may well be the matters that clients initially concentrate upon in talking about workplace issues and problems. The majority of difficulties and disputes in organizations are described in terms of grading or pay disputes, role confusion and reporting disputes, competition for formal power, equity, equal opportunities, and against favouritism or mistreatment by senior colleagues and against bullying. However, at the heart of many of these concerns are anxieties about the standing, integrity and value of the individual staff member as a person in his/her own right in that organization. These fundamental concerns stand over and above the employee's ability just to do a specified job. Such psychological aspects of work are increasingly being acknowledged as critically important matters to consider. There is now a greater realization among managers that if they are left unattended, they will adversely affect the performance and capability of an organization. The notion of the 'psychological contract' (Hay, 1992) between an employee and employer has re-emerged as an important contemporary consideration, perhaps prompted by the difficult employment market of the 1990s and from the increasing number of publicly reported cases of poor treatment of staff by employers. In turn, this may have been exacerbated by the increased pressure on staff to perform to increasingly exacting financial criteria and to meet high performance targets – but with fewer staff in post – leading to high levels of stress and tension within organizations. Counsellors consequently need to have an understanding of the company's:

- Organization structure.
- The key roles in the organization.
- How the hierarchy of decision-making operates.
- The levels of formal authority.
- The payment and reward systems in use.
- Recent re-organizations or other changes.

Counsellors should have a copy of the terms and conditions of employment and any other information, such as a statement of values and a mission statement, if these exist. Counsellors need to be aware of the formal documents that set out the business of the company and what it stands for. This material tells workplace counsellors a great deal about how the company sees itself. It provides an invaluable clue into the culture of the organization, especially when what is formally presented is in sharp contrast with what actually is happening. An awareness of such areas of knowledge is essential if counsellors wish to understand the organization and how it functions – and consequently, how this will influence the employees who work there.

   Workplace counsellors may find discrepancies in the formal organization structure – the way the organization should function – and the *informal* structure – the way the organization operates in practice, the unconscious, organization at work. Such discrepancies can be a source of great tension and stress at work which can be exacerbated when employees' acknowledgement of these discrepancies is denied or frowned upon when raised for discussion.

Less Formalized Aspects of your Organization

It is very convenient to have a neat organizational structure that is backed up by carefully worded practices that purport to show how the place works. However, organizations develop their own informal ways of working, some of which are in line with the formal organization and some of which run counter to it.

Within organizations employees develop their own informal patterns of influence, power and authority. On joining an organization, newcomers often find out very quickly who to go to for reliable guidance and support, and who the informal leaders in the organization are.

The formal models of organization introduced earlier in this chapter focus on what can be seen in the organization and what it is that those in positions of authority and influence purport to be the guidelines for decision-making, for action and for strategy. For example, it may be declared formally within the organization that it has the appropriate structure and people to do the work that is needed but this is not always the case in practice. For whatever reasons things get messed up and suddenly it can become apparent that the reward structure is encouraging some employees to work in ways that do not help other departments, or perhaps that managers are encouraged to be so performance-oriented that they begin to treat their staff as if they are just cogs in a machine.

We know also from Harrison's work (1972, 1993) how there are productive and disruptive sides to the cultural types he has proposed and so productive and constructive organizational practices and policies can – in the extreme – become dysfunctional and potentially destructive. Perhaps we are back to the management of dilemmas that remains one of the preoccupations of Hampden-Turner (1994)! All of these possibilities are relevant to workplace counsellors because they impact upon the clients whom they see in that organization.

Workplace counsellors need to have some knowledge about the potential for dysfunctional behaviour in organizations and of the undercurrents that exist. Many organizations have a counter-culture and, in order to build up a good enough picture of the internal life and experience of the company from which their clients are coming, workplace counsellors need to appreciate these aspects of an organization's workings. Without these understandings counsellors are left in a partial vacuum in which to work and without a sufficient understanding of what it means to be in the system from which clients are coming.

But there are other equally dynamic and important determinants of behaviour in organizations which are not so readily seen or set out in company policy, procedures and protocols. Indeed, some of these other potent organizational

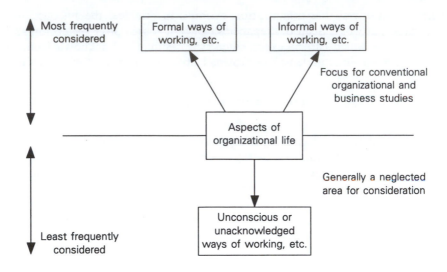

Figure 6.6   *Three 'aspects' of organizational life*

influences are not acknowledged, not seen, perhaps even denied by those who are nevertheless a part of them.

Figure 6.6 suggests three 'aspects' of organizational life. First, the more formal ways in which the company is set up, and the formalized ways in which it is organized and run. Next there is the informal organization which often reflects the way in which the formal arrangements have to be adjusted in order to get anything done. It is these two dimensions that get most of the attention and it will be aspects of these that will show themselves as part of workplace issues which clients will bring to the counsellor. However, it is the third area of interest – the area below the horizontal line in Figure 6.6 – which also offers valuable information and insights for the workplace counsellor about the organization's culture and what goes on.

These are the hidden processes and dynamics that can – and do – take over from time to time but which are very elusive to define and tie down for observation and study. For example, Trist and Murray (1990) show how social structures and cultures of organizations can be used unconsciously as defences against anxiety (see also Menzies, 1959) and how inner conflicts of the individual members can be projected into the organizations in which they work. If this is so, it follows that any change to the organization will tend to disturb these projections, which are important for maintaining the identity of the individual. They go on to observe how such insights – about the social structuring of psychological defences – have not gained immediate acceptance and are still largely ignored by the majority of researchers in organizational behaviour. For the workplace counsellor, these possibilities have considerable significance in working with clients in the organizations which employ them.

For many employees, organizations have far more meaning than solely holding a job for which payment is made. Much has been written about the ways in which some employees 'live' for the firm and invest a great deal of themselves in the job. Employees can come to identify with the company so strongly that they will resist change even when, on the face of it, the change is in their interests. In cases such as this, workplace counsellors need to consider the possibility of unconscious – in addition to more apparent – organizational processes which may be influencing the perceptions and behaviour of the organization as a whole, and its members individually. Again, with this possibility in mind, counsellors are better placed to consider more deeply some of the issues and concerns being presented by their clients. Without allowing for the possibility of unconscious work processes, however, counsellors are reduced to reflecting primarily on the formal and informal aspects of organizational life and thus may be missing a third valuable way of looking at that organization's culture and how it impacts on employees.

In Fenichel's (1945) view, the membership of an institution affects the personality structure of its members to the extent that they begin to identify strongly with the institution. Zaleznik (1970) has illustrated how patterns of unconscious anxiety affect the political workings of organizational life and can prevent those in prominent leader roles from accepting help and advice. Such behaviour, on the face of it, would seem bizarre and confusing until the possibility of unconscious processes is considered, but when considered, allows workplace counsellors to consider what these processes and influences might be, and the effect they may be having on their clients.

As individuals, we are influenced by our own unresolved, unconscious and unacknowledged processes, which shape our thinking, feeling and doing. Given that we take with us this treasure trove and storehouse of our history wherever we go, it is inevitable that at some stage it will come into play in our organizational interactions. Our psychodynamic composition will condition our perceptions and experiences at work – both conscious and unconscious – and will exercise an influence on organizational behaviour of which we may only partially be aware. These aspects of ourselves will find their way into the counsellor's room.

As Morgan notes, 'Patterns of meaning that shape corporate culture may also have unconscious significance and the common values that bind an organization often have their origin in shared – unconscious and unstated – concerns and unresolved issues that lurk below the surface of collected conscious awareness' (1986). While the workplace counsellor will work with the material presented by the client, not only is it necessary that these other dimensions are considered, in the light of the formally presented culture of the organization itself, but also that some consideration is given to the unconscious processes and dynamics of organizations too.

Facets of 'Management'

To be effective, workplace counsellors have to meet the needs of two quite different constituencies: first, they provide for the professional care for the client, and secondly, they exercise the counselling responsibility in ways which

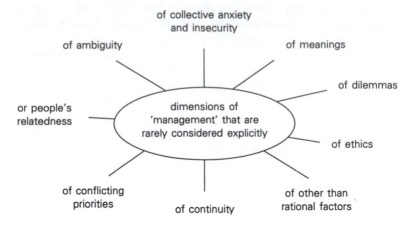

of collective anxiety
and insecurity

of ambiguity

of meanings

of dilemmas

or people's
relatedness

dimensions of
'management' that are
rarely considered explicitly

of ethics

of conflicting
priorities

of continuity

of other than
rational factors

Figure 6.7   *Dimensions of management that are rarely considered*

are realistic and practical in the light of the organization in which they are working. The scope for dissonant or incongruent ways of working exist and to avoid these workplace counsellors need to develop understandings about the nature of 'management' within the host company. Traditionally, 'management' has been taken to mean the organization of work, the arrangements through which employees work together and the bases on which performance and achievement are formally set out. These are all aspects that are likely to be seen as part of the 'formal' organization. However, so far as workplace counselling is concerned, while these matters are part of the structure within which the counselling provision is given, they are not, in themselves, the major concerns for workplace counsellors. The counsellor is more likely to be concerned with the types of management issues shown in Figure 6.7. In part, these are about the ways in which the client as an individual relates to others, but they are also about the ways in which the organization's culture determines how members will 'see' things.

Many aspects of a person's experience of what it means to them to work in an organization are, one way or another, managed by that organization. However, this aspect of business management and organizational behaviour often goes unrecognized in the emphasis on the logical-rational side of business. One of the consequences of this neglect is that matters which affect the well-being of employees are ignored and some of these may surface with the workplace counsellor. To be in a position to appreciate and understand the experience of the client – in that organization – workplace counsellors need to know how matters such as those set out in Figure 6.7 are handled.

Conclusion

The impact of an organization's culture on counselling provision is profound, and the more workplace counsellors can make themselves informed about an organization's culture, the more likely they will be able to offer a better, more informed and firmly grounded service for their clients.

The culture of an organization will affect how people do their professional work, the quality of the relationships they have with their sponsors in the organization, or with professional colleagues, and the degree to which they can be themselves in doing their work in a careful and professional manner. As Gitterman and Miller put it, 'Some clinicians [that is, workplace counsellors] distance themselves from their organizations, as if they were doing private practice in an organizational context. Their work consists in maintaining client contact and that is it. But is it? Does being organizationally isolated serve the clients or even one's own interests?' (1989). They consider the viability of other relational possibilities, such as an over-identification with the organization, but conclude that perhaps what is needed is for the counsellor to be alive and open to the pulls, pressures, ways of doing and of making sense of things which characterize the organization in which they are working. To do this, however, requires the workplace counsellor to understand and value the key features of the organization in which they work, and to appreciate how these may impact upon employees, while at the same time retaining the professional independence and integrity of a workplace counsellor.

References

Argyris, C. and Schon, D. (1974) *Theories in Practice*. San Francisco: Jossey-Bass.

Crandall, R. and Allen, R.D. (1982) 'The organisational context of helping relationships', in T.A. Will (ed.), *Basic Processes in Helping Relationships*. London: Academic Press.

Cummins, A.-M. and Hoggett, P. (1995) 'Counselling in the enterprise culture', *British Journal of Guidance and Counselling*, 23 (3): 301–12.

Deal, T. and Kennedy, A. (1982) *Corporate Cultures*. Reading, MA: Addison-Wesley.

Egan, G. (1994) *Working with the Shadow Side*. San Francisco: Jossey-Bass.

Fenichel, O. (1945) *The Psychoanalytic Theory of Neurosis*. New York: Norton.

Galbraith, J. (1977) *Organization Design*. Reading, MA: Addison-Wesley.

Gitterman, A. and Miller, I. (1989) 'The influence of the organization on clinical practice', *Clinical Social Work Journal*, 17 (2): 151–64.

Hall, E.T. (1959) *The Silent Language*. New York: Doubleday.

Hampden-Turner, C. (1990) *Corporate Culture for Competitive Advantage: Management Guide*. London: Economist Publications.

Hampden-Turner, C. (1994) *Corporate Culture*. London: Piatkus.

Harrison, R. (1972) 'Understanding your organization's character', *Harvard Business Review*, May–June.

Harrison, R. (1993) *Diagnosing Organizational Culture*. San Diego, CA: Pfetffer.

Hay, J. (1992) *Transactional Analysis for Trainers*. Maidenhead: McGraw-Hill.

Kets de Vries, M. (1991) *Organizations on the Couch*. San Francisco: Jossey-Bass.

McLean, A. and Marshall, J. (1988) *Cultures at Work*. Luton: Local Government Training Board.

Menzies, I. (1959) 'The functioning of social systems as defence against anxiety', *Human Relations*, 13: 95–121.

Morgan, G. (1986) *Images of Organization*. Beverly Hills, CA: Sage.

Peters, T. and Waterman, R. (1982) *In Search of Excellence*. New York: Harper and Row.

Trist, E. and Murray, H. (1990) *The Social Engagement of Social Science*. London: Free Association Books.

Trompenaars, F. (1993) *Riding the Waves of Culture*. London: Nicolas Brealey.

Walton, M. (1994a) 'Designer clothes and labels – or those that "fit"?' in R. Casemore, G. Dyos, A. Eden, K. Kellner, J. McAuley and S. Moss (eds), *What Makes Consultancy Work – Understanding the Dynamics*. London: South Bank University Press.

Walton, M. (1994b) '"Being" in Organizations', School of Psychotherapy and Counselling, Regent's College, London. Unpublished MA dissertation.

Weisbord, M. (1978) *Organizational Diagnosis*. Reading, MA: Addison-Wesley.

Wilkins, A. (1989) *Developing Corporate Character*. San Francisco: Jossey-Bass.

Zaleznik, A. (1970) 'Power and politics in organizational life', *Harvard Business Review*, 48: 47–60.

7

The Counselling Consultant's Role in Assessing Organizations for Counselling

Michèle Deverall

Assessing an organization for counselling is a process which involves the development of a consultancy relationship between the individual representing the counselling organization and the individual representing the potential client organization. This relationship is likely to be as important, if not more important, than the counselling relationships that are subsequently developed in the organization. The individual representing the organization providing the counselling service will be referred to as the counselling consultant. The nature and strength of the counselling consultant's relationship with the employing organization effectively facilitates the entire counselling process. This is not always easily managed because there is a dilemma that is inherent in the juxtapositioning of the two relationships. This is especially evident when the counsellor is also the counselling consultant, and occurs because the nature of a consultancy relationship varies significantly from the nature of a counselling relationship. The need to 'wear two hats' can prove stressful; it is also the most productive aspect of the relationship between counselling organization and client organization in that it oils the wheels for the effective use of the counselling service.

This chapter will focus on the consultancy relationship and process between the two organizations. Where a traditional management consultant is gathering information about the organization, both formal and informal, the counselling consultant is gathering the same information, but, in addition to this, is also on the lookout for information about the unconscious, and therefore unstated, world of the organization.

The overall assessment needs to take account of the rational conscious organization and the apparently irrational unconscious world of the organization. The consultant's judgement is vital and the ability to intuit 'what's going on' when dealing with the organization is central to the process. The more accurate the consultant's assessment, the easier it will be to create the most appropriate counselling service for that organization.

However 'benevolent' an organization is, it is ultimately contemplating using counselling for its own benefit rather than for the individuals within it. If the service does not provide the required outcome for the organization, then it will not be continued. Obviously, the counselling consultant needs to establish why the organization wants counselling and gauge whether or not

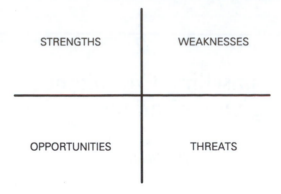

Figure 7.1   *SWOT analysis*

counselling is the best solution to its problems. To be cynical and go ahead with a counselling assignment when it is unlikely to solve the problem, will only build up problems for the counsellor at a later date. It does not do much for the reputation of counselling in general either.

The assessment process should draw together three areas of analysis and examination. A SWOT analysis is a helpful way of going about this (see Figure 7.1). This is a method of assessing an organization in terms of the strengths, weaknesses, opportunities and threats that present themselves to it. This will allow the counselling consultant to gain an impression of the stresses and conflicts that are likely to be inherent within an organization at the time, as well as some idea of where the organization is in the process of change. In order to do this the counselling consultant has to gather pertinent information about the organization and categorize it in terms of it being a strength, weakness, opportunity or a threat.

Organization Culture

It could be argued that most psychological stress or difficulty, resulting in the decision to get help, is due to some form of change in the world of the client. Indeed, the changes that most organizations have gone through this century have been phenomenal. The changes of the last decade have been particularly difficult because they have impacted the same population of employees who have worked through a period of growth, technological advancement and then recession. Assessing the nature of the change that the organization is going through, as well as the stage they have reached, is not always straightforward, but it is important to do so because it helps to define the culture of the organization and the extent to which that culture is being eroded. When an organization's culture comes under threat, it is usually because the organization needs to change in order to survive. Some organizations resist change where others embrace it. Both present difficulties, but for consultants, it is important to know which type of organization they are proposing to work with. As with individual clients, resistance and 'being stuck' are usually harder to work with than the client who is actively struggling with change.

I will use the work of the Italian political philosopher, Wilfredo Pareto, to help gauge the culture because I find his approach useful in that he emphasizes the dynamic of change as well as offering a measurement of change, and suggests ways of thinking about behaviour without producing an overly complex classification which might prejudice the analysis by imposing too rigid a set of categories. Essentially, Pareto was the first theorist to recognize the significance of the 80/20 ratio in the change process. He related this statistic to personality types within the organization and their impact on the likelihood of change occurring.

Seeing organizations as necessarily being involved in change, Pareto argues that at different stages of development, organizations attract different types of individual in terms of their behaviour within the organization. Essentially, their significant behaviour ultimately relates to their attitude to change: behaviour that is future-orientated, creative, unstructured, risky and revolutionary is ascribed to Foxes, and that which is past-orientated, methodical, structured, risk averse and reactionary to Lions. His view is that it is the tensions that are created as the organization struggles not only with the differing types of people, but also with the different structures, procedures and behaviour styles introduced by each type, that brings about change and in turn causes problems. I will use Pareto's Fox/Lion analogy to explore organizational culture and to help to assess the organizations' attitudes to change, drawing on my use of this concept in my work.

Foxes are typically found in flexible environments and Lions in bureaucratic environments, the former tending to be young and the latter more established organizations. When an organization is staffed by 20 per cent of Foxes, they overthrow the Lions and take over the organization. The same applies to Lions when the situation is reversed. For example, many companies that have succeeded over the past 30 years, such as Anita Roddick's Body Shop, may well have started out as Fox companies. The original members often recall the company's early years when the business was driven by the personal enthusiasm of the founder and the support of the few people around them. Founders often refer to their early years with fondness when they recall a company with few formalities, a lot of hard work, where many mistakes were made along the way, but where the overall intensity and commitment was satisfying and fun. War stories abound where deadlines were only just achieved and all sorts of dramas took place in order to succeed. The Fox personality thrives in this type of fast-moving environment where the aim is to grow successful and really become established. The future holds no fear, but is full of promise.

In contrast, a Lion personality is less comfortable with the future, which is seen as something of a risk and something full of danger to be insured against. The Lion looks to the past for security. The way things have always been introduces a sense of certainty and security. Lions like routine and find the Fox way of going about things quite unsettling. Once an organization becomes established it needs structures and procedures to stabilize it and prevent its failure. Interestingly, many organizations fail at the point where they need to introduce more formality. This is often due to the Fox's natural aversion to this style of operating. Those organizations that succeed often do so because they have recognized the need to bring in Lions to organize them. However, it is the very process of organizing that restricts the Fox, eventually making the most Fox-like individuals leave. These are replaced by Lions. Pareto surmises that when 20 per cent of the organization are Lions, they assume control of the organization and in time drive away the Foxes.

This perspective on organizations is especially useful in describing common organizational scenarios in the 1980s and 1990s. Many traditional organizations became hidebound and, as such, vulnerable to predators. Others perceived the need to change their management style in order to remain competitive. These Lion organizations then attracted a Fox to run them. The Fox, in turn, hired more Foxes who were charged with the task of bringing about change. Impatient with the Lion approach to management, many of the incumbent senior Lions were removed. The remaining Lions would become threatened by the changes being imposed upon them, for example the very successful WPP Group. WPP (Wire and Plastic Products, Hastings,) a manufacturer of supermarket shopping baskets, was purchased by the aggressive Martin Sorrell, ex-Finance Director of Saatchi's. Using it as a holding company, he went about buying above and below the line businesses in the communications sector, including J. Walter Thompson and Ogilvy and Mather, becoming the largest agency in the world in the space of three years (1986–89). These agencies may have been Fox organizations in their earlier years but, getting on for a half-century later, had become rather hidebound in their management if not their creativity.

Pareto's work makes the point that different types of people are stressed by different types of event, context or situation. For example, if the Lions were to complete a questionnaire asking them to name key life events experienced over the past year and had to name more than two, they would probably have experienced a great deal of stress, for Lions find change of any sort stressful and disturbing. Foxes responding to the same questionnaire would feel stressed if they had not experienced any of these key life events. Thus, a Lion organization undergoing change is a highly stressful place. The Lions would feel out of control without the familiarity of their routine and procedures. The Foxes would be frustrated by the Lions' inflexibility. In time, the organization would become all Fox. For a while the dynamism and creativity that this generated would be energizing and fun. But eventually the Foxes would become bored with the predictability, and as the organization grew and prospered, the more Lion-like Foxes would start to appreciate the need for some structure in order to capitalize on the gains made from the revolution that had taken place. The prospect of operating in a more disciplined environment would be unappealing to the Fox mentality, who would hire Lions to carry out key functions. This would work well initially, but as the number of Lions grew, the Foxes would feel that the company was no longer the one that they had joined. They would begin to feel bored and hemmed in and would drift off to other environments, eventually leaving the Lions to take over the business. And so the cycle continues.

Implications for Counselling Provision

Because the Lion response to stress is different from the Fox response, the type of counselling service provided will need to reflect the different types of culture if it is to survive and play a constructive part within that setting. For assessment purposes, it is significant whether the organization is becoming more Fox-like or more Lion-like, particularly when deciding what form a counselling service should take and at what level it should operate. The 80/20 ratio is an extremely useful guideline and tends to be valid in a number of circumstances. However, this is only a guideline and should not be overplayed as a method of assessment.

In contrast to a Lion culture, in a Fox organization counselling tends to be more effective when focused on key individuals. A formal counselling service would not be trusted by the Fox who would not like to conform to an imposed bureaucratic structure. For a Fox, discretion is less important than the adventure of trying something new. The extent to which counselling is accepted into a Fox organization will depend upon other organizational factors. The main determinants will be the product or service provided by the organization, the department in which the individual operates and the personal crises he/she is encountering. Many Foxes view personal development as being central to their success. Thus they would not welcome a 'counselling' approach that implied that they were not healthy or were dysfunctional. They would prefer to take a self-improvement approach whereby their aim would be to maximize their potential. It is these aspects of the organization that need to be ascertained during the assessment phase.

Some of my clients are Chairmen or Chief Executives of companies and as such are my only client within their company. In such cases, I do not have to carry out an assessment of the organization. However, an increasing number of organizations are focusing on the entire senior cadre when exploring methods by which to provide them with support. The Fox client tends to take a very different view of the counselling process from the Lion client. The former is often careless of boundaries but takes the process seriously. Seeing it as an investment, he/she wants value from it, viewing it as being as much his/her responsibility to gain benefit as the counsellors to provide the service. The Lion is more cautious initially, preferring to place him/herself in the counsellor's hands as the expert. He/she operates in a more structured way, taking notes, seeking advice and even writing agendas!

Lions are more risk averse and prefer the anonymity of a discrete external service. The Lion organization would be reluctant to accept the possibility of counselling as developmental, preferring to see any 'different' behaviour as dysfunctional and to be dealt with by experts elsewhere. The sort of concerns a Lion organization would have about counselling would revolve around adverse effects that the service might have. A common one would be the possibility that individuals being counselled would want to leave the organization. Foxes would be less inclined to see this as a threat in that if someone left in a positive frame of mind he/she would be a good ambassador for the organization. Lions would feel threatened by the departure – surely anyone normal would want to stay?

In order to gauge what sort of a counselling service an organization requires, if any, two sets of information need to be collated. One set relates to the potential user organization and the other set relates to the counselling organization or counsellor. These sets of data then need to be explored in the light of a dynamic process that matches the information from the perspective of the motives of the two parties concerned, that is the user organization and the counselling organization – in this case Foxes and Lions 80/20.

Most organizations requiring a counselling service of any sort are organizations where change has been a major influencer on the behaviour of individuals within the organization. Many organizations have tried to impose completely new management styles and attitudes, and have experienced great difficulty in bringing about such change. The resistance within the organization is often great, and the suffering within the organization can be quite extreme. The Fox/Lion, 80/20 analysis is useful in assessing this. It is important to use a model for understanding organizational behaviour that assumes healthy organizational behaviour, even if it is only healthy for some of the members. However, many Lion organizations going through change will experience problems with their staff who will show classic symptoms of stress – physical and mental – thus encouraging them to take the view that they need a service to remedy the illnesses they are experiencing. Fox environments are more likely to experience aggressive behaviour and high labour turnover.

Assessing the Organization

Let us return to the SWOT analysis. One needs to find out what the organization's own view of its situation is, particularly with regards to stresses and conflicts. This will help one to assess or to begin to assess the type of organization that one is dealing with, because, as is often the case with individual clients, their own personal analysis of what their problem is often proves to be very different from the real problem that emerges during counselling. The consultant needs to gain some sense of the extent to which the organization really wants to know about its real problems or is quite happy for it to be couched in some 'acceptable' diagnosis. Some organizations experience difficulty in coming to terms with the possibility that the organization itself has a problem, and prefer to believe that certain individuals within the organization have problems. If the consultant is aware of this, it will be easier to manage the relationship with the organization more effectively. The consultant will have to be sensitive as to when, if ever, to broach the real issues. In order to carry out a SWOT analysis, one needs to establish both material and cultural data about the organization. This will be especially helpful in assessing the Fox/Lion split. Other specific cultural factors are also valuable.

The Age and History of the Organization

This is important in order to gauge the traditions that are inherent in an organization. For instance, one of my client companies was founded around 100 years ago and has a long tradition of a paternalistic and highly moralistic management style, providing 'jobs for life' and a whole battery of staff benefits and welfare facilities. The company has always been run along the lines promoted by the Human Relations School of Management. The significant element of the Human Relations School here was the tenet that a happy worker is a productive worker, thus by looking after the welfare of staff, productivity would be maintained.

Recently, the company has been taken over by an aggressive American company. Individuals in the company are experiencing great difficulty in adapting to the requirements of the new powers that be. Because of the perceived need for a rapid change in attitude and behaviour, the managers selected by the American company to bring about change are aggressive, dynamic and future-orientated. The sense of history and pride in that history makes the changes harder to bear for the English company. For instance, I held a number of discussions with key members of the Board in order to gain a sense of the organization's culture. The Marketing Director happened to mention a potential new advertising campaign. The proposed advertisement involved a short fantasy story about the company itself. Some of his department, especially those from the American company, were enthusiastic, but the Marketing Director, who was from the English company, was concerned that the advertisement would be seen as self-indulgent. He viewed his company as an organization that had always taken pride in its socially responsible attitudes, and while the product was designed to indulge others, the company saw no merit in indulging itself.

To this organization, being socially responsible and serious was extremely important, and under normal circumstances a counselling service for such an organization would be a formal off-site service operating discretely as part of the welfare function of the company. However, the aims and objectives of the incoming company was to bring about a culture change so that these people could recognize that their traditional approach to managing their people was no longer viable in today's highly competitive marketplace and certainly was not compatible with the management style of the incoming organization. For them, the ideal counselling service would focus on key individuals at a senior level who were experiencing difficulties in 'shaping up' to the new ways. The ability to understand the issues and their attitude to what was happening would enable them to gain a handle on the situation and thus be able to choose a response.

What Does the Organization Do?

Is it a service organization, or is it a manufacturing organization? Is it sales, marketing, product- or skill-led? Is it labour or capital intensive? If it is labour intensive, what sort of people are crucial to its performance? Dimensions such as these need to be noted in looking at the potential client organization. In fact, this company was manufacturing based with an unspoken commitment to lifetime employment. This had changed in more recent years as production moved from automation to process, thus becoming capital rather than labour intensive. The people who were crucial to its performance were now the management team. The issues emerging from the SWOT analysis suggested that the threats and challenges facing the organization were those that would emanate from management decisions and would be generated by an increasingly competitive marketplace undergoing a difficult period economically.

How Well is the Organization Performing?

This needs to be assessed both financially, relative to the market, relative to past performance and relative to public opinion (especially if it is not a profit-centred organization). The organization was not performing as well as it had been in the past and the product was less easy to differentiate from those of its competitors, so that its future performance depended largely on management skills and decisions, for example those affecting product differentiation and new product development. In addition, the financial performance of an organization will influence the internal sense of confidence and belief in the company's future. When morale is low because of a lack of faith in the organization, a Fox will probably leave to pursue his/her interests elsewhere, whereas a Lion is more likely to sit tight, often unable to function at all effectively because of the stress he/she would experience.

What is the Size and Geographical Spread of the Organization?

In this case, the organization was sizeable with an international reputation, but the key sites for the newly merged company were based in the traditional manufacturing site in the Midlands with a shared head office function in London. Because it was decided that management issues were crucial for the future performance of the organization, it was the head office location in London that was the most commonly used location for counselling the senior management team.

A Range of Personnel Statistics Will be Required

These will include the number of employees and their distribution, both geographically and hierarchically. Is it white or blue collar? Is it professional or craft based? What is the predominant educational and social profile? Other personnel statistics will include labour turnover, average length of service, remuneration. The employment contract will vary from organization to organization and is a good indicator of the organization's attitude and culture. For instance, some organizations reward individuals for services rendered or tasks achieved and consider that their responsibility for the individual ends there (usually Fox). At the other end of the spectrum are organizations which recruit people with the expectation that they will employ the individual for the duration of their working life (Lion). These employers often believe that they have a duty towards their employees and provide them with a range of services and benefits which are especially welfare orientated. The traditional Japanese large company typified this model, as did the British Civil Service and the Armed Forces in the UK. Recently, these types of organization have tended to move away from this model of employer concern for their employee, preferring their employees to face up to life's fundamental insecurities. I believe that much of the stress experienced in the organizations with which I am familiar at the moment has to do with commitment. The employer still expects their employees to work as hard as they did in the 1980s, but is not prepared to offer the same level of reward or any real degree of permanence. Employees are experiencing difficulty in coming to terms with the removal of the mutuality of commitment that existed earlier in the relationship.

What is the Organization's Management Style?

How would you describe the culture? This will impact heavily on the way in which employees view themselves and take responsibility for themselves. In the paternalistic organization, which Lion organizations often become, the employees will be quite child-like and take little responsibility for themselves, whereas in a more aggressive individualistic culture, which is typically Fox, the best performers are often the most likely to vote with their feet if they feel that the company is not meeting their career requirements. This means that these companies often run the risk of ending up as 'mediocricies' where they had intended to be 'meritocracies'.

One large international professional partnership is involved in a continual struggle to protect itself from losing its best performers. Interestingly, this does not only involve looking after its best people, it involves being supportive to even the weakest performers. Possibly because the age profile is very young in the organization, and employees are from similar social and educational backgrounds, their ambition was often tempered with concern for their friends in the Partnership, who were often perceived as having been unfairly treated in some way. These star performers were very marketable outside the firm, which realized that it was important for them to leave as good ambassadors if they were to leave at all – both in terms of client development and in terms of future recruiting. Thus, as part of this need to support staff, different kinds of counselling were available. Remedial for those who were obviously experiencing personal and career difficulties, and developmental as a matter of course, emphasizing the best performers.

Has the Organization Been the Subject of Takeover, Merger or Move?

Has the organization decided to change its style to meet the demands of the marketplace? Obviously, this will be highly significant.

Nationality

This is obviously important to take into consideration, especially where there may be language difficulties.

Other Information

This would include the organization's mission statement (if any). The absence of a mission statement could also be significant and this would have to be explored. Does the organization have a plan? If it does, is it three, five, ten or twenty years? What are the organization's objectives? An organization that has a clear view of where it is going is going to be in better control of its destiny than an organization that is fumbling along. The organization that has not actually focused on where it is going, and how it is going to get there, is probably not going to be in such good shape. Having said that, one has to recognize that many companies in this country tend not to have clear plans for the future and if they have a mission statement at all tend to play lip service to it.

Assessing the Sponsor of the Counselling Service

Finally, one has to take a view about the sponsor of the counselling service. Would the counselling consultant be able to work with this individual? At what level in the organization does he/she operate. What are his/her motives for introducing such a scheme? Is he/she just paying lip service to trying to remedy the problem so that any solution will do? Are his/her motives personal or in the best interests of the company? A very important set of information relates to the motives of the organization. What does it really want the counselling service to provide? What does it consider the problems to be? How well formulated are these problems? What other solutions have been considered? Is the organization prepared to consider other solutions? If so, what would they be?

Where the existing management is responsible for change there is often a degree of discomfort, guilt and responsibility for having to bring about this change. It is important when change is being imposed to identify where the conflict is being generated. The location of stressed individuals is rarely synonymous with the generators of the stress. It is important for the consultant to take this into consideration when assessing the organization because if the consultant takes the option of providing counselling for all those who appear to need it, this could end up as no more than an 'elastoplast' function where it would be better occupied in working with the generators of stress.

Once one has gathered all this information the next step is to assess it for the SWOT analysis in terms of Strength, Weakness, Opportunity, Threat. For instance, a company that has household-name products and is well established is Strong in this respect. If it has lost its market position it has a Weakness. If it is seeking to diversify its product range, then it has an Opportunity and if it is vulnerable to takeover then there is a Threat to its existence in its current form. However, threats can often be opportunities. A takeover might give it the necessary strength to compete more effectively, and so on. This will give the consultant a real feel for the company in order to assess its potential for growth, and whether or not the organization itself feels the same way.

Whether or not the consultant decides to take on the role of counsellor involves the same decision-making process as for a private individual client. However, if the counselling consultant will be using other counsellors to carry out the counselling, then a review of these individuals and the service they will be providing will be necessary to assess whether the match with the client organization is a good one in terms of the likely effectiveness of the counselling.

Once all the collected information has been located with the SWOT grid (see Figure 7.1) you have a clearer idea of the nature and state of the organization with which you are engaging. The overview is vital in discussing and assessing counselling provision.

The Counselling Provider

Assessing the Organization for Counselling Provision

In the case of the organization providing the counselling, a number of questions need to be asked. The answers to these questions will be invaluable to the counselling organization when assessing whether or not the organization is ready for a counselling service. In any case, these questions will certainly be asked by the potential user organization in order to make its own assessment. They will also help to shape the counselling contract.

Shaping the Contract for Counselling Provision

There are several key questions.

1. How many counsellors are available and what is their availability? This is particularly pertinent in the case of a large or multi-site organization where the counselling organization needs to be assured that it can meet the demand for counselling. Similarly, the user organization needs the same reassurance.

2. Where are they located? Are the counsellors located within travelling distance of the organization. Companies are very sensitive to potential time delays or additional travelling costs. No doubt counsellors are as well. The counselling organization can face unnecessary internal conflict if counsellors do not feel they are being adequately compensated for travelling time. Conflicts in consultancy organizations risk leaking into client organizations.

3.   Where will the counselling take place?   Will the counsellors travel to the organization or does the counselling organization have its own premises. If so, are these single or multi-site, and how many counselling rooms are there on any one site? How accessible are the locations? Because of the sensitivity involved in counselling, counsellees are more inclined to complain to their company if they feel that they are not being held. Often, making the appointment with the counsellor requires courage – an unnecessary delay between doing so and the appointment itself or unavailability of rooms or last minute changes of locations often result in the service being criticized.

4.   What will the use of the counsellors cost the counselling organization?   The cost of the counsellors and their expenses need to be borne in mind when discussing possibilities with the client organization. Too often counselling organizations have put in cost estimates that are much lower than their competitors. Sometimes this is because they are allied to a training organization and use students under supervision as their counsellors. This can adversely affect the reputation of counselling in the commercial marketplace. Counselling organizations should seriously consider their marketplace carefully before proposing for business. Not only should they bear in mind which other counselling organizations might be competing for the business, they should also seriously consider what other solutions an organization might use apart from counselling. If they might use management consultants, or psychometric tests or a medical service, one needs to compare these costs, particularly where the alternative services are already established and respected. To be used simply because the service is ridiculously cheap, as is so often the case, not only runs the risk of the service itself not being taken seriously, it also adds to the difficulty the counselling world experiences in establishing itself as a profession. It is very important that the counselling organization has a sound understanding of its marketplace.

Another reason for assessing the costs to the counselling organization for the use of counsellors is to ensure that adequate funds are available for the use of the counselling consultant's time, which is likely to be considerable in servicing the contract.

5.   What are their qualifications?   Do any of the counsellors have specialist knowledge or experience that will be especially pertinent to the user organization? Companies often ask about qualifications. They do not really want to know that all the counsellors are psychodynamic, because this is unlikely to mean that much to them. They simply need reassurance that they are safe, and if being trained and/or qualified is the only assurance of that, then they need to know that this is the case. At the same time, they are more likely to be impressed with the non-counselling experience of the organization's counsellors. Such experience is often connected with relevant commercial or managerial experience or even experience of a particular type of organizational structure, for example a partnership. However, linguistic skills or international experience is becoming increasingly relevant as organizations become more international.

Fundamentally, organizations need to be reassured that the counsellors live in the 'real world'. There is still a perception, which is becoming lessened as the profession grows, that the counsellor's view of the world is unrealistic. Although one will often hear members of organizations saying 'My wife is doing a counselling course at the moment', further acquaintance with that individual sometimes reveals that this does not imply acceptance of counselling as worldly in the sense that it does not automatically follow that something his wife does involves a worldly or businesslike attitude, particularly with regards to understanding the subtleties of organizational life. Counsellors are often seen as individuals who cannot operate in an organizational environment and are therefore regarded with some suspicion.

From the counsellor's perspective, his/her own preferences are likely to make a difference to his/her performance with a client. The counsellor who is naturally drawn to a particular organizational structure or management style may have difficulty dealing with those from an organization far removed from that preference.

6. Are their qualifications uniform or diverse?   The counselling organization needs to know this because it is possible that the theoretical stance and depth of experience of a counsellor may have implications for the counselling outcome. For instance, a counsellor who views clients as patients, whether overtly or by implication, may be inclined to see behaviour as healthy or unhealthy. The counsellor who sees behaviour as appropriate to the environment or more appropriate in another environment will have a different experience with the client. A theoretical position that regards counselling as necessary to deal with pathological behaviour, with the intention of returning the client to 'normal', will operate most effectively in a setting that is consistent with these views. Similarly, a counsellor who believes counselling to be developmental rather than remedial will need to choose an appropriate working environment.

7. What are their value system(s) and are they uniform or diverse?   Are they Foxes or Lions? Can they operate flexibly or do they need a formal procedural and process-driven base from which to operate?

8. What sort of service is being offered?   Such issues include the availability of counsellors and the scope of the service. Should the service be contactable by telephone for all or part of the day? Is it remedial or developmental? Will it offer long-term or short-term counselling – or is there flexibility?

The answers to these questions will impact significantly on the type and number of counsellors being used. The same questions need to be considered if the counsellor is also the consultant. In this case the scope of the service to be provided is likely to be limited in terms of the number of clients the counsellor is able to handle. However, the nature of the service can be far more flexible and of enormous value to the organization if the counsellor has been careful to become established both in terms of the niche market being provided, the specific qualities and skills being offered and the nature of the service itself.

For instance, my area of specialization is senior management, which includes Board level and one level below the Board. Only in exceptional cases, or where the broader client base has been carefully specified, will I undertake a client brief which includes individuals further down the organization. This concurs with my value system in that I believe that the performance of an organization is largely determined by the attitude and effectiveness of the senior cadres of management and that these people probably need more help in their somewhat more isolated position within the organization. Because of their emphasis on achievement, independence and personal strength, these individuals find it harder to ask for help and therefore a discrete service aimed specifically at this level proves to be highly beneficial. This is also consistent with my previous experience within organizations.

At this point, the counselling consultant should have a really good feel for the fit between the counsellor(s) and the client organization. If the decision is made to accept the assignment, then the chances of success are improved because of the careful exploration of the issues involved. The organization will feel more comfortable because the process has allowed it a period of adjustment and it is forewarned of many of the problems that can arise. Similarly, the relationship between the counselling consultant and the sponsor of the counselling will have developed sufficiently to protect the service and thus the welfare of those using it.

Key Success Criteria

As stated at the beginning of the chapter, the success of the work will depend, to a great extent, on the counsellor's working relationship with the main point of contact within the organization. The nature of that relationship will depend largely on the agreed terms and conditions for carrying out the counselling. For instance, issues of confidentiality and general or specific feedback must be respected by both parties, particularly where feedback is encouraged. It must not be assumed that the need for feedback is sinister. Counsellors must use their judgement, so that they are able to trust the organization within reason. If they feel unable to do so, then they should not be providing the service. This is one of the issues where the consultant needs to think carefully about whether the organization is sufficiently mature or responsible to handle a counselling service.

The organization that is prepared to change when a problem is identified is often a better client than the organization that wants no feedback. The counsellor has to have assessed the representative of the organization to be sufficiently mature to be able to handle the information in a responsible way that is ultimately beneficial to the organization without being personally harmful to any individual. For instance, on more than one occasion I have been asked to work with a manager who is arrogant and high-handed with his staff. I have learned that it is important for the client and the main point of contact to be aware that as the individual begins to change, his/her department may well try to sabotage the process. The sort of people who are prepared to tolerate a difficult boss for a long time clearly need him to remain difficult. The support of someone in the organization is often very useful to help the person concerned, even if it is just to allow the continuation of the counselling after the 'change' has taken place. Certain types of organization are better able to manage changes such as this than others. The large bureaucracy, for instance, is often better off almost severing connections with its counselling service. It prefers to see individuals safely in the hands of experts and finds it hard to deal with issues arising from the service. Distancing itself from the process is its way of safeguarding itself from 'contamination'. Its natural respect for the professionalism of other disciplines will allow it to maintain a distance. However, the assessment needs to establish whether this stance represents a healthy distancing, or washing its hands of the problem – in other words dumping the problem on the counsellor.

In a mature organization that is attuned to people issues, feedback can be very valuable in helping the company to ensure that its management style and communication process is effective. What constitutes feedback needs to be scoped out; should it be attributable or non-attributable, it should not involve personal information without the counsellee's consent, the counsellee should be aware of the nature of any possible feedback, but not necessarily that non-personal feedback will take place as it would be too easy for the counsellor to be 'set up'.

The ability to persuade the organization that the generators of stress are not those who require the counselling largely depends on the organization's perceived need genuinely to solve the problem as well as the counsellor's credibility and skills of persuasion. For instance, the existence of most conflict might be in the upper middle management levels where the old culture clashes openly with the new. This is often because the old culture has not been weeded out to the same extent that it would have been in the top level of the company. But, because these individuals are involved in a battle, and so are able to try to 'do' something about their situation, the individuals who actually show symptoms of stress are sometimes further down the organization. This is because they can only witness goings on beyond their control, but are aware that the winning and losing can seriously affect them. Where an outside organization, and therefore a different management team, is responsible for the change, there is often a more pragmatic but less sensitive attitude towards the plight of the existing employees. The two attitudes impact significantly on the type of counselling service preferred. Similarly, a counsellor who is not in accord with the aims and objectives and motives of the company, would be best advised not to undertake such an assignment.

The consultant's judgement is his/her most useful tool during the assessment process. His/her sensitivity to the existence of unspoken issues and unconscious factors will help him/her to come to a decision on whether or not the organization is ready for any sort of counselling service. It is also important that the organization respects the consultant and the service. Without a relationship based upon respect, little of value will be achieved.

The same questions need to be considered if the consultant is also the counsellor. In this case, the scope of the service to be provided is likely to be limited, but advantages in terms of quality of service and consistency of feedback and a healthy working relationship are enormous, especially when an understanding of organizations is combined with counselling skills. The success of the work will depend largely on the working relationship with key personnel in the organization.

Is there a better solution than counselling? I believe that if a significant percentage of the organization appear to need counselling, it will not be an effective solution. In my experience this tends to be around the 10–20 per cent range. Following on from Pareto, 20 per cent would be the key point. Clearly, the organization itself has a bigger problem and is generating stress. Therefore, if counselling is to be undertaken at all in such an environment, it needs to be part of a larger solution. For example, one client organization, a subsidiary of a major international hi-tech group, decided to seek a counselling service due to major morale problems resulting from a poorly managed redundancy programme. This, combined with a lack of alternative employment in the area and poor redundancy payments, suggested that demand for the service would be excessive. I refused the opportunity to tender for this service, preferring a more discrete approach for senior managers, as it seemed that the organization had a management problem. The Managing Director did not understand the concept of developmental counselling and agreed to try being counselled. He found the experience valuable and agreed to introduce the service on the understanding that he selected candidates for counselling himself. Because of this, the service gained a cachet. Some of the feedback, which was non-attributable, was invaluable in the development of future business strategy. Another counselling service was subsequently introduced to deal with the stressed employees. This was extremely popular initially but became institutionalized and was seen as part of the welfare function and rarely used after a few months. However, it was of value during those months and ideally should have been withdrawn at the end of the process. Lane (1990) complains that a number of counselling programmes have been developed without the benefit of an assessment of need or any survey of employees' views at all. I would argue that it is more important to use an appropriate means of gathering information and that a formal information gathering process may not be the best route to take. It is important to understand the organization's culture. The survey approach works well in a bureaucratic environment aiming to provide a counselling service as part of the welfare function, but in a more flexible environment an intuitive approach is often more successful.

Conclusion

This chapter has focused on the role of the counselling consultant. The argument has revolved around the critical role that this individual takes and the tensions generated by the need to wear two hats when the consultant is also the counsellor. Great emphasis has also been placed upon the judgement of the counselling consultant. The ability that this individual has to intuit the state of the organization and its members, as well as to assess objectively the organization, is central to the success of the relationship that the counselling consultant has with the organization. The chapter has also examined the various factors that have to be taken into consideration when assessing an organization and the value of completing a SWOT analysis in this respect. The significant factors were the age and history of the organization, the product or service, performance, size and geographical spread, the management style, nationality and a range of personnel statistics. Assuming change to be normal, Pareto's 80/20 Fox/Lion model was used to help pinpoint the organization in the change process. This analysis helped the counselling organization to assess whether or not counselling was likely to be the best solution for the organization. The organization providing the counselling service would be better able to assess the likelihood of its being able to provide a service by having a clear understanding of who they are in terms of their own people and skills.

The chapter also considered the protection of the reputation of counselling as a profession, the maintenance of the integrity of the counselling consultant's relationship with the organization and whether or not counselling was the best, or even the right, solution to a company's management problem. The form that counselling should take was also extremely important. Two possible scenarios for counselling provision would be a discrete external service aimed at remedial support or a developmental service which also provides helpful advice to the organization in terms of management style or organization structure. The relationship of the counselling consultant with the main point of contact in the organization was also considered to be crucial to the success of the service, so it was important that the individual concerned was sufficiently senior or influential to ensure that the service was used effectively.

It may be helpful to think of the organization in psychotherapeutic terms whereby it represents a significant group or groups in a person's life. In individual, private therapy, my experience is that the family is likely to be threatened by any change in the person concerned, whether or not the family have recommended that he/she be helped. The same applies to the organization. Therefore it is important that the key point of contact is aware that often, where one person is changing, others around him/her may resist that change, or need support in coming to terms with the changes they themselves require. The impact of the individual's environment is extremely important to his/her development, and that when one has a good relationship with the organization, one has an excellent opportunity to influence the way the organization works. This is where the counselling function can really provide added value to all concerned.

References

Handy, Charles B. (1988) *Understanding Organisations* (3rd Edition). Harmondsworth: Penguin.
Lane, David A. (1990) 'Counselling psychology in organisations', *The Psychologist, Bulletin of the British Psychological Society*, 12: 540–4.
Pareto, W. (1996) *Sociological Writings*. Selection introduced by S.E. Finer, translated by D. Mirfin. London: Pall Mall.

8

Counselling as a Form of Organizational Change

Michael Walton

Introducing counselling into an organization carries implications for change. At one and the same time it is a supportive service for employees, and a threatening one. It is threatening in the sense that it has the potential for highlighting and unravelling issues and experiences that may be critical of the organization – messages and insights that the organization may prefer to discount, avoid or deny rather than consider and act upon.

Workplace counselling provides an opportunity – sanctioned by the company – for employees to raise personal matters in a professional and confidential setting; it offers the potential for personal change and the scope for personal development. It offers opportunities for clients to re-consider their work experiences and to ponder on what – if anything – needs to change. It sets in motion thoughts for a different future. Workplace counselling offers more than may often be expected; it is far more than a counselling session held within a company's premises. It differs greatly from the type of counselling that takes place within a private counselling practice.

Counselling and psychotherapy are, at their very heart, concerned with the dynamics of review and personal change. Counselling within the workplace carries with it the potential not only for client-generated self-review (which will then be carried forward into the organization at large), but also counsellor-generated feedback about that organization. Workplace counsellors exercise an influence, just by being there, on the organization. This can be a passive influence (because it will be known that workplace counselling is available within the company), or an active one (where the workplace counsellors become involved in stimulating the potential for change). One such 'active' opportunity, depending on the details of the counselling contract agreed, is presenting – in an aggregated and unattributable format – the work-related concerns collated from individual counselling work.

Workplace counsellors occupy a role that could be described as half-in and half-outside the organization. They have a pseudo-institutional role as the provider of a company-sponsored service, yet at the same time this is a private service, the details of which remain between the client and the counsellor. However, aspects of this personal client information, when aggregated, can be of considerable importance for the well-being of the company as a whole. A dilemma for workplace counsellors is how, without compromising client care and confidentiality, to remain true to their professional ethics and respond to requests for information about the state of the sponsoring organization.

Balancing Responsibilities: Riding the Individual and Organization See-saw

Organizations introduce workplace counselling provision for varying reasons. Some will be very aware that through workplace counselling they can enhance the quality of working life and perhaps stimulate positive internal change. Other organizations may prefer to see workplace counselling as an add-on support service so that needy employees will be able to discuss issues of a confidential nature with a professional workplace counsellor. In other cases, perhaps a major shock or trauma, such as a merger, a hi-jack, or a hostile take-over, may have prompted the decision – a recognition that the 'organization itself is in shock'! It may be that some organizations have supported workplace counselling provision because earlier management decisions to reduce numbers, introduce new technology, multi-skilling, etc., have seriously weakened the psychological contract that had formerly been in place between the employer and the employee (Schein, 1980). It may, too, have been prompted by a drop in morale by those who have survived the various job cuts, and who may be experiencing what has been described as 'survivor syndrome'.

Whatever the specific reasons may be, the primary purpose of introducing workplace counselling is to offer an employee counselling service. In some cases the organization may contract a workplace counselling service that extends beyond the individual client work to include regular 'insight summaries' about the state of the organization. Here, workplace counsellors, in addition to their individual client responsibilities, aggregate the main themes from their client work (over a given period) and present them as an overview – an insight – of the state of the organization at that time. In this way the sponsor of the workplace counselling can be made aware of possible emergent issues and concerns within the company.

Through their work, workplace counsellors become privy to some of the underlying issues affecting the performance of the organization. These could be deep-seated aspects of that organization's history and culture, or they could be the reactions to recent senior management decisions. Either way, workplace counsellors, in addition to their privileged access to the worlds of their clients, come to have insights about the organization itself which may not be available to many (if any) others within that organization. An immediate dilemma for the workplace counsellor is what, if anything, to do with this information. This is especially difficult if the counselling contract agreed upon does not include providing the type of 'insight summaries' noted above. In such cases, what is the workplace counsellor to do? Re-negotiate the contract? Stick to an individual counsellor–client contract? Choose not to see the wider picture that may be emerging?

The counsellor may begin to feel that some organizational procedures and practices are actually generating the clients coming to see them! Workplace counsellors may come to see how aspects of the organization at large are negatively affecting the well-being, not only of their clients, but perhaps of many other employees as well. It may be that the workplace counsellor reaches a view that the issues raised by clients can, in fact, only really be resolved through wider organizational change. Egan and Cowan (1979), for example, discuss the difference between (i) supporting clients and enabling them to regain composure, confidence, belief, etc., and (ii) seeking to identify and then influence the root causes that are leading to client distress in the first place. He uses the analogy of a stream to make the point that the counsellor can intervene 'downstream' (where the counsellor picks up those who have in some way been damaged already), or 'upstream' (where the counsellor tackles the core issues *before* employees become distressed).

The first option casts workplace counsellors in more of a conventional client-focused relationship within an organization. The counsellor is there to work with individual clients, irrespective of the surrounding contexts from which they come. The second option – the upstream one – positions workplace counsellors somewhat differently. In addition to the individual counselling role, 'upstream' work acknowledges the potential which workplace counsellors have for taking on a change-agent type of role. By trying to identify causes of client distress within the organization and by providing 'insight summaries' of collated (and anonymized data), workplace counsellors re-orient themselves into a more change-proactive position. One consequence of this is the dilemma of where, and to what extent, should workplace counsellors put their effort and attention. For example, should the workplace counsellor continue to concentrate on patching up and meeting the needs of the organizationally wounded who come to see them (downstream work)? Alternatively, should workplace counsellors, in a major strategic shift of role, concentrate on influencing company policy (upstream interventions) in order to bring about changes which may cause less internal harm and result in fewer organizationally wounded? If workplace counsellors do the latter, what will the consequences be for their clients who are likely to find out – perhaps with some horror and suspicion – that *their* counsellor is 'hob-nobbing' with the management? What client fantasies are likely to be generated when it becomes known that *their* counsellor goes to the Personnel Department on a regular basis, and what will the impact of this be in the consulting room? Where, clients may ask themselves, do the priorities and interests of workplace counsellors really lie – with their counselling work or in their (perhaps) desires to become part of the management?

A dilemma facing workplace counsellors is that, for the majority, their training and clinical practice will have focused almost exclusively on counselling within an individualized counselling framework, perhaps in preparation for setting up a private practice of their own, or for independent working within the framework of a private counselling service, or as a counsellor of an EAP. Workplace counsellors, however, are subject to, and influenced by, the organizational context in which they find themselves working. From the style of the offices, the furniture, the colours used, the facilities – or lack of them – the terms and styles that employees use to address each other, etc., workplace counsellors will become in some ways a 'part of the organization' and will be influenced by it. Workplace counsellors become attuned (consciously and subliminally) to the sights, sounds and patterns of engagements specific to that organization. As with employees, workplace counsellors are subject to the same socialization processes as their clients. A significant difference, however, is the capacity of workplace counsellors (through their training and experience) to be more aware, alert and attuned to what is going on around them in that organization. These processes combine with the workplace counsellors' increasing understanding and knowledge of company policy and practices.

The result is more 'organization-smart' workplace counsellors, but the ever-present danger is that workplace counsellors could merge too fully with the organization and risk losing their ability to maintain a distanced perspective on the organization. At one level they become more informed about the organization and its workings, which is an important prerequisite for effective and sensitive workplace counselling, yet at the same time they can be absorbed into the organization, thus becoming a part of it.

These considerations highlight an ever-present dilemma for workplace counsellors, that is, how to manage a balance between retaining sufficient distance (from the organization) and attaining adequate integration and understanding of the intricacies of the organization in which they are working. Carroll (personal communication) likens this to walking a tightrope – maintaining an optimum balance, being subject to the different pulls and pressures, yet having to work with both the client and the organization in order to move ahead. To achieve this balance involves (i) working with the individual client, (ii) raising emergent issues (on an aggregated basis) with the organization, (iii) perhaps contributing to employee policy, (iv) not getting too sucked into the culture of the organization, and (v) not falling over or losing one's balance and perspective, all at the same time!

Such conflicting pulls and demands co-exist. They impact greatly on workplace counsellors, who need to be able to manage and monitor their effects if they are to remain effective in their work with clients and, at the same time, be seen as viable and competent professionals in the eyes of the sponsoring organization.

Four Key Facets of the Workplace Counsellor's Role

Workplace counsellors have to:

1. Work at the level of their individual clients.
2. Work within the context of the organization.
3. Work with the organizational sponsor.
4. Manage their own professionalism as a counsellor.

Each of these aspects of the role of a workplace counsellor within an organization is important and each needs considered thought, attention and

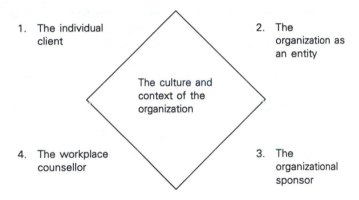

1. The individual client

2. The organization as an entity

The culture and context of the organization

4. The workplace counsellor

3. The organizational sponsor

Figure 8.1 *Four dimensions of workplace counselling*

management. Items 1 and 4 are likely to be the ones with which counsellors are most familiar. What makes counselling in organizations so different from counselling in private practice, however, are items 2 and 3. These aspects are illustrated in Figure 8.1.

The pressures involved in balancing the varying pulls of each of these different dimensions of workplace counselling is heightened when the role of workplace counsellors *as a force for organizational change* is superimposed on to the primary counsellor–client responsibility for individual counselling. Suddenly, workplace counsellors are perceived in a different light – they have the potential to deliver potent messages to senior people in the organization and are able to operate on a 'bigger stage' within the company.

Particularly difficult boundaries to manage are those between the counsellor and the client and between the counsellor and the organizational sponsor. What do I mean by the 'organizational sponsor'? I am referring here to the person (in some cases it will be a group of people) to whom the workplace counsellor(s), and the workplace counselling service as an entity, report. The sponsor is the person in the host organization whose responsibility it is to fund and support workplace counselling. He/she may be the line manager, for example where the counselling service is in a particular department. The organizational sponsor is the critical person in either enabling or barring workplace counsellors the opportunity to deliver the messages they may wish to present. Consequently, maintenance of a professional, focused and straight-forward relationship with the workplace counselling sponsor is crucial. It will probably be to the sponsor that 'insight summaries' are presented. It is likely to be the sponsor to whom the counsellor may propose a need for policy changes, or the introduction of additional policies designed to protect and safeguard employee (and the organization's) well-being.

Clues to deep-seated, but perhaps hidden concerns within the organization may be reflected through the counsellor–client interaction. It is as if the therapy engagement is a replication of that client's experience with his/her own organization. When the counsellor reviews client material as a possible 'parallel process', further insights beyond the immediacy of the client's material and about the wider organization become possible. To suggest that individual clients can be viewed as a 'mirror', perhaps a microcosm even, of their organization may seem to be stretching things a little too far, but nevertheless this possibility should be kept in the mind of workplace counsellors. Certainly, some issues that are brought to the counsellor will be owned by the individual clients whereas others may well be a reflection of wider issues of the organization itself.

When this possibility is allowed in by the counsellor, the role of workplace counsellors as a force for organizational review and (possibly) change is reinforced. In doing this, though, workplace counsellors then have yet another dilemma to grapple with. This one is to consider which issues belong to the client and which may be coded messages and reflections about the organization. Some client material will be both, but how does the workplace counsellor decide? And how do workplace counsellors keep sufficient distance and (relative) objectivity, first about the material they are working on with their clients, secondly, about their own experiences of what it is like to be a workplace counsellor in that organization, and thirdly, what is it that they should be picking up and reflecting back about the organization as a whole? It can be a muddle! Engaging with client material in these ways requires a major shift in the *mind-set* which workplace counsellors bring to their work.

In private practice the primary interactions go from client to counsellor and back again; interactions along a horizontal continuum. However, as soon as the context of the organization is introduced, and in addition the important relationship with the organizational sponsor noted above, the dynamics alter substantially. Suddenly the pattern becomes far more multi-dimensional and far less able to predict, control and understand. This complexity for workplace counsellors is a significantly different therapeutic–organizational proposition from that of counsellor–client interactions in a private practice.

Of the four main dimensions set out in Figure 8.1, each needs to be managed in relation to the others. So workplace counsellors need to consider not only their relationship with their clients, but also their own sense of themselves as part of the therapeutic relationship, and much more. A view of workplace counsellors as a force for organizational review and change will also be viewed differently by each of the four parts of Figure 8.1. Finding a path that accommodates these differing perspectives of workplace counselling is an ever-present and ever-changing challenge for workplace counsellors.

Coventionally, counselling and psychotherapy is about self-insight, self-review and the creation of a potential for change at the individual level. Counselling and psychotherapy also have much to say about collective and institutional change. After all, if the counsellor can enable employees to gain insight and 'change', and if employees are a sub-set of the overall organization, surely counselling approaches will have something to say about change at the organizational level too! All that needs to be done is to adjust and apply counselling insights, models and perspectives and re-orient them to the workplace. Depending on the theoretical orientation of the workplace counsellor, however, different diagnoses and thoughts about relevant interventions will be suggested. For example, Summerfield and Van Oudtshoorn (1995) provide a brief summary of several orientations and relate their usefulness to workplace applications.

Change and the Workplace Counsellor

Becoming associated with organizational change marks a significant extension of a counsellor's role away from that of a practitioner engaged solely with a client in a therapeutic relationship. However, whether actively promoting a need for change, or passively being seen to be a stimulus for organizational review, workplace counsellors lay themselves open to criticism. This could be on the basis that the role of workplace counsellors should remain firmly focused on individual client work, and therefore that a deviation from this is both inappropriate and perhaps unprofessional. On the other hand, the criticism could be that organizational change is very different from individual counselling and that different skills are needed, and that, therefore, it could be inappropriate for workplace counsellors to 'dabble' in the pond of organizational change. Still further criticism could be that it is inappropriate to aggregate client data, and recast it as 'messages to management' (that is, to the organizational sponsors), because it is, after all, still only individual client perceptions. There may even be unease that individual client data can be used in this manner – even with confidentiality safeguarded – and a risk that subsequent changes in the organization could be attributed (blamed even) on this aggregated client information. Irrespective of the validity of such claims, the impact of the possibility that a client working within the consulting-room confidentially with a workplace counsellor could be directly responsible for changes in workplace behaviour is an important matter to consider. In certain respects it could be said to alter, or at least to threaten, the basic sanctity of the private client–counsellor relationship.

For some workplace counsellors this broader potential to change in their work may be precisely why they decided to work in organizational settings. After all, some counsellors may claim that workplace counselling is really all about 'change' and about the leverage that workplace counsellors are able to apply (for the good of employees) through influencing management thinking and behaviour. On the other hand, this possibility may, for other counsellors, be full of dread. Dread that in some way the impact of their individualized 'private' work with clients may be seen by some to affect directly the work environment of others – for example, those who have not been their clients and about whom the workplace counsellor knows nothing. They may claim that their work is with the individual client and that that is where their responsibility starts and finishes. Whatever goes on outside the consulting room, and perhaps beyond the client session, is not relevant unless the client brings it into the counselling relationship.

There may also be a sense of dread at the responsibility workplace counsellors will have to take if they accept the wider impact that their counselling work with an individual client can have in the organization. After all, it could

Figure 8.2   *Possible reactions and responses to a workplace counselling service*

be argued that it is one thing working on matters within the capsule of the therapy room, but quite another if the client then applies his/her insights to a wider canvas of the organization. While this is no different from the possible outcomes from counselling in private practice, it can be experienced differently by the counsellor because the counselling occurs within an organizational setting and is funded by the client's employer. So with workplace counselling, the organization is always present and occupies a prominent facet of the counselling relationship, irrespective of the material brought by the client.

For some counsellors, contributing to the potential for constructive change is the major attraction of counselling in the workplace as it provides content for the 'insight summaries' noted earlier and enables the counsellor to contribute to the 'upstream' thinking noted by Egan and Cowan (1979). Workplace counsellors, however, whether they like it or not, become a *de facto* force for organizational review and perhaps change. It may be that as soon as a decision is taken within the firm to introduce a workplace counselling service a variety of expectations, views, emotions, and possibilities are triggered which immediately begin to affect that organization. Figure 8.2 suggests some of the reactions that could be expected within the organization once the decision to introduce workplace counselling provision is publicized.

Change holds the potential for release, developmental accomplishment, insight, transformation; it also holds the potential for collapse, disruption, fragmentation and regression. This is why the role of workplace counsellors is such a finely balanced and delicate one. Facilitating organizational insight and raising the potential for change on a macro level is a significant role to occupy, and insights from workplace counselling have much to offer management in guiding an organization that wants to facilitate change.

While insights from workplace counsellors have the potential for promoting constructive change, they are also likely to elicit deep-seated counter-productive defence reactions within the organization. After all, every organization is as it is now because in various ways that is what the organization cumulatively wants. If this were not so, then the organization would change. So, for example, if workplace counsellors draw attention to policies or procedures or management behaviours which are damaging morale and company performance, this will not be universally welcomed by those who like things as they are, warts and all.

Some of the reasons why people in organizations persist in dysfunctional, uncaring and inappropriate behaviour are due to powerful but unacknowledged tensions and influences within those organizations. Workplace counsellors may, through their counselling work, gain insights into these hidden dysfunctional influences. When they try to highlight these influences they may encounter stiff resistance and denial from other parts of the organization which may not want such matters highlighted, discussed or changed.

Workplace counsellors are participants in the processes of organizational review and change. Raising the need for change, however, could be considered irresponsible if this is not accompanied by insights, judgement and sensitivity about how organizations work and what they can come to mean, psychologically, to employees. To meet the challenge of this responsibility workplace counsellors need to be aware of how organizations:

- Maintain the *status quo* internally.
- Manage internal differences, dissension and dilemmas.
- Establish themselves as an institutional entity.
- Maintain *and* protect themselves against perceived external threats and disruption to the *status quo*.
- Structure and organize themselves.
- Are entities of politics and power.

While these areas of study – the field of organizational behaviour, occupational psychology and organization development – fall outside the remit of this chapter, they are fields of study which workplace counsellors need to be informed about and able to relate to their own workplace counselling responsibilities.

But what might the messages be that workplace counsellors could find themselves wanting to deliver to their sponsors and others in these 'insight briefings'? What could it be that makes this feedback aspect of workplace counselling so important yet so difficult to accomplish? Listed below are examples of the types of message that workplace counsellors may find emerging when they classify the work-related matters brought to them by clients:

- Messages about structure and organization.
- Messages about managerial practices.
- Messages about specific departments.
- Messages about morale.
- Messages about unethical behaviour.
- Messages about inadequate or mis-used policies.
- Messages about the need for specific employee policies.

Some specific items could be about sexual harassment in the workplace, about bullying, or about unreasonable and exploitative behaviour by some managers. It could be that the counsellor detects a growing sense of employee alienation and disenchantment, or that 'people don't care anymore'. These are the matters that touch the heart of an organization's capacity to remain resilient in the face of marketplace challenges. It may be that the organization is penalistic, a place where it is too dangerous to admit errors or mistakes, and thus where a lot of effort is diverted on to self-protection rather than task accomplishment. Such examples illustrate the types of theme and issue that workplace counsellors, when they have reviewed and aggregated client material, may wish to communicate to their organizational sponsors. Of course, some of these messages will not be welcomed, and there will be some risk that the standing and reputation of the counsellors will be put in jeopardy by raising such material.

Organizations, like most people, prefer to be given positive news and are therefore likely to defend themselves against critical comments. It is in the interests of the organization at large, and workplace counsellors in particular, therefore, that careful thought is given to how such material is communicated.

Communicating Key Messages

The messages to be delivered by workplace counsellors to organizations are likely to be critical in some way and perhaps controversial. If these 'insight summaries' are to secure the positive effects desired – in facilitating positive change – how they are communicated becomes a crucial matter for the counsellor to consider. When communicating sensitive and emotionally charged information it is depressingly easy for the key points to be mis-perceived and mis-communicated, and for the recipient to become so defensive that he/she is unable to hear what is being expressed. The more emotionally heightened the message is, the greater the potential for problems to arise during the communication. This can then lead to mutual frustration, mis-understandings and missed opportunities for constructive change.

Two challenges for workplace counsellors are first, how to present the messages so that they will be understood and valued, and secondly, how to pitch them so that they match where the listener has focused his/her listening-ear. Frustration, loss of energy, antagonism and even disengagement are some of the consequences that could follow if this information is mis-communicated or if there is insufficient 'tuning-in' by the counsellor to the needs of his/her management audience. It is one thing for the counsellor to have key messages to give, but quite another to facilitate the organization to listen, hear and understand them.

Let me illustrate what I mean. Let me assume that as part of the contract for workplace counselling there is a formal agreement that there will be a quarterly review to draw the company's attention to any emergent themes or issues, relating to the workplace, that the counsellor has discerned from their client work over the last three months. The themes will have come from several different clients and will have been re-cast into a series of issues, episodes, concerns, worries, etc., about the company. The workplace counsellor is now ready to share these and will have the aggregated information ready to substantiate the diagnosis reached.

So, where do you start? I'm not thinking here about which item comes first, although that is important, but about the level of focus which, as counsellor, you begin with in introducing the material you want to share. For example, a need for a policy on redundancy may have emerged from your client work but do you talk about the resources needed to draft a policy, or the timing of doing this, or do you relate the value of a comprehensive redundancy policy to the espoused values of the organization as displayed in the Mission Statement?

Sometimes difficulties arise because those communicating are not talking on the same wavelength to each other, yet are unable to recognize that this is happening. For example, if I am talking about apples and you are talking about pears the sooner we can recognize that we are both talking about different types of tree fruit the less confusion there will be, and the more likely it is that we will both decide to talk about apples first and then pears. Another possibility is when we listen so hard for an aspect of the topic that we consider a top priority – maybe a value statement, or a cost implication – that we miss the overall relevance of what is being communicated. One way out of such unhelpful cross-purpose communications is for workplace counsellors to make clear what aspect they are going to start talking about and how other aspects of the topic will be addressed.

Perhaps, like me, you have been in meetings where tensions have rapidly escalated to a very high degree because of vehement disagreements only for the protagonists to realize later – with some embarrassment – that they were actually talking at cross-purposes. When each party stopped trying to get their own way, they realized there was no substantive disagreement between them at all; they had been talking about different aspects of the same thing. This possibility is heightened when the material to be communicated and discussed is high in emotional content, such as feedback about how some employees feel and experience working in an organization.

Unless there is a straightforward way of ensuring that both parties talk at the same level (for example, both are talking about strategy, or actions), the potential for confusion and frustration is high. Figure 8.3 sets out a framework which differentiates between six different levels of attention, each of which requires some discussion. This framework can be used by workplace counsellors to help ensure that (i) all the parties are talking about the same things at the same time, and (ii) that sufficient attention is given to each of the levels specified. Discussion at each of these levels should be compatible with the others. For example, it is no good saying that policies will be introduced to cover sexual harassment at work if there are to be no resources allocated to make it happen or if there is no implementation date set out. Or that mentoring will be introduced but that top managers will have to squeeze it in when they can.

As well as helping to ensure that attention is directed to these different aspects of the material under discussion, Figure 8.3 enables workplace

1.	The PHILOSOPHY of it all	**generally given**
2.	The STRATEGY we should follow	**less attention**

3.	The TACTICS to adopt	**generally given**
4.	The RESOURCES we need	**most attention**

5.	The TIMING to go for	**generally given**
6.	The SEQUENCE to follow	**less attention**

Figure 8.3 *A discussion hierarchy*

counsellors to decide at which level to 'pitch' the messages. For example, in a discussion about the need, say, for a policy on managerial malpractices, would it be better to focus initially on the managerial philosophy of doing this, or on the first steps of an action plan to implement such a policy. So long as each of the levels is covered, it need not matter where you start. Having a framework like this can enable you – and the organization – to look in an ordered way at the sensitive issues raised by workplace counsellors. It can ensure that such issues are considered and worked with rather than brushed aside or ignored.

The emotional implications of the material presented by workplace counsellors may be difficult for the organization sponsor (and others) to accept as valid. They may prefer to believe you are making it up, or perhaps that all of your clients are in some manner hysterical, psychotic, or have deep-seated grievances against the company and thus are not to be believed. For some organizations, raising material critical of the company may be seen to represent the outpourings of an ungrateful workforce, whereas for others it could raise anxieties and despair about the need for wholesale structural change. Workplace counsellors need to be prepared to handle whatever reactions occur.

Coping with Reactions to the Material Communicated

To have value as contributors to change in organizations, workplace counsellors not only need insights into what needs to alter, but also the capacity to help others explore issues they might otherwise prefer to dismiss. Strong defensive reactions can arise when workplace counsellors share their insights about the organization to management. The range of reactions exhibited will be similar to the reactions each of us shows in response to emotionally charged information received in everyday life. What makes it so different within a business management context are the wider implications of the messages for an organization. For example, the counsellor's feedback messages:

- Hold implications for the organization as an entity in itself.
- Reflect (because they have been so derived) the client base of the workplace counsellor.
- May reflect in some way the competence and standing of the organizational sponsor.
- Put the counsellor in a position of vulnerability and risk (after all, the counsellor wants to continue his/her work).
- Expose 'hidden' dimensions of that organization in practice (as opposed to how people may say or pretend it functions).

To manage and cope with the myriad of personal and organizational interests which the above combination touches, generates considerable pressure on the counsellor during briefing meetings to soften or alter the messages to be shared. Workplace counsellors can expect extreme reactions during these meetings – for example, perhaps quiet acquiescence and passive acceptance (which may be a strategy to neutralize the potency of the points raised), or outrage and aggressive challenge, and all points in between. To maintain a sufficient grasp of what is going on, and where they are during the course of events, workplace counsellors need to be able to:

- Introduce the messages to be shared in ways that the recipients will understand and can relate to.
- Anticipate recipient reactions and be prepared to facilitate any dysfunctional ones so that the content can be heard and worked with.
- Keep in mind models about the nature of organizations and pay particular attention to the political and power dimensions involved (see Chapter 6).
- Follow through these messages with action (for example, facilitate teams, review policies, etc.) if requested.

Of advantage to workplace counsellors is their experience of working with their own anxieties and those of their clients. They will have an ability both to experience and remain aware to some extent at least, of what seems to be going on in and around them. This is critical material to hold on to because workplace counsellors may be able to use some of the reactions generated to authenticate some of the points raised for consideration.

From their research on reactions to change initiatives in organizations, Fink et al. (1971) summarized patterns of individual adjustment and personal change into four main reaction stages as shown in Table 8.1. Similar reactions can be applied to organizations and this framework can alert workplace counsellors to some of the reactions that their material could elicit and suggest some of the thoughts others may be feeling as they come to terms with the implications of the insights of workplace counsellors about their organization.

There is an underlying cycle that recurrs. First, there is an experience (within the organization) that, for some employees, causes angst and concern to the extent that, secondly, they see their workplace counsellor and work on whatever emerges as important for them at that time. In private counselling practices this cycle (or spiral) of engagement then repeats itself. With workplace counselling, however, there are additional stages on this cycle. Thirdly,

Table 8.1   *The four main reaction stages to organizational change*

Reaction stage	Personal experience	Thoughts
Shock	Threat	Denial, unwilling to reason
Defensive retreat	Defend	Plan for subversion
Acknowledgement	Uncomfortable and uneasy . . . but . . .	OK, but tell me what to do
Adaptation and change	Growing sense of security	More positive planning now

workplace counsellors distil from their work with clients organization-specific themes, which, fourthly, are fed back to the organization in some manner (for example, by 'insight summaries'). In turn, this produces a reaction and creates further potential for organizational review and possible change. In workplace counselling it is this more protracted cycle (or spiral) which then repeats itself.

Through meeting these two requirements – (i) having insights to offer, and (ii) enabling key managers to address and come to terms with the issues to be tackled – workplace counsellors can help relevant and constructive change to occur. In this way workplace counsellors can help prompt the introduction of new policies for employee protection and well-being, highlight dysfunctional work practices, and draw attention to dropping morale and increasing internal distress. Through these contributions – over and above their client work – counsellors can help the organization to anticipate the possible reactions and barriers to implementation of the desired changes too.

On the Politics and Ethics of it All

The issue at the heart of all this, though, may be less a question of whether or not counselling in the workplace is a force for organizational change, but whether it is appropriate that it is so. Perhaps the key issue is, is it *ethical* for a workplace counsellor to become involved in processes of organizational review? Even if clients are persistently presenting work-specific matters of great concern to them, where does the workplace counsellor draw the line? How does the counsellor mediate between and manage the boundaries shown in Figure 8.1?

If, however, through their work, workplace counsellors are inescapably drawn into considering the wider dynamics, organization and ways of functioning of the company, then workplace counsellors need to become as aware and knowledgeable about that organization as they can be. To appreciate and understand the matters brought by clients, workplace counsellors need to be able to relate specific client material into that organization's work context.

Organizations are not the static rational, and finely tuned machines that the literature – or top management – would have us believe. On the contrary, they are intensely dynamic and political entities, full of vested interests and entrenched personal positions. Over time each organization has evolved its present culture and constructed a preferred view of itself. Organizations project and hold on to images and descriptions of themselves that can be out of date and wildly inaccurate but which can remain unchallenged from within either because the discrepancy is not perceived, or because to do so would not be welcomed.

Change in organizations *is* a 'political' matter and through raising sensitive themes for discussion, workplace counsellors will invariably touch upon matters which are political or sensitive or taboo. The counsellors may touch on or uncover denied or purposefully camouflaged aspects of the organization that it finds difficult or harmful to deal with. For example, an organization that professes to follow an equal opportunities policy but where minority groups do not progress beyond the middle management levels can represent a harmful situation because it threatens the *status quo* and the political align- ments of the key players, and the sanctity (fragility even) of the corporate illusions.

In addition, workplace counsellors are vulnerable to manipulation by others and – as in all therapy situations – the counsellors need to be alert and alive to these aspects of their work. Knowing more about the organization at large is a way of both understanding the context and reducing the likelihood of becoming enmeshed in the internal dynamics and politics. But even then, Cummins and Hoggett warn of the dangers of 'counselling being used to sustain and camouflage austere and inhumane managerial regimes' (1995: 310).

The role and the work of workplace counsellors are not totally neutral. Their role is exercised within a complex and politicized work system – an organization. Workplace counselling will have its share of supporters and detractors, and it will not be immune to being used and exploited within the organization. So, again the question arises: 'Is it ethical for workplace coun- sellors to become involved in organization change?' For example, Gerstein and Shullman (1992) highlight ethical issues such as confidentiality, use of information, and boundaries of analysis, and they make the point that within an organization 'there can be pressure to share information in organisational settings [and] . . . inappropriate information sharing, however, although well intended, may harm individuals, work groups, or the organisation as a whole' (1992: 615).

The ethical dilemma for the counsellor is to ensure that no information is inadvertently devolved – even when it is being used in an aggregated form – so that it is incapable of being tracked back to a client. The *action* dilemma is to introduce the messages to management in ways where they will be considered and listened to appropriately, and the *personal* dilemma is that workplace counsellors maintain their own relative independence and boundaries as counselling professionals.

As in working with an individual client, an organization can become preoccupied, fixated even, through focusing on a particular aspect of organ- izational life and in so doing fail to appreciate the wider implications which would enable it to work through the dilemmas and difficulties being encountered. Workplace counsellors offer a way out of fixated thinking and behaviour within the organization. In addition, the way in which the workplace counselling service is itself set up and managed can contribute to the processes of organizational change. For example, how clients are treated and respected, how boundaries are managed, and how the service is organized and run can provide a model of a well-functioning organization.

Conclusion

In conclusion, this chapter is about the place and positioning of counselling as a force for review and change within an organization and thus it is concerned with the politics, the dynamics and the impact which material brought into debate by workplace counsellors have within organizations. Safeguarding client confidentiality, resisting pressures on the counsellor to reveal sources, withstanding invitations to become an 'agent of change' and of being captured and engulfed by the organization or used by it, are matters for workplace counsellors to be fully aware of and manage.

Clarity of the role, the limits, and the realistic expectations for counselling within the workplace amplify the importance of formally contracting for the services to be provided. Without such clarity counsellors in the workplace can find that they become susceptible to the political dimensions and pressures within the organization, and will become confused about their role and responsibilities to their clients, the organization, and to themselves.

Workplace counsellors have a unique contribution to make and a part of this can be considered as contributing to organizational change. The extent to which they can contribute to the constructive and sensitive review of the complexity of modern organizational life – and not add to the inherent confusion and ambiguity present – rests largely in how the workplace counselling service is defined and established.

Hind et al., in a paper about the importance of resilience in organizations, suggest that 'the psychological contract will need to be renegotiated in times of change' (1995: 3). They see this as an important component in coping with change – for individuals and within organizations. Perhaps through the implementation of workplace counselling services, organizations are seeking to care for their employees and safeguard themselves for the future. As for workplace counsellors, the dilemmas, challenges and tensions remain!

References

Carroll, M. (1996) Personal communication.
Cummins, A.-M. and Hoggett, P. (1995) 'Counselling in the enterprise culture', *British Journal of Guidance & Counselling*, 23 (3): 301–12.
Egan, G. and Cowan, M. (1979) *People in Systems*. Monterey, CA: Brooks/Cole.
Fink, S., Beak, J. and Taddeo, K. (1971) 'Organizational crisis and change', *Journal of Applied Behavioral Science*, 13 (1): 15–41.

Gerstein, L. and Shullman, S. (1992) 'Counselling psychology and the workplace: the emergence of organizational counselling psychology', R. Brown and R.W. Lent (eds), *Handbook of Counselling Psychology*. New York: Wiley.

Hind, P., Frost, M. and Rowley, S. (1995) 'The resilience audit and the psychological contract', City University Business School, London.

Schein, E. (1980) *Organizational Psychology*. Englewood Cliffs, NJ: Prentice-Hall.

Summerfield, J. and Van Oudtshoorn, L. (1995) *Counselling in the Workplace*. London: Institute of Personnel and Development.

PART 3

INTRODUCING COUNSELLING INTO ORGANIZATIONS

Part 3 takes up a number of themes that cluster around the general idea of introducing counselling into an organization. Michael Carroll explores the theme of educating organizations to receive counselling: this needs to be seen as more than a one-way process and counselling providers must be aware of how they can be educated to understand the needs of the organization. John Towler's chapter is specifically focused on how counselling provision needs to be managed and administered when set up within an organization. He looks at issues of contracting and negotiating, as well as understanding, counselling from the perspective of the organization. Catherine Shea and Tim Bond focus on the ethical issues emerging from this kind of counselling and highlight some of the unconscious dilemmas that may need to be considered. Carolyn Highley-Marchington and Cary Cooper conclude Part 3 by looking at how counselling can be evaluated within an organization. They are eminently placed to do so, having concluded a major evaluation project on workplace counselling.

9

Educating the Organization to Receive Counselling*

Michael Carroll

Setting up and maintaining a counselling service in an organizational setting, whether it is an in-house or external service, needs careful planning. It is, in a sense, the merging of two worlds, that of the organization and that of counselling. Like all mergers that succeed, there is a need for clear negotiation, for understanding the world of the other and for a credible anticipation of potential pitfalls. When two cultures merge, one either destroys the other or a third culture emerges from the integration of the two. This is why education is a two-way process: the counselling service learns about the organization of which it is a part, and the organization learns about counselling culture and management.

For the sake of this chapter, 'education' will be defined as 'the management of learning', that is all those elements that go into helping the learning process, whether that is for an individual or an organization. Education requires good teachers who understand how individuals and organizations learn and pitch their teaching to meet learning requirements. If 'all learning begins from the learner's frame of reference', then good teachers not only know what they are teaching but also the frames of reference of those whom they are teaching. In practice, this means accepting and starting to work with where the organization is, rather than where one might like it to be. It involves a shift into an empathy with the organization analogous to that which counsellors make in developing empathy with individual clients. To do this entails a great deal of observing, listening, communicating and building relationships with many key people in management, some of whom will be involved in, or tangential to, the organization of the new counselling system. Others will have authority or power in the organization. The learning relationship with key people takes considerable time and patience to establish, but will be a *sine qua non* of a successful counselling service.

Essentially, an organization that does not understand what counselling means will fail to use it effectively. This is what happened in a large multinational financial establishment keen to have counselling for its employees. Perhaps because the organization (and in this instance the Human Resources

* Sections of this chapter are taken from M. Carroll (1996) *Workplace Counselling: A Systematic Approach to Employee Care*. London: Sage.

department which had been given the task) knew little about counselling, or perhaps because it was not high on the list of 'things to be done', it decided to hire an in-house counsellor, give him/her a counselling room/office and let him/her get on with the job. A counsellor was duly appointed (there was no counsellor on the interviewing panel) and within a few weeks she had disappeared into the organization. She was psychoanalytically trained and worked long-term, she saw only a few clients, and because of her concerns around confidentiality, she never involved herself in the organization. She refused any invitations to be involved in training, to sit on any committees, or be part of any policy-making groups, insisting that it would endanger relationships with clients. Within a few months the word on the shop floor was that if you went to see her you were inevitably in for long-term (minimum of six months) counselling. This inhibited quite a number of people. The service was discontinued at the next annual review.

Without careful thought about the practicalities and guidelines in policy, procedures and marketing for counselling provision in organizational settings, problems will inevitably arise. An essential ingredient of introducing and maintaining effective counselling services in an organization is the educational processes that go into helping organizations understand what counselling is, how it works, how it is integrated into organizational culture, what to expect from it and how to evaluate its potential and value. This chapter will look at some of the steps of this educational process. It is based on several assumptions:

- That organizations, and key personnel in organizations, do not usually understand what counselling is about. There is often a vague agreement that counselling might help, and expectations can range from sorting out difficult personnel to 'counselling out' redundant employees. Education will help where there is a problem of ignorance, but not always where there is a problem of attitude. Ignorance can be cured by knowledge, not so attitudes towards counselling.
- That initial motivation for introducing counselling into an organizational setting may need reviewing. Knee-jerk reactions to crisis, matching company 'perks' to those of similar companies, avoiding litigation from overstressed employees and helping to facilitate the organization's redundancy programme are some of the initial reasons given for introducing counselling into organizations. Initial talks by the counselling providers can unearth a range of attitudes towards counselling and what it means in an organizational context. Deverall (personal communication) outlines this in a striking example:

 'In the case of an international firm of chartered accountants, only two partners turned up to the introductory talk given by the counsellor. One of the partners argued strongly that theirs was not an organization where people were weak and it was unlikely that they would either use such a service or needed such a service. His emphasis was on managing costs and he felt that anyone who availed him/herself of the opportunity to talk at length about his/her personal problems was not the sort of person the organization would want to have around in any case. The personnel director, who was highly influential within the organization, took these comments to reflect a need for counselling and a change of attitude rather than the opposite. The organization where these attitudes prevail is usually not suited to a counselling service but where certain enlightened individuals, in this case the managing partner and the personnel partner, want to change attitudes, then the situation is somewhat different. As it happened, the service was heavily used in the early months and one of the first clients was the partner who raised the objections.'

- That education is a two-way process. Not only will counsellors and counselling services need to learn from the organization about culture, bureaucracy, shadow-sides, organizational politics and dynamics, but the organization will need to be open to learning about counselling and how it can best serve the organization. As mentioned above, this takes time and patience.

- That setting up an educational process to help organizations understand and utilize counselling is a planned, step-by-step process that begins long before individual counselling is introduced and needs to continue throughout the life of the service.

Educating the organization to receive and utilize counselling services effectively takes place at all six stages of managing the counselling process within organizations (Carroll, 1996). These six stages are:

1. Preparing for counselling.
2. Assessing organizations and counselling providers.
3. Contracting for counselling.
4. Introducing counselling into organizations.
5. Evaluating workplace counselling.
6. Terminating the relationship between organization and provider.

This chapter will review each stage, concentrating on how educating the organization can be the focus of that particular stage.

Stage 1: Preparation for Counselling in an Organization

The preparatory stage of counselling in organizations often begins with an idea. Someone within the organization, a department and/or committee, a crisis or a series of crises, or an amalgamation of these, propel the organization, and key people within it, to begin thinking about the strengths of introducing a counselling service for its employees, its consumers, etc. It is at this stage that education begins. An effective counselling consultant or provider will help the organization to learn about counselling and how it can work in a number of ways. I would suggest that an organization that has never had a counselling service before begins by thinking through carefully what it wants. This can be done in several ways:

- By setting up a small, representative team from within the organization to steer the discussions and negotiations for providing a suitable counselling service for this group. It is crucial that this group be representative and if staff councils or unions are part of the workforce that they, too, have delegates on the team.

- By engaging an independent consultant (who understands counselling) to work with the team to help them assess what they want. This consultant should not be employed by a counselling provider or be someone who would be involved in the counselling work itself with this organization. He/she could be a monitor of the whole process and, indeed, could well evaluate the service at a later date. But the value of the consultant to the organization, at this stage, is to facilitate the search and provide education when necessary.

- By finding out what the organization needs from counselling: internal or external provision, or a combination of both?; what minimum requirements it has from a counselling provider?; what qualifications it needs from counsellors?; what facilities it needs for the service?; what budget it has to manage the service?; and how it sees the counselling service contributing to organizational support and change? It is essential that the counselling provision is seen to be congruent with the prevailing management practices.

- By reviewing the cost of counselling and investigating the costs of different counselling provision.

- By checking how committed the key people in the organization are to counselling. Hoskinson has put this well; 'One of the most important components . . . is the organizational investment or *commitment* to provide such services systematically, uniformly and to professional standards – and to perhaps position the service as in the interests of *both* the well-being of the employee *and* the performance of the business' (1994: 3; emphasis in original). Actively engaging that support from key people in management, as well as within unions and particular departments, is an effective way of ensuring that the counselling service has a chance of success.

- By drawing up a list of potential providers to be interviewed. Potential providers can be discovered by asking other companies that have organized counselling and use providers and by getting lists of counselling providers from EAPA (Employee Assistance Providers Association). Besides reviewing those who offer counselling services, the organization can learn from examples of counselling services in similar organizational settings. Precedents are always a good way of learning and can forestall making mistakes already made by others as well as learning from the experiences of others.

At this early stage, before the search has begun for a counselling provider, the organization will have defined what it means by counselling, whether or not counselling will be part of a wider provision, including such elements as advice, welfare, information, etc., or stand on its own, and will have reviewed the motivation of the organization in seeking to implement counselling as part of its resources. When they begin the assessment part of the search, they will already have clear concepts of what they want and where they are headed.

Before beginning the process of assessing and negotiating with an organization, the counselling provider (this could be an EAP provider, a group of counsellors, or an individual counsellor) needs to have a structure in place that enlightens an organization about what it might do and provides a basis for negotiation. This structure includes the following:

- Explanations of how they might work (theoretically).
- A clear programme of services offered.
- Supervision arrangements.
- Method of keeping statistics and giving feedback.
- How the relationship between individual clients, counsellors and the organization is agreed and maintained.
- Clarity around contracts.
- Clarity about insurance.
- Issues of referral, emergencies, etc.
- Other roles.

Before beginning the actual process of assessing and contacting, preparations involving the above will help to prevent any misunderstandings and will have the potential to offer guidelines for both parties.

Counselling providers need to have policy statements outlining their purpose, the provisions they offer, restrictions and limitations, and finances involved, where applicable. Wright (1985) has outlined the policy and procedures necessary for an EAP, which is very applicable to counselling provision in general. Such policy statements ideally contain:

- The purpose of counselling.
- A statement on counselling philosophy in the workplace, that is, how counselling is seen as beneficial in the workplace, why it is needed, and what benefits it will provide for both individuals and the company.
- What is needed to provide counselling within an organization: support by highest authority, budget, premises, a steering committee, a contact person within the organization, supervision for counsellors, publicity, etc.
- How counselling within an organization provides other resources: training, consultancy, welfare, etc.
- Who is covered by counselling provision (employees, family, dependants, particular customer groups, etc.).
- How referrals take place: self-referral, referral by others, recommended or mandatory.
- A confidentiality statement, which clarifies when confidentiality could be broken with or without the consent of the client.
- What to do in emergencies.
- How counselling services can be evaluated.
- The criteria for the background and training of counsellors, and their qualifications.

- The roles and responsibilities of different groups and personnel: steering committee, the counsellors, managers, departments, employees, etc.
- The codes of ethics to which the counselling service and counsellors subscribe. In this respect it would be helpful to have a code of ethics for the counselling office, a much missed area that can be open to professional abuse (see Clarkson, 1994 for help on setting up a code of ethics for the counselling office).

Policy statements need to be clear enough to be understood and flexible enough to adapt to different organizations. By providing sample policy statements, counselling providers show that they have thought through organizational issues and are prepared for negotiation.

Good preparation on the part of the organization and of the provider goes a long way in helping clear negotiation. It also shows how seriously both parties take the exercise. Preparation forces organizations and providers to spend time thinking about what they want and what they supply, and forces them to articulate these in statements and policies. At this stage the educational process is well under way, with the organization learning about counselling, counselling providers and examples of counselling in organizational settings. At the same time, the potential counselling provider is learning about the organization and how a counselling service might best be integrated into its particular culture.

Stage 2: Assessing an Organization for Counselling

This is a crucial stage in setting up counselling in an organizational setting. It involves the organization in assessing those who would provide its counselling and it entails the provider evaluating the organization. Counselling providers, and organizations themselves, need skills and competencies in a number of areas:

- Recognizing from the outset that the uniqueness of each organization demands that the counselling provision be 'tailor-made' to suit size, culture, the nature of the work of the organization, its location, and its particular workforce. There is no single model that covers all these. Examples can be seen from the organizations that have an existing counselling service.
- Defining and answering key questions that will affect the counselling provision. Summerfield and Van Oudtshoorn (1995) have suggested 11 questions to help organizations decide about the right kind of counselling for them. Table 9.1 lists their questions.

These and a number of other areas need consideration to understand how best to enter and set up counselling in a particular organization. Organizations may need help in assessing some of the following questions.

Table 9.1   *Questions to help decide on organizational counselling*
(Summerfield and Van Oudtshoorn, 1995: 16)

---

1. Who or what has driven the initiative?
2. What do senior management want from the provision?
3. What does the human resource function want from the provision?
4. What do individual employees, including management, want from the provision *for themselves*?
5. For each of the above three interest groups, what are the priorities?
6. What structures/support systems are already in place?
7. What are the logistical and economic constraints?
8. What level of quality assurance is required, and how will quality be monitored?
9. How will the programme be marketed?
10. How will the programme be evaluated?
11. How will the programme fit in with the organization's culture?

What is the Organizational Culture of the Group?

How is that culture expressed? How might this particular company respond to counselling? Having some idea of what kind of culture is involved should help ascertain what kind of counselling provision may be best suited to this group of people (see Chapter 4). There are a number of ways of assessing the culture of an organization. Spending time within it, talking to different groups and individuals, reviewing policies and statements, being acquainted with the organizational decision-making process and reviewing the power structure are all ways of getting a 'feel' for the ideology/ecology of an organization. More formal psychometric assessment is also available, for example the *Organizational Culture Inventory* (Verax (Human Synergistics), 1991) or *Diagnosing Organizational Culture* (Harrison and Stokes, 1993). It may be, for several reasons, that the culture of a particular organization is, at this time, alien to the introduction of counselling, and that attempts to do so may result in negative responses from employees, for example where counselling is seen as a management tool for managers who want to avoid their responsibilities towards managing crippling stress.

What Are the Counselling Needs of Employees?

Some sort of needs analysis should open up the kinds of problems employees face: stress within the work environment, personal issues brought into the workplace, etc. It may also help to evaluate whether or not counselling is the best method of meeting these needs. It could be that 'organizational change' consultants may deal more effectively with what is happening, or involving an outplacement counselling firm may be more effective.

Cooper and Cartwright (1994) have suggested a 'Stress Audit' as a helpful way of assessing some of the organizational needs. One method of doing this is to use the *Occupational Stress Indicator: Management Guide* (Cooper et al., 1988), which has been used as a diagnostic tool in occupational stress. Data from this instrument can be used to assess employee needs and to match those needs to helpful interventions whether those be counselling, training or something else.

Why is the Organization Looking for Counselling Just Now? How Will the Provision of Counselling Affect what is Happening?

Answers to these two questions will often reveal whether or not counselling is required for a particular area (for example, a building society that is mostly interested in helping employees deal with armed raids), and what kind of counselling might best help (for example, post-traumatic stress disorder counselling).

How Does the Organization Understand Counselling?

An awareness of how counselling is described will help dispel myths (for example, that counselling will create a happier workforce), and will also help the organization to face up to its real and unreal expectations of what can and cannot be achieved through counselling provision.

How Committed to Counselling Provision are the Top People?

Wrich is clear that support from the top is essential: '. . . many attempts to establish an EAP never really get off the ground specifically for lack of active management support from the very top of the organization on down' (1985: 171). He goes on to clarify that support is not just about not opposing the venture and he uses terms like 'active advocacy', 'casting a positive vote', 'providing a substantial contribution' to describe what support means. It is also a good idea to identify the individual or group who initiated the idea of counselling: their active support could be invaluable in the future. Indeed, it might unearth reasons for suggesting counselling not in keeping with what counselling is about. It is worthwhile trying to understand how employees might view the introduction of counselling by top management. In some instances it might be seen as a method of social control, or as a way of preparing people for major change with job losses.

What Facilities Will be Provided for Counselling?

Rooms to see clients, secretarial support, confidentiality provisions, budgets, etc. are a few areas that need to be considered carefully by the organization. Is the organization aware of what is needed financially to run a counselling

Table 9.2   *Assessing organizations (Deverall, this volume)*

1. The age and history of the organization.
2. What does the organization do?
3. How well is the organization performing financially relative to the market, to past performance and to public opinion (especially if it is not a profit-centred organization)?
4. What is the size and geographical spread of the organization?
5. Personnel statistics, for example, personnel turnover, remuneration, etc.
6. Statements, policies, plans.
7. What is the management style of the organization?
8. Has the organization been the subject of a take-over?
9. Who is the organizational contact with counselling provider?

service effectively? Wrich (1985) has pointed to the need of adequate funding for the venture and has offered advice on what services may be more cost-effective for different sizes of organizations. It is here that the counselling consultant needs to be aware of, and empathic with, the economic pressures on the organization.

Who is the Organizational Contact With the Counselling Service?

Who is line-manager if the service is internal, and who will be the contact person with the external provider? Managing the service is a key factor in how well it works. Hoskinson (1994) suggests that ideally this management function is best supplied by an 'advisory committee'.

Critical to the success of counselling in organizations is the contact person within the organization who will liaise with the counselling service. It is vital that this person is aware of the implications and administrations of the counselling service, how feedback is given, the nature of confidentiality and an awareness of the kinds of problems that can arise in the relationship between counsellors and organizational personnel.

How Will Counselling be Integrated into the Organization?

It is too easy for counselling services to become appendages to organizations rather than integrated into their lives. Organizations can be helped to see how counselling can do more than simply deal with individuals in crisis, and can be a process for organizational change (see Chapter 2).

Deverall (this volume) has summarized an extensive list of areas that should be covered when an organization is interested in introducing counselling. Table 9.2 outlines these.

At this stage of assessment, counselling providers can take one of several stances. First, the company is ready for a counselling service and has the infrastructure (attitudes, motivations, personnel, budget, facilities) to begin negotiations. A second stance is that the company is not ready for counselling provision but needs more help from a consultant to build up awareness of what counselling means and how it might be integrated into the organization. It is quite important throughout this process that counselling providers retain their freedom to refuse to provide counselling if they consider the situation is wrong and that counselling has little chance of succeeding.

Assessing Counselling Provision

As counselling providers (or counsellors) will want to assess the organization and its readiness for a counselling service, so organizations will want to assess the group or individual(s) who will provide their counselling. What should they look for? Good providers will have information available for organizations and will meet to clarify issues and/or give further information and answer questions. Deverall (this volume) suggests the following areas for assessment:

- How many counsellors are available and what is their availability?
- What are their qualifications?
- Do counsellors have experience of working in organizations?
- Are qualifications uniform or diverse?
- What are the value systems of counsellors and are they uniform or diverse?
- Where are counsellors located?
- Where will counselling take place?
- What sort of service is being offered? Is it 24-hour, remedial, developmental, long-term/short-term?
- What will be the cost to the organization?

In brief, the assessment side of counselling in organizations contains key educational aspects. Hopefully, it will end with both the counselling provider and the organization being more aware of each others' dynamics and ways of working. It will also explore possible clashes and pitfalls within culture, values, ethical stances and practical considerations. This mutual education process will lead to appropriate services being contracted for the counselling needs of a particular setting.

Stage 3: Contracting for Counselling in an Organization

The assessment stage allows both participants to find out information about each other and make initial judgements about suitability. The next stage is to draw up a more formal contract or agreement that covers roles and responsibilities as well as the practicalities of working together. Most organizations have legal departments that are skilled in formulating contracts but here, too, it may be that they will want some guidance from the counsellors themselves, for instance, examples of other counselling contracts (Carroll, 1996).

Contracts can include as much or as little as participants want. Some cover essentials but will generally include agreements on:

Table 9.3   *Setting up a counselling service (Bull, 1995)*

- Identify the needs of the staff and the organization.
- Compare the service costs to those of alternative strategies.
- Agree services to be provided.
- Obtain the backing of key people and groups within the organization.
- Establish guidelines for access to the service, that is type of referral.
- Establish lines of accountability.
- Establish boundaries for confidentiality.
- Devise methods of data collection and record-keeping.
- Ensure a confidential location for counselling.
- Establish an ongoing strategy for publicizing the service.
- Identify a local referral network.
- Agree the number of sessions.
- Establish administrative support.
- Agree hours of service availability.
- Provide external clinical supervision.
- Ensure counsellors have professional indemnity insurance.
- Establish quality assurance systems.
- Evaluate the service.

- The philosophy of the counselling service: this will include the purpose of the programme, the elements involved, who can use it, how confidentiality is defined and understood, and what qualifications the counsellors will need.
- Objectives to be attained.
- Policies.
- Procedures.
- The contact person within the organization and/or steering committee.
- Publicity of the service: this will include an announcement of the programme and publicity material for each employee.
- The responsibilities of all parties (counsellors and organization).
- Provision for supervision and ongoing training.
- Evaluation of the counselling service, record-keeping, reports and feedback. How will individual appraisal take place?
- Counselling budget and financial responsibilities.
- Integration into company policies.
- A code of ethics for the counselling service.

Bull (1995) has summarized areas that require consideration when setting up a service. These can be used as a useful checklist by an organization (Table 9.3). What is essential at this stage is that both parties to the counselling agreement are satisfied that they have discussed and negotiated all aspects of implementing counselling into this organization.

Hay (1992) uses the work of Eric Berne to highlight three levels of contracts that are applicable to counselling in organizations:

1. Administrative contracts which outline the various arrangements with such issues as responsibilities, payments, timing, publicity, etc.

2. Professional contracts which revolve around policies, objectives, tasks and roles of various individuals and groups, and methods of implementation and evaluation.
3. Psychological contracts which are based on respect and trust and are more concerned with the various relationships involved. Unhealthy psychological contracts exist because of unresolved issues between participants, underlying dynamics and politics that influence behaviour. Psychological contracts allow different parties to deal with any blocks, individual or group, conscious or underlying, that might harm the programme.

Often it is the third of these that is most neglected and, in the long run, can have the most influence. It is recommended that all three be considered in some detail when negotiations around workplace counselling are taking place.

Stage 4: Introducing Counselling into an Organization

However, contracting to bring a counselling provision into the workplace is only the beginning: the really hard work starts in working out and implementing a strategy for introducing counselling to the organization. This involves a number of areas, all of which should involve educating the organization to what is happening.

Managing the Counselling Process

Many counsellors are well-trained in clinical work but have little expertise in counselling management, that is how to set up a counselling system that works within another system. These are skills beyond those of working with individuals and groups in a therapeutic way, and demand the ability to think systemically and practically about the full implications of counselling work in the context of the organization. This, too, needs to be part of the training for organizational counsellors and part of the educational process for organizations that are thinking of providing counselling services. Counselling management covers such areas as:

*   What physical arrangements are needed to provide confidential counselling to clients in this setting? Where will the counselling room be placed? How will it be furnished? Klarreich (1985) reckons that after confidentiality, location of the service is the most important ingredient in successful workplace counselling. Suitable counselling rooms and adequate office space will enhance not only the service but also the image of the service. I have heard stories of clients having to walk through offices or reception areas and being asked why they were 'here', as well as rooms with glass doors so that there is little privacy.
*   How will clients contact the counselling service? Can they be referred by others? Will the counsellor accept referrals and appointments from sources

other than the client, for example colleagues, managers, supervisors, disciplinary boards, personnel, etc. And what are the circumstances in which referrals will be made?

- How will the counselling service be advertised/publicized?
- In what circumstances would a counsellor not accept a referral, for example, when a manager wanted to give a formal warning and insists on counselling to help the employee change his/her behaviour.
- What happens when the client contacts the service? Who is the first contact? What information does the first contact require?
- How is the client assessed, and what referral points are appropriate?
- What does the client (and the appropriate manager) need to know about the counselling service?
- What kind of contract is made with the client?
- What notes are kept on the client? Where are they kept? Who else besides the counsellor has access to these notes? How long are notes kept after the counselling has terminated?
- How are statistics kept within the service and how are they publicized?
- How will the counsellor organize his/her time in respect of clients, publicity, training, contacting?
- Will clients be seen for a specific number of sessions, or will some be long-term clients?
- If the counselling provision is within a department (for example, occupational health or personnel), what are the relationships involved? What contact will the department have with clients? What will they need to know about the clients, if anything?
- What contact will the counsellor have with referral agencies? When will a client be referred for specialist help?
- What methods will be used to evaluate the counselling service?
- When will the counsellor contact other professionals (for example, a doctor, psychiatrist, social worker) with or without the client's permission?
- What insurance (indemnity) is it appropriate for the counsellor to have (personally and/or organizationally)? What should this cover be?
- What supervision arrangements are essential (desirable) for the counsellor to have?
- What will the counsellor do in the case of an emergency?

This may seem a 'hefty' agenda for the beginning counsellor who needs to have worked through most of these areas before beginning to see clients. However, these items by no means exhaust all the areas that need to be established in setting up a counselling service. Not to have thought them through and worked out some answers will result in boundary issues, clients feeling unsafe and unsure, and the counsellor making up answers as the occasion arises. Counselling management is a prerequisite to good counselling provision, as is seeing clients, as part of an overall safety structure provided by good counselling practice. Counselling training courses need to be aware of the need for training in counselling management as well as interpersonal skills.

Publicizing Counselling Services

There is little point in having a counselling service in an organization if it is not known about by all employees, and if the image it is intended to have is not one in the minds of consumers. Fisher's research highlights some of the images that counselling services should avoid: 'There is still a lot of suspicion about personal counselling, and it's still seen here quite a lot as a failure if you need counselling . . . the very concept of counselling sends most people into a corner, saying where's the crucifix and garlic' (1995: 34). Marketing the service is crucial on several points. Hopefully, it ensures that all those for whom it is intended know of its existence, how to contact it and what it will provide. Often, organizations are well geared towards providing in-house communication bulletins and magazines. These can be used as a means of publicity and contact with counsellors.

It will be essential to have an 'announcement' day or event formally to introduce the service and its personnel. In one company (Klarreich, 1985) a letter endorsed by the executive director of medical services was sent to all employees. Publicity is also a way of explaining what counselling does. Employees need to know what will happen when they present themselves in the counsellor's room, what are the limitations of the service, and what confidentiality means in this context, etc. Francek has indicated that marketing EAPs is a complex process and has isolated a number of factors to be considered: 'In truth, the diversity and complexity of the targeted organizations, coupled with the need for versatility and adaptability on the part of the marketing experts, suggests a dynamic interplay that makes simple solution next to impossible' (1985: 24). His recommendations are that the organization be assessed to understand what publicity will work within this particular group and culture. How does communication typically take place? Where do individuals and groups meet? What is the best method of accessing the information flow within the organization? Good assessment should uncover how best to publicize: individually, through groups, newsletters, meetings, etc. It will also reveal the key individuals within the organization who need to know what counselling is about and how to refer to it. Francek (1985) uses the term 'organizational networking' to describe setting up relationships with all levels of management and departments within the organization. Working with the 'shadow-side' of organizations is a further skill to help promote services (Egan, 1994).

Clear strategies for publicizing need to be outlined: What needs to be said? How is this best communicated with the group? How will it be said? What particular groups will be targeted for publicity? This will differ from organization to organization. The size of the organization may be one variable in how publicity will take place. Once the strategies are clear they can be implemented and monitored to see how well they are working. Evaluating publicity will help counsellors know where knowledge about the service is located. It may be, if only women are coming for counselling, that publicity will target male employees.

High visibility and good work are the best promotional methods. Interviewees in Fisher's research talked about ways of publicizing their counselling service: 'I think we have to go and make some positive personal relationships, with more senior managers . . . I see it as fundamental to my role that I am known to as many key stakeholders as I can be' (1995: 36). In the long run satisfied clients will take over as the main publicizers of counselling, and referral by clients themselves is ideal. However, other strategies can help. It is always helpful to update information as a way of periodic publicity. This can be done through individuals or departments, as well as in-house magazines. Making presentations on the counselling service to different groups is a further method of good publicity and often a way of establishing personal contacts. Including the counselling service in policy statements, for example on equal opportunities, sexual harassment, stress management or Health and Safety policies, is a way of indicating how the service has been integrated into the organization at all levels.

Obviously, how counselling is introduced to the organization as a whole is a critical task. The right publicity gets across the image intended. Publicizing counselling services rarely rates highly in counselling training courses. The skills of publicizing are not the same as those of working with clients. What is needed in publicity is:

- The ability to produce clear written formulations: brochures, polices, statements.
- Good oral skills in presenting the service.
- Very good interpersonal skills to facilitate meeting key people in the organization and establishing personal contacts.
- Assertiveness skills to ensure the service has a high profile.
- Organizational skills to assess how best to publicize the service in the organization.

Stage 5: Evaluating Counselling in an Organization

Evaluation is a key element in counselling provision. Not only is it a way of ensuring that clients receive an effective service that is monitored for its effectiveness, but it also helps to convince organizations that they are getting value for money. However, there is little formal evaluation of counselling in organizational settings (Highley and Cooper, this volume). Masi (1992) has estimated that less than one per cent of the Employee Assistance Programmes in the USA have been evaluated. Here, too, educating the organization on how to evaluate its counselling service can be of tremendous value. Reddy (1993) has offered a range of questions to help focus evaluation:

- Have we achieved what we set out to do?
- Is it proving successful?
- Are we getting value for money?
- Can we measure the impact of the EAP in terms of qualifying changes?
- Can we quantify a cost-benefit ratio?

Clearly, organizations are under economic pressures as never before. This is, in itself, a good motivational boast for evaluation.

The organization may need convincing that evaluation is an important element in the overall provision of counselling. Counselling providers can marshall the existing evidence and the methodologies to convince organizations of the value of counselling services and how they might be implemented. Ways in which organizations can be helped to set up evaluation procedures include the following:

- An effective record-keeping system that gives reliable information on numbers, age groups, etc.
- An individual client evaluation process. Individual clients, as a matter of course, evaluate the counselling they have had through a format that allows generalizations to be made.
- An organizational evaluation of counselling. This type of evaluation can include reviewing the other roles and responsibilities of counsellors in the organization, performance appraisal of counselling staff, how other people in the organization view the counselling service and the effect counselling has had on the organization as a whole. Outcome evaluation can monitor how counselling has affected employee performance, for example absenteeism.
- Supervisor evaluations which can be integrated into organizational evaluation.
- A process evaluation to ensure that the service is meeting its own objectives and a method of reviewing procedures within it.

Throughout, the organization can be helped to clarify the objectives of evaluation: *who* evaluates, *how* evaluation takes place and how the conclusions of evaluation can be *implemented* to provide an even better service.

Stage 6: Terminating Counselling with an Organization

Contracts are either renewed or ended. In some instances counselling comes to an end. This can happen for several reasons: the company has decided to change its counselling service; the counselling provider is not renewing the contract; mergers have taken place; a company is closing down. Whatever the reason, it seems important to help the organization prepare for this termination effectively.

Termination with individual clients should be considered carefully. Even though the formal contract has ended, provision must be made for individuals who are still in counselling. Generally, dates will be negotiated for ending, and referral may take place as a result. Ethically, it is clear that individual clients must be ended in a satisfactory and measured manner.

Termination time is also a good opportunity for feedback. Companies can be asked for information on the counselling service, why they are not continuing the counselling provision, and how they found working with the counsellors. Likewise, counsellors can give feedback to the company on what they have learned from working with them. If the contract and contact between the two parties has been good, they will already have shared many of these issues and surprises will be unusual. This is a good educational opportunity to learn from the experience by both organization and the counselling service.

Employees, in general, need to be told about the ending of the service. Just as the service was introduced formally, so termination is best done formally. A letter from the Chief Executive or Managing Director will give the news with an explanation of why the decision to end has been made.

A small group can be set up to deal with practicalities of ending: what happens to notes and files; who owns what; and what counsellors have a right to take away from the company.

Conclusion

Counselling in organizational settings is more than just introducing counselling. To create an effective counselling system within an organization requires a process of education whereby the organization begins to learn about counselling, what it means, how to use and evaluate it, and how to relate to a counselling service not as an appendage to its work but as an integral part of it. Counselling consultants and providers would do well to heed the importance of this side of their work. Educating the organization in how it chooses the counselling services best suited to itself and its culture will have long-term results. Problems in understanding, with boundaries, with roles and responsibilities and with the relationship between the organization and the counselling service, can be anticipated and dealt with before they become entrenched. In this way the two worlds of counselling and organizations do not collide, but integrate.

References

Bull, A. (1995) *Counselling Skills and Counselling at Work: A Guild for Purchasers and Providers.* Rugby: British Association for Counselling.

Carroll, M. (1996) *Workplace Counselling: A Systematic Approach to Employee Care.* London: Sage.

Clarkson, P. (1994) 'Code of ethics for the office', *Counselling*, 5 (4): 282–3.

Cooper, C.L. and Cartwright, S. (1994) 'Healthy mind, healthy organization – a proactive approach to occupational stress', *Human Relations*, 47 (4): 455–71.

Cooper, C., Sloane, S.J. and Williams, S. (1988) *Occupational Stress Indicator: Management Guide.* Windsor: NFER-Nelson.

Egan, G. (1994) *Working the Shadow-Side: A Guide to Positive Behind-the-Scenes Management.* San Fracisco: Jossey-Bass.

Fisher, H. (1995) 'Plastering over the cracks?: employee counselling in the NHS'. MA dissertation, University of Keele.

Francek, J.L. (1985) 'The role of the occupational social worker in EAPs', in S.H. Klarreich, J.L. Francek and C.E. Moore (eds), *The Human Resources Management Handbook: Principles and Practice of Employee Assistance Program.* New York: Praeger.

Harrison, R. and Stokes, H. (1993) *Diagnosing Organizational Culture*. San Diego, CA: Pfeiffer. (Available from Roffey Park Management College, Forest Road, Horsham, West Sussex, RH12 4TD.)

Hay, J. (1992) *Transactional Analysis for Trainers*. Maidenhead: McGraw-Hill.

Hoskinson, L. (1994) 'EAPs: internal versus external service structures: the key differences and potential synergies'. Paper presented at the European EAP Conference, Augsburg, Germany, October 1994.

Klarreich, S.H. (1985) 'Stress: an intrapersonal approach', in S.H. Klarreich, J.L. Francek and C.E. Moore (eds), *The Human Resources Management Handbook: Principles and Practice of Employee Assistance Program*. New York: Praeger.

Masi, D.A. (ed.) (1992) *The AMA Handbook for Developing Employee Assistance and Counseling Programs*. New York: American Management Association (AMACOM).

Reddy, M. (1993) 'The counselling firmament: a short trip round the galaxy', *Counselling*, 4 (1): 47–50.

Summerfield, J. and Van Oudtshoorn, L. (1995) *Counselling in the Workplace*. London: Institute of Personnel and Development.

Verax (Human Synergistics) (1991) *Organizational Culture Inventory*. Hampshire: Verax.

Wrich, J.T. (1985) 'Management's role in EAPs', in S.H. Klarreich, J.L. Francek and C.E. Moore (eds), *The Human Resources Management Handbook: Principles and Practice of Employee Assistance Program*. New York: Praeger.

Wright, D.A. (1985) 'Policies and procedures: the essential elements in an EAP', in S.H. Klarreich, J.L. Francek and C.E. Moore (eds), *The Human Resources Management Handbook: Principles and Practice of Employee Assistance Program*. New York: Praeger.

10

Managing the Counselling Process in Organizations

John Towler

Managing the counselling process in organizations requires considerable diligence and expertise on the part of the counsellor, who needs to be a manager, a consultant, a counsellor who uses brief therapy interventions, a negotiator, a publicizer, a monitor of professional issues and an assessor for both the organization and the individual. The job description should always include 'the ability to laugh at self and others'! The role is demanding as counsellors need to:

- Juggle with their multi-faceted roles.
- Work to maintain the dynamic focus within clearly defined contracts.
- Work to maintain boundaries and accountabilities.
- Inform themselves and the organization of how all the parties interact and affect each other.
- Ensure regular and sufficient supervision for themselves.

Because the situation of all parties will always be unique, managing the process will constantly be challenging, often exciting, sometimes confusing and overwhelming. The organizational counsellor will remain forever the pioneer par excellence.

There is an interactivity and an interrelatedness between the practice of counselling and the organization in which it takes place (Crandall and Allen, 1982). Reflections will be offered from my experience in working as a supervisor to counsellors in various organizational settings, as a counsellor in a Human Needs Consultancy, as a teacher of workplace counsellors, and as a manager of a counselling service. While my intention will be to paint as wide a picture of the issues as possible, space will allow for more focused attention on particular aspects of the process. What will not be addressed is a discussion of how different elements of managing the counselling process relate to different counselling orientations.

Managing the counselling process means preparing for and facilitating those elements of the counselling provision to enable safety, clarity and information for all involved in the delivery of the service. Six main areas will be considered:

1. Negotiating and defining services.
2. Contracting with the organization and clients: some ethical considerations.

3. Identifying the client group.
4. Assessing the client, deciding on appropriate responses and issues in terminating counselling.
5. Exploring the nature of short-term counselling.
6. Exploring the influence of organizational culture and dynamics.

Each area will be addressed and the underlying themes and influences which arise will be traced. The focus throughout will be to draw attention to the connections both implicit and explicit between the management of the counselling process and the context in which it takes place.

1. Negotiating and Defining Services

Viewed from either end of a spectrum, by introducing a counselling service does the organization wish to promote health or is it looking for a sticking plaster? The question may seem cynical – maybe it is – but an honest answer will greatly influence the effectiveness or otherwise of the counselling service to be initiated. Even to have asked the question of the 'initiator' will be influential. The answer is a first step in helping organizations be clear about what it is they hope to achieve in setting up a counselling provision.

Rationale for Services

There are many reasons why an organization may want to introduce a counselling service, for example:

- Growing litigation proceedings resulting from severely stressed employees, for example, the Bloomsbury Health Authority Case 1994, may well force many companies into thinking seriously about the issue.
- Where counselling is seen as a way of reducing absenteeism, thus increasing both morale and maintaining realistic profit margins (Douglas, 1995).
- Where counselling is seen as a tool of management it could be construed as a legitimate way of implementing company policy, and thus manipulating employees into 'toeing the line'.

Such considerations will inevitably raise the question 'what is and what should counselling be in an organizational context?'. The following notions may suffice to give a broad indication of the activity of counselling in organizations:

- Helping employees find their own solutions and ways through currently experienced problems affecting their performance at work.
- Bringing greater freedom from stress and related issues.
- Helping employees manage more effectively both their personal problems and those generated from working within the organization.
- 'Nudging employees back on to the road of recovery' (Denton, 1993) from a crisis, for example bereavement, bullying, or issues which have necessitated an absence from the workplace.

A British Association for Counselling (BAC) definition of counselling is instructive of its potential: 'to provide an opportunity for the client to work towards living in a more satisfying and resourceful way' (BAC, 1993: paragraph 3.1). Organizations need to be clear that they create counselling services in an atmosphere where potential clients can capitalize on such 'an opportunity'. The BAC (1993) helpfully distinguishes this activity of counselling from the use of counselling skills in befriending/supportive relationships and other allied strategies. The dilemma frequently experienced by counsellors in organizations is determining who is the client – what is client and what is organizational dysfunction?

Organizational dysfunction can include inflexible managerial practices which cause unremitting stress for the individual and unrealistic expectations of an individual's performance, and a refusal by the organization to change aspects of its culture. As an example, an employee in a large public service was made redundant following 15 years' service in a high-risk role because he found it almost impossible to adapt to more 'normal duties' following accumulated trauma. Managers and clients will speak of 'bad chemistry' or 'personality clashes' which result in the individual being removed from the organization. Adams (1992) cites numerous examples of individuals being exited from work through those whom the organization have chosen not to tolerate!

Clearly, those setting up counselling provisions in organizations have a challenging task ahead as they seek to clarify the organization's expectations of what precisely counselling will provide. Orlans (1986) highlights the potential conflict between the expectation of the organization to want to control its employees and the function of counselling as that of increasing a sense of self-control and personal freedom for individuals. Counsellors are often faced with the referral from line managers who send employees to counselling for 'bad attitude problems', with the expectancy that they will change their behaviour overnight and become the compliant employees that the line expects! The role of counsellors in negotiating a service is:

- To determine the expectations of the organization.
- To educate managers and supervisors about the boundaries of what is possible in short-term work.
- To promote the service as independent of management control.
- To clarify the relationships between other carers in the organization, for example the company doctor, occupational health personnel, human resource managers, etc.

Implications for Counsellors

What then are the implications for counsellors faced with these dilemmas? The following are possible, though not exhaustive, responses:

1. Refuse to cooperate with the organizational dysfunction.
2. Engage the organization in a process of education about the implications of its behaviour.

3. Work with and hold the concerns of the organization and the client in a 'creative tension'.

Sugarman (1992), in exploring the ethics of referral, provides some useful distinctions which those initiating counselling services could usefully consider:

1. The mandatory referral – managerially controlled and thus could be seen to conflict with the ideal of the essential voluntary nature of counselling. She comments that it may be 'justifiable' in cases where termination of employment or suspension from the organization are the only alternatives.
2. The suggested referral – managerially suggested where the client's performance is seen to deteriorate through perceived personal problems external to the organization.
3. The voluntary or self-referral – client chosen based on sufficient trust in the safety, integrity and competence of the service.

Those appointing potential counsellors in organizations need to take careful account of the following factors:

- That the boundaries between counsellors and other deliverers, for example managers, occupational health professionals and human resource managers, are identified so as to avoid duplication, role conflict, role ambiguity, etc.
- That the employer is clear about what is and is not possible within the prescribed professional, time and financial limitations.
- That measures will be in place to monitor the throughput of clients so that counsellors are not overwhelmed by unrealistic case loads.
- That the boundaries of accountability are understood by counsellors in relation to their employers to avoid a breakdown of trust in the counselling services.
- That cognizance is taken of the various roles expected to be undertaken by the counsellor, for example educative and preventative, counciliator, welfare officer, etc.
- That adequate finance and time are negotiated for the professional support and supervision of the counsellors.
- That counsellors have sufficient understanding of the implications of working in organizations and skills to work assertively, maintain self-confidence and evaluate services (McGill, 1986, cited in Sugarman, 1992).
- That counsellors can deliver the style of counselling required, especially in short-term mode.

Managing the counselling process requires careful research and negotiation in the setting up and defining of services. Those to be employed as counsellors should consider their negotiating stance, their willingness to be flexible without compromising the ethics of their profession, and an ability to be proactive as well as reactive agents of change (Rogers, 1983).

Figure 10.1 *The three-cornered contract*

2. Contracting with the Organization and Clients: Some Ethical Considerations

Egan reflects the nature of making contracts when he writes: 'If helping is to be a collaborative venture, then both parties must understand what their responsibilities are' (1994: 62). English (1975), Hay (1992) and Micholt (cited in Hay, 1992), working within the School of Transactional Analysis in Organizations, provide a way of separating out the different parties in contracting within 'The Three-cornered Contract', that is, the individual client, the counsellor and the organization (represented by one or more third parties within the organization or having a functional relationship to it). Figure 10.1 shows the relationship between the parties.

Hay (1992) identifies three interrelated parts of the contract:

1. The administrative.
2. The professional.
3. The psychological.

In negotiating and in the practice of the counselling service these facets need to be considered explicitly.

1. The Administrative Contract

The counsellor will need to determine all the physical arrangements to provide a safe, confidential setting for the counselling to take place. Information on all advertising material must state clearly how the service can be accessed. Initial contacts with the service may vary from a specially staffed 'contact line', which then initiates the services of a counsellor, to a drop-in facility where a counsellor can be seen almost immediately.

Clarity is needed about opening times, the boundaries of the client group, a procedure for managing trauma or crisis, the number of sessions offered, including 'locally negotiated differences', for example suspended employees awaiting completion of disciplinary procedures, and the relationship of the counselling service to other personnel, for example human resource department. Sole in-house counsellors need to ensure that arrangements are in place for their annual leave or prolonged absence through sickness. One organization uses an EAP for such occasions.

Organizations often need educating about the professional support of its counsellor workforce. While they may not provide sufficient time and finance to support the BAC Code of Ethics requirements for counsellor supervision, that is one hour of supervision for six hours of counselling, counsellors need to make sure of a basic minimum, for example two company counsellors receive 1½ hours per fortnight and counsellors in a large public organization receive one hour individual and one hour group supervision on alternate weeks. Counsellors should insist on corporate indemnity cover for their counselling activity. Resolution of such issues is vital in the initial negotiating stages to avoid problems at the implementation stage.

2.   The Professional Contract

On the one hand, it is about the nature of the counselling process between counsellor and client, and on the other, the nature of accountability to the organization of information sharing and the possibility of organizational change and development. Some organizations have adopted a simple 'statement of understanding' which outlines the nature of confidentiality, areas of client disclosure required to be known by the organization, for example criminal activity, abuse, financial irregularity, etc., the number of sessions available, and missed appointments. This is presented in the first session for agreement and signature by the counsellor and client. Where counselling is contracted by an outside company this statement should reflect the original negotiated contract to mitigate against the worst features of breaking confidentiality.

In counselling terms, the professional contract includes the sharing of expectations of all parties, the negotiated goals of counselling, homework assignments, the number of sessions, the relationship with other related departments, for example the company doctor, occupational health, etc., and, as importantly, what counselling is not, and what will not happen, for example that some client issues which require longer-term counselling will not be specifically addressed.

3.   The Psychological Contract

Clients as counsellors arrive in the counselling room with imaginings about what each needs to contribute to the relationship. While some clients are referred with such prescriptions as 'get your problem sorted!', others may arrive as part of a disciplinary process. Whatever the route, clarity around the expectations of client, counsellor and organization can minimize unhelpful and protracted outcomes.

Case Study

The following client was a managerial referral.

Brian is 50, white, a lorry driver, and works for a hi-tech company. He is referred by his line manager because of his poor work attendance record, and regularly arriving at work smelling of alcohol. His line manager, while wishing to help him, has to ensure the health and safety of other employees and company clients. She refers him to the company counsellor.

The counsellor sees him for six sessions in which she works with Brian on arriving for work drink free. This goes well.

Subsequently, he is again absent with flu which causes his line manager to contact the counsellor to say that she is considering terminating Brian's employment.

In supervision, the counsellor expresses concern about her client's health if he is sacked. She feels that his line manager is going to act unjustly. A confusion emerges – the counsellor and the client had agreed to work on Brian arriving at work drink free, not giving up drinking altogether, a misconception of the line manager!

With Brian's permission the counsellor writes to the line manager setting out the facts of the agreed contract; to keep open the options for a possible case conference between counsellor, line manager and the personnel manager; and to express her concern at the potential effect of Brain's dismissal.

Ethical issues.   This example raises important ethical issues about the motivation of the client for counselling, the boundaries of confidentiality, the exercise of power of the organization and the counsellor with the client, the meaning of the referral for the client, the seemingly unrealistic expectations of the organization on the counsellor, and the differing roles the counsellor is expected to perform – negotiator, counsellor, advocate, educator, and supporter of the line manager. Maintaining these different boundaries is like a rather delicate juggling act. To maintain the balance of honouring the needs of the client and the organization is one the most demanding tasks of counsellors. Micholt (cited by Hay, 1992) introduces the notion of maintaining an equality of 'psychological distance' between client, counsellor and organization.

Using Micholt's model we can posit three possible distortions which are best expressed diagrammatically. Figure 10.2 illustrates the counsellor allied with the client. In Figure 10.2 the counsellor can unhelpfully collude with the organization, usually through a third party, for example the manager/referral agent. The counsellor's sense of accountability can be reduced, thus alienating both the client and the counsellor from the organization, its policies and

Figure 10.2   *Counsellor closely allied to client*

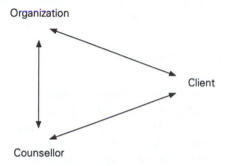

Figure 10.3   *Counsellor closely allied to organization*

procedures. The counsellor's empathy for Brian draws her closer to him, and triggers feelings of concern at the unjust nature of the organization's decision to sack him.

Figure 10.3 shows the counsellor allied with the organization. It demonstrates how the counsellor can defend the organization, thereby distancing herself from the client and reducing the level of trust in the therapeutic relationship. The telephone call from Brian's line manager draws the counsellor into a supportive contact with her, and an empathy which seduces her to the company's decision to sack her client.

Figure 10.4 shows the organization allied with the client. It illustrates a situation in which a counsellor can be alienated from a client and organization when client and organization (third party) are working consciously or unconsciously against a counsellor, for example when the organization uses a counsellor as part of a process of exiting an employee and needs a 'welfare' report to support the organizational stance.

The distortions are reflected in the confusion Brian's counsellor brought to supervision. The counsellor needs to work towards maintaining the equality of 'psychological distance' as illustrated in Figure 10.1. Time spent on careful

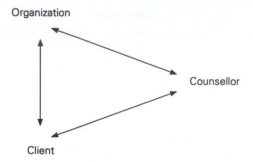

Figure 10.4   *Organization closely allied to client*

contracting can raise the level of trust between the counsellor, the individual and the company. It can serve to reduce the distortions illustrated in Figures 10.2 to 10.4, thus enabling the counsellor to manage a careful balancing of honouring client and company needs.

3.   Identifying the Client Group

In identifying the client, that is the individual and/or the organization, 'there is the risk that the employee becomes the patient or the one who needs treatment rather than the organization' (Hopkins, 1994: 13). This corrective statement by Hopkins goes to the heart of what may seem a self-evident question with which counsellors are faced. In the example of Brian, we can identify the individual, his line manger and the personnel manager (both representing the organization).

Third-party involvements are frequent in organizational counselling. For this reason, it is imperative that counsellors are clear about what agreements they are making with referral agents and other allied departments which might influence the counselling process and its outcomes for the client and the organization.

The following example, taken from a large national public service organization, serves to illustrate that counsellors may find themselves embarking out on serving one client and discover that they are being asked to manage several.

Case Study

Dianne is a service photographer whose main occupation includes taking photographs of victims of crime. She is referred by her departmental head because she recently broke down during a photographic session at a particularly gruesome scene of a crime.

The counsellor assessed that Dianne was exhibiting symptoms of post-traumatic stress – not sleeping, showing reluctance at returning to work for fear of facing distressing cases, sudden outbursts of uncontrollable tears, etc.

The counsellor agreed to work with her for six to eight sessions to help relieve the symptoms of her post-traumatic stress and to help her return to work.

Following agreement with the client, the counsellor spoke with her boss, recommending that she was given maximum support in her work, and the freedom not to have to attend particularly distressing situations. Also, that if she could not manage a photographic session, she could withdraw without recrimination and pressure from the department.

This arrangement worked well for two weeks. The counsellor was then contacted by the client's Head of Department who complained that he could not sustain this agreement any longer because he was understaffed. The counsellor was understanding, and emphasized that the client was not ready to assume full duties.

At the next counselling session the client arrived anxious and upset at the 'macho' taunts and pressure from her managers. Though somewhat reluctantly, the client was precipitated into seriously considering a career move.

The counsellor agreed to see the managers, whom she found aggressive, unsympathetic to counselling and inflexible in their attitude to Dianne's situation.

While it is clear that the client Dianne was temporarily incapacitated, the attitude of her managers was such that it was a major factor in precipitating a further crisis in the client's life. Here, we can identify three clients:

1. Dianne, suffering from post-traumatic stress.
2. Organizational line managers acting out their frustration at being unable to be flexible over staffing.
3. A seemingly defensive and resistant organization that requires maximum output from all its colleagues, stressed or not!

The counsellor is faced with the dilemma of being asked to work with all the constituent parties, that is the client Dianne and her line managers. While continuing to work with the client, the counsellor sets up a few sessions with the managers to help them through their current dilemmas. We might counsel the counsellor not to have become engaged with the managers but this didn't happen.

It is important that we pay attention to what was happening in the wider organization, and how this was affecting the counselling process. In supervision, it was possible to identify the interrelatedness of the predominant organizational culture, the way the managers were behaving, the effect of this on the client Dianne and how this manifested itself in the work of the counsellor and subsequently in the supervision group – an example of 'parallel process' (Crandall and Allen, 1982). The managers were acting out the symptoms of post-traumatic stress – irritability, restlessness, hypersensitivity to their superiors, anger, feeling out of control (that is not being able to manage their work differently), and resistance to working differently (minimizing the effects of stress on themselves). At an organizational level the counsellor's Head of Service was able to meet with Dianne's departmental bosses to inform them of the potential consequences of their actions on behalf of the client, and sensitively indicate levels of support for themselves.

Organizations as Clients

We note with growing interest the expanding list of psycho-pathological descriptions ascribed to organizations, for example anorexic, addictive. Such descriptions give point to the notion that organizations are a category of clients that need a response, as does the individual client. The organization may be another individual, for example a line manager, a team, a division or a department. The crucial issue for counsellors managing the counselling process is their role in helping to identify the source of organizational stress or dysfunction, how this is affecting their client and his/her dysfunction, and what appropriate responses can be made.

It is all too easy for organizations to assuage their lack of responsibility in managing distress or change by setting up an internal counselling programme or an external EAP. The image of the 'identified patient' from the world of systemic therapy is significant in this context. The projective identification of the organization (third party) on to the client is apparent as the organization is unable to face up to its own level of distress, and hence projects this on to the already vulnerable employee.

4. Assessing the Client, Deciding on Appropriate Responses and Issues in Terminating Counselling

In determining what is essential in assessing clients, a number of authors draw attention to the following different and important aspects:

- That 'poor assessment can result in a lot of time and effort wasted on what is not needed' (Carroll, 1995: 28).
- That the initial assessment session may last longer than the traditional first session (Nelson-Jones, 1991).
- That assessment contributes to the learning process, and hence, potentially, in increasing the client's options (Egan, 1994).
- That a useful question for exploration is 'what is keeping this person from managing his/her life just now?' (Lewis and Lewis, 1986).

Answers to the following questions provide significant clues to why the client is seeking help now:

- Why this counselling organization within this work setting? For example, the client might be trying to speak indirectly to the organization about something which a more explicit statement would label them as inadequate and poor performers or sick. Or alternatively, why this external counselling organization? For example, a student may decide that the college counselling service is not 'safe' enough, and therefore uses a more independent service.

- Why right now? An event or experience at work, home or elsewhere has triggered the client coming for help. For example, a row with a partner, tearfulness at the work desk, a broken relationship, a burglary, etc.
- What does the referral (self or organizational) mean to the client? For example, the client comes willingly or has been sent by a manager to 'get his problem sorted', and therefore may come with resistance.
- What is the client's level of motivation for wanting change and difference in his/her life? For example, it is important that the client has some notion of what a contract for change and difference might mean.
- What helping strategies will need to be employed in helping the client? For example, there are a variety of options – coaching, skill training, practical help, medical help, etc.
- Can the client's expectations be met within the boundaries of time and money set by the organization? For example, the goals of counselling need to be focused and realistic, with mutually contracted and understood outcomes for client and counsellor and, where appropriate, the organization.
- Can the client's problem find better resolution by trying to change the situation? For example, where the problem is clearly the result of a dysfunction of another, offering counselling is an unrealistic and unethical option.
- Is the problem able to be managed 'in-house' or will it require a referral outside the organization? The counsellor needs to decide that the problem is within his/her sphere of competence; if not, the client needs to be referred for alternative help.

In obtaining answers to these questions the counsellor's assessment will be informed and deepened.

Assessing the Suitability of the Client for Short-term Work

An ongoing dilemma for the counsellor at the time of assessment is, 'Is this client a suitable candidate for short-term counselling?' A critical question arises – 'how much of the client's dilemma is caused by the client's dysfunction (for example, personal pattern, insensitive interventions, unclear thinking) and how much of the client's dilemma is attributable to the dysfunction of others either at home (for example, bereavement, illness) or at work (for example, bullying, unrealistic expectations of the organization)? A growing body of practitioner experience is validating short-term approaches, such as (an assessment session plus six sessions with the option of up to six more. Some of the following notions need to be borne in mind at the time of assessment:

- That the client is not psychotic or borderline and needs psychiatric referral.
- That the client shows signs of a sufficient level of motivation for working and is unsuitable for counselling.
- That the counselling is specifically focused in the dynamic of change by action, choices, insight, etc.

- That the agreed outcomes, whether behavioural, cognitive or affective, are realistic, specific, manageable and measurable.
- That the counsellor will be working on here-and-now client issues using the past to inform the process.
- That the short-term nature is reckoned to be valid in itself, and not necessarily as a preparation for longer-term counselling.

Whatever the number of agreed sessions, the boundary of time continues to be a major influential factor affecting outcomes for the client.

Who Assesses the Client for Counselling?

Practice varies as to who assesses the client. Using a different assessor other than the counsellor may mean:

- 'Two starts' for the client, and hence a break in the therapeutic alliance.
- That resistance is set up in the client with the counsellor.
- That many counsellors wanting to rely on their own assessment, repeat the exercise, and thus valuable counselling time can be lost.

Many counselling companies, for example EAPs, use separate counsellors for these roles. Where an external referral is warranted, care needs to be taken that the client is enabled to make the transition without a sense of rejection.

Most organizations set a limit on the number of sessions available for clients. Others allow undefined time with a primary focus on completing counselling within short-term limits, for example one year. Psychometric tests such as a PF16 or SL90 can provide a useful addition to the counsellor assessment, and a more 'scientific' instrument, providing added confidence to organizational purchasers of counselling services for employees.

As counsellors within organizations often combine the counselling role with others, for example welfare, occupational health, etc., it is essential in assessing the client to determine the appropriate strategy or strategies with which the counsellor will work or need to refer, such as information giving, advisory work, advocacy, practical and emotional support (befriending), coaching or mentoring, in order to respond accurately and avoid confusion.

The Nature of Referrals

Some counsellors experience frustration in the length of time it can take to make a referral to an outside agency. Frequently, counsellors may have a 'holding brief' to help the client make appropriate transitions. Organizational counsellors do well to make effective internal links with fellow professionals, for example the company doctor, and to create a local referral resource bank, for example a Citizens Advice Bureau, an Alcohol Advisory Service, etc. The counsellors of one public organization, for instance, experienced constant difficulties with an internal psychiatric service. Following referrals, letters arrived from the psychiatrist couched in impossible 'psycho-babble' with implicit expectations that the counsellor would help clients with long-term psycho-pathological issues. Counsellors can become the unwitting victims of other professionals' pressure as they seek to expedite as many cases through the system as quickly as possible.

Many clients face the ignomy of not being able to afford the specialist care they require – a cost that organizations are increasingly unwilling to take up. This is especially invidious when the individual dysfunction is a direct result of an employee's normal duties and responsibilities at work.

Terminating the Counselling Process

Terminating counselling can bring its own dilemmas. For example, a client in the final session of her nine-session contract, disclosed that she was a survivor of child sexual abuse. The counsellor validated the client's courageous disclosure, acknowledged the potential journey remaining for the client, and negotiated three further sessions with the company on behalf of the client to assist her in making a closure and determining the next steps.

Being explicit about the end of counselling from session one allows the client consciously or unconsciously to pace him/herself towards the identified outcomes of the counselling. In addition to the normal processes of endings, for example managing loss and separation, maximizing learning, increased self-efficacy, etc., the organizational setting can pose other difficulties, such as:

- Where the organization terminates employment of the client while he/she is working towards a closure.
- Where recurring crises occur, precipitated by organizational dysfunction – for example a client who is pressurized to return to work before he/she is sufficiently functional to do so.
- Where the organization displays considerable anxiety to the counsellor about the client returning to work having only partially achieved resolution of the perceived problem(s).

Such instances may well involve the counsellor acting as the client's advocate with the organization, which may result in an extension of counselling or a change in organizational behaviour.

- Where a client punishes the organization consciously or unconsciously in insisting that he has an extension of counselling (it will cost the company!).

Here the counsellor has a responsibility to challenge the client's distorted beliefs.

- Where the organization perceives that the client has not achieved the expected outcomes.

Further discussion with the organization will be needed to clarify this.

The emerging critical factors demand clear contracting, thorough initial assessment and a flexible counsellor response.

5.   Exploring the Nature of Short-term Counselling

The nexus of the conflict faced by organizations and professionals in counselling is: 'Can short-term counselling really effect change for the individual, and at the same time be beneficial to the organization?'. The latter begs the meaning of 'beneficial' to the particular organization; the former the definition of 'short-term' or 'brief'.

What is 'Short-term' Counselling?

The literature of short-term therapy evidences anything from one to forty sessions (de Shazer, 1985; Hobson, cited by Barkham, 1989; Firth-Cozens, 1992; Malan and Osimo, 1992). Based on the notion that short-term counselling is valid in itself, de Shazer (1985: 5) highlights the distinction between brief therapy (as defined by time constraints) and brief therapy as a way of solving human problems. The purpose is to enable the client to get back to functional living as soon as possible, rather than working within a time constraint. As he points out, counsellors can then see more clients within the same period of time – hence, the growing demand by many organizations for this solution-focused, cost-effective approach.

Two elements in short-term counselling need constant attention – the establishment of goals and the maintenance of the focus for each session.

Characteristics of Short-term Counselling

Whatever the counsellor's orientation, short-term approaches have a variety of characteristics:

- They focus on achievable, measurable outcomes of behaviour or changes in thinking or feeling.
- Many are increasingly solution-focused.
- Change or development are often seen as precursors to enable clients to resume work, and maybe to move into longer-term therapy.
- They helps clients manage their work situations better and thus contribute to a reduction in absenteeism, and an increase in company morale and profits through increased effectiveness and efficiency.

Contracting – Goal and Focus

Assessment and contracting become critical to establishing realism in the counselling process. While listening to the presenting concern, the counsellor may inquire of past experiences which might serve to illuminate the current concern. As a consequence, goals need to be stated in terms which are clearly formulated, achievable, viewed by the client as important, and stated in terms as something new and good rather than old and undesirable (de Shazer, 1990). The case study example of our client Brian (p. 172) may help to illustrate a number of points in this area.

Case Study

Brian is not dismissed but the counsellor is contacted by the client's personnel manager and line manager wanting an update on the client's progress. Meanwhile the counsellor has referred the client to an outside alcohol consultant, a company service initially set up by the personnel department. On referring the client, the consultant said he would send 'the usual report' to the personnel department!

The counsellor arrives in supervision feeling overwhelmed, confused and used by the organization by being expected to act as the mouthpiece of authority within the organization, that is telling her client what to do, and thus she feels compromised in her relationship with her client. In supervision she questions:

1. Who is my client?
2. What are the boundaries of confidentiality with the client, the personnel manager, the client's line manager, the consultant?
3. What are the boundaries of the confidentiality of the organization with the outside consultant? (Hence the alarm about 'the usual report!' – sent to whom? stating what? agreed by the client?)
4. How is this affecting the dynamic focus of the counselling?
5. How should the perceived conflicting goals of the client and the organization be managed? That is, the personnel manager in the recent telephone call with the counsellor seems to have 'moved the goal-posts' by now insisting that the client must agree not to drink at weekends either, because he says 'the client has a drink problem'.

The organization provides six sessions plus one for review three months following session six. The client was referred by his line manager. The client goals were agreed – to assist the client in working towards managing his alcohol drinking during the week, ostensibly to help him manage a level which will enable him to operate at work following his drinking. Both counsellor and client understood that this goal was the same as was expected by the organization. The contract with his manager was to inform her of his attendance. There was no explicit contract between the counsellor and the personnel manager. The focus of the work with the client was person-centred in approach and behaviourally based. The counsellor acted as an information giver to the line manager, and towards the end of the contract as an advocate for the client. Somewhere along the process the personnel manager changes the goal-posts of the concurred contract by extending the expected behaviour of the client beyond weekday drinking to the control of weekend drinking.

The client was facing a crisis of personal confidence and lack of self-esteem, and was stuck in a chronic pattern of expecting others to resolve his dilemmas.

In maintaining her boundaries between all the parties, the dilemmas for the counsellor are that she:

- Is new and proving herself.
- Is accountable to the client and the organization.
- Feels increasingly that she is becoming the mouthpiece for a 'disciplining organization'.
- Feels she can easily jeopardize her counselling relationship with her client by sharing information not previously negotiated with her client.
- Does not know what kind of contract the organization has set up with the company in employing the services of an outside consultant.

Clear contracting, ensuring that the goals of the client are concurring with those of the organization, would have helped to minimize the difficulties being encountered. It could be suspected that the organization was using this counsellor to help dismiss the employee by changing the goal-posts. Maybe some form of 'statement of understanding' between the counsellor and client and counsellor and organization would have helped to alleviate the worst features of such a dilemma.

The short-term counsellor is required to assist the client in reframing the goals into ones which are manageable and realistic, while continuing to trust the client that he/she knows best. Counsellors in supervision often report anxiety about whether goals are concurrent with those of the organization. Changes which appear to conflict with organizational expectations demand that counsellors help clients explore the potential consequences of such changes – not to deter these changes – for action and decision remain with the client.

6.   Exploring the Influence of Organizational Culture and Dynamics

Building on a 'systems approach' in understanding organizations, Morgan (1986) posits three pragmatic issues for our consideration:

1. The organization does not exist in a vacuum; it is part of, and related to, the environment.
2. The organization comprises a number of interrelated sub-systems.
3. The organization needs an internal congruency between the sub-systems for it to flourish.

A counselling service is a sub-system of the larger organization. As such it has the potential to espouse the values and beliefs of its 'product', ones of being people-centred, caring, supportive, cooperative.

Culture has been defined as 'shared meaning, shared understanding, and shared sense making . . . a process of reality construction that allows people to see and understand particular events, actions, objects, utterances, or situations in distinctive ways' (Morgan, 1986: 128). Lane (1990) argues that introducing counselling programmes into organizations that experience dysfunctions, for example too much stress, or which exhibit a high degree of absenteeism, is a sure way of maintaining the levels of organizational dysfunction. Organizational interventions that deal with the causes rather than the symptoms are liable to be more effective in the long term than responding to symptoms with counselling.

The Relationship of Culture to Counselling Programmes

Van Oudtshoorn (1989) focuses attention on the predominant culture of the organization as indicating the use to which the counselling programme will be directed. She identifies four roles for counselling programmes and their 'fit' with organizational types:

1. Power cultures in which there is little or no impact of counselling on the prevailing culture.
2. Role cultures in which counselling is kept as a separate activity with little or no feedback to the organization.
3. Achievement cultures in which counselling will be evaluated according to results, and thus have a limited effect on culture.
4. Support cultures in which counselling will be seen as integral to the well-being, and thus the prevailing culture, of the organization.

Prevention and Education

Hopkins (1994) expresses a growing concern among service providers and practitioners about the dangers of companies using counselling services outside the workplace as 'sticking plasters or laundry baskets'. There is an increasing demand on counsellors to promote preventive and educational programmes as part of their role by feeding back to the organization trends and themes in their work with clients. Here, organizational dysfunction can be addressed, and consequent significant change effected. This slow 'drip feed' process requires working with various levels of management from a place of respect, non-judgement and trust, that is counselling the organization. Failure to address such issues is tantamount to operating double standards and is ethically suspect, where, for example, employees can be edged out of the organization through the fear of bullying, suffer serious illness and burnout resulting from unrealistic expectations of managers, etc.

The situation of Dianne outlined above (pp. 174–5) exemplifies the lack of 'fit' between the role of the counsellor and the predominant 'power culture' of the organization, leading to the client being faced with a choice of staying in an unsympathetic work situation or leaving. Organizational demands, for example corrective behaviour on the part of an employee, dealing with a personality clash or coping with a bully, can place the counsellor in conflictual situations with the organization. In such cases the counsellor needs to be 'up front' with the client and the organization about the potential boundaries of such help or, alternatively, suggest a referral outside the organization.

Labelling Clients

Experience shows that labelling a client as being in need of 'a psychiatric assessment', while being in the client's interest, can result in the organization perceiving the client as being seriously ill, being a weak link in the chain, being someone to be watched, or as being a suitable candidate for exiting. Counsellors need to think carefully about how they talk of their clients within organizations; be alert to ways of initiating preventive work; and to remind themselves that often organizations need to defend themselves from the numerous imagined projections which a counselling provision can trigger.

Parallel Process

Counsellors meet the organization in their clients as they experience 'parallel process' (Crandall and Allen, 1982), a concept from the world of clinical supervision. Here, the relationship between counsellors and clients is 'played out' or 'mirrored' in the relationship between supervisors and counsellors. The following example may help to ground the concept in practice:

Case Study

An able organizational counsellor presented the case of a young employee who had broken the company code of conduct in respect of abusive treatment of a customer. The client was referred to the counselling service via management. The company had already initiated a disciplinary procedure for the client.

In presenting his client in supervision, the counsellor exhibited considerable anxiety and aggression, which the supervisor also experienced. Further intervention and exploration determined that the anxiety and aggression was experienced by the counsellor in working with the client.

Here, it was attention to the process of the supervision session which provided an insight into unconscious processes at work in the counsellor, in the client and in the organization. Morgan (1986) suggests that organizational culture represents the unconscious of the organization.

Adapting ideas from Gestalt Therapy, Critchley and Casey (1989) illustrate a familiar theme in individuals and organizations – that of 'stuckness'. They argue that organizations 'get stuck,' like individuals, at various points on the gestalt cycle. It may well be that organizational 'stuckness' will exhibit itself within the counselling process mirrored by the client and in projecting its 'stuckness' on to the client.

A supervisee in the course of supervision constantly exhibited fears and anxieties in having open communication with his boss. Further exploration identified that he had chosen a number of bosses and organizational cultures that exhibited similar traits to those of his father and his family – 'The Frightened Organization – Interrupted before Action' (Critchley and Casey, 1989: 7). He found himself 'stuck' in the way he related to his boss, in the same way that he found himself stuck the way he related to his father – by always being devious out of fear of risking open communication. Neither the boss nor the supervisee ever achieved what they wanted from each other. The supervisee's way out was always to be looking for other posts, a way of behaving that he recognized for the first time as being 'well past its sell-by date'! Organizationally, while there was a lot of business, they found it very difficult to take decisive action.

Summary

Managing the counselling process in organizational settings is both a challenging and complex task for practitioners. Thorough preparation and attention to realistic contracts with the organization, often identified as 'third parties', and clients by counsellors will help create manageable boundaries and expectations within which to practise with relative sanity.

Identifying and dealing with the unconscious and conscious processes of both the individual and the organization is often complicated and confusing. While supervision is dealt with elsewhere, its importance for organizational counsellors cannot be over emphasized as a vital tool to enable practitioners to function well. Where there are relatively few counsellors working within organizations, feelings of isolation and being undervalued and misunderstood are common.

Assessment which pays careful attention to contracting, levels of motivation of the client, the influence of the organization (particularly through referral), identifying manageable and realistic goals, and appropriate closure, can be vital in enabling the client's and the organization's needs to be honoured. Whatever the outcomes, they must always be by the choice of the client.

While organizational practice varies according to the number of sessions afforded to individual clients, time creates a significant boundary. Counsellors must be constantly alert to how this can be influenced by organizational expectation and intervention.

Recognizing that organizations contain systems within systems, that they are a mixture of conscious and unconscious processes, and that this is the context for managing the counselling process, what happens in the counsellor's therapy room is an interlacing and interconnection of these various energies and processes. While the mixture is rich, the drink can be extremely intoxicating – even, dare one say, 'addictive'. Regular and effective supervision is essential to maintain healthy functioning for the counsellor. Establishing an appropriate feedback mechanism from the practice of the counsellor to the organization (and vice versa) demonstrates the essential relatedness illustrated in the Three-cornered Contract (English, 1975) between client, counsellor and organization.

References

Adams, A. (1992) *Bullying at Work: How to Confront and Overcome it.* London: Virago.

Barkham, M. (1989) 'Exploratory therapy in two-plus-one sessions. I – Rationale for a brief psychotherapy model', *British Journal of Psychotherapy*, 6 (1): 81–7.

British Association for Counselling (1993) *Code of Ethics and Practice for Counsellors.* Rugby: BAC.

Carroll, M. (1995) 'The counsellor in organizational settings – some reflections', *Employee Counselling Today*, 7 (1): 23–9.

Crandall, R. and Allen, R.D. (1982) 'The organizational context of helping relationships', in T.A. Will (ed.), *Basic Processes in Helping Relationships.* London: Academic Press.

Critchley, B. and Casey, D. (1989) 'Organizations get stuck too', *Leadership and Organization Development Journal*, 10 (4): 3–12.

de Shazer, S. (1985) *Keys to Solution in Brief Therapy.* New York/London: W.W. Norton.

de Shazer, S. (1990) 'Context. From Problem to Solution: A Conference with Steve de Shazer and Insoo Kim Berg', 10–11 May.

Denton, M. (1993) Personal communication with the author in supervision group.

Douglas, D. (1995) 'Beyond the bottom line', *Journal of Counselling at Work*, Summer: 11.

Egan, G. (1994) *The Skilled Helper* (5th Edition). Monterey, CA: Brooks/Cole.

English, F. (1975) 'The three cornered contract', *Transactional Analysis Journal*, 5 (4): 383–4.

Firth-Cozens, J. (1992) 'The effectiveness of short-term counselling'. Occasional paper.

Hay, J. (1992) *Transactional Analysis for Trainers.* London: McGraw-Hill.

Hopkins, V. (1994) 'Is counselling for the organization or employee?', *Journal of Counselling at Work*, Spring: 13–14.

Lane, D. (1990) 'Counselling psychology in organizations', *The Psychologist, Bulletin of the British Psychological Society*, 12: 540–4.

Lewis, J. and Lewis, M. (1986) *Counselling Programs for Employees in the Workplace.* Monterey, CA: Brooks/Cole.

Malan, D. and Osimo, F. (1992) *Psychodynamics, Training and Outcomes in Brief Psychotherapy.* London: Butterworth-Heinemann.

Morgan, G. (1986) *Images of Organization.* London: Sage.

Nelson-Jones, R. (1991) *The Theory and Practice of Counselling Psychology.* London: Cassell.

Orlans, V. (1986) 'Counselling services in organizations', *Personnel Review*, 15 (5): 19–23.

Rogers, C. (1983) *Freedom to Learn in the 80s.* Columbus, OH: Charles E. Meril Publishing.

Sugarman, L. (1992) 'Ethical issues in counselling at work', *Employee Counselling Today*, 4 (4): 23–30.

Van Oudtshoorn, L. (1989) *The Organization as a Nurturing Environment.* Oxford: Van Oudtshoorn Associates.

11

Ethical Issues for Counselling in Organizations

Catherine Shea and Tim Bond

It is tempting for a counsellor and client working together in privacy to lose sight of the forces which impinge on their relationship from the other side of the closed door. The fantasy of a wholly private space guarded by professional ethics has a substantial degree of reality if the counsellor is an independent practitioner seeing a private client who is solely responsible for payment. However, counselling ethics become much more complex when counselling takes place in an organizational setting. A third entity, an organization, which is composed of many different people, expands the dyad into a triad, or even more complex constellation of relationships. We will argue that although the third entity, the host organization, may not always be as visible within the counselling room as the counsellor and client, it would be unwise to neglect the ethical implications of this invisible presence in the counselling relationship. As host, and usually a major contributor towards the cost of the counselling, the organization has real power to enhance or undermine the ethical and, thus, the therapeutic basis of the counselling relationship.

The influence of the organization operates at different levels. We have classified these into three types. The first level includes the immediately apparent issues which are relatively easily addressed by professional codes and guidelines in which ethical principles can be converted into logistical strategies. The codes of the British Association for Counselling (BAC), the Counselling Psychology Division of the British Psychological Society (BPS) and the United Kingdom Council for Psychotherapy (UKCP) are particularly relevant. The second level is more subtle and relates to matters of ethos, which are the underlying philosophy, values, beliefs and attitudes which inspire and shape the stated ethical frameworks and day-to-day practices in the host organization and in the counselling within it. The visibility of this level will vary between organizations but the counsellor should not have too much difficulty in discovering the organizational ethos or detecting its influence in the disclosures of clients. The third level is much more shadowy and holds much of its power in its continuing to remain invisible and to pass unquestioned. We have identified this level as the organizational unconscious. Before we consider the ethical implications of each of these in turn, it is worth making some preliminary observations about the current state of counselling ethics in the organizational context.

The provision of counselling and the ethics of counselling are both relatively youthful in comparison to most other caring roles in the British context. Counselling was introduced into the UK from the USA in the 1960s. The first published statements of counselling ethics occurred in the early 1980s, leading to the first published code in 1984 by a national professional organization (BAC, 1984). This code underwent major revision in the late 1980s and a revised version was published in 1990, with minor revisions in 1993. An examination of the membership of the standards and ethics committee of BAC reveals that many of those who contributed to the writing of the codes had experience of providing counselling in organizational settings, especially within education, the voluntary sector, the health service and social services. In comparison, counsellors working in the commercial sector, within employee welfare services and on Employee Assistance Programmes (EAPs), although not wholly absent, are relatively fewer in number. This probably means that some logistical issues have not been given the consideration they deserve, but in our opinion the greatest gap in current thinking about counselling ethics relates to matters of ethos and the organizational unconscious. Their influence may be much more apparent in the diversity of the commercial sector.

It is also probably indicative of the relatively early stage of the development of counselling ethics in the context of organizations that the greatest discrepancies in published guidelines within the talking therapies relate to therapists and counsellors working in organizational contexts, and especially with regard to the ethical requirements for disclosure to professional colleagues within the same organization (see below, p. 192). Although this chapter will concentrate on the dilemmas and differences within organizations which host counselling, the discrepancies in the guidelines of BAC, BPS and UKCP on the management of confidentiality are a timely reminder that organizational discrepancies exist between the organizations which seek to regulate counselling and psychotherapy. These discrepancies may be evidence of divisions of ethos and of unconscious forces at work within the counselling and therapy, which cannot be considered as ethically united over counselling in organizations in comparison to guidelines for independent practitioners. There is a sense in which the increasing provision of counselling within organizations is testing our ethical maturity as individual counsellors cope with greater accountability and visibility to colleagues within the organization, as well as greater levels of complexity created by the need to take the host organization into account. Discrepancies in the guidance from professional organizations which represent us collectively may indicate that we are still in an early stage in our maturing process as a profession expanding provision within organizational contexts.

As authors with a combined interest in counselling and professional ethics, we want to advance the state of awareness of the ethical issues raised by providing counselling within organizations, without necessarily being too definitive about how dilemmas can be resolved. To this end, we (especially Catherine Shea) have gathered examples of the kinds of dilemma encountered by counsellors in actual practice, and we will use anonymized summaries of these to illustrate ethics. It is not within our scope to prescribe how such dilemmas might be obviated or resolved. It is simply our intention at this stage to foreground the kinds of issue which both counsellors and employing organizations may wish to be forewarned in order to be proactive about the efficacy of the service they provide. We will start our exploration with the sorts of issues most easily considered within professional codes and guidelines.

Established Ethical Principles and Guidelines

Published codes and guidelines establish the client's interests as being of paramount importance in ethical decision-making by counsellors, which raises an important issue for counsellors in organizations.

Who is the Client?

One of the first issues to confront a counsellor working in an organization is 'who is the real client?' Is the client represented by the organization who pays for the services of the counsellor and, thus, the most powerful participant in the triangular relationship of counsellor, client and organization? The fact that the organization is composed of many people does not preclude it from being the real client. The organization can be regarded as a social organism in its own right which is best understood by maintaining an overview of the processes and interactions within it. There are precedents for regarding the organization as the client in the context of counselling. In 'business counselling', the counsellor's primary commitment is to the success of the entire organization rather than any individual within it. Confidentiality exists between the organization and the counsellor rather than a single employee and the counsellor. It has also been argued that the client of a student counsellor is the education institution rather than any particular individual who may be seeing the counsellor. This view posed considerable problems for the counsellors concerned, because it threatened student privacy and confidentiality when seeing a counsellor. In fact, the ethical and legal arguments favourable to counselling prevailed (Bond, 1992; 1993: 184–9) and it is clear that the primary responsibility of the therapeutic counsellor in law and ethics is owed to the individual who seeks help.

The ethical primacy of the individual(s) seeking the counsellor's help creates a duty on individual workplace counsellors to ensure that the basis on which they construct their relationship with the organization recognizes the counsellor's primary obligation to the individual client. The nature of some organizations requires some limited qualifications to the ethical primacy of the client. For example, counsellors working in the health service are usually subject to a limitation where the health of patients or staff is at risk. Counsellors employed by the police may have limitations relating to criminal activity committed by the police. In heavy industry, there may be legitimate limitations relating to the safety of employees and the public. Some, but not all, organizations exclude serious criminal activity directed against the organization itself. So far as we know, there have been no decisions taken within the counselling profession as a whole about what constitutes an acceptable limitation. The ones which appear to have become established arise directly from the core activity of the organization, seek to prevent a substantial harm, and can be reasonably precisely defined.

Where such limitations as these exist, they should be clearly established within the agreement between the counsellor and the organization and should be known to clients.

Basic Principles

The next question which confronts the counsellor in organizations is 'what principles should guide my ethical decision-making?'. Bond (1993) has written extensively about the implications of four primary principles. These are:

- Respect for autonomy. What maximizes the opportunities for everyone involved to implement their own choices?
- Beneficence. What will achieve the greatest good?
- Non-maleficence. What will cause least harm?
- Justice. What will be fairest in the distribution of counselling?

These were the principles which were to the forefront of the minds of the authors of the current code for counsellors (BAC, 1993). However, it is not an exhaustive list and as we will be arguing that there are aspects of counselling in organizations which are not currently adequately addressed in current codes, and perhaps never could be adequately encompassed within professional regulations, it is worth considering the nature of these additional principles. Andrew Thompson (1990), in an extremely informative *Guide to the Ethical Practice to Psychotherapy*, argues for six principles which includes the addition of:

- Fidelity. What does the counsellor promise implicitly and explicitly and how should these promises be honoured?

Included within this principle is attention to dual relationships (see below, p. 194), and promises of confidentiality. It directs attention to the trustworthiness and integrity of the counselling relationship. In his order of priority, this principle closely follows the principle of autonomy, which is paramount.

His sixth principle is, perhaps, the most surprising, which is identified as 'self-interest'. He argues that the counsellor's self-interest is much better considered explicitly than left unacknowledged and as a hidden force in any ethical decision-making. Self-interest is not the same as selfishness but an appropriate recognition of the circumstances required for the counsellor to function effectively.

Each of the other principles are relevant to defining the content of self-interest. For example, the components of a principle of self-interest include:

- Self-autonomy – promoting professional autonomy.
- Self-fidelity – being able to trust one's promises to one's self.

- Self-justice – seeking appropriate rewards as a professional and in the struggle between professions.
- Self-beneficence – being appropriately good to one's self and seeking opportunities for self-improvement.
- Non-maleficence – self-protection from physical or psychological harm or from unnecessary litigation.

We have given some attention to this principle because it is particularly relevant to counsellors working in organizations.

The dependence of the counsellor on the organization for resources and status creates a potential for overt conflicts of interest to arise to the disadvantage of client, counsellor or organization. However, other more subtle forces can arise, creating similar effects due to the ethos or unconscious within the organization which are more likely to be actively considered if the counsellor's appropriate 'self-interest' forms part of the ethical decision-making process. Therefore, this principle has particular relevance within organizations because the counsellor is not independent of the total dynamic but a significant contributor.

The Primacy of Autonomy

The nature of counselling means that one principle takes precedent over all others. Respect for the client's autonomy is the foundation stone upon which the professional ethic of counselling is constructed. This is essential because counselling is an activity which is only possible with the active involvement of the client. A rather corny joke contains an important truth:

Q: How many counsellors does it take to change a light bulb?
A: One. But the light bulb has really got to want to change.

Therapeutic process is directed to enhancing the client's autonomy, the capacity for self-government, inside and outside the counselling relationship. Our professional commitment to the principle of respect for a client's autonomy has a number of practical consequences:

1. Counselling as a voluntary activity. Counsellors in organizations sometimes have people sent to them to be counselled. Usually this requires two responses. The counsellor would give the client time to consider whether he/she really wants counselling and on what basis, in order to establish the client's right to make autonomous choices. The counsellor may also seek to educate the 'sender' of the client or the organization about more appropriate ways of making referrals.
2. The importance of clients making free and informed choices within the counselling relationship. This requires that care is taken over ensuring that the client has the necessary information to choose about the method(s) used within the counselling, the availability of other methods or counsellors and to review periodically these decisions.
3. Matters of importance are clearly contracted between counsellor and client. Issues such as the arranging and keeping of appointments, any

payment, and restrictions on the number of sessions available would all normally be part of the contract. Confidentiality is a recurrent concern within organizations and may require special attention (see next section). Often these issues can be dealt with in an information leaflet about the counselling rather than negotiated on an individual basis. However, agreement about therapeutic goals which are also part of the contract can only be negotiated with clients on an individual basis. A counsellor's attentiveness to the therapeutic expectations of the client and periodic review of progress brings respect for individual autonomy into the heart of the relationship.

4. Maintaining a clear division of responsibilities between counsellor and client. The client holds responsibility for the way he/she uses the counselling in his/her life. This is sometimes referred to as responsibility for the outcome (Rowan, 1983). The counsellor is responsible for the methods used within the counselling and has to take care that these are consistent with the therapeutic elements of the contract agreed with the client. The division of boundaries means that the counsellor cannot claim responsibility for 'producing a breakthrough' or 'curing' a client as these are ultimately things that the client does for him/herself, albeit facilitated by the counsellor.

5. Exercising care over confidentiality, the maintenance of clear boundaries within the counselling relationship (especially the avoidance of exploitation) and externally (especially dual relationships). These all impinge on the client's sense of safety and capacity to act autonomously, but are important ethical issues to be considered separately.

Confidentiality

The management of confidentiality is probably the most recurrent concern of counsellors within organizations. Clients are often concerned to protect personal information about themselves from colleagues and employers within the organization as well as from people on the outside. Clients need privacy and confidentiality in order to be sufficiently open and honest to make the counselling worthwhile. On the other hand, there may be pressures on counsellors to communicate progress reports to referrers of clients, to other members of an interdisciplinary team, and to be accountable to the organization for the time and resources used by the counsellor. Some pressures to disclose confidential information are well intentioned from people who want to help the client. Other requests for information may be less benevolent and directed towards exposing a client's deficiencies, perhaps for a disciplinary hearing. Experience suggests that it is important that the counsellor treats all requests for personally identifiable information about the client on the same basis, regardless of whether the request is for or against the client's interests.

The general principles over confidentiality are well established. In general, confidentiality has to be protected. Confidential information about clients should only be disclosed with their informed and free consent, given either in the contract or negotiated for specific circumstances. Ideally, the disclosure of confidential information should be made by the client directly, but this is not always appropriate, or the counsellor is being asked to confirm the client's disclosures.

Some situations can be distinguished as requiring different kinds of response:

1. Routine disclosures to the third parties. These are universally prohibited without client consent.
2. Routine disclosures to team members. For example, the counsellor may be working in a team of counsellors or as a member of a multidisciplinary team. The minimum ethical standard required varies between professional organizations. BAC requires client consent or at the very least that the client is informed about such communications (BAC, 1993: ss. B4.3, 4.6). BPS merely requires that psychologists 'endeavour' (an ambiguous term) to inform the clients about disclosures to colleagues (BPS, 1993: s. 4.2), although counselling psychologists are subject to more stringent guidelines (BPS, 1995: s. 1.5). UKCP makes the decision to disclose to colleagues a matter of professional judgement in the best interests of the client and is ambiguous about the client's knowledge of the disclosures to the client's GP and relevant psychiatric services (UKCP, 1993: s. 2.5). In our view, anything less than seeking the client's prior consent undermines the ethical principles of fidelity and autonomy and requires a major countervailing ethical justification.
3. Routine disclosures to sources of help for the client. These can be distinguished into: (a) receiving a professional referral from another agency or unit to which some feedback about the progress in counselling is owed. It is considered optimal practice to inform the client about the content of such feedback and maybe to adjust the content to meet the client's wishes. Self-referred clients do not raise this issue; (b) making referrals to other agencies which may be able to help the client. The client's free and informed consent is usually required. 'Informed' requires knowledge of the agency's policies over confidentiality and the kind of help available. The counsellor may need to have preliminary discussions with the agency to obtain this information without revealing the client's identity.
4. Ethical and legal imperatives which override the client's right to confidentiality. Reasonably foreseeable limitations should be included within information leaflets and the contract with the client. Most professional codes recognize that the duty to protect the client from serious self-harm (BAC, 1993: s. B4.4; BPS, 1995: s. 4.3; UKCP, 1993) and the protection of others from serious harm (BAC, 1993: s. B4.4; BPS, 1995: s. 4.3) may (not must) override the duty to confidentiality. The legal and ethical requirements are complex and have been extensively discussed elsewhere (Bond, 1993; 1994a).

The management of an effective confidentiality policy within organizations requires attention to the counsellor's (and support staff) contract of employment, policies about record-keeping, preparation of brief statements to inform client about their rights, a more comprehensive policy agreed and supported by the organization, an internal complaints procedure and a programme of staff training. Some of the recommendations developed for alcohol and drug services are directly relevant to all counselling within organizations (Standing Conference on Drug Abuse/Alcohol Concern, 1994).

Honouring Boundaries in Relationships with Clients

Attention to boundary issues with clients is particularly important in organizations because the counsellor is to a greater or lesser extent part of the client's working environment and vice versa. The obligation to avoid exploitation of clients financially, sexually, emotionally or in any other way is well established in counselling. The dangers of sexual relationships with current and former clients is well established (Pope et al., 1993; Russell, 1993; Bond, 1994b; Jehu, 1994) among counsellors but is unlikely to apply to most other workers. Boundaries over finance may be more problematic in an organization. The involvement of a third party as paymaster rather than the client increases the potential for conflicts of interest to arise which work against the client. For example, the method of accountability for use of resources could undermine the client's confidentiality directly by requiring disclosure of names, or indirectly by requiring details which allow the identity of clients to be deduced. This is ethically undesirable.

Dual relationships are a frequent occurrence within organizations. Dual relationships arise for counsellors whenever we have another, significantly different relationship concurrently with one of our clients. The greatest potential for dual relationships arises when the counsellor also undertakes other functions within the organization, which often include training or contributing to policy-making about personnel and welfare issues. Each situation needs careful consideration to assess whether there is potential harm to clients or counselling relationships. Some discussion of the issues can be found in Herlihy and Corey (1992). Sometimes counsellors are asked to see clients as part of a disciplinary process. Often these referrals are well intentioned and designed as an alternative to disciplinary sanction. However, it is difficult to maintain the dual roles of counsellor and disciplinarian satisfactorily. It is much better that the employer distinguishes the disciplinary process from the counselling by stating exactly what is expected of the client and any sanctions if this is not achieved. A concerned employer may offer counselling to assist the client but the disciplinary procedures should be independent of whether or not the employee attends for counselling.

Counselling Supervision

The ethical requirement that counsellors receive regular and ongoing supervision regardless of their level of experience or training is a British tradition which is being increasingly adopted in cognate professions in this country and abroad. A number of reasons have been offered for this commitment to supervision which include the difficulty of being both involved in the counselling relationship and simultaneously keeping an overview of the counselling process, the need to unload the personal impact of working with other people's distress and the need to be regularly challenged and stretched in one's practice.

The tasks of supervision have been identified by Inskipp and Proctor (1989) as:

1. Formative. The learning of new skills and theory, reflection on experience, and imparting of knowledge about specific issues raised by clients.
2. Normative. The monitoring of the implementation of ethical standards, the quality of the counselling and consideration of feedback from the client.
3. Restorative. Dealing with personal issues and stress arising from counselling, validating achievements.

The challenge posed to the counsellor of needing to consider his/her relationship with both the client and the organization suggests that an additional task may be required:

4. Perspective. An exploration of the relationship between counselling and the organization and other sources of help for clients.

This last task takes on a particular significance when one adds to the challenges of managing the counselling process within the less tangible but very powerful forces at work in any organization which impinge on counsellor and client alike. These are the subject of the next two sections.

Issues Associated with Ethos

The implications of an organization's ethos for counselling ethics has not had the attention it deserves. The ethos can be identified by the characteristic shared attitudes within the organization and the beliefs and values which inform interactions within the organization. The practical examples offered to us by counsellors to inform the writing of this chapter suggest that the relationship between counselling ethics and organizational ethos is not simple or easily predictable. However, we will attempt to outline some preliminary observations before we consider the practical implications for counselling ethics.

The first observation is self-evident from the previous section. Counselling has its own distinctive ethos represented collectively within its professional organizations, promulgated in training, and reinforced in its literature. The ethos which prevails within counselling in Britain is characterized by valuing the individual over the collective, being more attentive to subjective experience rather than objective accounts of actions, and being more responsive to people's distress and difficulty in comparison to success and achievement within organizations. The established principles about respect for individual autonomy and confidentiality, the care taken over dual relationships, are all manifestations of an underlying ethos which pervades counselling, albeit with some differences of emphasis between major therapeutic orientations and national professional organizations. Viewed from the outside, the counselling ethos can seem perplexing or counter-cultural within an organization. A critic of the counselling ethos might well consider it to be individualistic to the point of ignoring social context, naive about politics and power within organizations, obsessed with discovering personal problems and unnecessarily secretive. The presence of such views within an organization is usually indicative of the existence of differences in ethos between counselling and the organization.

Working in an Ethos Compatible with Counselling

In organizations with a high degree of compatibility with the counselling ethos, situations can arise which are a source of legitimate ethical concern. For example, too consistent a coherence between the language and concepts valued within the organization and the method of counselling may be oppressive of some clients.

Case Study

Bill, a senior sales executive, is becoming increasingly disillusioned with his work and its purpose and has become depressed, perhaps as part of mid-life crisis in which he feels unable to perceive the changes which would bring new meaning to his life. The counsellor in staff health works exclusively with motivational approaches to problem-management and solution-focus therapy as models most compatible with the culture of an organization which requires a highly motivated sales force in order to succeed. Both counsellor and client fail to recognize that part of his problem is his disenchantment with motivational language and concepts and the counselling increases Bill's depression. His elusive sense of wanting more from life, in his relationships and spirituality, goes unrecognized until he is admitted to an acute psychiatric unit and experiences alternative therapeutic approaches.

The case illustrates how too great a compatibility between counselling and organizational ethos may blind both counsellor and client to important issues, sometimes to the considerable disempowerment of the client. It would be going too far to deduce that a counter-cultural element in counselling would be beneficial to clients and the organization, but it does suggest that counsellors, supervisors and organizations actually need to consider the possibility of blind-spots in situations where there is a high level of compatibility between counselling and organizational ethos.

Sometimes the compatibility of ethos between the host organization and the counselling may be more apparent than real. For example, a shared language may be misleading.

Case Study

A hospital selected the three-stage problem-management approach developed by Gerard Egan (1994) for training nurses in counselling patients and to offer peer counselling to colleagues. The model was selected because of its compatibility with the three-staged model of patient care in which the nurses were already trained and the increasing emphasis on patient-centred approaches to nursing. In a subsequent review of the use of counselling supervision by the nurses, it was discovered that the personal qualities (or core conditions) considered essential to the model were abandoned as it was coopted to a medical approach to nursing and counselling. Counselling supervision was also modified to fit the prevailing medical ethos which was hierarchical and discouraged disclosure of feelings, especially about the personal vulnerability of the counsellor.

In this example, the similarity in language and concepts concealed a clash of ethos in which a predominant medical ethos won out. Perhaps a greater awareness of the potential differences between the nursing and counselling model and the implications of attempting to challenge the dominant culture would have enabled a more effective implementation of the counselling ethos to the benefit of patients and colleagues receiving counselling. It may be that a greater degree of discrepancy between the counselling and nursing ethos would have helped this process by making some issues more visible.

Working in an Ethos Different from Counselling

Differences in ethos can also create challenges for counsellors. Some examples may illustrate the ways in which a different ethos within the organization may contradict accepted ethical practice within counselling, particularly over attitudes to client autonomy.

Case Study

A school counsellor is working with a 12 year old pupil who discloses that she has been cutting herself in moments of despair. She is anxious that no one else should know about this, especially her teacher or her parents. The counsellor considers that premature disclosures to either of these will add to her despair but she is also conscious of the ethos of being protective of young people in schools in general, and the expectations of parents and teachers to be kept informed about such significant concerns.

The case is typical of many situations which counsellors encounter when working in organizations providing care for young people. The ethos which has pervaded the development of counselling ethics is a set of values and beliefs appropriate to the autonomous adult. Relatively little attention has been given to the ethical principles appropriate to young people, especially within organizational contexts. A counsellor faced with this dilemma ought to be aware that ethically and legally the guiding principle ought to be the child's welfare, and an assessment of this ought to take into account a young person's request for confidentiality, but the existence of such a request, although important, does not carry the same weight in comparison to working with adults. The significance given to such a request increases with the young person's maturity and understanding, but the paramount principle is acting in the best interests of the young person. Although the principles are relatively easily stated, their application in specific situations is often problematic. In this situation, a great deal will depend on the relationship between the counsellor and other key figures within the school, especially the head teacher. A relationship based on mutual respect and trust in each other's competence is more likely to create the possibility of an appropriate decision being made in consultation with the pupil. A less secure relationship may result in a universal requirement to disclose all reports of self-harm or the counsellor retreating into inappropriate levels of secrecy and, thus, leaving some young people unnecessarily vulnerable.

Some clients may be perceived as being so discredited morally that they have forgone their right to autonomous decision-making and the protection that this provides.

Case Study

Peter has disclosed to his counsellor that he has discovered a way of transferring money from his employer to his own advantage and that he has been doing this over a significant period of time to fund a drug habit. There is no prior condition in the contract between the counsellor and client, or between the counsellor and Peter's employer (who funds the counselling) that limits confidentiality in these circumstances. The counsellor realizes that the embezzlement and the absence of any limitations on confidentiality are the result of the ethos of high levels of trust in each other within the company.

The counsellor is in an invidious position. A strict interpretation of professional ethics would suggest that she has to maintain confidentiality, but in doing so she is aware of her own moral complicity in betraying the trust placed in her by the employer in a way which is analogous to the employee's abuse of that trust. This is an instance where the ethical dilemma is rooted in matters of ethos rather than the rules. Perhaps a more forward-looking counsellor would have anticipated this situation and negotiated a clear agreement with the employer and client, but the absence of such an agreement leaves the counsellor sitting uneasily between values and beliefs about valuing trust and betrayal of trust. Some counsellors work in organizations where the client group is collectively considered to be morally discredited, such as sexual offenders, that the organizational ethos requires that all clients forgo any rights to confidentiality or privacy. This can be problematic for counsellors because the ethos of their working environment may be so different from the ethos which prevails in the profession which would tend to reject any discrediting of individuals, especially on a collective basis.

Counsellors who work in organizations which cross cultures encounter some considerable challenges over the values and beliefs which inform counselling. Some cultures have a much stronger sense of collective identity based on family, location or social grouping. In these circumstances, a professional ethic based on individual autonomy may be perceived as 'Westernizing', or may be incomprehensible as the basis for professional ethics. Some cultures diverge over their attitudes to gender and sexuality. Again, a white British counsellor will be aware of working from a professional culture which could be significantly antagonistic to the culture of the organization or client. As society becomes more culturally diverse, the possible permutations between counsellor, client and organization and the negotiation of such differences grows. There is an increasingly well-established view that all counsellors should be sensitized to and trained to respond to differences in race and culture (Lago and Thompson, 1996). It may well be that counselling has much to learn from the international commercial sector which has needed to consider cultural diversity and its impact on the working environment (Hofstede, 1980).

The Ethical Implications of Differences in Ethos for Counselling Ethics in Organizations

It is possible to list some preliminary conclusions:

1. We are at a relatively early stage in understanding the nature of divergences in ethos and their implications for counselling ethics. Counsellors working in organizations are often working in relative isolation and are relatively few in number and therefore relatively powerless to change the organizational ethos, even if this was considered appropriate. The current state of counselling ethics offers little specific guidance on how to respond to issues which arise from the ethos adopted by the organization or the client.
2. It may be that there is insufficient awareness among counsellors that counselling has its own distinctive ethos, which may be inappropriately monopolistic and insensitive to divergences within its own membership. It is probable that the predominant ethnic and class status of counsellors (white and educated middle class) has blinded us to the potential for variations in the ethos of the counsellor, client, organization and within the occupational culture of counselling.
3. It would be too simplistic to assume that ethical dilemmas are avoided where there is considerable compatibility between the organizational ethos and the beliefs and values of counselling.
4. There is considerable potential for research on the relationship between ethos and counselling ethics, especially where the counselling is provided within organizations.

The Organizational Unconscious

An organization characteristically takes on a life of its own which is more persistent than the contributions of any of its individual contributors. The organization is a social construction which can be viewed as a social entity with a series of inner dynamics analogous to the psychological and social dynamics of the individuals who create and sustain it as an organization. The conscious elements, which are usually readily accessible to the counsellor, are contained in the explicit regulations and agreements which bind the organization together. Matters of ethos may be readily apparent, or at least are more likely to be readily acknowledged when attention is drawn to them, and therefore lie above or immediately below the surface of organizational interaction. In contrast, the organizational unconscious, or at least those parts of it which are discernible, because some may be too hidden to become conscious, requires greater intellectual and emotional effort to surface. The unconscious can often be elusive or ambiguous and this may be resistant to exposing it. The existence of the organizational unconscious is significant for counselling ethics because it contains drives and valences which support or undermine the overt ethical discourse of the organization. As with individuals, the psychology of the organization is seldom an integrated and harmonious whole; rather it is likely to be fractured by varying degrees of splitting and discontinuities with areas of energy and commitment sometimes existing in opposition to each other. A few examples may illustrate the significance of the organizational unconscious for counselling ethics.

The Drive for Self-perpetuation

One of the basic drives in an organization is to perpetuate itself.

Case Study

A counsellor working in occupational health notices that there is a higher incidence of stress-related illness in one section of the company. She is becoming increasingly worried for the individuals concerned, some of whom are becoming suicidal. She is also aware that the entire company is vulnerable to takeover and that any failure in productivity within this section would threaten the independent existence of the company.

This is a relatively common scenario in many organizations. If other sections of the company are committed to survival and the management is optimistic and purposeful, there are good prospects of the employees obtaining additional support in their difficult role. The counsellor's role may be to assist the employees mobilize these resources for themselves as the organization's healthy will to perpetuate itself is an asset to client and counsellor. However, it may be that these clients are the most visible sign of an organization which is so overstretched, besieged or exhausted that it has lost the will to survive. In this respect, individual thoughts of suicide are symptomatic of a wider organizational malaise. In such circumstances, the options open to the clients are rather different, and any attempt by the counsellor to instil optimism may be to delay or prevent a healthy process of adjustment to the inevitable. Often the counsellor will not be in a position to make such assessments about the future of the organization. But when she is, her professional ethical commitment to working to the benefit of her clients is relevant to the decisions she makes about responding to her clients.

Sometimes, the drive of organizations to perpetuate themselves can lead to unconscious blindness to unethical behaviour within the company.

Case Study

A counsellor becomes aware through her clients that a unit manager is causing considerable distress to those working under her by systematic bullying of selected individuals. The particular manager is viewed by senior management as highly effective as her unit maintains its productivity and therefore there is no desire to disturb a part of the organization which is achieving its objectives. Attempts by individuals to alert management to the situation have either been disbelieved or resulted in discrediting the complainant.

Studies of bullying within organizations suggest that this kind of scenario is disturbingly commonplace (Adams, 1992). This is only one of several possible examples which illustrate the general point made by House that 'much of the dysfunctional nature of organizational behaviour is a result of avoidance and collusive denial of the real difficulties and conflicts that exist within organizations' (1996: 43). We will return later to the issue of how far does the counsellor share in a responsibility to alert the organization to dysfunctional behaviour which is harming clients.

Potential for Destructive Dynamics

The need for organizations to divide into sub-groups according to function and expertise is often essential. Many organizations are too large to function as a single unit. However, the existence of divisions creates ideal circumstances for other aspects of organizational unconscious to come into play. Groups within the organization may be subject to the projection of negative images. Some groups may only hold together because of fantasies about the competitive nature of other groups, conspiracy theories or a sustained unconscious paranoia towards the whole organization.

In some ways, counsellors are often well placed to recognize some aspects of the organizational unconscious. Most counsellors have a theoretical framework which sensitizes them to the potential for unconscious processes. Some counsellors with training in group dynamics, especially large group dynamics, are particularly well placed to identify unconscious processes at work. However, there are ethical doubts about how far a counsellor should take on the role of identifying the organizational unconscious to the organization, even when there are good prospects of a positive outcome. To take on this role is to change the focus of the work so that the organization, rather than the individuals within it, becomes the client, even if this is only temporary. As a consequence, the counsellor takes on a dual relationship with individual clients because the counsellor is seeking actively to change the client's work environment at the same time as the client is being empowered to exercise his/her influence over the environment. This need not undermine the client's autonomy where the dual role has the explicit support and informed consent of the client. However, there are other reasons for caution.

Counsellors are not independent of the organization in which they work. By accepting a role within it, they and their clients have, to a greater or lesser extent, endorsed the systems and authority contained within the organization. At both conscious and unconscious levels, others will attach significance to this apparent endorsement which may mean that a counsellor's comments on the unconscious will be seen as a betrayal of the perceived endorsement or as coming from vested interests as a member of the organization. This carries the risk that an important message will be less carefully considered from an in-house counsellor than from an equally well-informed independent consultant who can speak as an outsider. Notwithstanding these objections, there may be circumstances in which it is appropriate for the counsellor to intervene judiciously to minimize or correct some dysfunctional aspect of the organization's life. In some organizations, it is expected that the counsellor will work in collaboration with management in developing policy within the organization. Counsellors who undertake to work in this way usually only do so with safeguards to protect the privacy and confidentiality of work with individual clients, especially if they are the employees of the organization. However, notwithstanding the existence of adequate safeguards, the counsellor will be subject to different fantasies in the organizational unconscious in comparison to the counsellor who takes a more restrictive view of her role. The effectiveness of either counsellor will in part depend on her sensitivity to the organizational fantasies about herself and her role, and how this impinges on her relationship with clients and the organization itself.

Our final case study highlights a particular aspect of unconscious psychodynamics which can make it very difficult for a counsellor to achieve the psychological distance suggested above. This is a phenomenon which we will call organizational counter-transference. We have observed this dynamic operating, particularly in organizations whose *raison d'être* is to provide counselling, often to a specific client group; it is likely, however, that it is also present to a lesser extent where counselling is a secondary provision. In the former situation it seems that the kinds of counter-transference which are frequently individually recognized between counsellor and client can come to be writ large in the organization culture. For instance, working with people who have been raped or sexually abused can be potent in eliciting a whole range of counter-transference reactions in counsellors, from messianic impulses to being the client's saviour or good parent through to persecutory feelings. In the organizational culture these can become 'split', the positive counter-transference becoming focused on a glowing rhetoric about clients and the services provided to them, and the negative being acted out between management and staff.

Case Study

A voluntary organization providing counselling services for alcohol and drug users advocates a person-centred approach to working with this client group in advertised contrast to what it perceives to be the 'aggressive' medical-model provision of the parallel Health Authority service. In its publicity material and in its overt attitudes to clients, it works hard to resist the common negative stereotypes attributed to substance users (for example, that they are deceitful, devious and manipulative). The organization's history reveals, however, that there is a pervasive climate of mistrust between management and staff and vice versa; that it has employed increasingly authoritarian and aggressive management strategies which conflict deeply with the 'person-centred' ethos upheld in the counselling room; and that there have been an increasing number of disciplinary hearings in which staff have been accused of deceit, deviousness and insubordination. Managers question staff loyalty and competence, while counsellors feel disenfranchised, caught between the need to offer one ethos to clients and finding themselves subject to a climate which denies staff precisely these same values. They either feel powerless to protest, become ill on leave; or they become paranoid and reactive. Their position begins to imitate many features of their client's experience.

This case study encapsulates many of the issues we have touched upon in this section:

• It foregrounds splitting as a common feature in multi- or interdisciplinary work.
• It illustrates the consequences of adopting a counselling ethos in a way which sees it against instead of alongside other approaches.
• It demonstrates the consequences for unconscious organizational dynamics of adopting an excessively 'positive' view of human behaviour in the counselling room – applied to counsellor or client – that these, being negative experiences, are excluded, deflected and projected only to surface elsewhere with a particularly vicious vigour in which counsellors or other groups can become scapegoats.
• It argues the importance of paying attention to organizational dynamics because they enact and shed light on (in parallel process and often in amplified form) the unconscious forces which both shape and respond to what happens in the privacy of the counselling room.

The Ethical Implications of the Unconscious in Organizations

The ethical implications can be summarized in a few statements:

1. The power of organizational dynamics has largely gone unnoticed in ethical guidelines for counsellors but the examples indicate that they impinge on both counsellor and client to a considerable extent. The organizational unconscious intrudes into the privacy of the counselling

room with beneficial or destructive valences on the ethical and therapeutic environment.

2. Some counsellors may be well-placed to recognize the organizational dynamic although their role in responding to it may be problematic and perhaps better undertaken by an independent person. Some useful insights and suggestions can be found elsewhere (Obholzer and Roberts, 1994).

3. Although we have used psychodynamic terminology in developing the description of the dynamics at work, most therapeutic models have concepts which illuminate the dynamics of the organization and provide a language for describing the forces which impinge upon the counselling relationship.

Conclusion

In this chapter we have attempted to extend the usual discussion of counselling ethics beyond matters which are relatively easily the subject of professional regulation to matters which move beyond the sphere of regulation and involve complex ethical assessments by counsellors. Counsellors working in organizations face the complexity of moving from a dyadic relationship with the client to a triadic relationship which includes the organization. In addition, matters of ethos and large group dynamics become important in assessing ethical decisions. These contextual issues cannot be ignored when counselling in an organization. This raises a fundamental ethical question. Counsellors are required to work within their competence. This is usually considered in terms of their training to work with clients with some sensitivity to contextual issues. The issues presented to us by practising counsellors raise some important questions for us as a profession. Can counsellors working in organizations be considered competent without some training in ethos and organizational dynamics? Can counsellors discharge their ethical duties without considering ethos and organizational dynamics alongside the ethical requirements of our published codes and guidelines? The case studies suggest that the duty to the client cannot be adequately considered in isolation from the organizational context. There is also a corollary for counsellors working in organizations.

The challenge for the counsellor working in an organization is sometimes represented as looking in two directions simultaneously, that is taking regard of the client and the organization. This appears to be an oversimplification because the conscious and unconscious forces at work in organizations require an additional third point of attention, the counsellors themselves, in their actual and perceived relationship with the client and the organization. Counsellors working in an organization are neither neutral nor invisible, and have to take themselves into account in ethical decision-making. In the dance between counsellor, client and organization, there is often the possibility of strengthening the ethical and therapeutic basis of counselling, but there is also the possibility of undermining these. This is a daily ethical challenge of providing counselling within organizations.

References

Adams, A. (1992) *Bullying at Work: How to Confront and Overcome It*. London: Virago.

Bond, T. (1992) 'Ethical issues in counselling in education', *Symposium: Ethics in Counselling Practice, British Journal of Guidance and Practice*, 20 (1): 51–63.

Bond, T. (1993) *Standards and Ethics for Counselling in Action*. London: Sage.

Bond, T. (1994a) *Counselling, Confidentiality and the Law*. Rugby: British Association for Counselling.

Bond, T. (1994b) 'Ethical standards and the exploitation of clients', *Counselling, Journal of the British Association for Counselling*, 4 (3): Stop press 2–3.

British Association for Counsellors (1984, 1990, 1993) *Code of Ethics and Practice for Counsellors*. Rugby: BAC.

British Psychological Society (1993) 'A code of conduct for psychologists', *Code of Conduct, Ethical Principles and Guidelines*. Leicester: BPS.

British Psychological Society (1995) *Guidelines for the Professional Practice of Counselling Psychology*. Leicester: BPS.

Egan, G. (1994) *The Skilled Helper: A Problem-Management Approach to Helping*. Monterey, CA: Brooks/Cole.

Herlihy, B. and Corey, G. (1992) *Dual Relationships in Counseling*. Alexandria, VA: American Association for Counseling and Development.

Hofstede, G. (1980) *Cultures Consequences: International Differences in Work Related Values*. Beverly Hills, CA: Sage.

House, R. (1996) 'General practice counselling: a plea for ideological engagement', *Counselling, Journal of the British Association for Counselling*, 7 (1): 40–3.

Inskipp, F. and Proctor, B. (1989) *Skills for Supervising and Being Supervised*. St Leonards on Sea: Alexia Publications.

Jehu, D. (1994) *Patients as Victims: Sexual Abuse in Psychotherapy and Counselling*. Chichester: John Wiley.

Lago, C. and Thompson, J. (1996) *Race, Culture and Counselling*. London: Sage.

Obholzer, A. and Roberts, V.Z. (1994) *The Unconscious at Work: Individual and Organizational Stress in the Human Services*. London: Routledge.

Pope, K.S., Sonne, J.L. and Holroyd, J. (1993) *Sexual Feelings in Psychotherapy: Explorations for Therapists and Therapists in Training*. Washington, DC: American Psychological Association.

Rowan, J. (1983) *The Reality Game – A Guide to Humanistic Counselling and Therapy*. London: Routledge Kegan and Paul.

Russell, J. (1993) *Out of Bounds: Sexual Exploitation in Psychotherapy and Counselling*. London: Sage.

Standing Conference on Drug Abuse/Alcohol Concern (1994) *Building Confidence – Advice for Alcohol and Drug Services on Confidentiality Policies*. London: SCODA.

Thompson, A. (1990) *Guide to Ethical Practice in Psychotherapy*. New York: John Wiley.

United Kingdom Council for Psychotherapy (1993) *Ethical Guidelines*. London: UKCP.

12

Evaluating and Auditing Workplace Counselling Programmes

Carolyn Highley-Marchington and Cary L. Cooper

In the USA, the financial and other benefits of stress-care are widely recognized and most of the Fortune 500 companies have employee counselling services in place. UK companies are now also recognizing that by helping employees cope with stress they may be able to reduce absenteeism, improve morale and ultimately boost profitability. Employee Assistance Programmes (EAPs) and workplace counselling programmes in general, are human resource strategies which may help to combat the now well-recognized human and organizational costs of workplace stress, and with the growing acceptability and use of counselling in UK organizations, there is an increasing demand for information on the effectiveness of workplace counselling programmes.

The potential benefits of counselling for the individual in distress include improved mental well-being, better functioning at work, and enhanced job and life satisfaction; and for the organization they potentially include a reduction in sickness absence, unwanted turnover and accident rates, and improvements in internal communication, Health and Safety, and external PR (in being perceived as 'caring employers'). Most larger companies in the UK are therefore beginning to see counselling in the workplace not as an additional cost, but as a possible investment. This is almost certainly true in the medium to long term, although convincing measures of the benefit are not yet available in the UK. Because no conclusive evaluations have yet been done in this country, some UK employers are sceptical about the benefits, particularly financial, of stress counselling schemes.

Since most EAPs were created in an era of increased accountability and because of their relationship to cost-consciousness for profit organizations, one would expect EAPs to generate many evaluation studies. In fact, researchers (Knott, 1986) in this field seem to be still searching for identity, direction, methodologies and information. Most EAPs attempt to assist employees in a variety of ways, and this mixture of hard and soft benefits, and their simultaneous provision to the same employees, makes the identification of a clear 'outcome orientated intervention' model difficult, if not impossible. The greater the variety of interventions and services provided to employees, the greater the vagueness of defining the impact and outcome of such interventions.

In the UK, evaluations tend to be almost exclusively qualitative in nature, other than basic statistical reports on usage rates and the like. However, in the USA there has been a move away from such anecdotal evidence of EAP effectiveness towards insisting upon hard data (that is cost-benefit ratios). 'Almost every company with an EAP in the US is subjecting it to close scrutiny in terms of cost-benefit, utilisation and success rate. All sorts of bottom line questions are being asked' (Bickerton, 1990). In the future, this type of hard data is likely to be demanded by UK companies as well.

US Studies

A number of evaluations has been conducted in the USA, with varying degrees of scientific rigour.

One of the most ambitious and sophisticated cost-benefit evaluations was undertaken by the US Department of Health and Human Services 'Employee Counselling Service' (ECS) Programme. It required the cooperation of ECS programmes in 16 operating units throughout the USA, that were providing services to the Department's 150,000 staff. ECS counsellors saw in excess of 2,500 troubled employees during the 30-month period of evaluation. The evaluation had a number of important aspects: confidentiality of clients was guaranteed; the evaluation was compatible with existing policies and pro-cedures; the minimum burden was placed on EAP staff; feedback was given to management to aid decision-making; the design was rigorous so that results were credible (this was achieved by collecting individual level data); and the emphasis was on outcome (that is, cost-benefit). Employees who had not used the EAP were the control group and were selected in terms of unit, sex, age and salary level. Cost-benefit analyses revealed that: the estimated cost per client was $991; the estimated benefits in six months was $1,274 per employee served; and for every dollar spent the return in six months was $1.29. Ultimately, the programme should realize a $7.01 return per dollar invested (Maiden, 1988).

McDonnell Douglas (1989) commissioned a financial impact study which was an independently conducted, scientifically valid cost-benefit analysis. It involved the longitudinal analysis of the costs associated with healthcare claims and absenteeism for a four-year period (1985–88), before and after an EAP intervention. Each client was matched to 10 other employees on six demographic variables, thus establishing an appropriate control group. The research did not try to measure the financial impact of factors which could not be objectively and concretely measured – soft dollar items such as produc-tivity, job performance level, replacement labour costs and other subjective data were ignored. The result was therefore the most conservative possible study outcome. The overall saving for the EAP population (compared to the control) was $5.1 million and the return on investment was 4:1 dollars.

McClellan (1989) reports on the cost-benefit study carried out as part of an overall evaluation of the Ohio State EAP. No evidence of reduced health insurance costs were found and no reduction in sick time or employee turnover was evident either. Again, no control group was employed. All in all, the direct dollar value of the Ohio State EAP probably did not off-set its cost to the state government. However, the employees were very satisfied with the service, and so as an employee benefit, it had some value.

Nadolski and Sandonato (1987) examined the work performance of employees referred to the EAP for counselling, over a six-month period, at the Detroit Edison Company. The measures used were lost time (instances and number of days), health insurance claims, discipline warnings and accidents, all of which are generally accepted as accurate work performance measures. A measure of work productivity was also developed for use with those clients referred by their supervisor. A longitudinal, comparative study was used and data was collected for employees at initial entry to the EAP (for six months up to that point) and for six months following treatment. A sample of 67 employees was used – 31 supervisory referrals and 36 self-referrals. Instances of lost time had reduced by 18 per cent and the number of days had reduced by 29 per cent. There was a reduction in health insurance claims of 26 per cent and written warnings had improved by 13 per cent. There was also a 40 per cent improvement in suspensions and a 41 per cent improvement in the number of job-related accidents. In addition, the quality of work had improved by 14 per cent, the quantity of work by 7 per cent, peer relationships by 7 per cent and relationship with supervisor by 13 per cent. Unfortunately, no control group was used with this piece of research.

Chicago Bell credits its EAP for slashing its poor performance ratings from 28 to 12 per cent. In 1984, the EAP saved the company almost $500,000 in reduced sickness and disability absences (Pope, 1990). Masi (1984) summarizes that overall 'EAPs average a 3:1 return on the dollar'.

UK Studies

Even though findings from US studies have indicated generally positive outcomes, calls for good quality and independent evaluative research are increasing. Despite the enormity of the potential benefits of services, there is still a paucity of information about workplace counselling services in the UK, and an even greater lack of robust research substantiating their effectiveness, although more and more research is being commissioned.

One of the first evaluations to take place in the UK was carried out in the Post Office (Cooper and Sadri, 1991). The study systematically assessed the impact of stress counselling among postal workers, from shop-floor level to senior management. The research found that there were significant declines, from pre- to post-counselling, in sickness absence days and events, clinical anxiety levels, somatic anxiety and depression, and increases in self-esteem. The sample was 250 employees who had counselling over a one-year period. A control group was used and showed no changes over the study period.

The first nationwide independent evaluation of British EAPs and workplace counselling programmes has just been completed at The Manchester School of Management (Highley and Cooper, 1995). This research was commissioned by the Health and Safety Executive in order to evaluate what the effects of counselling were at both the individual and organizational levels. This research is presented in detail in Chapter 16, but the results are summarized here.

The mental and physical health of clients was found to have improved significantly from pre- to post-counselling. However, there were no effects on job satisfaction or perceived stress at work. An un-matched control group showed no significant differences for mental or physical health. Thus, while the mental and physical health of clients improved after counselling, no improvement was detected for the control group. There were some differences in terms of the results for internal and external counselling services. The data from this research suggested that the internal counselling services are having the greatest effects. There was a significant reduction in both the number of absence events and the total number of days absence, from pre- to post-counselling, but there was no such reduction for the control group.

Intuitively, one would expect that if a significant proportion of employees are reporting the early resolution of potentially serious problems and returning to work, then this must show up on the bottom line. It is a virtual impossibility to obtain purely quantitative proof, and so the decision to give an EAP or workplace counselling programme a try is still more often a leap of faith than a measured decision. Given that many employers in the UK, are not just concerned with showing a return on investment, this is likely to remain the case. Many UK companies are, quite rightly, primarily concerned about the human factor.

Evaluation

The importance of evaluating a workplace counselling programme (whether provided externally or in-house) cannot be overestimated. Many programmes must be assessed to justify their existence to some external authority, and even if this is not the case, they should be evaluated to ascertain the extent to which they are reaching their objectives, and to find ways to improve their effectiveness. The goals of any workplace counselling service or EAP should be built in from the beginning, and it is essential for organizations to be able to evaluate whether or not those goals are being met.

Outcome Evaluation/Effectiveness

Workplace counselling programmes rely on the premise that well-run services do help staff in distress, and, as a consequence, help the organization and pay for themselves in the long run. However, this assumption should not be made automatically, as every organizational context is different. It is essential to evaluate the 'whole service', in order to show that this assumption is indeed valid in the particular organization involved. *Outcome evaluation* is needed to ensure that the service is correctly designed for the organization in which it is operating, and that it is meeting the needs of that organization and its employees. Encompassed within this should be an analysis of organizational 'bottom-line' personnel data, such as sickness absence and unwanted turnover, because it is necessary to be able to establish a link between counselling employees and personnel performance criteria (Reddy, 1993). Outcome evaluation can encompass a whole range of activities which include evaluating effectiveness, cost-benefits, cost-efficiency and cost-effectiveness.

Maiden (1988) believes that one of the critical concerns of this constantly growing field is the need for comprehensive programme evaluations to demonstrate the cost-effectiveness and cost-benefits of EAPs and workplace counselling in general. Indeed, there is increasing pressure, both political and economic, to evaluate the cost of interventions. As workplace counselling becomes more of an everyday occurrence in the UK, organizations will increasingly be expected to justify their spending and evaluation is essential for this.

Effectiveness of counselling is concerned with whether those who receive treatment improve. Pre- and post-counselling comparison is one way of evaluating effectiveness, the aim being to show that a change has occurred following counselling. However, difficulties arise in attributing change solely to counselling, because counselling is not the only thing which is taking place – other major influences may account for the change. To help address this a proper control group is needed (Barkham, 1991).

Cost-benefit analysis aims to evaluate costs and benefits solely in monetary terms. However, there are doubts about the validity of converting psychological outcomes into monetary terms (Barkham, 1991). It is useful to distinguish between 'hard' and 'soft' data. Hard data (for example, absence and performance) tends to be quantifiable, whereas soft data (for example, client self-report measures – both quantitative and qualitative) is less easy to verify independently. However, verification is possible using third-party sources, so that reliance is not being placed solely on the client's perspective.

Cost-efficiency involves comparing two or more interventions in terms of the cost of achieving a specific outcome (for example, getting an individual back to work) and *cost-effectiveness* looks at more unspecified outcomes (for example, psychological well-being). The aim of the latter is to establish which intervention achieves the best therapeutic results in relation to the cost of implementation.

In light of evidence of diminishing returns as the number of counselling sessions continue (Howard and Szczerbacki, 1988), decisions have to be made as to how limited resources are best utilized to achieve the maximum therapeutic effect for people at work (Barkham, 1991).

The evaluation of counselling services/EAPs is the goal of both academics and business alike (Megranahan, 1993). Counselling providers simply want to prove that counselling works and has some quantifiable benefit so that organizations will buy counselling services. Such a motivation gave rise to many of the US studies cited earlier and, as a consequence, many of the studies are methodologically weak and somewhat biased since they have been undertaken by organizations wanting to show particular results (Megranahan,

1993). Academics attempt to measure scientifically the counselling process and to give insight into the value of counselling by showing something which is tangible from an activity which is intangible.

Process Evaluation/Audit

Companies need to know that the EAP or workplace counselling programme is running smoothly and that the efficiency and quality of the service is high. While such *process evaluation* or *audit* is an essential basis for continued improvement and development of the service, it does not measure 'value for money' or whether the service is effective, as with outcome evaluation.

Audit is concerned with assessing the running of the service and includes scrutinizing procedures, checking that counsellors are sufficiently well trained, and ensuring that the organization is getting what it is paying for. Such audits are invaluable, but must be carried out independently of the provider and the organization. Audit allows the quality of the service to be monitored and changes made where appropriate. Workplace counselling programmes need to be audited/assessed in terms of the appropriateness, effectiveness and efficiency of internal operations. In the USA all EAPs are regularly audited and some organizations in the UK have also commissioned audits.

Audit of this type is based on the premise that a quality workplace counselling programme, which has a consistent and effective service delivery, also needs to have a coordinated and standardized set of policies, procedures and services for both the administration and operation of the service. These need to be developed in response to programme objectives and organizational needs. A programme designed in such a way should prove both viable and effective for customer organizations and their employees. Audit is concerned with verifying that this is the case. Auditing policies and procedures serve to improve the quality and effectiveness of workplace counselling programmes.

The numbers and qualifications of staff must match programme needs and all staff must be qualified to perform their duties and have clearly defined descriptions of their roles and responsibilities. The quality of provision of a counselling service depends on the professional qualifications, training and experience of its practitioners and counsellors. Staff competence is critical to programme success. In addition, there is a need to match the client, who has an identified problem, with the appropriate level of support. Accurate assessment, intervention or referral will increase the likelihood of employee well-being and improved job performance.

Workplace counselling programmes need to be positioned in order to maximize the value of their benefits in the human resource and organizational areas. There is a need to ensure that the service functions as an integral yet independent part of the organization and that it offers support to all involved in change and other company developments. It needs to be positioned at an organizational level where it can be most effective and where it can gain support and endorsement from all levels of management. Workplace counselling programmes operate at their optimum when they are fully integrated with internal organizational structures. Linkages within the organization should maximize programme effectiveness. All these issues are addressed as part of a comprehensive audit.

Methodological and Practical Problems Associated with Evaluation

Clearly once the decision has been made to go ahead with an evaluation, there are many obstacles to be overcome. Evaluations which are not rigorously designed are difficult to compare with other findings because:

- Problems exist in terms of defining what constitutes a problem.
- The nature of the counselling process varies.
- There are inherent differences both between and within EAPs and workplace counselling programmes.
- There is no universally accepted definition of success.
- The way in which services are costed varies.

Sonnenstuhl and Trice (1986) expand upon the possible reasons for the paucity of counselling evaluation research. They too believe that it is understandable for a variety of reasons. Evaluation research is both time-consuming and expensive, counsellors are generally more orientated to treatment than research, and the issue of confidentiality has made it difficult for outside researchers to evaluate programmes. The relative lack of evaluation is also due to the difficulty which researchers have in gaining access to programmes. Counselling services are particularly sensitive research sites because programme staff, management, union representatives and clients are all likely to resist the encroachment of outside evaluators. Those who attempt to conduct research in occupational contexts are often put off by the relatively complex relationships that must be negotiated. Evaluation studies require effort and cooperation among researchers, work organizations and counselling service providers. It also requires the recognition that they have a common obligation (moral and legal) to protect the employees' rights to privacy and the anonymity of the programmes studied. However, without access to the everyday experiences of managers, employees and counsellors, researchers cannot understand what happens in workplace counselling services and cannot develop concepts reflective of reality or useful to practitioners. In addition, counselling service providers do often attempt to evaluate their own programmes, but this is a practice fraught with the irresistible temptations to make one's programme look good.

Holosko (1988) closely examined the literature and found that the lack of attention directed towards why workplace counselling works or does not work is conspicuous. More specifically, there is a distinct literature void related to scientifically based evaluations of workplace counselling.

The major practical problems with carrying out counselling evaluation research in organizations are: questionnaire administration; selecting a comparison group; confidentiality; extracting 'hard' data from company records; and gaining access to providers and organizations.

The questionnaire. Although self-report measures are a useful means of determining the level of effectiveness of counselling, if too many different measures are used, then it can be difficult to compare different services. It is better to devise a 'core battery' (for example, the Occupational Stress Indicator or the General Health Questionnaire) for which normative data is available (Barkham, 1991).

When designing evaluation questionnaires there is a need to balance the length of the questionnaire against the depth of information gleaned from it. If the questionnaire is seen as too lengthy by providers, organizations and/or counsellors, it is likely to affect adversely the response rate. The effective use of multivariate, inferential statistics requires large sample sizes. So, for findings to be of value, it is essential that enough individuals who have been through the counselling process are assessed, to enable meaningful statistical analyses to be carried out.

A customer feedback section for those individuals who have gone through the counselling process collects users' views of the service (in terms of perceived helpfulness of counsellors, perceived quality of service provision and perceived positive benefits both at home and at work). This section can be viewed quite sceptically by some counsellors, who believe that this may be used to monitor their individual performance.

The control group. One of the common criticisms of research evaluating the effectiveness of programmes aimed at enhancing well-being, is that many factors other than the treatment programme itself can influence the results. This criticism is particularly valid when no comparison group is used. In order for an evaluation to be strong methodologically, the research therefore needs to demonstrate not only that benefits exist, but that these benefits can be attributed to the provision of counselling. Without comparative data from individuals who have not used the programme, it is extremely difficult to disentangle effects due to the counselling process from those due to factors related to the individual being counselled.

However, the controlled experimental approach is comparable with the clinical trial in medical research, and the use of this approach requires a situation in which it is possible to deny the programme to some individuals (control group) and the researcher randomly assigns individuals to each group. One cannot withhold treatment from a group of potentially stressed people, particularly when the basis of workplace counselling programmes is largely voluntary self-referral.

Even in situations where controls do exist, they may not be comparable. There is a need for longitudinal research which incorporates time and repeated measurement, both of which are necessary if we are to learn whether or not positive results are maintained.

Shapiro et al. (1993) believe that workplace counselling evaluation research is promising, but not conclusive. They see the main problem as being the absence or inadequacy of control groups. Those individuals who seek psychological help have massive fluctuations over time, and also tend to seek help when they feel at their worst. As such, improvement over time is somewhat inevitable, whether counselling occurs or not. A comparison group over a similar period is needed to demonstrate the effectiveness of the help received. However, they are unhappy about using a comparison group of people not seeking help, because these people are likely to be much more psychologically healthy to begin with, so improvement over time is less likely. They assert that control groups of this type therefore tell us very little about the effectiveness of the treatment. According to Shapiro et al. (1993), more studies are needed which randomly allocate those seeking help to one of two groups, either immediate or delayed help. However, this is a virtual impossibility given that British workplace counselling programmes operate on the basis of self-referral and immediate access to counselling.

Swanson and Murphy (1991) believe that, in reality, every member of an organization where a workplace counselling programme is present is a waiting-list control, since they may at any time refer themselves to the service, and there is no reason to assume that those who do not refer themselves are less stressed, because in a free choice situation not everyone who may benefit from counselling will opt to use the services. Ideally, though, one needs more than one control group, maybe from another site of similar size, engaged in a similar activity, from the same organization, where the service is not available. In the absence of this possibility, normative databases are an appropriate comparison group for some outcome measures, but the organizational factors specific to each case will be ignored by this.

Barkham (1991) suggests that each client can be used as his/her own control if at least one baseline measure is established, for each client, at some time prior to counselling. With only one pre-counselling measure it is not possible to determine how stable the measure is, whereas two pre-counselling measures give a summary about change so that it is possible to gauge whether or not improvement is occurring because of the client's expectation of counselling. However, three pre-counselling measures is ideal, according to Barkham, because it gives a much better idea of stability.

The use and selection of the comparison group, therefore, is a major problem. In addition, providers are generally unwilling or unable to select these individuals from company records, because they then have access to the names and addresses of people not using the service. When a comparison group is being used, the questionnaires should be sent to the employees' home. This ensures that individuals are not wrongly assumed to be using the counselling service by other staff members, who may catch sight of the questionnaire and jump to the wrong conclusion.

Confidentiality. A longitudinal research design can present problems on ethical grounds. This relates to the issue of confidentiality, the main barrier to rigorous evaluation designs. It has been suggested that trust in confidentiality and the perception of a service being truly confidential is the cornerstone of a successful workplace counselling programme (Feldman, 1991). Employees have a right to confidentiality, where any data from them is protected from others.

Balgopal and Patchner (1988) believe that there are a number of obstructions that a researcher will encounter in conducting an evaluation, and perhaps the most difficult issue is that of confidentiality and employee privacy. Because of societal values about many problems, employees are reluctant to seek assistance from counselling programmes. This reluctance is further compounded if they are not guaranteed that the data shared by them will be kept in complete confidence.

Since the assurance of confidentiality is crucial to the success of the service, many providers are understandably wary about releasing sensitive employee data to researchers. Masi (1984) reinforces the fact that the reputation of the programme could be destroyed if employees perceive the evaluation negatively. Strict adherence to the principle of confidentiality, in some way, limits the amount of data an evaluator can obtain, but preserves the integrity of the employees, the programme and the researcher.

While preserving the confidentiality and respecting the privacy of employees, the evaluation process should be conducted openly, with the purpose of the research fully explained. There is a need to clarify that evaluation results will not reveal the personal identity of any employees. Having a comparison group of individuals not using the service can create problems because the individual may accidentally be perceived as a client by others. It is thus essential to protect all individuals taking part in the study. Unfortunately, these procedures are perceived as additional chores by providers/counsellors, who therefore resist participating in evaluation research involving rigorous methodology. There is no easy solution except that the benefit of such research has to be conveyed as a payoff for all.

Organizational level data.   For evaluation at the organizational level, access to individual absenteeism/sickness absence rates is desirable, because such measures enhance the rigour of the evaluation by minimizing the dangers inherent in relying on subjective, self-reported data. However, many UK organizations do not monitor absenteeism. A 1991 survey by Arthur Anderson estimated that 40 per cent of UK business fall into this category. This is despite an estimated annual cost of absenteeism to UK industry of £6 billion. Adequate evaluations cannot be conducted objectively unless adequate data is recorded by companies to make the evaluation of 'hard' data possible. However, organizational data, even in summary form, is still useful.

Even if records are available, access to individual employee records is not always seen as acceptable by organizations, on ethical grounds. There are severe problems, therefore, in gaining access to records. Even if access is granted, there is always some debate about exactly who should extract the data. The extraction of such data is very difficult and requires detailed discussions with providers, the organization, the union and any other relevant parties, to come up with an acceptable formula. Internal counselling services tend to have an advantage in this respect. Internal counsellors, employed by the organization, have access to personnel records and can therefore extract the necessary data on their clients. They are also in a very good position to select comparisons, because they know what characteristics to match the individuals on. They are also bound by an implicit code of ethics, so confidentiality is ensured.

Access to providers and organizations. Traditionally, EAP providers in the USA, and here in the UK, have resisted any form of evaluation by stating that the benefits of counselling cannot be quantified. McDonnell Douglas believe that 'this myth is perpetuated because providers are fearful that results may not be favourable' (1989).

Knott (1986), who evaluates US EAPs, says that she hits 'a wall of resistance' when she talks to EAP providers, probably because evaluation is inherently threatening. Providers/counsellors may be hesitant about the evaluation outcome and concerned that the results may not positively reflect their programmes. Balgopal and Patchner suggest that 'these dynamics may not only bias the research, but also impede the endeavour' (1988). Swanson and Murphy (1991) have also suggested that EAP providers are unwilling to be evaluated by independent researchers because it is threatening to their business. Further, Sonnenstuhl and Trice (1986) believe that EAP providers often assume the effectiveness of their EAPs automatically, and EAP personnel are therefore apt to put a rather low priority on programme evaluation.

Kurtz et al. (1984) believe that providers and counsellors often do not see evaluation as part of their mission. By virtue of their professional training and commitment, they have confidence in the efficacy of their work and place low priority on the need to confirm the validity of their services. As Kurtz et al. suggest, 'if the evaluation is in the hands of independent outsiders who may not understand or be sensitive to the intentions of their profession, their enthusiasm is even more diminished' (1984). If a provider does not really want to participate, and hence their commitment to the research is lacking, there is no guarantee that the providers/counsellors will fully cooperate in facilitating data collection either.

Orlans (1991) points out that while the overall goals of different programmes may be the same (or a least compatible) the way in which the goal is met – staffing, basis for referral, assessment, implementation – might differ. Indeed, in a competitive market it is necessary for providers to be able to distinguish themselves from one another; therefore, no two programmes are ever the same. For competitive survival reasons and to be effective, the service must tailor its services to the requirements of the organization in which it operates and be responsive to the needs of the individuals within the organization. All these factors make a uniform evaluation of their effectiveness complex and open to the influence of any confounding factors that one cannot control. It also means that some providers are reluctant to allow an independent researcher into their organization, for fear that information may be passed on to others. It is thus important that independent researchers can demonstrate credibility, particularly in terms of confidentiality.

Client organizations. These can also be very reluctant to participate in research. Their reluctance stems from a number of different concerns. Some organizations implement a counselling service as a public relations exercise to 'show they care'. They may not, therefore, be particularly interested in its effectiveness. In some organizations, the usefulness of the service has been heavily motivated by a particular individual, who has fought hard to get the counselling service implemented. This person potentially has a lot to lose, therefore, if the service is shown to be either ineffective or not worth the cost. As discussed, 'confidentiality' can be a problem. Apart from the issue of client confidentiality, some organizations are keen that their name should not be associated with the research because they do not want to be perceived by the outside world as a 'stressed organization'. Also, most organizations take it for granted that programmes are effective. They are assured by providers that counselling is effective, and because other organizations have them they don't perceive a need to invest in their own evaluation.

Masi (1984) believes that confidentiality can be used as a defence against having an evaluation. People can be threatened by the thought of being evaluated and will try to think of reasons why an evaluation cannot be done. According to her, 'a major battle emerges between those who apply pressure for the programme to demonstrate its effectiveness and those who claim that documentation is impossible' (Masi, 1984). Unfortunately, providers often do not realize that evaluation can help them 'sell' their programmes. In most cases they are providing valuable, needed services and evaluations can help them demonstrate this.

Qualitative vs quantitative data. Due to the possible inappropriateness and problems inherent in trying to evaluate scientifically counselling at work, some authors are now calling for a more qualitative approach to be adopted, in conjunction with more quantitative approaches. Orlans (1991) believes that the evaluation literature provides insufficient data to assess the differences between schemes and relate these to research outcomes in any systematic way. Many aspects of human existence and experience are not objective, or easily quantifiable, and EAPs/counselling services are operating at precisely this level. In her opinion, increasing attention should therefore be given to qualitative research methods for gaining insight into what it is one is dealing with. She believes that it is no good solely concentrating on those factors that can be easily identified, when less tangible factors are certainly involved. By ignoring these less tangible factors one is not fully evaluating the effectiveness of workplace counselling. Certainly, soft factors are hard to measure, but that does not make them invalid or outside the scope of any research that claims to be evaluating the effectiveness of a counselling service. One commonly accepted view of stress is that it is in the eye of the beholder, so, according to Orlans, we should be talking to the people involved, getting their views and, having gained this insight, should not call it unreliable and put it to one side. Teram (1988) also calls for a greater emphasis on qualitative research methods and points to the value of such data in evaluations, precisely because EAPs usually have multiple interventions coupled with poorly defined success criteria.

Organizational framework of evaluation. Some researchers have pointed towards the need for more research before a service is introduced. Kim (1988) says that most evaluation reports are so much concerned with the specific aspects of components of EAPs that they tend to lose sight of the totality, context or framework of the evaluation. Utilization analysis is more informative and useful as an evaluative tool, if utilization rates can be compared to some pre-determined measure of 'need' (that is, prevalence of problems prior to the introduction of the service). One can only sensibly ask if a programme is being successful in meeting the needs of a particular organization's employees, if you have some idea of how many distressed employees you have got within the organization and what their needs are.

Outcome evaluation can thus make a significant contribution to the further development of good quality and 'value for money' EAPs and workplace counselling programmes in the UK. However, to what extent complete evaluations are demanded by organizations will depend to a large extent on the organization's reasons for initially implementing a counselling service. For some organizations, a workplace counselling programme is seen as a 'company benefit', which should also help their corporate image. In such cases, organizations are unlikely to feel the need for outcome research or the need to justify the cost of the service. Nevertheless, whatever the reason for implementation, companies should ensure that they receive value for money, that the service is being run efficiently and to a high standard, and that the service is designed in a way which best meets the need of the organization and its employees.

Conclusion

Myers (1984) believes that in the haste and enthusiasm which often accompany the development and implementation of workplace counselling programmes, evaluation planning is either ignored or assigned a low priority on the list of things to do. It appears that the importance of investing in evaluations has been temporarily obscured by the unprecedented growth and popularity of the programmes. However, as the novelty and excitement of the initial growth of the movement subsides, there will be an increased demand for documentation of the benefits of workplace counselling.

Research could help spur the growth of EAPs and workplace counselling programmes as management see financial benefits. Kurtz et al. (1984) summarize by stating that: 'In the end, quality evaluations will develop only to the extent that researchers are willing to adapt their approach to occupational contexts, programme staff take the lead in assisting researchers to navigate the politically treacherous current of the workplace and that organisational leaders accept such assessments as routine responsibility.'

References

Arthur Anderson Survey (1991) 'Absence rate is EC worst', *Independent on Sunday*, 20 October.
Balgopal, P.R. and Patchner, M.A. (1988) 'Evaluating Employee Assistance Programs: obstacles, issues and strategies', *Employee Assistance Quarterly*, 3 (3/4): 95–105. (Special Issue: Evaluation of Employee Assistance Programs).

Barkham, M. (1991) 'Understanding, implementing and presenting counselling evaluation', in R. Bayne and P. Nicholson (eds), *Psychology and Counselling for Health Professionals*. London: Chapman and Hall.

Bickerton, R. (1990) 'Why EAPs are worth the investment', in L. Stern (ed.), *Business and Health*, pp. 14–19.

Cooper, C.L. and Sadri, G. (1991) 'The impact of stress counselling at work', *Journal of Social Behaviour and Personality*, 6 (7): 411–23. (Special Issue: Handbook on Job Stress, ed. P.L. Perrewe.)

Feldman, S. (1991) 'Trust me: earning employee confidence', *Personnel*, 68 (2): 7.

Highley, J.C. and Cooper, C.L. (1995) 'An assessment and evaluation of employee assistance and workplace counselling programmes in British organizations'. Unpublished report for the Health and Safety Executive.

Holosko, M.J. (1988) 'Perspectives for Employee Assistance Program evaluations: a case for more thoughtful evaluation planning', *Employee Assistance Quarterly*, 3 (3/4): 59–68. (Special Issue: Evaluation of Employee Assistance Programs.)

Howard, J.C. and Szczerbacki, D. (1988) 'Employee Assistance Programs in the hospital industry', *Health Care Management Review*, Spring.

Kim, D.S. (1988) 'Assessing EAPs: evaluation, typology and models', *Employee Assistance Quarterly*, 3 (3/4): 169–87. (Special Issue: Evaluation of Employee Assistance Programs.)

Knott, T.D. (1986) 'The distinctive uses of evaluation and research: a guide for the occupational health care movement', *Employee Assistance Quarterly*, 1 (4): 43–51.

Kurtz, N.R., Googins, B. and Howard, W.C. (1984) 'Measuring the success of occupational alcoholism programs', *Journal of Studies on Alcohol*, 45: 33–45.

Maiden, R.P. (1988) 'EAP evaluation in a federal government agency', *Employee Assistance Quarterly*, 3 (3/4): 191–203. (Special Issue: Evaluation of Employee Assistance Programs.)

Masi, D.A. (1984) *Designing Employee Assistance Programs*. New York: AMACOM.

McClellan, K. (1989) 'Cost benefit analysis of the Ohio EAP', *Employee Assistance Quarterly*, 5 (2): 67–85.

McDonnell Douglas (1989) 'McDonnell Douglas Corporation's EAP Produces Hard Data', *The Almacan*, August: 18–26.

Megranahan, M. (1993) 'Editorial', *Employee Counselling Today*, 5 (5): 3.

Myers, D.W. (1984) *Establishing and Building Employee Assistance Programs*, Westport, CN: Quorum Books.

Nadolski, J.N. and Sandonato, C.E. (1987) 'Evaluation of an Employee Assistance Programme', *Journal of Occupational Medicine*, 29 (1): 32–7.

Orlans, V. (1991) 'Evaluating the benefits of Employee Assistance Programmes', *Employee Counselling Today*, 3 (4): 27–31.

Pope, T. (1990) 'EAPs: good idea, but what's the cost?', *Management Review*, 79 (8): 50–3.

Reddy, M. (1993) *EAPs and Counselling Provision in UK Organizations: An ICAS Report and Policy Guide*. Milton Keynes: ICAS.

Shapiro, D.A., Cheesman, M. and Wall, T.D. (1993) 'Secondary prevention – review of counselling and EAPs', Paper presented at Royal College of Physicians Conference on Mental Health at Work, 11 January, London.

Sonnenstuhl, W.J. and Trice, H.M. (1986) *Strategies for Employee Assistance Programs: The Crucial Balance*. Key Issues, No. 30, NY State School of Industrial and Labor Relations, Cornell University: ILR Press.

Swanson, N.G. and Murphy, L.R. (1991) 'Mental health counselling in industry', in C.L. Cooper and I.T. Robertson (eds), *International Review of Industrial and Organisational Psychology*, Vol. 6. Chichester: John Wiley. Chapter 7: 265–82.

Teram, E. (1988) 'Formative evaluation of Employee Assistance Programs by studying role perceptions and organisational cultures', *Employee Assistance Quarterly*, 3 (3/4): 119–28. (Special Issue Evaluation of Employee Assistance Programs.)

PART 4

RESEARCH INTO COUNSELLING IN ORGANIZATIONS

Part 4 draws together some recent research into counselling in organizations. Four of the five chapters are written from what were Masters dissertations. Catherine Carroll interviewed 12 employee counsellors and presents their views of how they see their roles and responsibilities in the workplace. Peter Martin, himself a counselling trainer, asked public sector managers to evaluate their training in counselling skills and its effects on their personal and professional lives. Annette Greenwood concentrated on how EAP counsellors viewed the stresses in their work-lives and traces connections between being a workplace counsellor and stress. Carolyn Highley and Cary Cooper present findings from their nationwide research into workplace counselling. Finally, Helen Fisher interviewed four managers of EAPs in the National Health Service and draws out themes and patterns in how they see their roles and their services.

13

Building Bridges: A Study of Employee Counsellors in the Private Sector

Catherine Carroll

I began this research prompted by a personal and professional quest. For five years I had worked as the in-house counsellor for the London office of a multinational company. Those years were marked by hard work, challenge, anxiety, excitement, exhaustion and satisfaction. Many times I felt as though I was treading unchartered waters, despite my strong medical and counselling background. It took quite an adjustment to adapt my counselling training into an organizational setting committed to making money.

Since my own experience raised a number of questions about employee counselling in the private sector, I wondered how others, doing similar jobs, would apply their knowledge and skills in this context. While counselling in the workplace is a growing industry, there are still relatively few in-house employee counselling services, especially in the private sector. In a sense, the few there are could legitimately call themselves the 'first generation' of employee counsellors. However, being first generation automatically means there are few maps to guide us, and we are, in a way, the pioneers for the future.

Hence this research. On the one hand, I wanted to document the experience of the first generation – tell it from their perspectives, be part of their struggles to make sense of their work. On the other hand, I hoped the research might supply a map, or at least some signposts, that future generations could use to build on the territory gained. This research is not about the employee counselling services that are provided as these are as diverse and as unique as the companies who parent them; it is about the counsellors, their thoughts and feelings, their values and principles, their views and perspectives.

A qualitative research method was chosen as the one best suited to undertake the task of entering the internal and subjective worlds of employee counsellors in the private sector. This methodology seemed to offer a number of advantages over more traditional quantitative methods. First, by allowing for no hypothesis, it looked towards illuminating what was there: there were no pre-suppositions about what might happen or what might be said. Secondly, there was no manipulation of the setting or the subjects: interviewees would talk for themselves and their perceptions would be the data of the research. And thirdly, this method seemed more in keeping with the whole area of counselling itself. Researcher and researched were on a quest together for meaning, making sense of, trying to understand, exploring, finding patterns. Such is the very stuff of counselling itself. The qualitative researcher has been likened to a caring companion in an empathic search.

Writing a chapter of 6,000 words from a research dissertation of 20,000 words presented dilemmas. I decided that the richest and most powerful part of the work was where employee counsellors were allowed to speak for themselves: so I have concentrated on the results section. Briefly, I interviewed 12 employee counsellors (six male and six female) from 12 different companies in the private sector. There were few, if any, other private sector companies employing in-house counsellors. Using a semi-structured interview, I asked them about:

1. Their perceptions of their roles and responsibilities as employee counsellors.
2. How they saw the interface between organization and counsellor.
3. What they thought were the training needs and requirements for being an employee counsellor today.

Each interview took approximately one and a quarter hours, was audio-taped, transcribed exactly, and copies sent to each interviewee with an invitation to change or amend. The transcripts were coded according to Grounded Theory (Strauss and Corbin, 1990). This entailed generating labels from the interviews, reducing these labels to underlying categories, and testing these categories/ themes against the data (using an expert in qualitative data analysis). What is included here are the categories and themes gleaned from the data. Direct quotations from interviewees are in italic. An overview of the categories and sub-categories is contained in Table 13.1.

1.   Roles and Responsibilities

The roles and responsibilities seen by employee counsellors as part of their jobs are presented under four headings: multiple roles, working with clients, agents of change, and personal responses to these dimensions.

1.1   Multiple Roles

The study revealed that all 12 participants were engaged in diverse roles within their organizations. The main roles were as follows:

- Ensuring counselling provision (all 12 interviewees).
- Advising line managers on approaching troubled employees (all 12 interviewees).
- Employee counselling (10 interviewees).
- Training and health education (10 interviewees).
- Advising the organization on policy matters (6 interviewees).
- Managerial responsibilities (6 interviewees).
- Welfare (5 interviewees).

Table 13.1   *Overview of categories and sub-categories*

1. **Roles and responsibilities**
   1.1   Multiple roles
   1.2   Working with clients
   1.2.1   Counselling orientation
   1.2.2   Support
   1.2.3   Client issues
   1.3   Agents of change
   1.4   Personal responses to multiple roles

2. **Counsellor attributes**
   2.1   Flexibility
   2.2   Pioneering
   2.3   Assertiveness
   2.4   Coping strategies: supervision and networking

3. **Organizational/counselling interface**
   3.1   Organizational culture
   3.2   Underlying motivation for counselling services
   3.3   Who is the client?
   3.4   Mediation
   3.5   Confidentiality
   3.6   Who owns clients' notes?

4. **Training needs**
   4.1   Personal qualities
   4.2   General counselling training
   4.3   Specialist areas
   4.4   Professional qualifications

- Case-work supervision (4 interviewees).
- Facilitating organizational change (3 interviewees).
- Critical incident de-briefing (3 interviewees).
- Research (1 interviewee).
- Advising on equal opportunities (1 interviewee).

There were a series of other roles that were intrinsic to the counselling services:

- Publicizing the provision of services.
- Educating staff about the role of counselling.
- Developing counselling provision.
- Monitoring effectiveness.
- Administration.
- Referral.
- Mediating between client and organization.

1.2   *Working with Clients*

Eleven interviewees emphasized that their primary task was to ensure counselling provision for staff. The twelfth, a medical social worker, saw formal counselling as a secondary task:

- *I suppose that the steady bit is the counselling work*
- *the main anchor of the role is the personal counselling*
- *I see my job as offering individual, confidential counselling*

1.2.1 Counselling orientation. A humanistic eclecticism was the preferred approach of 11 respondents: the twelfth was a cognitive-behaviourist whose remit is working with post-trauma. Most felt their eclectic stance was open to criticism by purists: *it sounds arrogant to say we are eclectic because that is usually an excuse for a mishmash of things which isn't the case.* However, interviewees believed firmly that the range of clients and issues presented warranted this theoretical approach. Most clients present with here-and-now crises requiring facilitative, focused, short-term work. The clients' needs determine the response:

- *we use a number of different approaches in particular problem areas, e.g., Egan, Murray–Parkes, Kubler–Ross, Heimler, depending on the client and their need*
- *I think each (approach) has its place depending on whatever the person is presenting and the resources of the person*

Most clients came for short-term problem-solving rather than for long-term therapy, and this was seen as appropriate for workplace counselling. Clients, too, perceived short-term work as both important and appropriate:

- *I have clients who come and they have one or two sessions and it is the most exhilarating thing in their life*
- *most clients are not looking for major personality restructuring*

Four counsellors had freedom to work in the long term with clients when warranted. Most of the respondents emphasized the establishment of a genuine therapeutic relationship with clients:

- *I'm more focused on the personal qualities: a preparedness to listen, a sensitivity, compassion, non-judgemental about them and their issues*
- *I don't think I could do what I am doing if there wasn't a genuine and sincere connection with the people who come*

The counselling relationship was seen to provide a boundaried and emotionally safe environment for the client.

1.2.2 Support. Several participants spoke of the importance of offering a 'supportive role'. These counsellors surmised that other practitioners may disapprove of this role, and interpret it as 'propping up', but there was a strong thread that in the workplace setting clients at times just needed support and a 'safe place to offload'. Such support allowed the individual to remain working through difficult times (*counselling is sometimes just ongoing support . . . some people might pooh-pooh that. I think, well, if it keeps the person in work and functioning, then it is worthwhile for a business to have it*). Interviewees saw themselves as not only offering a therapeutic counselling relationship, but providing *a more humanitarian space, and an oasis in an organization that is not very human at times*).

One participant, although not religious, likened counselling at times to being a military chaplain, or working in a MASH unit where the tough environment called for *the quick, decisive intervention, the slap-on-the-band-aid and get them back*. This analogy fits with all the respondents who see themselves as regularly dealing with clients in crisis, requiring a swift but correct assessment followed by appropriate intervention:

– *I have a lot of experience in terms of assessment and I think that's one of the key things in our job . . . its working in crisis and not being panicked*

These crises can be personal or directly work-related, especially in dealing with the occupational hazards of armed robberies.

1.2.3 Client issues. The various services from which interviewees came provided counselling on a range of personal and work-related issues. These included family as well as personal and work relationships, and ill-health. Legal issues and debt counselling also featured, although most services had made arrangements for appropriate referral. It was often the counsellor's task to act as 'gatekeeper' for such functions.

One interviewee wondered whether or not counselling and advice services could co-exist comfortably (*on the one hand you are saying to people I can help you, I've got knowledge and I will tell you what to do and where to go. But I am also a counsellor and I won't do that*). Most programmes had built up advice and information services, and saw this as a logical complement to counselling.

1.3   Agents of Change

All participants saw themselves as agents of change. A recurrent theme of influencing change within the organization emerged. Six respondents were actively committed to this while others looked to develop this aspect. Facilitating organizational change was perceived as a proactive, preventive measure to complement reactive responses to distress:

– *I would far rather be involved in mending the road to the cliff, so that people don't keep going over the edge . . . that work is very much to do with group intervention*
– *I think the biggest reward from it all has been the ability to change what was a very paternalistic, very traditional, conservative, and rather stubborn organizational approach to their staff, and therefore to their working practices*

1.4   Personal Responses to Multiple Roles

A strong sense of personal and professional satisfaction emerged from all counsellors. This was particularly true in regard to their counselling work:

- *I think for me the satisfaction is watching individuals grow . . . that for me is the biggest kick*
- *one of the things that energized me all the way through was seeing people change*
- *it feels great. I get enormous satisfaction about getting people better. I'm not ashamed to admit it*

In addition, participants saw their job as affording them the opportunity to embody deeply held personal beliefs:

- *I was able to try to fulfil one of my ideas about how life could be within the workplace*
- *it's fulfilled my own personal dream . . . intellectually, professionally, and from a personal point of view it's extraordinarily rewarding*
- *the rewards are putting something in place which I thought and talked and lectured and researched for a long time, and that's a tremendous buzz*
- *one of the reasons I work within a company is because everybody in that can get service free at the point of issue, and that's something I feel very strongly about*

All participants liked having a repertoire of roles in which to engage. Although these were professionally and personally demanding in terms of time and energy, there was a sense in which they enjoyed this challenge:

- *the biggest buzz is not knowing what the hell is going to happen . . . the variety in this job, particularly*
- *I go through that door with some pleasure and wondering what's in store*
- *you've got lots of things just on the simmer, on the boil, and you've got all these pots you've got to keep your eye on, and you've just got to encourage them at the right moment . . . it requires a lot of effort and attention as well*

The one relationship that participants felt would preclude a counselling relationship was that of friendship:

- *if I was a friend with somebody in the company, somebody else may be inhibited because they would think I would share [anything they might say] with the friend*
- *keeping the specialized counselling role available to people means having close professional relationships but not exceeding those*

Three counsellors referred to material benefits gained from working in the private sector. These included access to resources and working environment. They were particularly impressed by the trust, autonomy and care they experienced in the business world: 'people in business, for all the myths about it being hard-nosed, competitive, aggressive, they actually take far more active measures to look after staff than the so-called caring public services'.

2.   Counsellor Attributes

The in-house counsellors interviewed were generally well trained in several relevant professional and academic fields and were experienced in working with clients from a variety of backgrounds and with a variety of problems. A number of personal characteristics emerged from the interviews. The most frequent were:

● Flexibility.
● Pioneering.
● Assertiveness.

2.1   *Flexibility*

Flexibility and crisis management emerged as qualities seen by interviewees in themselves. Not being easily scared and responding in adaptable ways were seen to be necessary to workplace counselling. Being confronted by an anxious manager, dealing with stressed, depressed, psychotic, suicidal, panic-stricken, traumatized, or bereaved employees were part of the experience of being a workplace counsellor. Responding in a calm, professional way and choosing appropriate interventions, borne out of training and experience, was seen as a necessary characteristic of workplace counsellors:

– *the ability of a counsellor to be flexible, to be open to a role not as tight as a psychotherapist/counsellor*
– *you have to be someone who learns on their feet, really. I think I am like that, that happens to suit me. If you are somebody who gets panicked by that then I imagine at times it's hair-raising because you want more stability and structure round you*
– *I know what my constraints are and where my boundaries are in terms of my role and it's extremely flexible*

Two interviewees linked this flexibility to the culture of their respective companies:

– *what that reflects is the flexibility of work roles within the organization . . . there is a tradition . . . in a company so young of somebody getting on with tasks in whichever field they happen to be in*
– *this organization changes constantly . . . it's proud of the fact that it innovates and changes constantly which is of course hard for people. It challenges them, I mean that challenges me as well*

2.2   *Pioneering*

Seven of those interviewed had actually set up the services they managed, while the others saw themselves as inheriting and developing young services. This gave a theme of 'pioneering' to interviewees. They not only ran, but marketed the counselling provision, establishing its ethos, its boundaries and purpose, and grounding it, almost literally, in the organization. Some had no fixed counselling room to work from, particularly those who were peripatetic. Nearly half of the interviewees worked from wherever and whatever was available, when needed. They coped with this by working hard to develop more suitable service provision. One experienced counsellor commented that she was *prepared to work in a shoe-box if needed*:

- *I look back over my history and I am forever setting things up . . . that's what excites me, trying to create something out of nothing*

One aspect of being an initiator is the ability to work autonomously. Each individual, whether in a team or solo, revealed an ability and a preference for working independently. Although part of large organizations, these particular roles set them apart from the mainstream, and tolerance of isolation was necessary:

- *I have a reasonable amount of autonomy at work . . . and that is important*
- *you have your work to do it as you want to do it . . . and your priorities are your priorities and not the company's*
- *I think of myself as a pretty lonely cog*

2.3   Assertiveness

Assertiveness was viewed by many as a key characteristic for this particular job because of the organizational aspects of the work:

- *it needs somebody very strong, at least to be prepared to stick out for what they know is right and to go for it*
- *you've actually got to be tough and be able to stand up for your own profession and assert it*
- *you just need somebody who isn't afraid of standing up for what they believe is right*
- *you have to be a bit brave*

In this context assertiveness also meant an ability to communicate clearly and respectfully one's own needs as well as reflect the needs of the other party. It also calls for an ability to use language that will be understood:

- *it's bringing the caring, committed approach and putting it in a business language they will understand*
- *if you come on strong with the authority, you know, in our role that is not very helpful. So you have always got to stay in touch with your facilitation bit*
- *what is very important is to be patient in your negotiations and deliberations with companies*

2.4   Coping Strategies: Supervision and Networking

There were three main sources of work-related stress for employee counsellors: working within organizational structures, heavy case-loads and 'aloneness':

- *it is stressful, and I have certainly lost sleep some nights . . . but mostly the stress has been caused by organizational pressures, by dealing with the particular structure of the business. From bitter experience I've learnt about consulting the right people where and when and how*
- *I've learnt that the politics of life didn't sit terribly easily with me as a counsellor*
- *you work at somebody else's pace, not your own . . . you work at the company's pace*
- *it can be so totally exhausting and overwhelming*

Coping strategies were needed to deal with particular difficulties associated with their roles. 'Aloneness' was one such difficulty and even counsellors in teams experienced varying degrees of 'aloneness', whether as a necessary accompaniment to being the 'keeper of secrets', or as the reverse side of autonomy. While having some disadvantages, most accepted this experience:

- *you have this triangle between you, the client and the employer, and you are the sort of isolated person in the company*
- *what I experience is . . . not being able to get too close to people. I would not go for a drink with people in work or go to lunch on a regular basis with anybody . . . I see it as a necessary part of the job*
- *this is a very lonely occupation*

Employee counsellors can carry the burden of considerable amounts of confidential information:

- *my experience was quite terrifying in a way because I contained vast amounts of highly confidential information from all levels of the organization and that was a real balancing act*
- *I'm privileged to an enormous amount of information in my position and that sometimes weighs quite heavily on me*

Three interviewees, who had been counsellors in organizations for several years, spoke about having experienced symptoms of burnout. Two main factors emerged as essential coping strategies for counsellors: external supervision, and social and professional networking.

Ten out of the 12 counsellors were in ongoing supervision. Only one experienced counsellor had no formal supervision, although an informal channel was used. Supervision took place in a variety of ways: a large number, seven, had external supervision, some had internal supervision, some had combinations of both, and individual and group supervision formats were used. Supervision was seen by counsellors as a forum to discuss boundary issues, to enhance self-awareness, to monitor efficacy and ethical decision-making:

- *we have an external supervisor which brings a balance, a neutrality about it . . . I think it is essential*
- *I'm lucky in having a very good supervisor who can support me in that . . . without the good supervision, it would have been a disaster*
- *what was useful to me in supervision was that there was someone to go to*

and talk about these organizational issues and the frustration I encountered, particularly straddling two organizations

A particular value for those in external supervision was the provision of a 'safe place' for the counsellor to come when weary. It was also a place to bring the irritations caused by organizational issues. However, there was an impression given that finding suitable supervisors with experience of supervising within an organization context was difficult.

Social and professional networking were viewed as an important support for employee counsellors:

- *I saw clearly when I interviewed for the job that I would need peer support*
- *I manage it personally by having a very informal network away from work . . . I've used colleagues within the service, colleagues outside, to offload and get rid of my frustration*
- *basically, the more professional support you have the better*
- *I am a very social person. I have been lucky enough to have a very strong social life outside of work . . . and I take advantage of those because I know I am not going to get that sort of interaction in work*

3. Organizational/Counselling Interface

3.1 Organizational Culture

Of the 12 companies represented by interviewees, eight had strong traditional British bases and four had international traditions. They ranged from financial services to highly technical production and marketing businesses. All were successful and well established, although all had been affected in some way by recession.

The word most frequently used historically to describe these companies was 'paternal'. Other terms used were 'protective and supportive', 'generous', 'caring':

- *a very strong company culture of looking after people*
- *we were offering, way back when, basically a magnificent welfare-service from a very kindly, patriarchal, kind-of-paternalistic company*

However, these same organizations were described as being in transition, changing 'shape' from hierarchical, bureaucratic structures to more devolved lines of communication and often more open decision-making. Such dramatic and necessary changes have both positive and negative impact on employees. Uncertainty is seen as rife: uncertainty of job security and uncertainty around job role. Change is now the only constant:

- *it's a fast-moving company where people have to change fast or leave . . . the human impact of a dynamic constantly evolving company is one of uncertainty*

3.2   Underlying Motivation for Counselling Services

While some employees thrive, responding to an inner drive to progress and achieve, others are less able to adjust or learn new technology. This is an area where casualties can occur:

- *I see people winding themselves into all kinds of stressful roles, having to prove themselves*
- *they live in a culture where you never have any certainty of how long your job is going to go on for . . . not knowing what their role is, not knowing what their career structure is, because like any organization it has become flatter*
- *the company has a reputation for forcing people, but actually I think most people force themselves*
- *the stress on people of change being the norm can be huge. I think at times the company may overestimate the ability of particular individuals to change and develop with the company*

There was a belief that the organization established counselling services out of a tradition of responsible care for employees' personal and work-related needs:

- *they [the organization] have not put in place a counselling service to save money. They've put a counselling service in because of a genuine concern of their staff for people . . . it's not been put in place because of absence or poor performance, it's been put in place to deal with genuine distress*
- *I don't think anybody has successfully shown me any statistics whereby you can prove that employing us is really going to make a lot of difference to their budgets*

This was balanced by a recognition of the need for the business to be successful:

- *clearly the business has a right to expect added value from what we're doing*
- *they are in a business that has to make a profit and has to make some fairly tough decisions at times*
- *at the end of the day there is a certain service or product which has to be produced . . . that is what the organization is about*

There was a general consensus that employee counselling services were of high value to both the employee and the organization:

- *I like to feel the client is getting a good deal out of it and the company is getting a good deal out of it. Its a win–win*
- *I think counselling in employment is a very valuable tool . . . not to provide it is a missed opportunity both to individual employees and for the employer*
- *if they can be more freed up without all these problems, how much more they can be beneficial to the organization as individuals*

3.3   Who is the Client?

In general, employee counsellors regard their primary client as the individuals who walk through their doors whether for personal counselling or for some other reason, for example organizational advice, liaison, training. Their emphasis is on the individual in front of them irrespective of their reason for being there.

Nine participants made specific reference to the need to recognize the *organizational context* and acknowledged some tension around balancing needs between the individual and the organization. They generally believed that attending to the needs of the individuals would benefit the company:

– *well, this is a very difficult one . . . usually I try to put the needs of the client I am seeing first . . . but I try to balance the needs of the company and the needs of the client . . . I find most of the time helping the client and helping the company go hand in hand*
– *the individual [pause], because I think the organization, by employing me, has put me in the role as an officer to help the client*
– *the client is my focus. However, I represent a service that takes place in an organizational context*

3.4   Mediation

Eleven counsellors saw an important role for *mediation* between the individual client and the company when the circumstances required, and the client gave express permission. The one dissenter came from the most recently established service. Even this participant, in subsequent months, decided to allow for general feedback (personal correspondence).

The reasons given in support of a mediation role were that the counsellor had the skills and impartiality to help both sides develop realistic notions of each others' needs. This was likened to couples counselling:

– *if you have got to be a mediator between husband and wife, at times, then why not between employer and employee*
– *I think, if you've got somebody that you have been counselling and seeing for a fairly protracted period and then you are talking about going back to work, then you've got to have an input, and I would always try to persuade clients to let me write something about what I have been doing with them to the manager so that the manager understands better*

In these situations expressed verbal permission from clients is essential, and in some cases specific written permission is required. This was seen as giving the client choice and control over their personal information:

– *no information is released without the client's signed consent and that specifies to whom the information may be released, for what reason it is to be released, and over what period of time it will be released*
– *very occasionally the client gives permission for me to intervene directly with line management*

A notable feature of mediation was that counsellors found that most requests for information from line managers was frequently prompted by human concern rather than interference or business needs:

- *the context in which people talk to me about clients is almost invariably, this person is having problems, how can I help*
- *the typical manager is only looking, very often, for support to provide the human approach*

Counsellors were aware of the precariousness of their position and did not want to be used by either client or company, or both:

- *it's a service run for staff and could be seen as another ploy, or another management tool, in some way to control or manipulate*
- *the thing is to try not to become a conduit or a go-between*

3.5 Confidentiality

There was almost complete unanimity that the principles enshrined in the British Association for Counselling (BAC) *Code of Ethics* pertain in workplace counselling, with confidentiality being the cornerstone and the credibility of the service. One service had its own individual code of ethics which was in general agreement with the BAC code, differing only in one aspect: it did not offer confidentiality where there was a serious breach of the company rules:

- *I make it plain to people when I see them that what they're telling me is for us unless they are going to reveal something of a criminal nature or abuse*
- *no information is disclosed without the client's permission, we do not provide feedback to the company unless the client should ask us to do so*
- *I think this is the most important fact, that when the door is shut nothing goes out of here, but nothing, absolutely*

All interviewees see themselves as offering a safe place for clients to bring vulnerable issues (*I think I am the human face in the company, if it has one*). If the client(s) revealed grave or criminal danger to the client or another person, the counsellor would feel morally absolved from holding the material as confidential. Occasions when confidentiality had to be breached were rare:

- *I am only aware in, what twelve years, of one instance where we actually had to divulge some information that the individual was reluctant . . . and that was seriously endangering the life of a third party, and we had no alternative . . . we're talking 140,000 clients, that's not a bad track record*
- *in the time I've been here there have been three occasions where I've had to take a decision . . . and use my knowledge of the client to make a situation safe*

All participants were explicit in explaining the boundaries of confidentiality to clients and three negotiated written contracts.

Protecting confidentiality can extend to not acknowledging clients when the counsellor meets them in the building (*I could break the confidence in just saying hello and using their name. I let them know I would pass them without acknowledgement and that goes along with the confidentiality).*

Despite the competitive, profit-making nature of these companies, counsellors generally experience respect and support both personally and professionally for the boundaries of confidentiality:

- *we have people on the board who have a lot of awareness about personal problems and a lot of sensitivity to the value this sort of thing has to offer*
- *generally speaking you are dealing with a supportive environment*
- *most of our interfacing with the organization is quite positive*
- *once they understand you're professional and why you are not saying anything they won't push it*
- *my boss would never ask me to do things that I see would compromise my professional responsibilities . . . he will sit down and talk it through with me*

3.6   Who Owns Clients' Notes?

Who owns clients' notes and what happens to them when the counsellor leaves the organization? These questions were intended to probe the practicalities and boundaries of confidentiality. Most counsellors were initially thrown by the question and had to work through their answer. Their hesitations were around the practical and ethical complexities involved in the questions.

Seven initially saw themselves as owning the notes. On reflection, two changed their minds and acknowledged that notes were owned by the counselling service.

Four said that they would shred the notes if no counsellor of a similar ethical stance replaced them. One service automatically shredded notes when clients left counselling. Two counsellors felt strongly that there was little to be gained in handing over notes because each therapeutic relationship was unique and was often better not influenced by prior knowledge.

There was also uncertainly around the legal position. Some of the counsellors had been involved in legal tribunals at the request of their clients and talked of the need to be conscious of this.

One counsellor remarked that there may well be room for a *Code of Ethics* specifically to deal with workplace counselling:

- *we are embarking on what is evolving . . . and it will require the development of a whole new set of ideas and perhaps beliefs and attitudes*

4.   Training Needs

Despite a range of professional and academic qualifications, none had training in workplace counselling. All had learned to apply their existing skills and knowledge to the workplace environment. All were supportive of a training programme in employee counselling. When asked to identify the training requirements to equip in-house counsellors for the demands of their multiple roles more than 73 suggestions emerged! These have been categorized into four groupings:

- Personal qualities.
- General counselling training.
- Specialized areas training.
- Professional qualifications.

4.1   Personal Qualities

Participants gave particular attention to the personal qualities required to be an employee counsellor. They saw the personality of the counsellor as the main therapeutic tool: the credibility of the counselling service was integral with the ability of the counsellor to be both human and professional. In summary, the following qualities were identified:

- Self-awareness.
- Assertiveness.
- Awareness of boundaries.
- Flexibility.
- Openness to learning.
- Responsiveness to crises.
- Humanness.
- Intuition.

Other terms used included 'warm', 'pastoral', 'patient' and 'stickability'. Personal therapy was seen as an important ingredient in developing these personal qualities.

4.2   General Counselling Training

Less attention was given to general counselling training. This may have been the way the question was occasionally phrased (for example, 'If you could design a course for yourself, what would it include?'). Nine interviewees specifically mentioned the need to be 'skilled' in counselling. Four spoke of their concerns with counselling courses which seemed to offer varying standards of knowledge and skills as there is a general sense of unreliability and/or uncertainty about the level of competency gained. Being trained to use supervision effectively was also stated as an important element in training.

4.3   Specialist Areas

Organizational psychology was most frequently mentioned as the area most useful to counsellors. Participants believed that a general awareness and understanding of the powerful dynamics within organizations were essential. Knowledge of the particular culture and policies of the company for which they worked was an important element but it was felt this could be picked up once in the post:

- *I'd like to know more about organizational psychology . . . because it would have probably made it a bit easier for me to deal with the organization, but probably, by having the experience, I learned enough for me to deal with it*
- *you have to have people with a capability of learning and understanding [the workplace] . . . the organization has a character of its own and you have to understand its quirks and the problems it can cause, it is an extraordinary powerful being*

Other specialist workplace issues mentioned were: stress management; dealing with job loss and managing change; responding to trauma; performance appraisal; disciplinary issues; and alcohol dependency.

Training in couples and systems therapy was suggested because they provide a helpful model for when organizational interventions are appropriate and, in particular, mediation situations between individuals and the organization:

- *I don't think it is enough to focus on individuals and individual models of distress . . . you need to start thinking about people in systems*

Knowledge of specialist areas such as the nature of work, job design, leadership and delegation, motivation, and health psychology were considered helpful by one interviewee. No one expressed a belief that experience of the business world was very important. What made a difference was the ability to learn from the situation.

Implicit in much that was said involved guidance in setting up, developing and monitoring an in-house counselling service which included identifying needs, engaging management support, establishing boundaries, writing policies, and pinpointing location and suitable counsellors. This includes the skills of training and presentation-giving, particularly when marketing the service. No one mentioned training in collecting and presenting statistics, even though there is no standard formula for collating such information.

4.4 Professional Qualifications

A professional background in areas such as social work and/or nursing was seen as providing two important ingredients necessary for in-house counsellors: a knowledge and skills base in assessment, and an extensive, practical experience of working with a wide variety of people undergoing a range of difficulties and crises:

- *Ideally, somebody who has a social-work, streetwise background. That combination of practical and definite skills in learning to be out-there, to holding things that seem like crises, to actually make decisions*

It was recognized that in order for someone to acquire such perfection of knowledge, skills and ability, it was likely to be a long journey. One interviewee commented, *you might think they are all crotchety and arrive here in a wheelchair . . . they don't . . . I suppose the average age is early 40s.*

Discussion

Reviewing the transcripts shows that beneath the four main categories – roles and responsibilities, counsellor attributes, organizational/counselling interface and training needs – are two elements that continue to reappear as fundamental to all of them. These are the personality features of workplace counsellors and their personal experience of doing the job. They are the continual basics that seem to account for this set of categories, and which are not immediately obvious from reading the texts of the interviews.

Personality attributes of the employee counsellors seem to explain why they were able to hold a number of roles in amicable tension; not only to work with multiple roles but to receive a great deal of satisfaction from doing so. Rather than be dismayed with a trend that in traditional counselling is frowned upon, experience has taught them that this was the most effective way to work in this context. Employee counsellors learn to be flexible, assertive, pioneering, and they develop coping strategies to help them survive in this difficult world. They chose to be employee counsellors because of their blend of personality attributes and personal experience and training. These two features may be an explanation of why these particular people are engaged in workplace counselling at this time in the history of counselling in industry, and how they manage their roles and the ethical issues that emerge.

Personality factors and workplace counsellors' experience of working within organizations are expressed in a number of ways. Employee counsellors are open to constant and ongoing negotiations around almost all aspects of their lives. This gives rise to a flexibility in their work and a willingness to change direction when needed. They move continually between polarities, the individual and the organization, the values of two worlds, the counselling and the business world, the counselling versus other roles. Their roles revolve around building bridges between counselling and business: a task at which they seem to be very adept.

Conclusion

Employee counsellors, in their own unique services, work with the common motive and purpose of bringing together the world of work with the world of counselling. There is not only a deeply held belief, but also a wealth of practical experience, to confirm that they give valuable and effective service to individuals and companies. This is not romanticism but realism. Their jobs are backed up by sheer hard work, a constant juggling of roles and walking fine lines. Yet this is also part of the reward. Most important is seeing that employee counsellors make a difference, that they mediate and translate professional and personal values into the real world and enable clients to regain a sense of self.

This research is, in my view, only a beginning point: I can see so many areas that would yield further insights, whether about the best training for workplace counsellors, the most appropriate counselling approach in this area, the boundaries of confidentiality and the legalities and usefulness, or other- wise, of record-keeping. In particular, I would like to see further exploration into how we make ethical decisions and resolve ethical dilemmas as employee counsellors. Answers to some of these questions are the grounding for best practice in the further development of counselling in the workplace.

References

British Association for Counselling (1984) *Code of Ethics and Practice for Counsellors.* Rugby: BAC.

Carroll, C. (1994) 'Building bridges: a study of employee counsellors in the private sector'. MSc dissertation, City University, London.

Strauss, A. and Corbin, J. (1990) *Basics of Qualitative Research: Grounded Theory, Procedures and Techniques.* London: Sage.

14

Counselling Skills Training for Managers in the Public Sector

Peter Martin

There is very little research available on the effects of counselling skills training on public sector workers. Much of my own work as a freelance trainer and management consultant has been in the public sector. I decided to conduct a rigorous analysis within a County Council on employees who had recently undergone counselling skills training in the hope that such research might provide useful pointers for the future.

Context

The public sector differs from the private sector in several respects. Unlike many private firms, employees in the public sector have many masters. These include those who intervene from central government and the wishes of the majority of elected members on governing committees, as well as the normal hierarchy of paid employees. The outcome, too, is more diffuse than in profit-led industry. Although there has been considerable pressure on local government to rationalize its resources, the 'output' will to some extent represent major policies and political necessity, as well as the forceful influence of the press and of public opinion in general. There has to be an attempt to be fair in the delivery of goods and services to the public. Measurement of good care of the elderly may, for example, be more complex than profit figures for shareholders in a private business. This is reflected in another possible difference. There is a long tradition of public service with all its attendant ethical and practical considerations, which again may be distinct from the motif of profit through good service which is predominant in many firms. So there is a measure of distinctiveness about public service which the present chapter seeks to illuminate, though a comparative study has yet to be conducted.

Review of Literature

An exhaustive search on the Institute of Personnel and Development (IPD) database produced no articles or research on the response of managers to counselling training. 'Psychlit', a Psychological literature database, produced only one article (McDonald, 1991) which referred to training in the public sector. This concerned the training of unqualified social work staff in counselling skills and is referred to in the discussion at the end of this chapter.

The wider context of counselling at work, however, is increasingly well represented in the literature. Reddy's assertion that '. . . the centre of gravity of the counselling universe is moving inexorably to the workplace' (1993: 15) does not, however, specify what kind of counselling provision is likely to predominate. Charles-Edwards (1989: 118) delineated between counsellors whose main work is line management, those who work 'sometimes' as a counsellor, and the work done by external consultants. Indeed, the current interest in Employee Assistance Programmes eclipses the earlier enthusiasm shown for the manager as counsellor. Some alarm has been expressed about the very concept by Novarra (1986: 4) who asks 'Can a manager be a counsellor?' This caution arises properly from the very delicate issues surrounding ethics in a company. The high value placed on profit for instance, may be at serious odds with the needs of the individual within the company. The public sector is no exception to the problems of role conflict. Orlans (1989: 4) makes a plea for recognition that the 'traditional base' of counselling is radically different from that of the business setting. There have been many attempts to solve this particular conflict with some believing that 'Counselling Skills' and not 'Counselling' as such can be conducted by the manager (Newby, 1983). The research this chapter reports does not support this idea.

However, there are voices on the side of the argument for the bona fide counselling manager. Writing as early as 1979, Stewart, with a National Health Service background, insisted that counselling should not be 'hived off' to specialists because there is a need to 'deal with the action where it originates' (1979: 18). Making a related but different point, Hughes considers that the sheer availability of the counselling manager, and the normality of the context is important to a good outcome (1991: 26). Reddy (1993: 75) argues against the notion that a trained counsellor 'is necessarily better' anyway. Both Megranahan (1989b) and Egan (1986) noted that the majority of helping skills, including counselling, is offered by people who are not counsellors.

A diversity of approach, however, is well represented in the literature, which indicates that there is a high transferability of counselling skills to other areas within management. Scott, in Watts (1982), spells out some applications such as mutual objective-setting, appraisal, interviewing and discipline. Novarra (1986) quotes Reddy's 1985 Report saying that counselling in appraisal training and career development is contributing to a general increase in employee effectiveness. Pickard, however, insists that a clear distinction needs to be made between related activities such as mentoring, advising and appraising: the counsellor must be able to distinguish one from another (Pickard, 1993). The research represented in the body of this chapter would confirm this finding, and also illustrates it with numerous practical examples.

The literature on training in counselling skills at work is less plentiful. Davis (1981) breaks training down into stages, some of which are applicable to skills training. Relevant also here are the various attempts to come to terms with the competency approach (Burgoyne, 1989; Carney, 1992; Crouch, 1993). It may well be that skills training as opposed to the wider process of counselling lends itself to the competency model. Whichever method is used, Fowler (1991) advocates that a counselling component is present in any supervisory or management programme. This view is backed by Charles-Edwards (1989) who claims that counselling skills have a central role in both management competence and training. Unfortunately, the material available does not illuminate the particular features of counselling skills training as it affects public sector employees by comparison with the private sector. Neither does it treat the possibly increased sensitivity presumably experienced by the public sector employee, as a section of the workforce very much under public scrutiny. That is a field open to further research.

The Background of the Study: Research Question and Methodology

My own research was centred on Oxfordshire County Council where I regularly worked as a management trainer. A substantial number of senior and middle managers had been through one of two counselling courses. One course was a counselling skills module within a wider human relations management course, whereas the other was a stand-alone counselling course which was designed to implement the council's sickness monitoring scheme. The number of people involved in a 15-month period on both was 74.

I made the decision to use Strauss and Corbin's (1990) qualitative research model. The research was focused around the question: *What are the effects of counselling training on public sector managers?* The purpose of this question was 'to give flexibility and freedom to explore a phenomenon at depth' (1990: 37). The goal was to analyse responses to questionnaires using first 'open' coding, then 'axial' coding. Open coding is a process of breaking down, examining, comparing, conceptualizing and categorizing the data. Axial coding is a set of procedures in which data is put back together in new ways after open coding. This is done by using a coding paradigm which involves conditions, context, action/interactional strategies and consequences. This process is the 'ground' from which theory is developed, hence the name.

The questionnaires were sent to all course participants. They were asked:

1. What benefits they saw from the modules?
2. What was not helpful?
3. What, if any, skills they learned which might be transferred to other areas of work not normally associated with counselling?

The length of most responses indicated that those replying gave a considered response. Seventy-seven per cent returned questionnaires. After analysis, a summary of findings was sent to each respondent. Of the original respondents 70 per cent replied to this: 27 per cent said the report represented their views

Table 14.1 *Overview of categories and sub-categories*

1. **The benefits of training**
   1.1 Focus
   1.2 Perceived acquisition of knowledge
   1.3 Skills acquisition
   1.4 Boundaries of counselling
   1.5 Human relations aspect of management
   1.6 The use of counselling skills in organizations

2. **Unhelpful elements within the training**
   2.1 The context of the module
   2.2 The structure of the learning experience
   2.3 Conceptual muddles
   2.4 Techniques used in learning and teaching

3. **The transfer of skills**
   3.1 Skills arising from Egan's framework
   3.2 Use of skills in other organizational spheres
   3.3 Personal and relational issues

'completely', 62 per cent 'mostly' and 10 per cent 'only partly' No one said the report represented their views 'not at all'. Finally, the data and summary was sent to a nationally recognized psychologist in the field of counselling at work who validated the results.

The Results from an Analysis of Answers

Table 14.1 presents an overview of the categories and sub-categories derived from analysing the answers. In the subsequent sections, direct quotations from respondents are in italic.

1.   The Benefits of Training

1.1   Focus

'Focus' was seen by many to be important. The training for one person focused on the 'non-rational issues of an organization and behaviour in contrast to feelings in the workplace'. This understanding of what Egan (1993) calls the 'shadow side' of organizations led some trainees to consider the possible conflict between organizational and individual goals. Another important issue was the notion of partnership between manager and employee. Some people from Social Services noted that the module helped them to think about colleagues' needs as well as those of clients. Several had found it useful to focus on the main content and intention of the counselling interview, while two respondents were particularly glad to have identified the need to establish priorities within such an encounter. One respondent was pleased at the opportunity to focus on the difference between an intuitive approach that had been up until now used, and the Egan model offered in training. The limitations of the training in this model were also noted:

- *there is a danger of people now thinking that they know how to do it, and jumping in with both feet, which could have the wrong result and only make things worse*

This trainee (and others) was afraid of undue confidence which might lead some managers to regard themselves as trained counsellors. This could lead to disastrous consequences for the employee.

1.2   Perceived Acquisition of Knowledge

This cluster of comments included many who felt they already had counselling skills but were glad to have a refresher course. For those new to the field, there was an appreciation of the 'possibilities of counselling' but more specifically a greater understanding of the management task in counselling. This was developed by other responses which quickly noted the 'need for a structured approach, and the dangers of unstructured, intuitive work. Used inappropriately, counselling can at least be unhelpful and at worst damaging. Several respondents related the learning to their own inner process, saying that they were now more able to pick up on observations, were wanting the employee to solve their own problems, and were learning as a manager to say 'no' sometimes. One reflected inner experience by commenting:

- *I actually feel part of the session rather than someone looking through a window*

This would seem to indicate that this person, and those who responded like him, had begun to understand the key Egan skill of empathy.

1.3   Skills Acquisition

The next cluster around 'skills acquisition' fit neatly around the three stages of Egan's (1986) model.

Stage 1:   Exploration (using active listening).
Stage 2:   New understanding (having established priorities).
Stage 3:   Action (support for meeting realistic goals).

It was particularly noticeable how many respondents felt that the Stage 1 skills of empathy, establishing rapport, but especially active listening, were important. Several people were also appreciative of learning the skills of pacing in Stages 2 and 3 'recognizing the need to move into action'. A few replies included a positive view of the techniques of learning, including role play and what one person called 'practical guidance'.

1.4 Boundaries of Counselling

The cluster on the boundaries imposed by the counselling approach were usually signalled by a deeper understanding of what counselling skills are not:

- *I think I've become clearer about the ways in which boundaries can be drawn between public and private worlds and some of the appropriate ways of dealing with 'personal' issues in the context of work!*

Included in the new understanding of what counselling did not involve, was giving answers or getting involved 'in an unprofessional way' (such as intervening too much, or too personally), prejudging and 'responding antagonistically'. These responses were important in defining a positive concept of counselling skills. In this way, counselling skills such as empathetic listening, reflecting back and paraphrasing, were retrieved and defined away from a great many other general communication skills.

1.5 Human Relations Aspect of Management

Many replies went straight past skills acquisition and the definitions and into the heart of the nature of the counselling relationship. One comment sums up several responses on regarding others as humans:

- *they were not just people at work, but were human beings living their lives*

Others spoke of the need to care, of a 'more trusting partnership' of 'more sympathetic listening – less hardhearted'. Specific shifts in situational responses were cited, including 'emotional blackmail dealt with more maturely' and 'calmed an explosive situation'. Responses in this cluster were fulsome and all listed benefits to human relations in areas which would be helpful throughout any organization. 'Tackling potentially difficult problems at an early stage' would, for instance, be a much needed skill in terms of the efficient running of an organization, regardless of its human relations implications.

1.6 The Use of Counselling Skills in Organizations

The cluster around uses of counselling skills concerned many respondents. Immediate applications were made to mentoring, staff induction, continuing personal development and 'promotion disputes and repercussion'. Useful, though hard to categorize, was the comment that the module helped one person in 'finding what is appropriate and not appropriate to deal with at work'. Another found the module a cornerstone to her behaviour within the organization, indicating its usefulness in 'building a belief that an employee can change things'.

2. Unhelpful Elements within the Training

2.1   The Context of the Module

Some of the comments about the context of the module related to the problems of using counselling skills within an organization. 'Too much sympathy
and not enough emphasis on the organization/task' was one comment, while
another felt the problems of role conflict between the counselling stance and
the responsibility for overall management had not been fully discussed.
Indeed, there were many comments on the course being too short, and one
said that it could have come too late anyway:

– *by the time we have had the training we may have left a trail of devastation*

  Need for follow-up was expressed. The placing of the counselling module at
the end of the nine-day management course was criticized in that it came at a
point when there was no opportunity to follow up. Respondents were specific
about what they thought was missing from the course, and these nearly always
related to the organizational context. These perceived omissions related to the
presumed lack of opportunities for counselling within the present organizational structure, room facilities, etc. They related as well, to the pressures put
on all managers in the organization, as a result of rapid change with its
consequent re-prioritizing. It was suggested that the trade unions should have
been involved in the sickness monitoring programme and that there needed to
be back-up from the Council procedures in implementing this scheme. (There
had, in fact, been full trade union consultation, and procedures had been put
in place.) 'Contemporary' issues such as redundancy were referred to. Specific
skills were asked for in dealing with 'scornful' employees and in dealing with
anger in the manager, 'induced by employees'. Again the ever-present potential conflict between the values of the organization and counselling values was
implied or spelled-out in these responses.

2.2   The Structure of the Learning Experience

Comments in the cluster about the structure of learning concerned both basic
values and technique, for example, 'Too much reliance on technique – this is
artificial without genuineness.' Another said that there was need for a wider
debate asking 'Where does empathy and commitment fit in with technique and
behaviour?' Again there was a call for more practical applications and less
theory. The level of the course was questioned, with some experienced people
feeling that they needed more challenge and others pointing out that the
learning 'could be overwhelming for the inexperienced'. One such person said
that more thought should be given to the 'stressful nature' of the module.

2.3   Conceptual Muddle

Questions were asked about the place of counselling skills in various types of
interview, and what in particular was the overlap between counselling and

mentoring? One person summed it up by asking, 'When do you use counselling, and when another approach?'. Other questions concerned when to refer. 'When can empathy be counterproductive?' This seems to be tapping the deep root of organizational effectiveness versus individual development. None of these confusions seem incapable of clarification, but might suggest the need for some kind of follow up to the original training. It is perhaps worrying that these confusions continue to exist up to 15 months after the completion of the training.

2.4   Techniques Used in Learning and Teaching

The last cluster emerging from this question relates to teaching and learning techniques. Replies concentrated largely on role play. Criticisms were about 'unequal pairings' for role play where one course member was more experienced in counselling skills than the other. Several people, however, said that they wanted more role play and contrasted it with what was thought to be unrealistic scenarios on commercial training videos. The comment was made that 'more direct feedback' was needed after a role play, where the comments of the course leader seemed to be given more value than those of peers. This was reflected, to a degree, in the comment of the course-member who would have preferred demonstrations given by tutors over course-member role play. One person said, 'I didn't learn much from inexperienced trainees'. The theme all the way through was the need to reproduce counselling experience, as the primary route to learning.

3.   The Transfer of Skills

3.1   Skills Arising from Egan's Framework

A good number of replies indicated that the Egan framework (see pp. 243–4) was useful outside the workplace counselling context. One person summed it up with the adage, 'Don't solve a problem before identifying it!' Others were less general: one person used the structure to manage meetings. Listening skills, including paraphrasing and summarizing, were felt to have many applications elsewhere, as was the notion of 'finding new perspectives'.

3.2   Use of Skills in Other Organizational Spheres

The cluster of replies around the use of counselling skills in other organizational management 'theatres' was plentiful. Respondents suggested 22 areas which included managing change, grievance situations and coaching, as well as team management, supervision, delegation and negotiation. More predictable was the application of the skills to recruitment, mentoring and appraisal. Some people gave very specific examples of where the skills had been useful to them, such as 'Land disputes – finding a remedy within enforceable law but being sensitive to personal feelings'. More general but still valuable to the organization was, 'Understanding the layman/expert communication problem' and 'diffusing hostile situations'. There were many such examples given.

These responses were so positive and ubiquitous that they might form a compelling rationale for including a counselling skills training in any management programme, regardless of whether counselling were part of the declared values and infrastructure.

3.3   Personal and Relational Issues

The cluster around personal and relational uses of the skills was also well and fully represented in the replies. The sickness monitoring module produced the response that one was 'more aware of a relationship', that 'sympathy and understanding reduces the likelihood of confrontation', and that one saw the need of 'not being biased'. The general module produced evidence of a change of perspective:

- *it's more a matter of awareness of what people are saying to you and how the manager can respond that*

Several people said that they felt more able to gain the confidence of a colleague, while one man said he could now 'manage in a more humane and patient way'. About one-third of the respondents made the point that there had been an increase in their interpersonal skills as judged by their own perception of their interactions at work. Some more were willing to say that the major gain had been in their home life. One person was especially enthusiastic about the training, saying:

- *the counselling module is something all staff would benefit from doing for their personal development*

The data having been categorized in terms of 'open coding', enabled the research to continue to the next stage of 'axial coding'.

The Results from Axial Coding

Three principal findings emerged:

1. A short counselling skills training course brings about a heightened awareness in terms of framework, structure, and the focus of counselling skills.
2. After a short counselling skills training course there is evidence that managers show a high level of spontaneous transfer of counselling skills to other management scenarios.
3. A short counselling skills training programme has a greater effect than its stated purpose on trainees and on their organization.

Discussion

1. *Heightened Awareness of Framework, Structure and Focus of Counselling Skills*

That a course on any subject should produce heightened awareness is not particularly surprising. More important, however, is that this awareness appears to have stayed with trainees for up to 15 months after the training. This may be because counselling skills training had become meshed in with other aspects of their work and life, and came to have more meaning for them, as the discussion under findings 2 and 3 explores.

(a) Framework of counselling skills: the place of counselling skills within the organization. A heightened awareness of the framework of counselling skills involves for each trainee a dialogue between what they have learned and the organization for which they work. McDonald makes the point that such training must not only 'be conducted in a way that is compatible with counselling values' but must also have regular feedback (1991: 13). The 'feedback' in this case comes from the context of the Country Council, and the procedures and policies that it administers (see p. 251 below).

Interaction between the skills and the organization was frequently referred to in the response. It applies especially where sickness monitoring was concerned and the plea was made for more management backing for procedures in the workplace. This circular process seems to imply a need to devote at least as much time on a course to the application of such skills, as to the teaching of the skills themselves. While this would usually be possible, it does have implications for both the depth of the coverage given, and the extent of the overview of the skills in a short training course. It would certainly mean that fewer skills could be learned and that these skills would need to be taught with the specific objective of using them in context.

Role conflict in using the skills in an organization The applied use of counselling skills in an organization inevitably illuminates the potential for role conflict. Many of the respondents quickly focused on the inherent conflict that may be said to exist in counselling activities at work. It may be that this conflict will never be fully resolved in theory or even in practice, but it is very important that trainees should be aware of the dilemma and begin to work out their own way of handling it. Nixon and Carroll contend that the conflict cannot be directly resolved but that managers can use counselling skills without an inherent ethical problem: 'Managers cannot be counsellors but need to build up their counselling skills in order to be fully effective in their management roles' (1994: 7).

There are attempts to produce what I would call a 'vertical' category in which counselling skills, counselling, and depth professional counselling are in a kind of hierarchy. Bond (1989) reflects a possible caveat to this argument. He points out that 'counselling skills' are themselves subject to many different

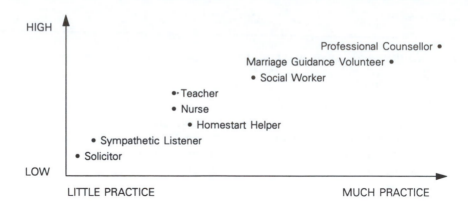

Figure 14.1   *Mapping the field (Pearce, 1989)*

understandings. At one end of the continuum he notes that counselling skills are seen simply as communication skills, and at the other end as a synonym for counselling. Bond's categories encourage a less status-conscious model such as that put forward by Pearce (1989: 194). Here she categorizes counselling in terms of trainings and practice required for different scenarios (see Figure 14.1). This model is, in a sense, 'horizontal': the *same skills* are used by different practitioners at different levels of expertise, and according to the needs of the counsellees. She would see counselling for managers operating at a relatively basic level with less practice and skill than that required, for instance of a marriage guidance counsellor. The training required of a manager would be at a similar level, she says, to that needed by solicitors. The term 'counselling' could, however, be applied to all such activities, whether by manager, marriage counsellor or professional counsellor. The adjustment in understanding the type of counselling being offered would be quantitative in terms of training and practice rather than representing a completely different category of activity.

The question in practice is that if a manager using counselling skills is talking through a particular problem with a particular employee in a particular place, in what sense would that activity be anything other than counselling? An attempt to make a firm distinction between counselling and counselling skills seems premature. It was, however, important that trainees were able to grasp what counselling could potentially involve and to become more aware of their own limitations as well as their possibilities within that context.

An acceptable role?   Having accepted that caveat, most respondents seemed also to believe that the sheer availability of a manager with counselling skills was an advantage over the professional counsellor. Murgatroyd (1985: 5) believes in the 'demystification' of the counselling role. The plethora of newspaper reports concerning national disasters where 'trained counsellors' are employed did not seem to make respondents feel they had nothing to offer in the day-to-day atmosphere of the County Council. Many examples were given of where an intervention which involved counselling skills proved effective, at least in the eyes of the trainee.

The framework for the use of counselling skills fits squarely in the host organization (see p. 249). Having confirmed the valued possibilities which the application of counselling skills offers, the next task was to understand better the structure of the skills themselves.

(b) Structure of counselling skills. That course participants had learned the structure of the Egan model is well attested to by the responses. But the plea was often expressed that more practice was needed to put that structure in place in their own experience. It would seem that this had been done in the workplace if the ubiquitous transfer of skills is anything to go by. Most of what have been called 'conceptual muddles' seem to have been caused not by the difficulty of the material itself, but by the shortness of the course. These related particularly to the boundaries between counselling skills and other related activities, such as appraisal. It is evident that although this problem worked out in practice, the trainees wanted to feel that they had a clearer concept at the time of the training. The suggestions such as 'more discussion of types of interview', and the question 'when do we use counselling, and when another approach?' may well still concern very experienced counsellors, but more could be done on the initial course to consider such matters more fully. However, unless the organization was willing to devote more time, this could only be done at the expense of other learning.

Course duration Coopers and Lybrand (1993) consider a week to be an ideal time in which to teach the skills and presumably also the organizational context for the skills (see p. 249). Steddon (1991) claims that even half a day can 'empower' the manager to make useful interventions. His objectives in such a short course are mainly to give the manager 'permission' not to be certain of all the issues involved in the employee's problem before the counselling interview begins. In his view, the critical skill is for the counselling manager to learn to listen effectively. Further research could usefully examine the outcome of courses of various course durations against their declared objectives. It may be difficult to decide on an optimum length since the readiness of the organization to espouse counselling values might well be another significant variable. What this research seems to indicate is the need for staged training, where the trainee can develop relevant questions after the initial training, which can then be addressed at a second or subsequent point. As was noted above (p. 247), some confusions about the applicability of the counselling approach in various situations still existed 15 months after the course was concluded. Staged training would ameliorate this difficulty. It may be that Fowler's (1991) suggestion that counselling skills training should always feature in a general management programme would allow for the staged development of counselling concepts as the general course progressed, and encourage useful cross-fertilization.

The question of the duration of the course, and how much learning should take place then, and how much afterwards is particularly important where the internal processes of the trainee are concerned. One of the issues that is crucial to the counselling manager is what work and personal material of the employee he or she is willing to deal with in the counselling context. One respondent specifically notes that it was during the course that she was able to decide where those boundaries should be (p. 245). In this case she decided that she was only prepared to listen to work-related issues. She would then feel free to concentrate on these without being burdened by the unease of material she was uncomfortable with, or by guilt because she had not examined the issue and come to a clear conclusion. Although this is partly a cognitive process, it is also an emotional one. As McDonald (1991) points out, support and understanding of the trainee by the trainer is needed. This may have implications for the size of the training group which are beyond the scope of the present chapter.

Techniques   The responses are consistently concerned about techniques. There was considerable enthusiasm for the techniques of active listening, para-phrasing and summarizing, but again the suggestion was that these should be given more time in practice. This research asks no questions about the effectiveness of the use of that technique on their employees. There is now, however, plenty of research to suggest that counselling in organizations by professional counsellors has a worthy success rate (see Cooper et al., 1990; and Reddy, 1993). The only indication that the teaching of technique may have been successful for the managers in this study is the many reported uses trainees made of it. There is opportunity for more research in this area.

Referral   The gap between the manager with counselling skills and the pro-fessional counsellor is best met using the strategy of referral. Many trainees wanted to know more about when and how to refer. Megranahan sees referral skills as failing because the manager may not recognize the need for referral and may be tempted to persist in a counselling relationship where he or she is not competent or trained. This error may be the result of the training which the manager has originally undergone and which has not taught when and how to refer. 'Managers who are properly trained and clear about their objectives for the training should be clear about the limitations of their counselling in their role' (Megranahan, 1989a: 170).

It may well be that the trainee who was concerned about counter-productive empathy (see p. 247) was in fact signalling a concern for better referral skills. A misunderstanding of the appropriate counselling role could impede the more general management role.

(c)   **Focus of counselling skills.**   All training is designed to provide focus on a given skill or area of knowledge. The experience reflected in responses in this research, however, suggested delineation and distinctiveness of the precise boundaries and content of counselling, mentoring, advising, etc., are hard to achieve. It would seem that many respondents reached a view of what counselling skills were, and where to use them, by 'negative' means, for example, they come to an understanding that counselling outcome is about self-direction, and is not a response to persuasion by the managers.

By defining what counselling was not, many of the respondents seemed to be able to develop a 'feel' for where it might be appropriately used. This is especially important in view of the many and diverse ways that the skills are capable of being employed. As is discussed later, the trainees were very able to see where counselling and other skills intersect (for example, appraisal, disciplinary skills), but it is equally important that they should be clear where they are different and need to be kept separated.

The 'feeling' base in the counselling approach   Another issue which caused several comments was the focus on the feeling base in the counselling approach. This appeared to be a new insight for many trainees, and indeed is a departure from the 'rational' model of management which many employees and managers still cling to (see March, 1987: 91). The interest shown by trainees in the 'non-rational issues' in the organization or in 'behaviour in contrast to feelings in the workplace' indicate a developmental role for counselling skills training in moving towards a wider, and perhaps more profound, view of human beings in the workplace.

All of the questionnaires seemed to indicate that the battle through the conceptual and affective minefield was worthwhile. Although a few people said that they had not had the opportunity to use the skills, no one said that they felt they were unusable. Counselling skills used in practice would appear to be more robust than the debates (see Newby, 1983; Hoare, 1984; Novarra, 1986) surrounding them might suggest.

What kind of training for each trainee?   There are some remaining problems for the trainer. McDonald (1991) supports the need for participative training. There was, however, considerable comment about the mismatch of trainees, especially where role play exercises were concerned. A different learning culture within the organization might well have ameliorated the problem. A more rigorous selection of trainees could also help to achieve a more productive match between the skills and knowledge of the participants. There is a difficulty in selection where the course is a module within a general training programme since different trainees would be likely to be at different levels of competence and understanding in each area. The difference in ego-strength and self-confidence of trainees is also very relevant here. There were several people who felt the module could have been more challenging, but there were also fears about the 'stressful nature' of the course for some people. It may be that such difficulties are inherent in the training and that it is part of the process of the course to work through them.

2.   The Transfer of Counselling Skills to Other Organizational Spheres

The spontaneous transfer to other management areas was well evidenced in the responses to the questionnaire. The sheer enthusiasm of response is interesting to try to interpret. Perhaps these particular communication skills unlocked and made available to the workplace, interest, experience and drive which had previously been compartmentalized in the domestic and social domains? One general comment was that the skills made one respondent:

– *realize that talking to an individual is something that required thought if you want an individual to respond in a certain way*

Another was that the skills were used in:

– *conflicts between the need to take risks and to be sensitive to statutory obligations in elderly people's homes*

This was, in addition, to the many other more specific areas such as disciplinary situations and coaching scenarios. This was equally true of those who had done the focused sickness monitoring module as to those who had learned general counselling skills in the context of wider management issues. The question might well be asked why people attributed an increase in personal and relational skills to the counselling skills course as opposed to their many other experiences of life and of learning. It may be that counselling training, focusing as it does on dilemmas, uncertainties, exploration, and heuristic learning, is a very fertile source of wider life skills. It may also be that the focus of counselling on a dyad, elicits all sorts of other partnership dynamics within an organization. These may be between the manager and the managed, the client and the provider, the individual manager and the many project teams of which he or she is a member (see p. 257).

Counselling skills with a 'central role' in management training.   The outcome of client-directed behaviour may strike a very sensitive nerve in a period when 'empowerment' is a buzzword. Organizations, however, find it very hard to implement this practice. Counselling skills bring about a very different kind of relationship and it may be that their practice gives experience of a very different kind of power relationship. The responses to the first question (see p. 245) about gains showed a marked concern for the way that management relationships were conducted and the power balance within them. The comments that managers felt it was 'easier to approach others' and 'ensure that others state their viewpoint' are indicative of a change of approach, and suggest a key role for learning counselling skills in order to implement genuine empowerment.

   It may be that the spontaneous transfer of the counselling skills to areas not usually associated with counselling was an avoidance of using the skills for counselling *per se*. If this is so, it would not offend Jarvie and Matthews (1989) who list as useful outcomes of training, personal growth, good communication, high motivation, a high performance team, mutual responsibility, innovation and enterprise and synergy. Whatever the reason, the outcomes seem positive, with no one reporting a negative reaction except for the comment that: 'At the end of the first day I felt deskilled, but I had been warned!' Even if the working practice suggested that counselling skills were not used directly in counselling activities, Charles-Edwards' claim that counselling skills have a 'central role to play in both managerial competence and in training' appears to be borne out (1989: 118). The actual experience of the counselling approach in organizations, however, is very patchy. This may be accounted for by the difference that Argyris and Schon (1984) note between the 'espoused theory' of an organization and its 'theory-in-use'. The expectation that counselling values may reach the heart of an organization and change its values may be still a long way from fulfilment.

Counselling skills repercussing throughout the organization. More optimistically, the structures of counselling, such as the Egan framework (see p. 244), which was so ingeniously adapted by many respondents, gets an enthusiastic reception. This is perhaps because counselling skills have in most cases similar characteristics to any other management input. An input on customer care, for instance, would be expected to have repercussions throughout the organization. The same may reasonably be expected of counselling skills, in spite of its somewhat 'precious' approach when it was first introduced more than a decade ago. This early reluctance to admit to the confrontational, 'hard' use of counselling (see Pawlik and Kleiner, 1986) may relate to a prevalence of misunderstood and badly applied Rogerian principles in contrast to the more eclectic understandings now more in use. It would seem that counselling has now achieved a status on a par with other management learning, such as change theory, and it is treated accordingly by those learning the skills.

That there is a high transferability of counselling skills to other work areas need not surprise, but it does need to be capitalized upon. If this transferability is not recognized by trainers and management alike, its potential may be restricted to individual responses, rather than being nourished and enabled more widely by organizational structures and management practice. Fowler's (1991: 25) belief that counselling skills are best learned in a general management context would, for example, ensure the maximum use of remembered learning and a more productive cross-fertilization of ideas and behaviours (see p. 251). Indeed, Newby, in an early article (1983), proposed the distinction between 'counselling' and 'counselling skills'; he says that the distinction is useful because it differentiates between the process of the counselling relationship and the skills components of this interaction (see pp. 249–50). The distinction is made: 'precisely because there is a range of counselling-based activities [in training, in management development, in team-building, in the organizational intervention field] that do not fit in the traditional (counselling) framework' (Newby, 1983: 15). In other words components of counselling are used throughout the organization but, should not be considered as bona fide counselling.

Counselling skills without disguises. Newby goes on to explore the unhelpful implications of using 'semantic disguises' (1983: 17) in order to advance counselling in the workplaces. He emphasizes, however, that the distinction needs to be made clear to anyone who may benefit from counselling or make use of counselling skills. The present research evidence agrees with Newby that counselling does not need a disguise, and that the skills are powerfully functional in catalysing learning throughout management expertise. They exist in their own right but are surfaced, energized and honed partly by other mind-sets. This outcome is quite logical: the roots of the counselling approach are in helping individuals to tap their resources, release potential and to promote imaginative and creative action. This has been the outcome of counselling for individuals for decades. It follows that the same potential is available for organizations.

3. A Short Counselling Skills Training Has a Greater Effect Than its Stated Purpose

Disorder and unintended consequences.   J.G. March (1987) traces theories of choice and making decisions in organizations. He posits that far from being rational, decision-making often emanates from disorder. He says that the classical ideas of order in organizations involves a belief that 'events and activities can be arranged in chains of ends and means', and that 'organizations are hierarchies in which higher levels control lower levels, and policies control implementation' (1987: 95). He says the reality is more confusing. What is actually very often important is the unintended consequences of a decision. In the situation examined in this chapter, both the Council and the trainer made a decision to provide counselling skills training in order that managers might more effectively carry out a counselling role where appropriate in their jobs. As it turned out, the side-effects of the training appears to have been even more important than this stated purpose.

Counselling skills and organizational culture.   The unintended consequences of counselling skills training at Oxfordshire County Council appear to have been in two main areas: what impact the training may have had on the culture, and what the value may have been in terms of self-development in the individuals concerned. A look at the culture of any given organization might well begin with an understanding of Rensis Likert's systems approach in which all aspects of the organization should naturally support and reinforce each other. Orlans has pointed out that if counselling is to succeed in an organization, the 'recognition and commitment of senior management' (1989: 6) will be necessary. This research goes further and suggests that the culture itself may be affected by the skills learned: the movement is reciprocal. Ditton identifies why this impact is possible in that after counselling training 'management will benefit from treating the employee as a whole person and not splitting off the emotional from the rational' (1991: 28).

Orlans (1986) says that change is currently the most important stressor in organizations, and suggests counselling as an antidote, but Ditton (1991) sees the role of counselling in a much more positive light. He relates how the Ashridge Consultants have developed a Counselling for Change programme. This is taken up by Jarvie and Matthews, who claim that this approach to individuals within the organization brings about wider change: 'The manager becomes capable of enabling individuals to make decisions and to release potential energy for change and development' (1989: 10). McDonald (1991) focuses on the element of reciprocity inherent in the counselling process, one which in larger organizations may reflect a partnership relationship between managed and managers, between clients and providers. This by-product of counselling may yet be seen to be its most fundamental contribution to the fabric of a successful organization.

Partnership is worked out through communication. Communication is enacted through detailed and sincere attention to the employee. Hughes (1991: 2) says that up to 80 per cent of managerial time is spent in oral communication, so it is surely important that these encounters are of high quality and reflect organizational 'love'? Peters and Austen (1985) trace the effects of this kind of love on an organization, as does Egan who designates it as 'tough loving' (quoted in Ditton, 1991). In both cases, 'love' is not sentimental but has the effect of a good organizational outcome. Reddy (1993) sees the connection between such communication and the purpose of the workplace as inherent. The more industry engages with the counselling model, the more it will '. . . be grappling with the perhaps unsuspected depth of the relationship between counselling and the core business of the organization' (Reddy, 1993: 99). This view is supported in pragmatic terms by Orlans, who believes the relationship is more overt: 'It is . . . difficult to imagine that organizations would continue to offer counselling services on a large scale if they did not feel the company was reaping long-term benefits in terms of increased productivity and higher levels of morale' (1986: 23). It is not categorically evidenced in the present research that counselling can change the organizational ethos but the indications are that this is likely.

Counselling skills and self-development.   Self-development is hard to define within management training. Martin (1995) and Dorn (1992) argue that counselling can encourage the integration of career identity with personal identity. Such integration would not be hard to prove, so it should not be too much of a surprise to find that learning counselling skills that are work-based have personal repercussions. McDonald (1991) noted that the content of counselling skills raised issues for course participants on a personal level. It is, indeed, hard to provide without producing too much of what McDonald calls 'uncomfortable feelings' to be ethical. It would seem that this indirect route to self-development, taken by the researched courses, enabled trainees to have enough safety so that they could look into deeper human issues without being threatened head-on. They were able to look at themselves by learning how to cater better for the needs of others. There were many reports of using the skills learned at home to new insights into the nature of people at work, how to handle difficult feelings and how to correct their own tendency to want to solve rather than to be actively engaged with another person.

Many organizations now understand that they need more mature, better-rounded people to help to run a complex organization. Yet such qualities are hard to demand on an application form. It may well be that training which seems to produce an element of self-development is a good option. The modules were not designed for self-development in anything but a rather general way. Yet, that this was in abundant evidence is another indication that the benefits exceeded the stated purpose. In Reddy's summary comment on the present research, the training:

> allowed delegates to find new coordinates for themselves in all sorts of relationships. It seems to have granted them distance, allowed them new freedoms, protected them from manipulation, made some of them more sympathetic and approachable, others more challenging and assertive. (Reddy, cited in Martin, 1994: 27)

This seems to represent considerable self-development and, if it is true, the training has taken the participants well beyond the stated aims of the course.

Conclusion

This research suggests that new and useful learning occurs on short training courses for public sector managers, that these skills are readily transferred to other areas of managerial life, and that the repercussions of counselling training go well beyond its stated aims. There is a need for a comparative study in the private sector in order to draw wider theory across the field.

References

Argyris, C. and Schon, D. (1984) 'What is an organization that it may learn', in B. Paton, S. Brown, R. Spear, J. Chapman, M. Floyd and J. Hamwee (eds), *Organizations*. London: Paul Chapman.

Bond, T. (1989) 'Towards defining the role of counselling skills', *Counselling*, 69: 3–9.

Burgoyne, J. (1989) 'Creating the managerial portfolio: building a competent approach to management development', *Management Education and Development*, Spring.

Carney, P. (1992) 'Deconstructing competencies in counselling', *Counselling*, 3 (4) (November): 237–8.

Charles-Edwards, D. (1989) 'Counselling as a training resource', *Training Officer*, April: 118–20.

Cooper, C., Sadri, G., Allison, T. and Reynolds, P. (1990) 'Stress counselling in the Post Office', *Counselling Psychology Quarterly*, 3 (1): 3–11.

Coopers and Lybrand (1993) 'Counselling for managers', *Higher Education Briefing*, June.

Crouch, A. (1993) 'Coming out – happy to be humanistic', *Counselling Psychology Review*, 8 (1): 14–19.

Davis, V. (1981) *'Notes on counselling skills'*. Unpublished MA thesis, Keele University.

Ditton, A. (1991) 'Counselling for change', *Training and Development*, July: 28

Dorn, F. (1992) 'Occupational wellness: the integration of career identity and personal identity', *Journal of Counseling and Development*, 71 (November/December): 176–8.

Egan, G. (1986) *The Skilled Helper*. Monterey, CA: Brooks/Cole.

Egan, G. (1993) 'The shadow side', *Management Today*, September: 33–8.

Fowler, A. (1991) 'How to provide employee counselling', *Personnel Management Plus*, May: 24–5.

Hoare, I.D. (1984) 'Can managers counsel?', *Counselling*, 48: 7–13.

Hughes, J.M. (1991) *Counselling for Managers: An Introductory Guide*. London: Bacie.

Jarvie, D. and Matthews, J. (1989) 'A counselling approach to development management', *Training and Development*, August: 9–10.

March, J. (1987) 'Theories of choice and making decisions', in B. Paton, S. Brown, R. Spear, J. Chapman, M. Floyd and J. Hamwee (eds), *Organizations*. London: Paul Chapman.

Martin, P.A. (1994) *'The effects of counselling training on public sector managers'*. Unpublished MSc thesis, University of Surrey.

Martin, P.A. (1995) 'The secret agenda', *Human Potential*, Summer: 18–19.

McDonald, D.T. (1991) 'Counselling training for staff in homes for elderly people: problems and possibilities', *Counselling*, 2 (1): 12–13.

Megranahan, M. (1989a) 'Counselling skills in professional and organisational growth', in W. Dryden, D. Charles-Edwards and R. Woolfe (eds), *Handbook of Counselling in Britain*. London: Routledge. pp. 168–83.

Megranahan, M. (1989b) *Counselling: A Practical Guide for Employers*. London: Institute of Personnel Management.

Murgatroyd, S. (1985) *Counselling and Helping*. London: Methuen.

Newby, T. (1983) 'Counselling at work – an overview', *Counselling*, 46: 15–18.

Nixon, J. and Carroll, M. (1994) 'Can a line-manager also be a counsellor?', *Employee Counselling Today*, 6 (1): 10–15.

Novarra, V. (1986) 'Can a manager be a counsellor?', *Personel Management*, June: 48–50.

Orlans, V. (1986) 'Counselling services in organisations', *Personnel Review*, 15 (5): 19–23.

Orlans, V. (1989) 'Counselling in the workplace: a review and thoughts for the future', *Employee Counselling Today*, 1 (1): 3–6.

Pawlik, V. and Kleiner, B. (1986) 'On the job employee counselling: focus on performance', *Personnel Journal*, 65 (11): 31–6.

Pearce, B. (1989) 'Counselling skills in professional and organisational growth', in W. Dryden, D. Charles-Edwards, and R. Woolfe (eds), *Handbook of Counselling in Britain*. London: Routledge. pp. 184–206.

Peters, T. and Austen, N. (1985) *A Passion for Excellence*. New York: Random House.

Pickard, E. (1993) 'Designing training for counsellors at work', *Counselling at Work*, Autumn: 7–8.

Reddy, M. (1985) *Counselling Practices Survey* 90 Church Road, Apsley Heath, Woburn Sands NK17 8TR

Reddy, M. (1993) *EAPs and Counselling Provision in UK Organizations: An ICAS Report and Policy Guide*. Milton Keynes: ICAS.

Scott, D. (1982) '*The need for counselling in industry*', in A.W. Bolger (ed.), *Counselling in Britain: A Reader*. London: Batsford.

Steddon, P. (1991) 'Dealing with troubled employees', *Training and Development*, January: 14–15.

Stewart, W. (1979) *Health Service Counselling*. Tunbridge Wells: Pitman Medical.

Strauss, A. and Corbin, J. (1990) *Basics of Qualitative Research*. London: Sage.

Watts, A.G. (1982) 'Counselling in work settings', in A.W. Bolger (ed.), *Counselling in Britain: A Reader*. London: Batsford.

15

Stress and the EAP Counsellor

Annette Greenwood

This chapter is based on my research dissertation for an MSc in Counselling Psychology from the University of East London and upon my own experiences of working as an EAP counsellor within the National Health Service for the last four years. To date, there has been little research into the possible stresses and coping ability of EAP/workplace counsellors. The findings of this research have implications for the training, supervision and further development of EAP and workplace counsellors and the structure of the organizations they work for.

When I was appointed to the post of Senior Counsellor at Leicestershire Occupational Health Services' Employee Assistance Programme (EAP), I had the luxury of stepping into a newly created post. One of the undoubted benefits this brings is the opportunity to be creative. I saw my role as proactively promoting the counselling service throughout the NHS Trusts within the contract and to allay possible fears that potential clients of this newly created service may have had. At this time the NHS was in the process of major change, one such change being the pending closure of an established hospital and the transfer of staff to another unit. After consultation with both units, I delivered a series of workshops to teams of nurses, doctors and administrators, entitled 'Moving Forward . . . Carrying On'. These workshops brought into sharp focus the two different needs of the employees and the organization. The issues facing EAP/workplace counsellors became apparent and I have chosen to represent this as the conflict triangle (see Figure 15.1).

Figure 15.1   *The conflict triangle*

The Conflict Triangle

The conflict triangle may arise for EAP/workplace counsellors from what may be construed as the opposing expectations of the counsellors by the contracting organization on the one hand and the needs of the client on the other. For example, the needs of the organization may be to return a client back to work as soon as possible whereas the client's needs may be in conflict with this. At such times the organization may perceive that it is paying for a service that it is not receiving.

The implications of the conflict triangle for the counsellor can be a possible stressor. Boundaries are the framework of the therapeutic relationship and it may appear that they are vulnerable in the workplace context because of the differing expectations. Furthermore, regardless of a counsellor's theoretical stance, most counselling training educates the counsellor to focus upon the needs of the client. Within the conflict triangle as thus formulated, the counsellor may feel that he/she has two clients with potentially opposing needs.

Job-related Stress

Job-related stress has been a significant factor in studies within the caring professions. The early work of Maslach suggests that 'job-related stress and burnout can be a considerable problem for those employed in the caring professions' (1976: 16–22). Far from being a single monolithic experience, stress is an individual phenomenon, mediated by one's ability to cope with it, and is influenced by one's own perceptions and experiences of life (Cox and Howarth, 1990). There is, nonetheless, a growing body of research which has found that in the caring professions there are shared experiences of stress, and this has led some theorists to coin the term 'job-related stress' (Maslach, 1986; Leiter, 1991).

Stress at work has far-reaching implications. The Confederation of British Industry (CBI) estimate that absence from work, caused by stress, is an annual cost of £1.5 billion (Summers, 1990). The concept of job-related stress has now been recognized through our legal system. Following the precedent set in the USA, a social worker, John Walker, has successfully sued his former employer in 1994 (Northumberland County Council) and won £200,000 compensation on the grounds that his job was so stressful that he had to retire due to ill-health (Walker v. Northumberland County Council).

EAP/workplace counsellors may be similarly at risk from job-related stress, not only because of the emotional focus of the relationship with the client, a factor shared with other caring professions, but also, in consequence of this legal precedent, by the expectations of the organization that the counsellor may act, in some way, as an 'insurance policy' against expensive litigation from employees.

Despite the fact that there have been a number of studies of stress and burnout within both UK and US caring professions, there seems to be no evidence of any research into the possible stress and coping abilities of EAP/ workplace counsellors. Having identified this gap in the research field, which reflects the embryonic development of EAPs and workplace counselling, I undertook a research project which was initially conceived as part of an MSc dissertation. The research project utilized a standardized questionnaire, the Mental Health Professionals Stress Survey (MHPSS), which has been developed in a recent study of stress and the coping abilities of clinical psychologists (see Cushway and Tyler, 1994).

A formal study was undertaken to investigate stress and the coping ability of EAP/workplace counsellors in a more systematic manner. It considered coping mechanisms for the individual and structures for the organization, as well as considering the implications for the training of the profession. It drew upon both the many theories of stress and coping and formulated a hypothesis which included the multi-faceted nature of stress and recognized that personal and work issues have an impact upon the individual. The findings of this research have relevance to the role of workplace counsellors and to the development of training and supervision of these counsellors. This research forms the basis of this chapter.

The Role of EAP/Workplace Counsellors

There are three dynamics involved in EAP/workplace counselling (Figure 15.2). The triangle created within the framework of the counsellors' role has an impact at many different levels. All three have an impact on the other: the client is employed by the organization and is seen by the counsellor; the counsellor, while working with the client, is at some level involved with the organization (whether it is an in-house or external counselling service); and the organization pays for the counsellor. This interplay by the three sub-systems is an area of stress for the EAP/workplace counsellor (Carroll, 1993).

In essence, the workplace counsellor is often the catalyst for change. The clients who present for counselling are often feeling stuck or confused about what to do. The role of a counsellor is to allow the clients some space within a therapeutic relationship to explore some of the options they might have. This empowering of the client may result in change. Thus the counsellor often acts as the catalyst. Change in the client may be in conflict with the organization. It is a common assumption for management to have the expectation that an employee who goes to see the EAP/workplace counsellor will in some way become easier to manage. However, the employee may become more empowered and, as a result, could be perceived by management as being more of a problem. The consequence of such a change can mean the EAP/ workplace counsellors are held responsible. If this is the case, it can present a difficult and stressful situation for the counsellor because, as stated earlier, he/she has two contracts, one with the client (employee) and one with the organization which is paying for the service.

Figure 15.2   *The three dynamics of EAP/workplace counselling*

The strategy a counsellor employs for coping with this conflict may be a factor that can affect the amount of stress experienced. Alternatively, the client may perceive the counsellor as having loyalties to the organization which may then intrude upon the therapeutic relationship in that the client may feel guarded and unable to express his/her true concerns. A knock-on consequence may be that the counsellor picks up the conflict from both the client and the organization, and this may result in the counsellor feeling responsible in some way for that conflict. This could then promote feelings of self-doubt and lead to higher levels of stress for the counsellor. It may be that there is a link between how the EAP/workplace counsellor is viewed by the organization and the counsellor's feeling of conflict, self-doubt and stress. Such additional tensions for workplace counsellors may be different from those of counsellors in other settings.

Stress

What then is stress and how does it impact on our working lives. In trying to understand the multi-faceted concept of stress, we might be able in some way to minimize its effects. The concept of job-related stress has been acknowledged and described by many theorists (Maslach, 1976; Cooper, 1988; Cox, 1991). More importantly, it has been suggested that it may 'be a particular problem to those doing "people work"' (Maslach 1976: 16). In the last two decades there has been increasing evidence of this from studies into the effects of work-related stress on a variety of health professionals (for example, Payne and Firth-Cozens, 1987).

According to Cox and Howarth the concept of work-related stress 'is one that offers an economy of explanation in relation to the complex perceptual and cognitive process that underpin people's interactions with their work environment and their attempts to cope with the demands of that environment' (1990: 109). In effect, our ability to cope with stress is dependent upon our own perceptions of our abilities to cope, and our coping in other aspects of our lives. Work-related stress often comes about because of changes in the workplace and how it is structured, often described as 'moving the goal posts', rather than the stress associated with a particular type of work, for example the tasks involved in an Accident and Emergency department.

Work-related stress has been defined as the psychological state that is or represents an imbalance or mismatch between people's perceptions of the demand on them (relevant to work) and their ability to cope with those demands. This appraisal of the situation may also take into account the resources and support available to the person for coping, and on the person's control over the situation (Cox, 1987: 6), that is, the individual accesses the outcome of a demand being asked of him/her, and also takes account of the resources and support available and the amount of control he/she has within the situation. We know from the early work by Lazarus and Folkman (1984) that a person's perceived 'locus of control' is an important factor in the outcome of stress and coping with that stress. Work-related stress is often described as a person's experience of negative emotion, unpleasantness and general discomfort, and, in a slightly longer time scale, by changes in general well-being. These feelings may result not only from the experience of stress, but also from the effects of attempting to cope. In simple terms, it is a case of which comes first, the chicken (stress) or the egg (coping). In extending our understanding of stress and coping, it is important to remember that one is not mutually exclusive of the other.

While Cox and Howarth (1990: 6) do address the notion of work-related stress, their transactional model does not fully acknowledge that for some individuals the experience of stress at work may be more strongly correlated to stress and possible conflict at home, with a partner or family member, than to some aspect of the work situation. Lives are not always neatly compartmentalized with a separate professional and home life. Within my own organization, at assessment, clients are asked if work performance is affected by the presenting issue that brought them to the EAP counselling service. For many, this is indeed the case, but often, through the course of the sessions, it becomes clear that a pressure at home, for example, has changed their perceptions of being able to cope and now they feel not only stressed at home but also at work. Burke and Greenberglass (1987) seem to support the notion that the concepts of stress and burnout need to be examined within the context of both family and work life.

If one takes the concept of stress a step further (that is, if the feelings of stress are prolonged), the result can be a form of stress known as 'burnout'. 'Burnout' is a term that was first coined by Freundenberger (1974), whose original formulation of the burnout syndrome was focused on the emotional demands of human service work and the difficulties that individuals encountered in fulfilling professional role expectations. This disjuncture was conceptualized by the Maslach Burnout Inventory (MBI), which Maslach and Jackson 1986) developed as a measure of that syndrome. In essence, Maslach's thesis is that the therapeutic relationship which provides the basis for a wide range of human services is built upon a close, personal relationship between the care giver and the service recipient. The burnout syndrome results from the depletion of the service providers' emotional resources. The studies of burnout have implications for counsellors since the therapeutic relationship is based upon an emotional and often close working alliance. Moreover, the effects of burnout are often described as individuals feeling distant from the world, not being able to engage emotionally with work colleagues and patients/clients. It is as if an invisible wall is built between them and the world in an attempt to cope with their personal world. Psychologists use the term disassociation to describe the concept.

The systematic study of work-related stress has generated a large body of evidence that does suggest that it is a real phenomenon, but few studies have investigated 'how individuals deal with or manage the stress experience, and about effective methods of coping with work-related stress' (Driscoll and Cooper, 1994: 343).

Coping Abilities

Recognition of the phenomenon of stress has resulted in a smaller body of research into how individuals cope. Coping strategies can be both individual and organizational. Understanding the coping mechanism and its importance has been suggested by several theorists (for example, Aldwin and Revenson, 1987; Lazarus and Folkman, 1984; Cox and Ferguson, 1991), who have stated that coping behaviours can minimize the impact of stress and help alleviate the possible negative consequences. Leiter (1991: 124) goes further and suggests that 'prolonged maladaptive coping may ultimately induce a chronic, highly debilitating form of stress known as burnout'. These concepts link to the transactional models of stress that relate to how an individual perceives a situation as stressful. Drewe et al. have described coping as 'cognitions and behaviours adopted by an individual following the recognition of a stressful encounter, that are in some way designed to deal with that encounter or its consequences' (1993: 7).

In order to be able to deal with the effects of stress, it is important that we have an understanding of the ways in which individuals, within a profession, a professional body or as people, create and then employ coping strategies. To do so may be a useful starting-point in the development of organizational structures which can support and educate people in the very notion of psychological well-being within the caring professions.

Psychotherapists, Psychologists and Stress-coping

Research into stress and coping among health professionals has covered many areas and disciplines. Several US studies of psychologists (for example, Boyer, 1984; Laliotis and Grayson, 1985) suggest that the prevalence of distress and impairment among psychologists is at least as high and often higher than in the general non-professional population. A few studies have considered the effects of work-related stress of psychotherapists (Hellman et al., 1987) and clinical psychologists (Norcross and Prochaska, 1986a; Cushway, 1992; Cushway and Tyler, 1994).

The earlier studies of psychotherapists suggest that many practitioners perceived their careers as fulfilling but that the profession also generated personal and professional strain. Later findings suggested that age, experience and lighter case-loads helped alleviate work-related stress (Hellman et al. 1987; Kwee, 1990). Hellman et al., (1987) identified five stress factors associated with the therapeutic relationship:

1. Maintaining the therapeutic relationship.
2. Scheduling – time management.
3. Professional doubt.
4. Work over-involvement.
5. Personal depletion.

More recently, Cushway (1992), in a study of trainee clinical psychologists, estimated that the prevalence of psychological disturbance on the General Health Questionnaire–28 (GHQ–28) was 59 per cent, and 75 per cent reported being moderately or very stressed as a result of clinical training. These findings were similar to an earlier study in Scotland; Sampson found that 68 per cent of Scottish clinical psychologists were moderately or very stressed as a result of their occupation. The GHQ–28 estimated prevalence of psychological disturbance was 33 per cent lower than that of Cushway's trainees. This difference may also be due to the difference in the sample, that is, Cushway's trainees were less experienced and also would have the added stress of passing the clinical assessments. Sampson suggests that stress levels peak during clinical training.

Boundaries were emphasized as an important factor in efforts to understand the stresses and conflicts within the therapeutic role (see Hellman et al., 1987), the suggestion being that the nature of the therapeutic role leads to feelings of anxiety within the therapist and therefore clear boundary management is essential in the maintenance of the therapist's own psychological well-being. In considering the public versus the private sector, Hellman and Morrison (1987) found that public service therapists were less stressed than those in private practice. It may be that there are benefits from belonging to an organization which may give the therapist access to peer support and consultation. In the UK it is not unusual for workplace counsellors to work alone in their employment, regardless of whether it is NHS, public or private sector.

The Hypotheses of the Research Project

The research project that I undertook attempts to investigate the gap in the literature regarding stress and the coping abilities of the EAP/workplace counsellors. Within a quantitative research framework, five hypotheses (questions) were investigated:

1. Experienced counsellors will report less stress.
2. Women will report higher distress levels than men.
3. Behavioural strategies will be most frequently reported (for example, talking with others, sharing one's problem).
4. Avoidance coping, that is, strategies that attempt to reduce tension through, for example, smoking, drug use or keeping one's feelings to oneself, will be associated with greater levels of distress.
5. Counsellors who have partners or do not live alone will report lower levels of stress.

Discussion

The findings of the research hypotheses provided a useful benchmark by which to evaluate the levels of stress.

1. Experienced counsellors will report less stress

Contrary to the first hypothesis that experienced counsellors will report less stress, the results showed that 94 per cent of counsellors were experienced and reported feeling stressed. Clearly there was a bias within the sample, but it is of interest that experience in this group was not a predictor of reporting less stress. The stresses experienced by these counsellors may also be different from those of clinical psychologists in the comparative sample because the provision of workplace counselling is not a statutory requirement and thus it does not have the same organizational structure or developed culture within the NHS. It is also acknowledged that it is a newly developing field.

2. Women will report higher distress levels than men

This hypothesis was not proven. Men reported slightly higher distress levels than women (51 per cent of men on the GHQ–28 compared with 45 per cent of women). In this study all the participants had a partner or did not live alone. It may be that the buffering effect of having a partner to talk to, as suggested by Long (1984) and Cushway (1992), was an important factor for the women in this study. A gender difference may also be that men who work as counsellors may be more able to articulate their feelings of stress than men in other professions. This perhaps questions a dominant assumption that men are the 'copers'?

3. Behavioural strategies will be most frequently reported

In contrast to the expectation that behavioural strategies will be most frequently reported, the findings were unsupported. The highest scoring coping strategy was active cognitive coping. The two most-used coping strategies were: 'I tried to find out more about the situation' and 'I went over the situation in my mind to try to understand it'.

This finding is not consistent with the earlier findings of Cushway (1992) and Cushway and Tyler (1994), where behavioural coping strategies were the most reported (that is, talking with others). The structure of the EAP/ workplace counsellors' organization may be an important factor in the choice of coping strategy. If you work alone or in a small team, it may not be possible to employ behavioural strategies as suggested in Cushway and Tyler (1994). It may simply be that there is no one to talk to. The counsellors did, however, score higher on the amount of social support, but slightly lower on the quality of that support, than the clinical psychologists. This suggests that it may be the quality of social support and not the amount of support that is an important factor in the choice of coping strategy. The training of clinical psychologists may be another predictor to their coping strategies: most clinical trainee courses have clinical placements where trainees have supervision and support from more senior clinical psychologists and team colleagues. This early learning experience of the opportunity to talk things over with someone may influence their model of coping strategy.

4.   *Avoidance coping will be associated with greater levels of distress*

From the findings we can see, however, that avoidance coping will be associated with greater levels of distress. This is consistent with the findings of Norcross and Prochaska (1986b), Cushway (1992) and Cushway and Tyler (1994). One reason may be that those suffering from the highest levels of distress are unable or unwilling to use different coping strategies, or at this high level of distress other coping strategies may not be effective. Cox (1990) suggests that stress is often compounded by the use of ineffective coping strategies.

5.   *Counsellors who have partners or do not live alone will report lower levels of stress*

In this study all participants had partners or did not live alone. This may act as a buffering effect as suggested earlier. Although almost all of the counsellors had partners in this sample group, they still reported feeling stressed. The stress may be different from other studies and more related to organizational structure and process, professional self-doubt and home-conflict.

What Stresses EAP/Workplace Counsellors?

Evidence from this study suggests that counsellors do report high levels of stress due to the following factors: (a) workload; (b) organizational structure and processes; (c) conflicts with other professionals; and confirms the usefulness of the MHPSS as a diagnostic tool. The implications of these findings are that stress in EAP/workplace counsellors needs to be addressed not only at an individual level but also at an organizational level. Pines and Aronson (1981) suggest that organizational strategies for preventing burnout should include reducing staff–client ratios, making 'times out' available from particularly stressful situations, limiting hours of stressful work, increasing organizational flexibility and improving working conditions. The EAP counsellor, unlike the clinical psychologist, often responds to clients' requests for face-to-face counselling within five to seven days. This difference in referral time may be an additional stress for the EAP counsellors. It is not unusual for referrals to clinical psychologists to take between two to nine months. Working with clients experiencing such high levels of distress may be a factor in the accumulative stress experienced by some EAP counsellors. It may therefore be important that the EAP counselling service take note of this when developing its own organizational culture and support for the EAP counsellors it employs.

More recently Cox and Haworth (1990) has proposed strategies which will lead to the development of healthier organizational cultures and which will contribute to the alleviation of work stress. Cox contends that there is a need at an organizational level to acknowledge and address work-related stress issues and the organization can grow and benefit from sharing and problem-solving stressful issues that may be shared in some occupations. The benefits to the organization can be significant. The stressors associated with workplace counselling could be a resource if the problem-solving of individuals could be seen in the context of a shared experience across the counselling service. Then the organization could learn and create a healthier, more aware culture.

Job satisfaction correlated negatively with organizational structure and processes, relationships and conflicts with other professionals and the MHPSS mean. This finding is consistent with the earlier work of Cushway and Tyler (1994). The largest negative correlation with job satisfaction was organizational structure and process, emphasizing the importance of this factor to occupational satisfaction.

There was a negative correlation between the MHPSS and the amount of social support and client-related difficulties, which suggests that the amount of support was an important factor in reducing client-related difficulties. The MHPSS does not, however, consider work colleagues and peer support in the questionnaire with regards to social support. This may be an important factor in supporting and reducing levels of stress regarding client difficulties. For example, peers at work have a shared knowledge and experience of work-related stress. The quality of social support was significantly negatively correlated with the MHPSS, organizational structure and process, lack of resources, professional self-doubt, home–work conflict and the MHPSS mean. The findings suggest that when investigating factors for predicting stress in caring professionals, there is a need to include not only work-related stressors but also home-life and personal relationships, as suggested by Burke and Greenberglass (1987).

The GHQ–28 mean correlated with the MHPSS mean, which is consistent with the earlier study of Cushway and Tyler (1994). This result also suggests support for the MHPSS as a valid tool of assessing stress, as most people experiencing stress do seem to have psychological difficulties as identified by the GHQ–28 scale. Indeed, 47 per cent of the sample were cases. In particular, the counsellors significantly correlated between the sub-scale social dysfunction and self-doubt. This is in contrast to the clinical psychologist who most strongly associated with the sub-scale anxiety and insomnia.

The early work of Maslach (1986) and Hellman et al. (1987) has developed the concept that the therapeutic relationship itself may be stressful. It is important that a distinction is made among the different professions as 'people work' *per se* is a too broad a definition. While EAP/workplace counsellors may share some similarities with psychotherapists and clinical psychologists, further research into this area is needed.

Coping Strategies of EAP/Workplace Counsellors

Coping strategies are clear indicators of stress. As stress levels increase, a counsellor may employ an array of coping strategies in response. The importance of understanding coping mechanisms has been underlined by several investigators (for example, Lazarus and Folkman, 1984; Cox and Ferguson, 1991), who suggest that coping behaviours can minimize the impact of stress and alleviate its negative consequences (Driscoll and Cooper, 1994). The coping strategy that is employed is a significant variable in determining a positive outcome. Increased consumption of alcohol, for example, would be considered an avoidance coping strategy as it does nothing to address the underlying issues (and actually will result in a depressant response). For the counsellors in this study, active cognitive coping was the highest reported coping strategy, and this suggests that the process of understanding their role and being active participants in decision-making practices may be important factors in dealing with stress.

Although there have been methodological difficulties associated with research into coping strategies (Driscoll and Cooper, 1994), an understanding of how people cope will lead to a greater understanding of the whole concept of stress. This in turn will have direct relevance for the development of future organizational structures within workplace counselling providers, and the training and supervision of workplace counsellors.

Conclusion

The findings of this study have a number of implications for workplace counselling: first, the training of workplace counsellors, in addition to equipping the counsellor with the necessary skills, should include education about organizational behaviour and systems. A knowledge of the conflict triangle could give counsellors insight into possible areas of conflict and stress. A number of studies have shown that by giving information and understanding of a situation, individuals have a better sense of control.

In the UK today only four courses are specifically geared to counselling at work, and what training exists tends to be unsystematic (Carroll, 1996).

Orlans (1992) has argued that a counsellor needs a long list of understanding and skills beyond those of counselling.

Workplace supervision should be viewed as a coping strategy for the counsellor and it can be a significant resource for the counsellor to explore alternative ways of coping. There are few training courses available which address the particular issues facing workplace counsellors. Good supervision sessions will focus not only on the clinical work, but be a time to try to understand the organizational culture: 'enabling counsellors to understand the kind of organizational culture in which they are involved will help them be realistic about expectations' (Carroll, 1993: 9).

Supervision can also help counsellors to have an understanding of how an EAP can be set up and managed. The foundation of a good contract for the counselling service within an organization can empower counsellors to have a sense of their own boundaries.

Lastly, it is perhaps worth remembering that there is life outside workplace counselling and a more personal coping strategy may come from having personal and social support from various sources.

It is not a sign of failure to say we cannot cope. We also have a responsibility to ourselves to monitor our own stress levels – 'the very profession that teaches self-care so often fails to practise it' (Nichols, 1988: 50). While the profession of workplace counselling would do well to promote more education into the development of counsellors and supervisors, it is of equal importance that some effort is directed at the improvement of healthier organizational cultures.

References

Aldwin, C. and Revenson, T. (1987) 'Does coping help? A reexamination of the relation between coping and mental health', *Journal of Personality and Social Psychology*, 53, 337–48.

Boyer, C.A. (1984) 'The profession's response to distressed psychologists', in R. Kilburg, P.E. Nathan and R.W. Thoreson (eds), *Professionals in Distress*. New York: American Psychological Association.

Burke, R. and Greenberglass, E.R. (1987) 'Work and family conflict', in C. Cooper and L. Robertson (eds), *International Review of Industrial and Organizational Psychology*. New York: Wiley.

Carroll, M. (1993) 'Supervising counsellors in organizational settings', unpublished paper.

Carroll, M. (1996) *Workplace Counselling: A Systematic Approach to Employee Care*. London: Sage.

Cooper, C.L., Copper, R.D. and Eaker, L.H. (1988) *Living with Stress*. London: Penguin.

Cox, T. (1987) 'Stress, coping and problem solving', *Work and Stress*, 1 (1): 5–14.

Cox, T. (1990) 'Stress and organizational health', paper presented at Stress and Mental Health Conference, MIND, Whitehaven, Cumbria.

Cox, T. (1991) Editorial comment, 'Organizational culture, stress and stress management', *Work and Stress*, 5 (1): 1–4.

Cox, T. and Howarth, I. (1990) 'Organizational health, culture and caring', *Work and Stress*, 4, 107–10.

Cox, T. and Ferguson, E. (1991) 'Individual differences, stress and coping', in C. Cooper and R. Payne (eds), *Personality and Stress: Individual Differences in the Stress Process*. Chichester: Wiley. pp. 7–30.

Cushway, D. (1992) 'Stress in clinical psychology trainees', *British Journal of Clinical Psychology*, 31, 169–79.

Cushway, D. and Tyler, P. (1994) 'Stress and coping in clinical psychologists', *Stress Medicine*, 10: 35–42.

Driscoll, M.P. and Cooper, C.L. (1994) 'Coping with work-related stress: a critique of existing measures and proposal for an alternative methodology', *Journal of Occupational and Organizational Psychology*, 67: 343–54.

EAP Association (1995) *UK Standards of Practice and Professional Guidelines for Employee Assistance Programmes*. London: EAPA.

Freundenberger, H. (1974) 'Staff burn-out', *Journal of Social Issues*, 30, 159–65.

Hellman, I.D., Morrison, T.L. and Abramowitz, S.I. (1987) 'Therapist flexibility/rigidity and work stress', *Professional Psychology: Research and Practice*, 18 (1): 21–5.

Hellman, I.D., and Morrison, T.L. (1987) 'Practice setting and type of caseload as factors in psychotherapist stress', *Psychotherapy*, 24 (3): 427–33.

Kwee, M.G.T. (1990) 'Burn-out among Dutch psychotherapists', *Psychology Review*, 60: 107–12.

Laliotis, D.A. and Grayson, J.H. (1985) 'Psychologist heal thyself: what is available for the impaired psychologist?', *American Psychologist*, 40: 84–96.

Lazarus, R. and Folkman, S. (1984) *Stress, Appraisal and Coping*. New York: Springer.

Leiter, M. (1991) 'Coping patterns as predictors of burnout: the function of control and escapist coping patterns', *Journal of Organization Behaviour*, 12: 123–44.

Leiter, M.P. (1992) 'Burn-out as a crisis in professional role structures: measurement and conceptual issues', *Anxiety, Stress and Coping*, 5, 123–44.

Long, P. (1984) *The Personal Professionals: A Comparative Study of Male and Female Careers*. London: IPM.

Maslach, C. (1976) 'Burned-out', *Human Behavior*, 5: 16–22.

Maslach, C. (1986) 'Stress, burnout and workaholism', in R. Kilburg, P.E. Nathan and R.W. Thoresen (eds), *Professionals in Distress*. New York: American Psychological Association.

Maslach, C. and Jackson, S.E. (1986) *Maslach Burnout Inventory Manual*, 2nd edn. Palo Alto, CA: Consulting Psychologist Press.

Nichols, K.A. (1988) 'Practising what we preach', *The Psychologist*, 1: 50–1.

Norcross, J.C. and Prochaska, J.O. (1986a) 'Psychotherapist heal thyself – 1. The psychological distress and self-change of psychologist, counsellors and laypersons', *Psychotherapy*, 23 (1): 102–14.

Norcross, J.C. and Prochaska, J.O. (1986b) 'Psychotherapist heal thyself – 2. The self-initiated and therapy-facilitated change of psychological distress', *Psychotherapy*, 23 (3): 345–56.

Orlans, V. (1992) 'Counselling in the workplace – Part 1: Counsellors' perspectives and training', *EAP International*, 1 (1): 19–21.

Payne, R. and Firth-Cozens, J. (1987) *Stress in Health Professionals*. Chichester: Wiley.

Pines, A. and Aronson, E. (1981) *Burnout: From Tedium to Personal Growth*. New York: Free Press.

Summers, D. (1990) 'Testing for stress in the workplace', *Financial Times*, 6 December.

16

An Evaluation of Employee Assistance and Workplace Counselling Programmes in the UK

Carolyn Highley-Marchington and Cary L. Cooper

There have been only a handful of UK evaluations of workplace counselling programmes. The Post Office study (Cooper et al., 1990), which evaluated an internal workplace counselling service, is one of these few. This paucity of UK evaluation research led the Health and Safety Executive to commission an evaluation of UK workplace counselling programmes, which was carried out independently by the Manchester School of Management (Highley and Cooper, 1995). The primary aim of this research was to evaluate a sample of UK EAPs and workplace counselling programmes, at both the individual and organizational levels, and on a nationwide basis. A self-report questionnaire was designed and individual sickness absence data was collected. This chapter will describe the measures used, the methodology which was employed and the results of the research. There will also be a discussion of the possible reasons for the findings.

Method

Methodological Considerations

It was essential that the research evaluated the benefits of counselling at both the individual and organizational levels, because such services operate at the interface between the two and for the mutual benefit of both. At the individual level, a questionnaire-based study of stress and employee well-being was used. Mental well-being, physical well-being, job satisfaction, interpersonal relations at work, home/work relationship, self-reported absence and attitudinal factors were assessed. These are subjective measures which required self-report. Details of the questionnaire items are given later. At the organizational level, objective data such as sickness absence was collected.

One of the common criticisms of research evaluating the effectiveness of programmes aimed at enhancing well-being is that many factors other than the treatment programme itself can influence the results. This criticism is particularly valid when no comparison group is used, and measures are only taken at the point of entry into a programme and at a single point in time immediately after completion. There are several problems with such a 'before' and 'after' design when evaluating the effectiveness of counselling programmes:

1. Without comparative data from individuals who have not used the programme, it is extremely difficult to disentangle effects due to the counselling process from those due to factors related to the individual being counselled, or to the organization.
2. Because an individual is likely to be in a high-stress state at the time of entry into the counselling process, regression to the mean effects may influence findings (since, statistically, there will always be spontaneous movement towards the mean and away from the extreme).
3. The evaluation of benefits is limited to immediate impact when, in fact, the time lag between application of the counselling process and the manifestations of its effects is unknown.

Indeed, the 'effectiveness' of a counselling programme, from an employer's (and individual's) point of view, is likely to be defined in part by its ability to have a positive impact 'beyond' the time of contact. Given that the manifestation of effects is likely to vary between individuals, problem types and over time, it would have been unfair to those providing counselling services to restrict the assessment of benefits to 'immediate impact' only. For these reasons it was decided that a control group was desirable, as was the need to follow up clients some months after counselling had been completed.

One of the positive aspects of this research was the anticipation of working with a number of counselling providers, which would have enabled an evaluation of the benefits of counselling to employees in a variety of occupations and locations (provided sample sizes were large enough). This would have enhanced the overall external validity of the research and, consequently, its ultimate practical value to all parties. However, it also meant that 'treatment effects' may have influenced the results, because even though the overall goals of counselling programmes may be the same (at least compatible), the way in which these goals are met – the structure, implementation and operation of programmes – differs. Confidence in the overall results, and in the evaluations for each individual EAP/counselling provider, is therefore greatly increased if data collection is not set within the context of a single organization. It was decided, therefore, to collect data from at least two client organizations for each provider, in order to make the evaluation more meaningful. This had the effect of increasing sample sizes, enhancing validity and minimizing the possible influence of potentially unique organizational factors.

Linked closely to these design considerations, there were several potential sources of variance intrinsic to this study, which may potentially have confounded the results, and these must be considered.

As stated earlier, the benefits derived from counselling (outcomes) will vary between individuals, problem types and over time. 'Treatment' is also variable, since short-term, focused counselling is necessarily eclectic and responsive to the needs of the individual client. Furthermore, observed effects may be influenced not only by the experiences and personal qualities of the individual being counselled, but also by the experience, personal qualities and qualifications of the counsellor. Since one has no control over these factors, they can at best be measured and at least acknowledged as potential sources of variance. In recognition of these complexities the study included a short questionnaire to be completed by counsellors themselves (after the final session with each client), in addition to a section for clients' evaluation of the counselling process.

Finally, as with all assessments of treatment programmes, an individual's willingness to go for counselling and their expectations for therapeutic gain can influence results (selection effects). Since the majority of employees using such services will have referred themselves voluntarily (and not everyone who may benefit from counselling will elect to participate), self-selection into groups cannot be avoided. However, some measure of employees' attitude towards the provision of counselling was included on the questionnaire. Although this will not have eliminated selection effects, it did provide data on the perceived value of counselling, and ties in with the suggestion that such programmes can serve an internal public relations function simply by being in place.

Selection of Criteria Measures

Regardless of how creatively designed, well-controlled and smoothly executed a research design is, its ultimate value is largely determined by the measures from which data is derived The choice of what to measure and which measures to use had to be guided by the relevance of the variables selected to the goals and objectives of the research; standardization of the measurement instrument; technical features of the measurement instrument (reliability and internal validity); and feasibility in terms of access, time and cost constraints.

Given the multiple outcomes that counselling can produce, the definition of which criterion measures should determine 'success' demanded careful consideration. Take-up/usage rates are sometimes put forward as a measure of success. However, these rates are more accurately interpreted as an index of the demand/need for services and an index of the success of programmes in gaining employee confidence. Take-up rates are, therefore, a powerful statement in themselves: if 10–15 per cent of the working population feel that some professional assistance in dealing with difficulties they may be having will be of value to them, it has to be an option that is seriously considered by employers. On their own, however, they say nothing about the benefits derived from having been through the counselling process.

As stated earlier, the potential value of EAPs/counselling programmes to industry is that they offer benefits to both individuals and employing organizations. The outcome measures, therefore, needed to tap both these levels and reflect the interaction of the individual with the organization. As Roman et al. have stated in relation to evaluation, 'exclusive attention to individual employee outcomes can lead to neglect of an EAP's potential as a humane and reasonable mechanism for trying to stabilise both individual and organizational performance' (1987). To be of real practical value, measures should also have implications for organizational functioning.

The function of any evaluation is to assess effectiveness in achieving predetermined objectives. One of the main purposes of the preliminary discussions with providers and organizations with EAPs was to gain a deeper understanding of the issues involved and avoid omitting important areas of concern for providers and their clients. The starting point in deciding what to measure was therefore guided by those individual and organizational factors that EAPs/counselling programmes are said to impact upon. Potential benefits to the individual include: improved mental well-being, coping ability and interpersonal relations; and increased job/life satisfaction. Potential benefits to the organization include: increased 'morale' and improved interpersonal relations; decreased rates of absence/sickness, employee turnover, accidents and formal grievances; and increased performance (in terms of both quality and quantity).

Organizational-level measures – absence data. For evaluation at the organizational level access to individual absenteeism/sickness absence rates was desirable. Such rates are of serious concern to employers and are a relevant indicator of a programme's 'effectiveness': previous research has found a significant relationship between subjective and objective measures of stress and absenteeism, suggesting that any significant decrease in stress should, in turn, result in a decrease in absenteeism (Cole et al., 1982).

In addition, multiple and objective measures enhanced the rigour of the evaluation by minimizing the dangers inherent in relying on subjective, self-reported data. It was recognized, however, that many UK organizations do not monitor absenteeism: a 1991 survey by chartered accounts Arthur Anderson estimated that 40 per cent of UK businesses fall into this category. It was also understood that access to individual employee records may not have been acceptable on ethical grounds. However, organizational data – even in summary form – was still deemed useful. Existing performance indicators could also have formed outcome measures at the organizational level. This obviously required detailed discussion with client organizations.

Individual-level measures. When evaluating programmes which can produce multiple outcomes for the individual, all potentially relevant variables cannot possibly be incorporated into a single study. This would be far too demanding on respondents – even if identification of the relevant variables was clear cut. Individual outcome measures considered for inclusion in this study were: organizational commitment/morale; coping ability; job satisfaction; and mental/physical well-being. Of these, job satisfaction and mental/physical well-being were selected as outcome measures. These were selected for two important reasons:

1. They are the most common individual benefits said to be derived from the provision of EAPs/counselling services in industry.

2. There is extensive research evidence indicating their relationship with individual turnover, absenteeism and job performance (Griffin and Bateman, 1986), all of which are of obvious relevance for effective organizational functioning.

As stated earlier, it is imperative that measures reflect the interaction of the individual with the organization and assess the stated goals of EAPs/counselling. It is also the case, however, that the experience of negative stress – its causes and consequences – is unique to the individual. Personal characteristics and circumstances will influence whether and how distress is experienced. The benefits derived from counselling are therefore also likely to be influenced by these factors.

Personality characteristics implicated as having an important influence on 'stress' include: Type A/B; locus of control; hardiness; coping ability; and trait anxiety. Again, all these potential influences cannot possibly be included within the context of a single study. Furthermore, reliable existing measures designed to tap such characteristics tend to be lengthy. While it is undoubtedly important to endeavour to discover what makes one person more susceptible and/or able to cope with stress than another, it was not the purpose of this study. In order to minimize the time taken to complete the proposed questionnaire, none of the above characteristics were included in this study.

The personal characteristics selected were age, sex, educational achievement, and marital and parental status. Job characteristics and health habits were also included. In recognition of the subjective nature of 'stress', all respondents were asked whether they were experiencing stress in particular spheres of their lives at the time of completing the questionnaire and if so, to give these experiences a subjective stress rating. The selection of which life spheres to include was based on problem categories commonly addressed by EAPs/counselling services. This was viewed as more meaningful, and less time-consuming, than including a standard 'life events' scale which is both lengthy and not directly relevant to those problem areas addressed by counselling services.

A major strength of EAPs/counselling services lies in their holistic approach to well-being and their recognition of the fact that a clear distinction between personal and work-related problems is not possible: distress in one area is likely to affect adversely the other unless dealt with effectively. The degree of functioning at the interface of home and work domains is important because it is realistic that people will bring their personal worries to work at times, just as they will take work problems home with them. It was necessary, therefore, that this research included some measure of the home/work interface.

It was equally necessary that work-based pressures were assessed, because of the potential of EAPs/counselling to perform a proactive role in organizational well-being. While it was recognized that it is not within counsellors' power to change an employee's job, rate of pay, or how the organization is structured, EAPs/counselling services do have a potentially important role to play in alerting organizations to internal factors that may be inhibiting performance in groups of employees – these are, after all, the factors that employers have most control over and can change. Unless these factors are looked at, internal factors which may have important implications for effective organizational functioning will be overlooked. It was felt that concentration solely on personal stressors would not do justice to the potential which counselling services have for facilitating action that can enhance individual and organizational well-being.

The Measures Used

The questionnaire. The self-completion questionnaire designed for this research consisted of a biographical section and three sub-scales. The questionnaire measured:

- Individual variables which may influence the experience of stress.
- Major consequences of distress for the individual.
- Major sources of pressure (at the interface of the individual with the organization).

The decision as to which measures to use was dictated by the standardization of the measurement instrument, reliability and internal consistency of the instrument and time/cost constraints. Access to a large normative database was particularly important as the research was being conducted with diverse groups of people in diverse settings. The measures selected for use in this study are outlined below.

- *Current state of health: mental and physical well-being.* The GHQ–12 (Goldberg, 1972) and mental/physical health sub-scales of the OSI (Cooper et al., 1988) were selected for use in this research. Used in conjunction, they provided both a context-specific (work-related) and global measure of mental health (OSI and GHQ–12, respectively). The work-related nature of the mental health scale of the OSI was obviously of value given the objectives of this research. It was felt, however, that a more global measure of mental well-being, which could identify minor psychiatric disorders, was also needed.
- *Job satisfaction.* The job satisfaction scale of the OSI (Cooper et al., 1988) was selected for use in this study.
- *Demographic variables.* Personal and job demographic variables included age, sex, marital and parental status, education, job grade and tenure. Questions relating to lifestyle/health habits (alcohol and nicotine consumption) were also included. This section also included a question about stressful situations currently being experienced in seven different life spheres and asked for a subjective stress rating of those situations (where appropriate). Respondents were also asked if any changes/events were currently occurring within their organization which they perceived as affecting their job – either directly or indirectly. The purpose of this question was to identify whether any factors unique to that organization were exerting an influence on the findings.

- *Sources of pressure.*   Four of the six sub-scales of the OSI (Cooper et al., 1988) 'sources of pressure' scale were highly relevant to the nature of this research since they tap the interface of the individual with the organization and allow the identification of perceived organizational sources of pressure. The Likert-type response options for these sub-scales allowed an assessment of the extent to which each potential source of pressure was perceived by individuals.
  The four sub-scales were:

  1. 'Home and work relationship': considers whether home problems are brought to work and whether work is perceived as having a negative impact on home life. It does not address specific home or work-based problems, but assesses the extent to which the individual experiences a conflict between the two.
  2. 'Relationship with others': assesses perceived pressures arising from personal contacts at work. The sub-scale taps the issue of interpersonal relations and allows an assessment of changes along this dimension over the course of time.
  3. 'Organizational structure and climate': addresses problems which commonly arise from bureaucracy, communication problems and morale in organizations. The sub-scale is focused at the level of the organization.
  4. 'Factors intrinsic to the job': this sub-scale looks at workload, variety of tasks and rates of pay, and is focused at the level of the job itself.

  It was important to identify organizational and job sources of pressure in this research, since whether individuals perceive their main sources of pressure as coming from within the organization, or outside it, was likely to be a source of variance influencing the findings.
- *Other information.*   In addition to the scales outlined above, opinions regarding the provision of a counselling service were sought. The questionnaire included a short section on employees' attitudes towards the provision of counselling (perceived values of such a service for both individuals and the organization as a whole). In addition, individuals were asked if they had been absent from work in the last six months and if so, on how many occasions and for how long.
  An extra 'counselling evaluation' section was included for those individuals who had gone through the counselling process, so that their views of the service (in terms of perceived helpfulness of counsellors, perceived quality of service provision and perceived positive benefits both at home and at work) could be assessed.

Objective sickness absence data.   In addition to collecting self-report questionnaire data, it was necessary to consider whether the fact that individuals attended counselling had any impact on the organization. It was decided that sickness absence data may be one of the organizational statistics affected by the provision of counselling, so sickness absence data was collected.

Methodology

Evaluation at the individual level. The original methodology was a retrospective design comprising an 'experimental' (counselled group and a 'comparison' (non-counselled) group. However, data from those using the service was still desirable, and useful, even if it was not possible to select a comparison group. This in fact proved to be the case.

Pre-counselling and post-counselling measures were taken for the experimental group over a period of 8–12 months. Pre-counselling measures were taken at the first counselling session and post-counselling measures were taken after the last session (agreed between the individual client and counsellor). A comparison group (equal in size to the experimental group) was to have been selected at random from a list of all appropriate employees. The comparison group would have been given the same questionnaire. A follow-up measure was then given to the experimental group (and would have been given to the comparison group) after an interval of three months. Time restraints meant that follow-up measures could not be taken after a longer time interval in this study. Ideally, one would want to have more than one follow-up measure, over a greater time interval – even several years. While restricted, our follow-up period was sufficient to stabilize regression to the mean effects and identify the benefits of counselling to the individual beyond immediate impact.

The research design allowed the benefits of counselling for the individual employee to be effectively evaluated since it enabled an assessment of:

1. The immediate impact of counselling on individual well-being for those employees who chose to use the service.
2. The longer-term impact of counselling on individual well-being for those who had used the service, compared to their personal pre-counselling and post-counselling levels.

However, due to the lack of a comparison group, it was not possible to assess whether the changes seen in the experimental group were more positive than those seen in the comparison group.

Evaluation at the organizational level. Access to hard data was desirable, in order to assess the benefits of counselling at an organizational level. This would ideally have been individual sickness/absence records collected retrospectively for the six months prior to counselling and six months after completion of counselling. Any individual sickness absence data could only be collected with the informed consent of the individuals concerned. The absence data was collected in two forms – the first was the total number of days absence in the six-month period, and the second was the number of absence events in the six-month period. Where possible, control data over the same time periods was also collected.

Administration and Distribution of Questionnaires

The questionnaires took no longer than 30 minutes to complete. The way in which the questionnaires were administered to the experimental group was closely linked to the need to maintain the assurance of confidentiality given by counselling providers to their clients. The importance of keeping disruption to the counselling process itself to a minimum was also recognized. It was decided, therefore, that for the experimental group (that is employees who presented for counselling) questionnaires would be distributed by the counsellors themselves. The pre-counselling measure was distributed at the first session and the post-counselling measure at the end of the final session. It was also essential, however, to be able to match measures taken at pre-counselling, post-counselling and follow-up for each individual counselled. Each individual was therefore allocated a number by the counsellor at the beginning of the first session. The resultant list of identifying code numbers was held in strictest confidence by the counselling providers. This number was written on the first questionnaire by the counsellor and the same number used on questionnaires handed out at the end of the last session. Measures taken at follow-up were also distributed via the counselling provider, using the same code number. A cover letter explaining the purpose of the numbering system, as well as outlining the research, was sent out with each questionnaire.

By adopting this approach, the individual's right to confidentiality and anonymity was protected: only the counselling providers knew the identity of employees presenting for counselling. However, this required a great deal of commitment and cooperation from individual counsellors. In general, the counselling providers fully understood the reasons for this approach. In order to maintain confidentiality and encourage individual employees to respond, freepost reply envelopes addressed directly to the researchers were provided.

Results

Questionnaire data was collected from the clients of nine separate counselling services and EAPs, at three different time points (pre-counselling, post-counselling, and three to six months after counselling). Absence data was available from a further four companies. In addition, it was possible to collect questionnaire data from a sample of all staff in two of the nine companies. Both had EAPs. The data was collected at two time points – the first just after the EAP was introduced or re-launched, and the second 18 months to two years after implementation.

Individual Questionnaire Data

The key findings in relation to the pre-counselling, post-counselling and follow-up psychological measures were:

After receiving counselling (and at follow-up) clients reported significantly improved mental well-being and physical well-being, compared to before coun-selling. However, there were no reported changes for job satisfaction or any of the sources of pressure scales.

To a great extent this finding is not surprising. Counselling, whether internal or external to the organization, is aimed at helping individuals to cope with their personal and work lives better. As such, one would hope to find some change in a client's mental and physical health after receiving counselling. However, job satisfaction is concerned with an individual's satisfaction with various aspects of his/her job, and the sources of pressure scales are concerned with where employees perceive stress as originating from within the organization. None of these things are likely to change as a result of going for counselling, because counselling services are not organizational interventions, and it is therefore unlikely that any organizational issues are addressed. This results in the organization staying the same and the individual changing. Hence, one cannot expect to see an impact on job satisfaction or sources of pressure. In effect, individuals still view the workplace the same as they did before (because it is the same as it was before), so no changes result for job satisfaction or sources of pressure. However, individuals are able to cope better and therefore should be more mentally (and probably physically) healthy.

Similar findings were obtained when comparing pre-counselling and follow-up scores and this suggests that any psychological changes resulting from counselling are likely to be sustained over a period of at least three to six months after counselling. This is to be expected. Indeed, it has been suggested that the effects of counselling may continue well after counselling ends and therefore greater effects may be seen at some stage later.

Clients were asked whether or not they had been absent from work in the last six months and if so, how many days absence they had had. The results showed that after counselling less people had been absent from work in the last six months, and that those who had been absent had fewer days off.

At the pre-counselling stage, clients were asked who had suggested they use the service. The results were: 24 per cent – manager; 21 per cent – occupational health; 14 per cent – friend; 5 per cent – personnel; and 3 per cent – union. However, the majority (36 per cent) reported that they referred themselves.

Clients were also asked whether or not they thought that the provision of a counselling service was valued by staff: 88 per cent said it was definitely valued; 10 per cent believed that it was possibly valued; and 2 per cent said that it was not valued.

Clients reported their initial problems as falling into the following categories: 38 per cent – marital; 29 per cent – work; 26 per cent – health; 24 per cent – family; 18 per cent – colleagues; 11 per cent – legal; and 10 per cent – financial. Obviously, some clients reported that their problems fell into more than one category. For example, 44 per cent of clients were seen by a counsellor within one week of contacting the service and 86 per cent felt that this was quickly enough. The average number of sessions was seven, over an average of eleven weeks: 74 per cent of clients felt that the number of sessions they had was enough to help them and 89 per cent reported seeing the same counsellor throughout.

In terms of the effects of going for counselling on the clients' work and non-work life, the ability to concentrate on tasks, relationships with colleagues, family and friends, self-confidence, job performance, overall enjoyment of life, and decision-making ability, were all rated highly: 74 per cent of clients believed that counselling had not resolved the problem but had enabled them to handle it better and 85 per cent of clients would use the service again, if the need arose.

There were some differences in terms of the results for internal and external services. The data suggested that the internal counselling services were having the greatest effects, in terms of mental and physical health.

This may be due to some extent to the greater ability of internal services to deal with workplace issues. If an individual is counselled as a person within the workplace context and all the culture, policies and procedures of the organization are known to the counsellor, one would expect the counsellor to be more effective at helping the person to cope with both his/her work and home life. This more effective coping can be expected to have an effect on the person's mental and physical health. This may well be the case with internal counselling services.

In contrast, EAPs are less able to deal with organizational issues, primarily because the counsellors do not know enough about the organizations involved. Thus, clients seeing an EAP counsellor are likely to be counselled as individuals, but not within the context of the workplace. Therefore, the whole of the person's life is not being addressed. If only the individual's personal problems are being dealt with and he/she is no better able to cope with work-related issues, then a significant effect on mental and physical health is unlikely.

The somewhat surprising finding is that if an internal service does have the ability to feed back organizational issues to the company, one would expect there also to be an effect on the other variables contained in the questionnaire (that is job satisfaction and sources of pressure). The fact that this was not evident may be explained in at least three ways:

• The pre- and post-counselling questionnaires were completed by individuals at the start and finish of counselling. The time period between completion of the two questionnaires is therefore quite short (on average about 10 weeks, according to clients). Even if an organizational problem was picked up by a counsellor and fed back to the company, it is unlikely that any changes at the organizational level would be instituted before the client finished counselling. Therefore, one could not expect to see an impact on the job satisfaction and sources of pressure scales.

- Although internal counsellors do indeed have the opportunity to feed back issues of employee concern to the organization, it may well be that they do not actually do so in practice. It is quite possible that they use their knowledge of the company to help individual clients (hence the effect on individual well-being scores), but do not then feed back issues to the organization for them to address. If this is the case, then obviously no impact on job satisfaction or sources of pressure can be expected.
- It may be the case that even if the counsellor does feed back problems and organizational issues to the company, these may not be addressed by the organization. So although the counsellor has picked up on these issues and fed back on them, the organization may choose not to do anything about them. If this is the case, then obviously there would be no impact on an individual's job satisfaction or sources of pressure.

A further explanation for the differences found between the internal and external services may concern the sample sizes. Much more data was available from the internal services than from the EAPs, so the sample sizes, and hence the likelihood of significant findings were much greater for the internal services.

An unmatched control group of a sample of all employees within two companies showed no changes on the mental and physical health scales where changes were detected for counselled employees.

While these two groups of employees were not ideal as controls, they were considered to be suitable for this use, given the fact that data could not be collected from matched controls from within the same organizations as the clients. The fact that these controls showed no changes in the scores for the scales which the client group did, suggests that the effects found for counselled employees are likely to be due to some extent to the counselling process.

There were no significant differences from post-counselling to follow-up (three to six months after counselling) on any of the mental and physical health measures. However, clients did report significantly more stress as coming from the 'organizational structure and climate'.

As discussed earlier, there is a belief that counselling may well continue to have an effect for some time after counselling itself has ended. This suggestion is not borne out by the results of this research because no improvement in mental or physical health was found from post-counselling to follow-up. However, at follow-up, clients did report significantly more stress as coming from the 'organizational structure and climate'. Therefore the longer-term impact of counselling may have been obscured by the perception of more stress. Indeed, if employees are reporting more stress from work, but their psychological health has been unaffected, this is positive in itself, as one would have expected to see a reduction in mental health when more stress is being experienced.

Sickness Absence Data

There was a significant reduction in both the total number of days absence, and the number of absence events, from pre- to post-counselling. However, there was no such reduction for the matched control group.

The findings from the objective sickness absence data were in line with the self-reported sickness absence given by clients on the questionnaires. The self-report absence statistics revealed that after counselling less people had been absent from work in the last six months, and those who had been absent have had fewer days off.

The absence statistics (days and events) for the control group and client group were identical at the pre-counselling stage, but differed significantly at the post-counselling stage, when the client group showed significantly less absence compared to the matched controls.

These sickness absence results can be considered in conjunction with the questionnaire results on psychological health, in that essentially what is happening is that going for counselling is having an effect at the individual level. It is the individual's health (that is mental and physical well-being) and health behaviours (that is sickness absence) which appear to be affected by counselling, rather than organizational indicators (that is job satisfaction and sources of pressure). This is to be expected because counselling is essentially an intervention which focuses on the individual (not the organization), where the emphasis is on changing the individual's response to stress rather than changing the organizational sources of stress. It is therefore likely that the greatest effect will be shown for individual outcomes, that is absence, mental well-being and physical well-being.

Company-wide Questionnaire Data

The results from the company-wide questionnaires were:

The introduction of an EAP affects the individual being counselled but not the whole employee population, in terms of mental and physical health, job satisfaction and sources of pressure.

This finding is not surprising since an EAP is an individual, not organizational intervention. Hence no organizational impact can be expected. In order to have an organizational effect, an organizational-level intervention would need to be introduced, in addition to the counselling. An organizational-level intervention would enable the organization to identify its sources of stress and, where possible, to address them appropriately. Simply introducing an EAP in an attempt to affect organizational indicators is unlikely to work, since an EAP does not have any global effect on the organization, although it does help individuals psychologically and reduce their absence.

While this research offers support to the argument that a healthier work-force is likely to lead to a healthier organization (if we count sickness absence as an indicator of this), the company-wide data does not suggest that an EAP has any effect on the organization, other than reducing absence in those who use the service. This is not surprising since, if an organization is to manage stress effectively, it is essential to intervene at both the individual and organizational levels.

Individuals who have access to, but do not use, an EAP do not benefit psychologically, or in terms of their job satisfaction or perceived sources of pressure from knowing that it exists.

This finding is in direct opposition to what some organizations and/or providers believe, which is that simply knowing that help is available, should it be needed, can reduce stress. This is not supported by this data, which shows no effect on individuals who have not had counselling. In fact, the employees in one of the companies involved in the study reported being less satisfied with their jobs and seeing more stress as coming from 'organizational structure and climate', following the implementation of the EAP.

Conclusion

Workplace counselling has a very important role to play because individuals may suffer stress from both their personal and work life, and this will impact upon an employee's performance at work and his/her psychological well-being. The key is, that while the introduction of a counselling service may well be of benefit to individuals, psychologically, there is unlikely to be any impact at the organizational level, unless an intervention targeted at changing the organization is also in place. There is a need for UK companies to look much more closely at their reasons for buying counselling services. If their aim is to support staff, then the service is probably useful in this respect. However, if organizations are hoping to influence positively 'bottom line' indicators at the organizational level, then they are likely to be disappointed. The evidence suggests that there is little organizational impact beyond the reduction of sickness absence in those employees who use the service.

References

Arthur Anderson Survey (1991) 'Absence rate is EC worst', *Independent on Sunday*, 20 October.
Cole, G.E., Tucker, L.A. and Friedman, G.M. (1982) 'Absenteeism, data as a measure of cost effectiveness of stress management programs', *American Journal of Health Promotion*, Spring: 12–15.
Cooper, C.L., Sloan, S.J. and Williams, S. (1988) *Occupational Stress Indicator Management Guide*. Windsor: NFER-Nelson.
Cooper, C.L., Sadri, G., Allison, T. and Reynolds, P. (1990) 'Stress counselling in the Post Office', *Counselling Psychology Quarterly*, 3 (1): 3–11.

Goldberg, D.P. (1972) *The Detection of Psychiatric Illness by Questionnaire*. Oxford: Oxford University Press.

Griffin, R.W. and Bateman, R.S. (1986) 'Job satisfaction and organisational commitment', in C.L. Cooper and I.T. Robertson (eds), *International Review of Industrial and Organisational Psychology*. Chichester: John Wiley.

Highley, J.C. and Cooper, C.L. (1995) 'An assessment and evaluation of employee assistance and workplace counselling programmes in British organisations', Unpublished report for the Health and Safety Executive.

Roman, P.M., Blum, T.C. and Bennett, N. (1987) 'Educating organisational consumers about Employee Assistance Programs', *Public Personal Management*, 16 (4): 299–312.

17

Plastering Over the Cracks? A Study of Employee Counselling in the NHS

Helen Fisher

As a Staff Counselling Service Manager who was new to the National Health Service, I found the early months a challenging and confusing time. Despite my previous experience of employee counselling in industry, I was ill-prepared for the complexities of my new environment. Particularly helpful in this respect was to meet with other managers of similar counselling services within the NHS, where we could regularly discuss and debate the issues arising both from our managerial and operational perspectives. While these share many elements in common with other counselling services, I am aware that there are areas peculiar to employee counselling in the NHS. It was with this in mind that I set up a research project to access how service managers of counselling provision in the NHS saw their services, their own roles and their difficulties. Readers who want further details of that project will find them in my dissertation (Fisher, 1995).

What I want to do in this chapter is present the conclusions of the research, but a brief preliminary first of all is necessary to place them in context. The conclusions emerge from in-depth interviews with four managers of NHS Staff Support and Counselling Services. The interviews were transcribed and analysed using Grounded Theory. This allowed me to label the underlying categories and themes emerging across the interviews. Table 17.1 summarizes the main categories and sub-categories within them. This outline will be used as the format for the chapter, which will look in more detail at each of the categories before drawing out specific conclusions. The quotations in italics are direct quotations from the interviewees and are added to give their voice to the discussion.

1. Counsellor Fit

The four managers who participated in this study were in total accord about the importance of having appropriately skilled staff to deliver counselling and support services to the employees of the NHS. Each had learned by experience that the wrong choice of counsellors could have a major impact upon both the delivery and the carefully nurtured reputation of their services. The essential qualities identified consistently emerged during the taped interviews. These

Table 17.1 *Summary of the four categories*

1. **Counsellor fit**
   1.1 Experience
   1.2 Orientation
   1.3 Personal qualities

2. **Understanding the NHS Counselling Service providers' role**
   2.1 Boundaries
   2.2 Risks

3. **Fitting into the NHS**
   3.1 Understanding the culture
   3.2 Adapting operationally

4. **Overcoming the obstacles**
   4.1 Building relationships
   4.2 Developing the service
   4.3 Support for workplace counsellors/managers

pointed towards more than a certain standard of counselling skills, but to the counsellor's ability to understand and adapt to a particular environment. This collective learning was expressed by one subject this way:

– *with hindsight, knowing what kind of counsellor you need to work in this environment is very important and I didn't know that in the early days . . . very caring people who would go to the ends of the earth for the clients, but who didn't understand the need to fit in with the NHS*

Eventually the essential qualities described were sub-categorized under three headings: experience, orientation and personal qualities.

1.1 Experience

It was agreed by subjects that counsellors with specific experience in a workplace setting were most suited because they had an understanding of the conflicts at the individual/organizational interface. The credibility of their service depended upon clients feeling confident that counsellors had some understanding of organizational policies, procedures and practices and their effect upon clients.

Additionally, it was felt that the NHS was 'different' from other organizations and that therefore experience of the NHS also would be beneficial, although, in its absence, service providers thought this less important than work-based counselling experience.

– *a lot of the time we are dealing with work stuff and actually helping people explore and understand the context of the work*

Knowledge of occupational psychology and organizational dynamics was also cited by Carroll (1994) as an important feature for counsellors in organizations. This is seen as particularly important during early development, as the service strives to gain identity and acceptance. In addition to high levels of counselling competence, a range of necessary skills for work-based counsellors is listed by McGill in Sugarman (1992). These include:

- Awareness of how organizations operate and function.
- High levels of social skills and assertiveness.
- Knowledge about community agencies.
- Capability for specific analysis of data.

In this particular setting, subjects identified the changing and fragmented nature of the NHS, combined with the difficulties of many specialities competing for resources, and a hierarchical and controlling management style as some of the issues that their counsellors would need to understand to place client work here in context.

1.2   Orientation

In the course of this study it was noted that the counselling orientation of each of the subjects differed. Further, they did not state a preference for one theoretical orientation over another in their counselling staff. Consistent with the views in Carroll (1994), they were agreed, however, that experience of working in short-term or brief counselling was a necessity, with a strong emphasis on using problem-solving techniques. This was viewed by subjects as an important consideration in the recruitment of counsellors, who may previously have worked in environments where long-term therapy, with the aim of insight into unconscious processes, was the treatment norm. It was also felt necessary that counsellors were able to adapt to work with differing levels of client need, from crisis intervention to brief therapy or problem-solving.

- *there are people who are really coming for therapy and you can offer short therapy, but there are other people who are really coming to problem-solve. One just has to be able to adapt appropriately*

In addition to being able to work with a brief therapy model, subjects felt that it was sometimes in the interests of clients that counselling staff offer advice or information. Subjects felt that counselling 'purists' may be unhappy about this aspect, which service providers saw in some circumstances as a necessary part of their role. This was not, however, viewed as conflicting with the underlying ethos of empowering clients, to which these services subscribed. Rather, taking the view that 'the EAP Practitioner is an enabler as well', Cunningham (1992) also identifies that this aspect of work-based counselling, which deviates from most counsellor training, is a source of embarrassment to the EAP professional. She, however, offers some encouragement for what is probably the reality of 'real world' practice.

Conversely, service providers were aware that they and their counsellors felt that short-term counselling was also at times a constraint, where they believed the level of distress presenting in their NHS clients was greater than in other 'industries'. Partly, this was attributed to the inherently stressful nature of work in healthcare professions (Payne and Firth-Cozens, 1987; Ramanathan, 1992; Paxton and Axelby, 1994) and partly because they perceived that the

NHS attracted 'damaged people'. At their own discretion, and if it was felt that a significant improvement would be the client outcome, service providers allowed some flexibility about the number of sessions offered. This was also regarded as important for counsellors' job satisfaction and development, giving some substance to the therapeutic work. One subject also expressed an opinion that the effects of brief therapy were not sustained over time in this environment, a point supported by Ramanathan (1992).

Subjects and their staff had experiences of counselling clients presenting with serious levels of disturbance. Where, in the absence of other specialist agencies to whom they could refer clients immediately, for example, sexual abuse, alcohol, drug treatment centres or to psychiatric services, service providers had viewed it a responsibility to 'contain' clients, by providing support until appropriate sources were available. This role could also involve advocacy on the client's behalf, for example to their General Practitioner or social worker, etc.

1.3   Personal Qualities

The subjects of this study had experienced the negative consequences of having staff without workplace counselling experience or 'organizational savvy', resulting in staff turnover and the burden of having to shield counsellors from roles and tasks they found difficult. They also worried about what messages stereotypical counsellor images conveyed about the counselling services.

Realism was a personal quality that service providers felt was a prerequisite of work-based counsellors in the NHS, especially if they were to avoid disillusionment and burnout, a phenomenon that particularly affects 'helping professionals'. West cautions that 'requisite to being an effective employee assistance professional is the ability to recognise one's own limitations' (1992: 293–310). In a study by Pearson (1982) into 60 health care professionals, it was recognized that a prime determinant of job success and satisfaction was how subjects came to terms with disillusionment, value and loyalty conflicts.

– *if you wanted to measure what difference you make, I don't know. Not a huge difference. You can't realistically, even if you get 10 per cent of the workforce, what's 10 per cent of 4,000*

Today, work-based counselling services realize that to be effective they must provide a service that is not just plastering over the organizational cracks, in that they have a role in influencing the organization in its handling of 'problem employees'. Roman et al. (1987) report that the EAPs which are most effective are those that are fully integrated into the organization and its management control systems. Berridge and Cooper (1993) additionally propose that working at an individual therapeutic level only is nothing more than 'peripheral tinkering'. While the subjects of this study were in agreement with the principle, they were aware that it was a slow process, and acknowledged that their powers were limited to small successes, expressed as a 'drip-drip effect'.

Service providers recognized in themselves and in some of their staff, a quality likened to that of a 'crusader'. Defined by the *Oxford English Dictionary* as a 'campaigner against something recognized as evil – a concerted action to follow a cause', it is a term originating from medieval Christian military expeditions to recover Holy Land. This concept of going into battle to further a cause was seen as particularly applicable by three of the four subjects who had set up their services and who, over time, had adapted from this early view of their role to one that recognized that they were unlikely to succeed at winning any wars, but that victory was signified rather by persistence and determination to win successive minor skirmishes. In relation to their staff, one subject identified that this quality could manifest itself in counselling staff wishing to 'take up arms' on behalf of their clients, despite the counsellors' apparent understanding of role boundaries. Service managers had learned to contain this problem by constantly examining boundaries and considering the ethical pros and cons. Supervision also played an important role in containment.

2.   Understanding the NHS Counselling Service Providers' Role

Role boundaries define the limits of specific tasks or functions and dictate the expectations of both employers and those to whom we are providing a service. The managers involved in this study had learned over time that conflicts arose when NHS management and staff had expectations that were contradictory to the service providers' own ideas about the nature of a counselling service in an organization. While this may sound a simple statement of their learning, the reality is that realization had evolved through a constant process which had involved much soul-searching for the subjects and was not a simple matter of fulfilling a job description or a service brief – their roles were recognized as implicitly multi-faceted.

2.1   Boundaries

This role has been described in part as that of the 'constructive broker' role by Steele (1988) and demands that counsellors constantly balance the conflicting needs of employer and employee to provide a service that offers the greatest good to the greatest number. In a sense, the integrity with which this balance is maintained was central in their services. Participants of this study had evolved definitions of the boundaries of their roles. That is not to say, however, that these boundaries were static; with each new quirk and anomaly came the necessity to re-negotiate and re-define. Subjects, however, were in agreement that the primary client was the individual, accompanied by a philosophy that ultimately what was good for the client was good for the NHS. In practice, service providers found that each intervention required that they check out 'who is the client?' The company employing the counsellor, the supervisor making the referral, or the employee with a problem to resolve? It has been argued that service providers' roles include a responsibility for not only assisting the individual client, but also for promoting social justice and addressing social change (Levy, 1974). This was felt to be important so that the location of the problem, and therefore also the solution, did not rest solely with the individual client.

- *I'm very clear, it's about making them [the clients] better for themselves and not being an agent for making things better for the organization*

Roman et al. (1987) identified the 'double victim': the client is both the bearer of his/her problem and the source of the problem. Service providers were aware of the dangers of that, 'subtle coercions in the corporate setting may revolve around implied threats concerning promotions, continued employment, and future raises' (Lee and Rosen, 1984: 276–80). To ensure that their services avoid such situations, the management referral of clients was shunned in favour of voluntary self-referral. Service providers, however, were attuned to the fact that there were levels even of voluntary self-referral.

Another form of coercion that was recognized to exist by NHS service providers was the need to maintain homeostasis (balance) within the organization (Berridge and Cooper, 1993). Subjects perceived an expectation of their roles likened to that of keeping the machinery running smoothly. This was felt to reinforce the notion of the 'problem employee'. The subjects of this study avoided coercion by being clear about responsibility as service providers to clients and clear about their responsibilities to the NHS. Further, in the same way that they raised awareness of personal responsibility in clients, they saw a parallel function with the organization – in raising its awareness of practices, procedures and policies that were causes of employee problems.

It was recognized that attempts to involve service providers and their staff in coercion was not an activity limited to management. Subjects were equally aware of the propensity of some clients to use counselling and staff support services to further their own agenda. Service providers had, in the early stages, had negative experiences of being 'used' by clients. These instances had led to service providers being labelled 'subversive', despite their efforts to maintain neutrality. Subjects developed strategies to prevent these occurrences, ensuring that clearly stated boundaries and contracts were defined, and an attitude of caution adopted towards expressing opinions.

- *I present information, I present statistics. I talk about alternative climates. But I do not fire bullets when somebody says why are you not telling Senior Management? I say, why are you not telling senior management?*

Service providers were aware that during the early stages of service development they were under pressure to conform with unreasonably heavy workloads. In part, the pressure was perceived as self-imposed, created by the drive to succeed in establishing their services amid fierce competition for NHS funds. Service providers felt that they had, of necessity, acquiesced, and subjects recognized the inherent danger to themselves, ironically observing a parallel with their NHS clients, who were presenting with burnout symptoms which were perceived as being caused by a lack of resources to provide adequate care. There was very real pressure for subjects that was created by a lack of staff both to perform administrative tasks and to provide additional counselling, thus preventing the service manager from performing the developmental tasks such as planning, marketing, budgeting, defining policies and procedures, and establishing referrals networks. In effect, the service provider initially performed all of these roles, while simultaneously providing counselling, facilitation to support groups, presenting training courses and workshops, and attending key meetings to gather intelligence.

– *one of the arguments I have with myself is I could have said no, but how would I feel if they withdrew the contract. So while I do have a sense of boundaries, it's also that our freedom for manoeuvre is constrained*

Roman et al., discussing the pressures on EAPs to implement programmes when there is an expectation from above to do so, warn also of the temptations 'to engage in activities that are beyond their skills and training' (1987: 57–90) – a particular issue when working alone without the controlling influence of 'peer scrutiny'. This ethical issue is common in all professions, but especially tempting in new programmes, where demarcation lines may still be fluid and regulation by an appropriate line manager low.

– *that was hard – especially in the early days when you wanted to make the service viable. I said yes, when it would have been better to have said well I don't really think we ought to be doing this*

Ethical standards had been at the heart of many of the dilemmas facing service providers in the developmental stages, but practice has evolved, as is often the case, by trial and error.

Some authors have stated the importance of EAPs having a proactive and visible role in the organization (Frost, 1990; Milne et al., 1994). This role was seen as a necessity by service providers, who believed that this was an ongoing process of educating both individuals and the organization about the existence of services and their potential benefits. However, an argument against visibility has been identified by Roman et al. (1987), who see this need to 'drum up business' and thereby increase the service visibility as questionable ethically in that service providers may be introducing 'new problems' along with their accompanying solutions. It could be further argued that where a service is new, all business is 'drummed up' – problems in this context are not necessarily new, just unaddressed – as in the particular case of the subjects of this study who recognized that NHS reforms and the subsequent organizational changes had created a window of opportunity for counselling and staff support services in the NHS. The need was, however, not perceived to be as much to 'drum up business' where a need was manufactured, but rather to react to a rising current of concern in an appropriate way, while not ignoring what was seen to be gaining prominence in what was described as a 'vulture like' way by one subject.

— *I feel really good work has been done with staff that have been on the receiving end of some very difficult organizational changes. For us, that has given us a prominence within the various organizations in which we work which would have taken us much longer to attain*

2.2 Risks

Service providers had realized that there were also disadvantages to becoming more prominent in the organization. Both management and employees had high expectations that counselling and support services could serve them politically. Despite contracting with staff groups and individual clients about the boundaries, employees nevertheless often attempted to incite service providers to accept responsibility for mediating or advocating on their behalf with management. Likewise, the reverse situation could occur, when managers requested that counselling and support service providers act as messengers to staff. In either event, the service would ultimately be the loser as both these strategies meant that neither party were accepting responsibility for the situation. Therefore, when situations remained the same, the inevitable conclusion management and staff could draw was that the service was to blame – for being unable to change things as they desired.

— *if they* [the support groups] *didn't get what they wanted, they could say, the service was terrible. It hasn't made anything better, nothing has changed. And the reason why nothing has changed is because the service is no good*

While subjects were desirous of raising awareness of the interrelation between 'problem employee' and 'problem employer' in the organizations employing them. They were also aware of the personal/career implications of how far the EAP practitioners can press with human service values and perceptions without losing their credibility with both groups, or their jobs (Briar and Vinet, 1985).

Perhaps a further component of the tendency towards blaming in the context of the NHS has roots in what Menzies (1959) identified as a defence mechanism in nursing staff, who, in the face of death, pain and anxiety, projected their feelings of vulnerability on to subordinate staff, attributing to colleagues their own unconscious fears about their inability to cope. Blaming, therefore, became entrenched in the culture of the NHS.

Service providers had evolved assessments as a strategy to help them minimize the risks of inappropriate or conflicting role boundaries. Berridge and Cooper (1993) list some of the risks of multiple roles as overload, intra-role conflict and a lack of professional role clarity. A further risk identified by service providers as a possible outcome of these situations is being open to blame. Avoidance of blame was achieved through a combination of clearly defined boundaries – stated in policies, contracts, information sheets and brochures – and through problem assessment.

Accurate assessment is viewed as a critical factor of an effective EAP (Walsh, 1991). Guidelines for assessment can be found in the Employee

Assistance Programme Association's *UK Standards of Practice and Professional Guidelines for Employee Assistance Programmes* (1995). From a practitioner's point of view, what is difficult in assessment is predicting cause and
effect of service intervention. Service providers in this study had, by experience, developed an understanding of probable events, but this was perceived
as by no means 'fool proof'.

Assessment was of particular relevance to the issue of management referrals
to services. While self-referral was the method espoused by service providers,
they were aware that, in practice, self-referrals are often 'nudges from supervisors and co-workers' (Roman et al., 1987: 57–90), or possibly worse, of the
'garbage-can category of the personnel role' (Berridge and Cooper, 1993:
89–102), in that, not knowing what else to do about certain employees or
situations, counselling and support services were summoned to 'fix' the
problem. In earlier times, accepting roles to facilitate support groups or
provide stress management workshops were cited by subjects as examples
where, during pre-assessment days, they had 'walked into the lions den'.
Growing emphasis on systematic intervention into the stressors found in
organizations has made it incumbent upon service providers to offer multiple
assessment to ensure appropriate intervention and complete services.

– *there is a sense in which a counselling service can be an organizational
dustbin – we've done a lot of work to ensure that we don't get inappropriate
referrals*

3.   Fitting into the NHS

The subjects of this study were explicit about their needs for certain kinds of
staff to assist them in the provision of their services. They had also developed
a clarity about the role of their service within the host organization. But
underlying throughout this raw data was a consistent theme about the nature
of the environment in which they existed. Viewing this from a systems theory
perspective enabled me to understand what was being expressed at a deeper
level. As a newcomer to the NHS, it has been important for me to understand
something of the historical background to the changes now engulfing the NHS
in order to place client work into context – in essence, understanding that the
NHS is now having to adjust to operating a market economy, which entails
competing to provide cost-effective healthcare to local populations. Further
changes in the method of distribution of government money from national to
local level has created ripples of change throughout the NHS, in the same way
that a pebble does when it is dropped on to the surface of a lake.

Underlying the tasks of counselling and support service managers to provide an effective service to the NHS is a necessity to understand the context of
the organization in which they operate. This is in order that the interventions
offered are appropriate, relevant and acceptable to the NHS population. This
process has involved service providers developing an understanding of the
organizational culture.

— what I've come to understand over five years is what an incredibly complex organization it is, with umpteen different interests, lots of people working together. But answerable to all sorts of different areas, with lots of different agendas

3.1   Understanding the Culture

Culture is seen to have powerful systematic effects on both individual and social structures, shaping the day-to-day operations of organizations and communities, unfortunately, however, at a level at which we are rarely aware, providing 'a highly selective screen between man and the outside world' (Egan, 1979). McLeod (1993: 132) also discusses the many levels and layers of culture, the implication being that understanding is a complex task. In order, then, to examine the layers of culture, the concept of systems theory provides a useful model.

As a system the NHS is undergoing major changes. It is therefore incumbent upon service providers to understand the nature of the transition and its impact at the various levels of the system, in order to offer a service that is in context with the changing world of the NHS. Subjects were aware that the organizations in which they worked were complex, with many differing clinical and administrative specialities vying for precedence, where employees at all levels felt that instability was, in effect, the only constant (Traynor, 1994).

Prior to the establishment of 'official' staff support and counselling services, the subjects of this study were aware that counselling already existed within the organizations. Employees in occupational health, chaplaincy and personnel departments, as well as line managers, already felt that they were fulfilling this role. In addition, 'informal' counselling has taken place within this setting from peers and colleagues 'since time began'. This situation was problematic to the development of a systematic, integrated counselling support service. First, is the issue of professional jealousy and rivalry, particularly in an environment undergoing change (McLeod, 1993: 129). Secondly, the issue of conflict occurs for those acting as counsellor, whose primary role involves management accountability to the organization (Sugarman, 1992), because fulfilling 'dual-relationships' (McLeod, 1993: 169) creates unclear boundaries and conflicts of interest. Promoting the benefits of an independent service to employees without alienating other departments can require delicate handling by service providers, especially in the way they educate potential users about services.

— the NHS did not really understand the concept of providing support for staff and perceived that Personnel was doing that job very nicely thank you!

The NHS was perceived by subjects to have inherent cultural defence mechanisms which also impeded the development of counselling support services. Menzies (1959) identified two processes which operated at an unconscious level in nurses: those of objectifying patients, making them into external objects rather than individuals in their own rights; and of projection, that is making others responsible for their (the nurses') feelings. These coping strategies had been thought to have relevance in the NHS where culture dictates that vulnerability or inability to cope is routinely denied.

McLeod (1993: 133) links the key ideas of Menzies (1959) with the concept of 'parallel process'. In the case of the subjects of this study, parallel process was viewed as a phenomenon that affected NHS staff's usage of counselling services. One subject of this study described her service as like 'a split-off bit of personality', in which the feeling part of the organization was split off from the logical, rational, decision-making, management and patient services aspect. The NHS cultural undertone was felt by service providers to imbue NHS staff with a perception of counselling services being for 'the weak', for those who could not cope. If patients perceive a stigma attached to needing help with psychological or mental health problems (Jenkins and Shepherd, 1983), then how much more so healthcare professionals and NHS staff who feel they are paid to cope with those who cannot. At the macro level of systems there is also, in the UK, a traditional view that 'personal problems are not the organization's concern' (Orlans, 1986: 19–23). An additional difficulty also for service providers in the NHS is the term 'Counselling', which previously was a euphemism for a disciplinary meeting, thus requiring subjects to re-educate their employers and employees about their use of the term.

At the heart of the origins of attitudes towards staff counselling in the NHS was a general attitude about 'success and achievement against all odds'.

– *medicine is about surviving a gruelling experience and then when you get to the top you can kick everyone on the way up*

The stereotypical image of counselling among many in the NHS was an area of concern, described by one subject as 'the brown rice and sandals' label. This image of the caring and concerned counsellor, who was not quite worldly, was one that service providers worked hard to discourage. Adopting a pragmatic approach to their work was regarded as a necessity.

Being regarded by NHS staff as providing para-psychiatric services was felt by subjects to be detrimental to service development. Sbriglio et al. (1987) discuss whether an EAP and medical community can work together and point to the negative attributes displayed by physicians towards non-medical health professionals, the obvious implication being for service providers that there may not be many allies among medical staff. Where the dominance of the medical model exists this may make it difficult for counsellors to find acceptance for work with relationships or feelings (McLeod, 1993: 129). This tension in values, which is communicated at the meso level, obviously impacts upon the micro level of counselling.

In terms of adjustment to the NHS, a particular challenge for two subjects and some counselling staff had been that of adjusting to, and working with, a different and harder-nosed NHS culture. As opposed to their preconceived notions about NHS values and philosophy, where the ideal of caring for people was thought to predominate, service providers found that their pre-conceived beliefs about NHS values were not consistent with their observed reality.

– *I suppose I naïvely had belief, most people do, that the Health Service is about making people well, it's about looking after people*

The concept of parallel process has been referred to in relation to how services may affect client users. Service providers also recognized evidence of parallel process in themselves and their staff, in that they 'mirrored' the same pressures and anxieties as their clients. Research psychologists have identified a specific type of stress 'burnout' as a phenomenon that occurs in human service professionals (nurses, social workers, police, counsellors, etc.). Service providers were aware that they, too, were vulnerable to the same pressures, and that they sometimes displayed the characteristics of their clients, experiencing varying degrees of burnout.

– *we suffer the same pressure and anxieties as the people we are providing a service to*

Finally, in this category, from a systems perspective, the difficulties of not subscribing to NHS cultural norms cannot be overstated. Hampden-Turner states that 'all cultures are in fact responses to corporate dilemmas' (1984: 11). The NHS dilemma seems to be about providing increasingly costly healthcare to populations with increased expectation of health standards, while resources remain limited.

Advancing technology and medical science has given us the ability to treat many more diseases. However, a tension always exists between what we can do and what we are able to do, ultimately in order that the NHS balances patient needs with a limited budget. Service providers also 'mirror' the belief of many staff that we can always do more for clients, given the resources, time, staff, etc. The issue of meeting increasing demands with limited resources also manifests itself in the NHS system through a 'busy' culture that subtly transmits a 'this is how we do it here' message to members of the system.

– *we mirror what goes on in the organization, all the time unless we're very careful*

As with all cultures, service providers have learned that attempting to flout the cultural norm meets with resistance. A self-regulating feature of cultures is that they are used by individuals to reinforce ideas, beliefs and feelings, therefore discouraging and repressing statements or information that are not consistent with those espoused (Hampden-Turner, 1984: 12).

– *I do not want to become part of the culture because I do not think it is helpful. It is about martyrdom . . . perpetuating the system*

3.2 Adapting Operationally

An effect of the reforms in the NHS is that now NHS Trusts compete with other Trusts or agencies to provide services to the community. The advantage to purchasers is that they can select the required service from the most cost-effective provider, creating a necessity within NHS Trusts to operate within tight financial constraints. The changes engulfing the NHS are not the topic of debate in this study. However, from the perspective of systems theory, what cannot be ignored is the effect upon all levels and, ultimately, the effect upon the service provider and client.

Stability of funding is discussed in McLeod (1993: 138) in relation to voluntary agencies who rely on sources over which they have little control. Parallels can be drawn within NHS counselling services where they rely upon individual NHS Units, Hospitals or Trust Boards, who can withdraw contracts or funding and place services in crisis. On a day-to-day level, subjects' awareness of the 'potential instability' of funding created pressures, not only in terms of the activities undertaken, but in compromising their ideals of adequate service standards, examples of which included shared accommodation and telephone extensions with non-counselling services, insufficient funds to employ administrative staff or to obtain extra counselling staff to meet increasing demands for services. While the *prima facie* problem was limited resources, however, there was a perception among service providers that the issue of resources had a deeper significance. In terms of perceived 'rivalries', McLeod (1993: 129) identifies that in primarily non-counselling organizations these types of problem and dilemma can occur. Where traditionally NHS staff are expected to cope with the intrinsic stressors of their role, these forms of resistance may therefore be the result of flouting cultural norms. It may be the case, however, that 'even within public sector social services, efforts to ensure the fullest delivery of services are always approximations of the ideal' (Briar and Vinet, 1985: 342–59).

– *grudgingly, I was allowed to appoint one full-time counsellor after 6 months. I also said I can no longer share an office – I mean we were sharing a telephone! We're running a service and I haven't got a phone where people can contact me in private*

In order to make their service as accessible as possible to as many as possible, service providers were aware that they needed to operate flexibly to accommodate NHS staff's shift-work patterns. Listing 11 guiding principles of an effective EAP, Bergmark (1986) argues for 24-hour, year-round programmes staffed by professionals. Of the services in this study, only one provided a 24-hour service – with the benefit of hindsight, it was felt not to be a priority during the early stages of a service. Further, operationally it was found to be difficult and costly to coordinate and, in terms of usage, not fully warranted.

All service providers were as flexible as possible about individual appointment times, as group activities such as workshops and support groups created problems for NHS staff, particularly those staff involved with patient care where it would be impossible for whole wards or departments to attend. Experience had taught subjects that small groups/workshops on a rotational basis, carefully timed to coordinate with 'off-peak' activity, was most likely to ensure attendance. Venue was also difficult, subjects being required to provide *in situ* sessions in less than ideal conditions on wards, etc., to accommodate departments where minimal staffing levels prohibited attendance to off-site activities.

Despite these adaptations to the working environment of the NHS, service providers had become accustomed to staff groups – particularly at ward level – cancelling arrangements at short notice, usually due to unforeseen staff shortages, and causing subjects frustration at the loss of time involved in unnecessary preparation.

4. Overcoming the Obstacles

4.1 Building Relationships

Operating an in-house counselling service often feels like being an athlete participating in a hurdles event, with the knowledge that each obstacle successfully overcome will surely be followed by another. Some of the obstacles to successful implementation of workplace counselling services can be inherent and may pre-empt the introduction of services altogether (Briar and Vinet, 1985). In examining the background to implementation of counselling/support services, Briar and Vinet warn that service developers would need carefully to weigh the benefits of their services against the costs of hostility to management and the service itself. This is particularly true in organizations like the NHS which are undergoing rationalization or change. If implemented, however, service providers will find that they have to confront the undercurrent of employees' hostility and begin the process of establishing trust and confidence in themselves and their services. Vital in this respect was the subjects' ability to build and maintain good working relationships throughout the host organization.

Great emphasis was placed on building relationships with senior managers by service providers. First, because it was felt that a respected senior member of staff could influence and encourage other managers and staff to use developing counselling services, and secondly, if the services ever hoped to provide more than a 'band-aid' service, active support or a 'rubber stamp' from senior management should, at least in theory, enable services to perform more preventive work, by enlisting senior management support to facilitate changes in the environment (Orlans, 1986). Service providers also gained a sense of security from positive relationships with senior managers in that they felt they would act as advocates or ambassadors for the service, particularly in influencing issues of funding and resources, against fierce competition.

– *we need to have at the most senior levels a high level of awareness of what the service is about. So I see it as fundamental to my role that I am known to as many key stakeholders as I can be!*

A challenging aspect of the work of providers of in-house counselling and support services is that of balancing the needs of the client with that of the organization, while carefully protecting neutrality and impartiality in order that their services can be of value to both. Achieving this balance, however, in practice often requires confronting the distrust of trade unions and staff associations, as well as individual employees, particularly during times of organizational change or conflict, when counselling services may be perceived by unions and staff as palliative gestures. Levy suggests also, as an aid to confronting these conflicts, that 'practitioners should be scrupulous about not representing opposing parties' (1974: 207–16). Prevention of this type of conflict may also be achieved through the involvement of trade unions in the needs assessment and implementation stage of programmes, and therefore discouraging the view of services as being 'management orientated'.

Subjects of this study were very cautious about involvement in the organization, carefully choosing committees and meetings that preserved their image of neutrality. Equally, they were aware that representing individuals, for example in disciplinary hearings, would be problematic. Activities were therefore carefully weighed.

– *I am very careful which meetings I get involved in because if we're seen to be sitting too close to management, then where do our allegiances lie?*

As in building other relationships, gaining the confidence of staff requires time and effort. Ultimately, the service integrity becomes apparent when the espoused philosophy, policies and practices are congruent with its actions, through protection of employees' rights to confidentiality, avoiding management referrals and being careful in giving feedback to the organization. The question of 'Whose needs are served?' (Roman et al., 1987) is a central theme for workplace counsellors and is best managed through consistent adherence to stated contracts and clearly defined boundaries, with the guidance of supervisors and, when necessary, referral to legal specialists and British Association for Counselling advisers.

Issues of building individual relationships with senior management have been explored from a systems theory perspective, the mesosystem level, or the level of personal networks, including relationships with other professional groups. Berridge and Cooper (1993) describe Employee Assistance Programmes as a 'crossroads discipline', combining diverse inputs such as sociology and psychology. They also regard such services as residing in 'disputed territory' between personnel departments, professional therapists and finance departments, that are operating with widely differing values and methods. It is not surprising, therefore, that finding acceptance among these groups can be difficult. Subjects of this study had encountered problems of professional jealousy and disputed territory, which was felt to be exacerbated by the uncertain climate of the NHS and the competition among departments of their genre to discover wider areas of business. The physical location of services where apparent conflicts of interest may occur may also need careful consideration prior to implementation.

In practice overcoming these difficulties requires sensitive exploration of overlapping professional boundaries, coupled with an attitude of cooperation and reassurance that counselling services are a optional extra and not an alternative to existing employee services. Egan (1994) describes 'savvy managers' as those who understand the human condition and use their understanding to help individuals serve the business better and improve the quality of work-life, making the service provider/managers endowed with counselling skills possibly better equipped than most in these situations.

– *they saw us as taking away part of their work . . . the way to get around it is to show them that what you are offering is an adjunct to theirs*

4.2 Developing the Service

The subjects of this study were aware how, over time, their counselling and support services had developed and had become accepted within the NHS community. This transition had bought about the necessity of changing from the role of 'crusader' to one that was more stable and routine. Service providers had recognized a point at which they had needed to 'hand over the reins' to counselling staff and become more involved in consolidating their learning. This was in order to move from implementation, which was experienced by subjects as very much a reactive stage, to development. Consolidation required time-out to plan, to write formal policies and procedures, to consider areas of expansion and to set up administrative systems. This transition has been identified by McLeod (1993: 134).

With the formalizing of services, the emphasis of the subjects' role shifted from purely client work, to management and administrative functions, which necessitated service providers taking an active role in providing feedback to the organization. Both quantitative and qualitative input was required by NHS senior managers, not only to justify the existence of services and to create a sense of value for money, but also to give insight into potential problem areas. Service providers saw this function as vital as a basis of further preventive work. They were, however, very clear about confidentiality issues and presented information in a way that protected individuals from identification. Bond (1994: 129) has written on the conflicting obligations for counsellors in a workplace service, and recommends that in advance of counselling, agreement should be reached between employer, counsellor and employee representatives about the boundaries of confidentiality under which counselling is offered. This prevents counsellors from finding themselves in a situation of 'having to make decisions about confidentiality in isolation, without guidelines' (Bond, 1994: 129). An argument for EAPs or counselling services to be provided by an external organization has been that the potential for role conflict is lessened. The disadvantage, however, is that the counsellors are less knowledgeable about the particular organization and are thus less likely to be able to implement preventive strategies (Orlans, 1986).

– *we give feedback that doesn't jeopardize confidentiality but gives a real sense of how the service is being used. This involves a minimum of one-day preparation . . . for potentially 60 meetings per year. But then the whole awareness of the service becomes that much more powerful within the organization, and the sense that we are not actually just tinkering away on personal things*

4.3   Support for Workplace Counsellors/Managers

This study has explored the experiences of NHS counselling/support service managers and gives insight into the complexities of their roles and the organizations in which they work. Central to surviving what had been a combination of gruelling and exhilarating experiences was the need for support. Service providers were well aware of the effects of 'burnout' as a phenomenon that presented among their NHS client group. They were also aware that they too were vulnerable, if they did not make regular use of the networks of support that they themselves had developed, which included professional supervision and peer support.

Isolation had been a particular problem for the three subjects who set up their services, both in terms of their unique role in the organization and the requirement for confidentiality, which tends to exclude counsellors from the usual work friendships. This situation had abated when service providers had been able to employ other counsellors. Professional isolation was also experienced by being in the vanguard of in-house counselling service providers in the NHS. Even so, among peers, when competition for contracts is not an issue, there is a tendency to be guarded about the exact nature of one's work because of confidentiality constraints.

– *it's quite isolated in a sense – of necessity isolated from the mainstream of the organization – so it's very easy for your training, development and support needs to be overlooked*

The role of the supervisor in counselling is not one of inspection or managerial control, but rather is aimed at assisting the counsellors' work with clients through a role similar to that of a tutor or consultant (McLeod, 1993: 215). The three main functions of supervision are education, support and management, to ensure quality of work and thereby client safety, in addition to advising on the appropriate use of techniques and monitoring the progress of the client/counsellor relationship. Service providers felt that it was essential that their supervisors had an understanding of organizational issues, not only to explore the impact of the organization on the client, but also to explore the dilemmas created for the counsellor. This had been cited by subjects as particularly relevant in examining issues of role conflict, policies and procedures, and organizational culture.

– *we have group as well as individual supervision . . . from someone who is experienced in organizational issues and that has been really helpful*

Subjects had also sensed the danger of narrowed vision, encouraging service providers to make efforts to develop 'networks' with other counselling professionals. Participating in conferences, having active roles on committees, and continuing development through training and education were all viewed as necessary despite having to justify the costs to their employers. The NHS service providers participating in this study were consistent in their view that they had developed both personally and professionally as a result of their role. Mainly, they felt that they had gained great personal satisfaction from work with clients, where they perceived both the most tangible outcomes and received the most positive feedback. They found that working with the organization was the most frustrating and at times the most demoralizing part of their jobs. Subjects felt that the complex nature of their roles, coupled with growing demands to meet service users' needs with diminishing or unstable resources, took its toll. This led them to conclude that their work as service managers had a limited lifespan, not least because 'career paths' for service providers were limited in their organizations. Sadly, three of the service providers in this study expressed a view that they doubted they would want to continue to work in employee counselling.

– *working in this kind of setting demands that you are very OK and that you've got high energy levels*

The subjects of this study were very aware that they mirrored many of the conflicts of their NHS client group, who were also often distressed that they were not able to provide the standards of care they desired. Additionally, like the client group, service providers' roles were tremendously responsible, involving them in issues from the relatively simple, to ones where clients livelihoods or lives were in jeopardy (Walsh, 1991). These findings contrast with the experiences of EAP providers in the private sector, where perhaps the greatest difference was their 'strong belief around its [EAP services] value to the organization and to the individuals within the organization' (Carroll, 1994: 53). Sadly, NHS counselling service providers often felt that they were no more than a gesture – plastering over the cracks.

Conclusion

This study provides insight into the experience of NHS counselling/support service managers who work in the emerging UK profession of workplace counselling. Consistent throughout the work was the underlying sense of a parallel process occurring between the counselling/support services and their host environment. This phenomenon has been viewed from a systems theory perspective and indicates the importance for counsellors in this setting not only to be highly skilled and adaptable, but to be trained in organizational behaviour theory and practice. More explicit was a sense of the subjects' struggle to balance what was often the conflicting needs of the employing organization with those of the individual client.

It was apparent also in the work that on occasions the subjects had experienced disillusionment, coupled with a strong sense of having to compromise their ideals of service standards with the reality of life in today's NHS. It may be that counsellor trainers, who are remote from work-based counselling, add to the counsellors' sense of distance from the profession, by basing teaching on standards and practices more compatible with work in private practice or other independent agencies. The experience of both professional and personal isolation in their roles has created an understanding of the need for the support of other professional counsellors and also for supervision of counselling practice from someone who specifically understands organizational issues and the complexities of this kind of role.

Having had time in the year since completing this study not only to reflect upon this data, but also to observe the evolving day-to-day practice of managing an NHS counselling service, the statement of one of the subjects seems to convey the essence of our collective learning about this role:

– *it's all about boundaries and containment, I use these words time and time again. Containing the clients' **and** the counsellors' issues within this department . . . and having clearly defined contracts and boundaries with the organization and the clients is absolutely essential*

Further research is needed, building upon the intensive interview data gathered here, which would examine the generality of these findings across a larger sample. There are also implications for the training needs of counsellors entering the workplace who would benefit from the knowledge of organizational behaviour, systems theory, financial management, administrative skills, statistical/data analysis skills, and presentation and facilitation skills, in addition to being skilled counsellors who can adapt to work at a variety of levels to meet the needs of their clients. Finally, counsellors in this setting need the support of supervision from individuals who are not only experts in the field of counselling but who have experience of the way in which organizations function and impact upon services. They also need the support of other counselling professionals, gained from attending formal and informal conferences and meetings, with whom to share experiences and a sense of developing the workplace counselling profession.

References

Bergmark, R. Edward (1986) 'Employee Assistance Programmes: trends and principles', *Journal of Business and Psychology*, 1 (1): 59–65.

Berridge, S. and Cooper, C. (1993) 'Stress and coping in US organizations: the role of the Employee Assistance Programme', *Work and Stress*, 7 (1): 89–102.

Bond, Tim (1994) *Standards and Ethics for Counselling*. London: Sage.

Briar, K.H. and Vinet, S. (1985) 'Ethical questions concerning an EAP. Who is the client (company or individual?)', in S.H. Klarreigh, J.L. Francek and C.E. Moore (eds), *The Human Resource Management Handbook: Principles and Practice of EAPs*. New York: Prager. pp. 342–59.

Carroll, C. (1994) 'Building bridges: a study of employee counselling in the private sector', MSc dissertation, City University, London (unpublished).

Cunningham, G. (1992) 'The EAP counsellor: attributes, knowledge and beliefs', *Employee Assistance Quarterly*, 8 (1): 13–25.

EAP Association (1995) *UK Standards of Practice and Professional Guidelines for Employee Assistance Programmes*. London: EAP Association.

Egan, G. (1979) *People in Systems: A Model for Development in the Human Service Professions and Education*. Belmont, CA: Brookes/Cole.

Egan, G. (1994) *Working the Shadow Side: A Guide to Positive Behind the Scenes Management*. San Francisco: Jossey Bass.

Fisher, H. (1995) 'Plastering over the cracks: employee counselling in the NHS', MA dissertation, University of Keele.

Frost, Abbie K. (1990) 'Assessing employee awareness – a first step to ulitization', *Employee Assistance Quarterly*, 16 (1): 45–55.

Hampden-Turner, C. (1984) *Corporate Culture*. London: Hutchinson Business Books.

Jenkins, R. and Shepherd, M. (1983) 'Mental illness and general practice', in Bean, P. (ed.), *Mental Illness: Changes and Trends*. Chichester: Wiley.

Lee, S. and Rosen, E.A. (1984) 'Employee counselling services: ethical dilemmas', *The Personnel and Guidance Journal*, January: 276–80.

Levy, C.S. (1974) 'On the development of a code of ethics', *Social Work*, March: 207–16.

Menzies, I. (1959) 'A case study in the functioning of social systems as a defence against anxiety: a report on a study of the nursing services of a general hospital', *Human Relations*, 13: 95–121.

Milne, S.H., Blum, T.C. and Roman, P.M. (1994) 'Factors influencing employees' propensity to use the EAP', *Personnel Psychology*, 47 (1): 123–45.

McLeod, J. (1993) *An Introduction to Counselling*. Milton Keynes: Open University Press.

Orlans, Vanja (1986) 'Counselling services in organizations', *Organizational Personnel Review*, 15 (5): 19–23.

Paxton, R. and Axelby, S. (1994) 'Is stress your occupation', *Health Service Journal*, November: 30–1.

Payne, R.L. and Firth-Cozens, J.A. (eds) (1987) *Stress in Health Professionals*. Chichester: John Wiley.

Pearson, J.M. (1982) 'The transition into a new job: tasks, problems and outcomes', *Personnel Journal*, 61: 286–90.

Ramanathan, Chathaphuran, S. (1992) 'EAP's response to personal stress and productivity: implications for occupational social work', *Social Work*, 37 (3): 234–9.

Roman, Paul, Blum, M. and Terry, C. (1987) 'Who is served?', *Health Education Quarterly*, Special Issue, 14: 57–90.

Sbriglio, R., Livingston, S.T. and Millman, R.B. (1987) 'Can an EAP and a medical community work together for the benefit of both?' *Employee Assistance Quarterly*, 2 (4).

Steele, P.D. (1988) 'Employee Assistance Programmes in context', *Journal of Applied Behavioural Science*, 24: 365–82.

Sugarman, L. (1992) 'Ethical issues in counselling at work', *Employee Counselling Today*, 14 (4): 23–30.

Traynor, Michael (1994) 'Stormy Weather', *Health Service Journal*, June: 22–3.

Walsh, Stephen, M. (1991) 'Employee assistance and the helping professional, the more things change, the more they stay the same', *Employee Assistance Quarterly*, 7 (2): 113–18.

West, Michael (1992) 'Innovation, cultural values and the management of change in British hospitals', *Work and Stress*, 6 (3): 293–310.

PART 5

ISSUES FOR COUNSELLORS IN ORGANIZATIONS

Part 5 pulls together several relevant facets of counselling in organizations not considered elsewhere in the book. John Nixon tackles a controversial issue: What is the relationship between line management and counselling? Can managers engage in counselling with their staff? Eileen Pickard, in Chapter 19, looks at the present stage of training for counsellors in organizations and offers some theory and suggestions about improvements. In the final chapter Brigid Proctor takes the supervision theme and applies it to counsellors who are working within organizations.

18

Line Management and Counselling

John Nixon

Can a line manager also be a counsellor, really be a counsellor? Are the two roles compatible or incompatible? This chapter will tackle the issue head-on and take the stance that the modern line manager *cannot* be a counsellor any more than a mother can be a counsellor to her daughter, or a friend enter into professional counselling with a close intimate. Ethical codes point out that some roles are incompatible, and unethical. This chapter illustrates the need for managers to understand unequivocally what counselling is and is not, why role confusion must be avoided when managers combine roles, and how the mindful use of the skills of counselling have a crucial place in managers' work. It reveals the risks and responsibilities that accompany these skills as managerial tools and pinpoints the indispensable attributes of training courses in counselling skills.

Of all managers, it is line managers who cannot afford to fail when under pressure to deliver results. They have heavy responsibilities, being sandwiched between satisfying directives from above and ensuring effective teams below. As workforces get ever leaner and less permanent, it is the task of managers to orchestrate the relentless cycle of new working relationships which are central to project-focused team-work, said to be the route to success in the future (Peters, 1993). Only with well-developed people skills will managers be able to transform directives into tasks, solve problems, reach goals and lead their teams safely through the forming, norming, storming, performing and mourning cycle.

Here is an example where these issues converge:

Case Study

Jean, a new member to the team, asks to see the manager because she is distressed by remarks made to her. It's a busy day and the manager, Jim, has targets to achieve. He can see his output schedules are about to be upset, his targets are in jeopardy.

What options does Jim have? He can try to mollify Jean, persuade her the problem is not so important, convince her that the department's need is paramount, promise to deal with things later, even direct her to get on and cope. Whatever he decides, Jim is under intense pressure to contain the problem in favour of immediate operational needs and he will want to look at any 'quick fix' that may help.

Sometimes it is in cases like this that counselling is suggested as an appropriate approach for a manager to use. Unfortunately, the process of evaluating its potential is not clear-cut because there is a lot of ignorance of what counselling in the workplace actually means.

What Does Counselling Mean?

A major problem lies in the word itself. The term 'counselling' does not enjoy a universal understanding of what goes on between two people as does, say, 'talking', 'sympathizing' or 'arguing'. And writers on the subject fail to help by using a number of terms synonymously. Nelson-Jones (1988) prefers the word 'helping'; Thorne (1992) sees little difference between 'counselling' and 'psychotherapy'; The Samaritans 'befriend' their clients, and HIV/AIDS workers often combine advocacy, information giving and counselling. Some counsellors include information-giving as part of their role, and a recent book on counselling sees it primarily as an 'educational process' (Nelson-Jones, 1993a). It has even been suggested that much of the everyday dialogue engaged in in the workplace is counselling, but it is not being recognized as such (Redman, 1995). The disturbing extent of the problem is starkly revealed by Bull: 'most [workplace] help is unqualified and counselling is a synonym for anything from giving advice to disciplinary action' (1994).

It is quite wrong if a line manager infers counselling to be an entirely natural, spontaneous and everyday process requiring little depth of understanding. On the contrary, counselling is a purposeful activity, one which I have observed to have a profound effect on people. Professional counsellors undergo extensive and ongoing training precisely because counselling is such a potent process. So powerful is it that people make significant and often radical changes in their lives as a result of counselling. Any apparent contradictions in the nature of 'counselling' must be resolved or its value in relation to line management will be misunderstood.

A look at the most widely publicized definition of the nature of counselling will help here. The British Association for Counselling (BAC) *Code of Ethics and Practice for Counsellors* states: 'Only when both the user and the recipient explicitly agree to enter into a counselling relationship does it become "counselling" rather than the use of "counselling skills"' (1992: 3.2). This distinction between 'counselling' and 'use of counselling skills' is especially pertinent to line management and will be explored later. But for now, 'What is a counselling relationship?' is a valid question.

First, the BAC definition stresses that the activity called 'counselling' exists only when an *explicitly agreed* counselling relationship is entered into (1992: 3.2). In practice, this means it needs to be both verbally expressed and understood by both parties. Secondly, within this relationship, the *Code* says that counsellors must work with *integrity, impartiality and respect* as the very foundations of the work (1992: A.1) In effect, this means that counsellors must not be prejudiced by any outcome. Thirdly, and extremely relevant to line managers, is that the *Code* makes it the responsibility of the counsellor to clarify any ambiguity in the relationship with the client and to set boundaries (1992: B.2.2.5).

Looking back at our example with Jean, how much sense do these requirements of counselling make to Jim? Not much. In effect, he is being asked to say: 'For this meeting I am your counsellor to discuss this problem, with no part to play in whatever you choose to do; but when we finish, I will revert to being your manager, responsible for the results of your decision.'

This is as absurd as parents suggesting that their children's decisions will have no impact on family life. It is the unambiguity of the relationship that the BAC *Code* emphasizes and while it may well be viable for a manager in a staff role like human resources to be a professional counsellor, for a line manager role confusion will inevitably result from undertaking counselling with subordinates.

On the other hand, counselling offers seductive benefits. Recent research shows that people in organizations see workplace counselling as valuable for reducing stress, handling redundancy, performance improvement and as part of the process of organizational change (TDA, 1994). These are undeniable benefits for line management. So the question is posed by the line manager: 'If I want these benefits, how can I go about counselling my staff?' The short answer, given the BAC definition, is 'you can't', or more precisely, 'you run serious risks if you try'.

The Risks of Counselling in Line Management Situations

Unlike the USA, there is no UK legislation which prevents a manager taking the role of counsellor with a subordinate and so creating the potential for harm. Perhaps there should be. Sheila is an example of how damage can occur:

Case Study

Recently tasked with managing a busy administrative unit, Sheila learned that a member of the unit had suffered a panic attack at work a few days before. Having completed a course in counselling (in her own time), Sheila thought she should act as the person's counsellor on her return from sick leave. Naturally enough, Sheila was keen to help the person avoid further attacks and, as her line manager, was expected by the organization to sort matters out.

What harm came from her taking on the role of counsellor? First, professional counselling is discrete. Achieving this proved to be impossible. The length of time required, approximately an hour, meant cover had to be arranged for absence. An extra workload was thrown on workmates and this led to speculation, gossip and irritation, resulting in harmful backbiting. Then the cause of the panic attacks was alleged to be due to bullying by the other unit members. Acting within a professional counselling contract which requires confidentiality (BAC, 1992: B.4.1) and the relinquishing of control (BAC, 1992: 2.2.3), Sheila felt she could not use the allegations to take action. With no actions taken, the levels of work output expected from her unit remained unacceptable. A clear conflict with her responsibility to the organization was thus created. Also, as nothing was done, the bullying continued and the panic attacks worsened. Further, since professional counselling normally excludes the giving of advice (BAC, 1992: 2.2.2), Sheila refrained from advising, only to find herself in trouble with her manager who expected her to have told the employee what to do. Ultimately, the whole episode damaged Sheila's own career prospects.

This illustrates that the crunch for line managers comes with the issue of impartiality. Without doubt, many managers have integrity and respect for their fellow human beings. But for line managers, impartiality is not an option because of the power, authority and control that comes with the job. So, despite the various interpretations of the term 'counselling', it is essential that managers do not confuse it with well-intentioned chats or conversations containing advice or problem-solving discussions. Nor should it be used to describe the use of counselling skills, as we shall see later. It is vital that counselling is seen as a professional activity, undertaken by trained persons *who can safely put themselves in a position where they can operate within published codes of practice and ethics.* Understanding this point makes it obvious why line managers should not be counsellors to their subordinates.

I have presented the case that for line managers to attempt counselling is both impractical and unethical. But managers need the skills of counselling, first, to be more effective in communication with their people at work to maintain morale and performance and, secondly, to enable them to spot employees in or approaching a crisis point and to know what to do. It is to a discussion of counselling skills, rather than counselling that we now turn.

All Managers Can Benefit from Counselling Skills

Line managers are often completely unaware of how they are actually creating the very problems which make their jobs difficult. In my experience as a manager and when working with line managers, it is problems with employees that cause the most concern. Often, a lack of ability in handling people derives from line managers being good at something else before becoming managers. Egan makes this point somewhat firmly, if not sarcastically:

> Most companies choose people to be managers because they are good at something else. They are good accountants, good engineers, good lathe operators, good whatever. Then they give them no training in distinct managerial skills. Would you like to be operated on by someone who was chosen to be a brain surgeon because he or she showed excellence in the maintenance department? (1993: 34)

Egan is making the point that people skills are not necessarily a prerequisite for promotion to managerial positions. Communication skills, relationship-building skills and interpersonal skills are all bedrocks of managerial expertise. However, in many ways they are non-negotiables for future success. Without them, line managers become isolated, incapacitated and fearful for their positions.

And what can make things worse are the visible badges of status which can delude a manager over his or her abilities to manage people. Such delusion may take the form of: 'Of course I can manage people or they would not have given me this promotion.' Worse still, the longer the elapsed time from being promoted, the more conscious of status and the more unreceptive to training in people skills he/she is likely to be. It is deficiency in this area which lies at the root of many of the people problems which beset managers.

How does this deficiency cause problems? It may be an over-simplification, but problems occur when people fail to respect each other. In a social context we can choose with whom we mix and spend time. Not so in the workplace. Ideally, a manager 'gets on' with all of his/her team, irrespective of like or dislike, and is respected. But respect is a two-way thing which thrives on mutual understanding and good relationships. What really blows relationships apart is the sense by either employee or manager that the other 'does not have any time for me', 'doesn't listen', 'doesn't understand my position', 'doesn't care about me'. These are all undesirable reactions which counselling skills can help avert.

These skills are not mystical, nor are they exclusive to counselling. They include generic skills that some people possess naturally and use to help others. Many managers have abilities in listening to and building good relationships with their staff. Many are good communicators, constructive in their support of staff and proficient at helping them to make their own decisions. Yet, precisely because these abilities can be seen as 'innate' (IPM, 1992), the specific skills which go to make them up are not always recognized as definable skills to learn. Equally, their absence is also not always recognized. The point is that while many managers may be unconsciously competent at people skills, many too are unconsciously incompetent. In other words, they are unaware that they lack ability in this area.

It is because these same helping skills are fundamental to counselling and because counsellors have wished to know what makes effective counselling, that analysis has led to specific 'core' skills being identified, and hence the emergence of the term 'counselling skills'. The predictable outcome is that people now sell courses so that a manager can learn, practise and become proficient at using them, just like any other skillset.

Core Skills – Only Part of the Picture

Helpfully, there is much agreement on the core skills required for effective helping and on their affinity with communication skills (Reddy, 1987; Megranahan, 1989; Culley, 1991; Egan, 1994; Redman, 1995). Culley offers a useful definition of counselling skills as: 'competency or accomplishment in communication, acquired or developed in training' (1991: 3). She considers the 'foundation skills' to be attending, observing clients, listening, reflecting, probing and being concrete.

It is not my purpose here to describe each skill in detail or how to become proficient – that is covered in a number of widely available books (for example, Murgatroyd, 1985; Culley, 1991; Hughes, 1991; Nelson-Jones, 1993b). However, I have included Table 18.1 to illustrate the difference in a meeting when counselling skills are used by a manager.

Empathy – The Added Dimension for Effective Employee Care

There is a duty on line managers to care professionally for their employees but many do not know how to read the signs and spot an employee in or nearing 'crisis'. Counselling skills are a way forward to really effective staff support, not simply because of better communication, but because being skilled at interpersonal relationships delivers results.

Carroll (1995) uses the IPM *Statement on Counselling in the Workplace* (1992) to make this point with regard to managers:

> Much workplace counselling is not counselling in the modern definition of the term, but relates to situations which require the use of counselling skills. This increases their ability to deal more easily and quickly with employee issues, to recognise signs of distress or disturbance more quickly and to be able to relate to their staff in more humane ways. (Carroll, 1995: 23–9)

What is so special about counselling skills that increases this ability in managers? To reiterate, good communication, building good relationships and interpersonal skills are all core management skills, but within counselling skills there exists an additional momentous dimension of which managers are often not aware. Managers attending counselling skills courses are often surprised at the stunning effect of the approach to which they are introduced.

The effect that amazes them is how conscious attention paid to *feelings* during an interview gets results in bringing underlying problems out into the open. This can lead interviewees into new insights into their problems. For some managers the feelings dimension is an entirely new approach and takes them into a way of relating to people that is alien to them when at work. However, not all authors on the subject agree that it has merit. One well-established reference work on people skills openly discourages the notion of paying attention to emotions (Honey, 1988). The point is that paying attention to understanding a problem and discussing behaviours is a commonplace managerial style, but paying attention to a person's feelings is not. Active listening, open body language, summarizing and questioning are all effective techniques which clarify understanding. But when a manager investigates the *emotional* aspect of the situation, saying something like: 'how do you feel about that?', it is different and new because it moves the discussion away from the logical business of studying content (that is, the details of the situation) to 'process'. Process here means what a person

Table 18.1 *A comparison of two approaches*

'Power' approach	Skills	Alternative approach
Employee has to leave job to make appointment (control model of management).		Manager is often available at employee's point of work.
Manager sits behind desk during interview. Leaves door open. Sets timespan for interview.	*Attending*	Manager moves to 'neutral' seating, relinquishing 'power barrier'. Shuts door. Diverts telephone. Negotiate mutually acceptable timespan.
Manager sits, arms folded, looking intensely at employee and asks 'What's the trouble?'	*Observing*	Manager adopts open body language, looks relaxed, and asks if the employee would like the meeting to be confidential. Whatever, manager outlines limits of confidentiality and sets boundaries for the discussion.
Manager accepts telephone interruptions, fidgets, has poor eye contact.	*Listening* *Rapport*	Manager encourages employee to start whenever he/she wishes, listens without interrupting, keeps still, maintains comfortable eye contact.
Manager hears employee's concern and starts to address it mentally.	*Reflecting* *Empathic responding*	Manager uses active listening skills to let employee know that he/she is accurately and empathically understood.
Manager considers impact on his/her own or departmental needs and begins to formulate most expedient resolution, mentally, to meet those needs.	*Probing*	Using the minimum of appropriate questions, manager enables employee to express and clarify depth of feelings about the concern.
Manager interrupts employee in order to explain his/her own perceived solution and/or options for next steps.	*Reframing* *Paraphrasing*	Neutralizing his/her own feelings and worries about the concern and its possible consequences, manager assists employee to hear his/her own views and feelings about the issue, so as to promote self-understanding and to diminish the effect of excessive emotion.
Manager presses own preferred solution forward with powerful arguments to justify its adoption by the employee.	*Being objective* *Diagnosing* *Clarifying*	Suspending his/her own emerging judgement and solution paths, manager helps employee make explicit the specific and most important aspects of the issue.
Manager keeps his/her own agenda hidden from employee.	*Being congruent*	If employee's needs are in conflict with manager's agenda, manager is open about the conflict as appropriate within confidentiality boundaries agreed.

Table 18.1 *(cont.)*

'Power' approach	Skills	Alternative approach
Manager prescribes or gives strong recommendation as to what employee should do next.	*Intervening*	Manager helps employee to find his/her own ways forward, refraining from offering advice or guidance too early. If possible, manager accepts employee's solution through a process of clarifying pitfalls, exploring options and consequences, and negotiating round obstacles.
	Being self-aware Referring	Manager decides whether the employee's interests (and therefore his/her own) might be better served by another resource, e.g., personnel, staff nurse, professional counsellor. If so, makes suitable referral in appropriate style. Agrees with employee the extent of any information to be passed across.
Manager ends interview.	*Summarizing*	Manager confirms next actions as decided by employee and supported by manager, agrees timescale and sets date and time for review. Reminds about confidentiality.
	Ending	Manager enquires if interview is effectively over, if employee is all right to carry on. Interview ends.

experiences at an emotional level when exploring his/her problem. In normal interaction with their employees, managers seldom take notice of this dimension, preferring to concentrate on thoughts and behaviours. Figure 18.1 illustrates the impact of the added dimension.

The point is that failing to take account of the influence that feelings have on what we do or think, limits our understanding of what is happening for us and reduces the quality of our decision-making. So managers attending courses in counselling skills based on the Egan three-stage model of counselling (that is, exploration, understanding, action) will find themselves introduced to the feelings dimension quite early on.

Such training typically encourages them to be on the lookout for the key words, the physical signs and the inflections in tone which give clues to the emotional process going on within the other person. Managers learn about empathy, as the ability to feel another person's world as he/she feels it or, as I like to describe it, as being able to feel how someone's shoes hurt. Empathy is so effective at building rapport and trust that its use carries responsibilities, a subject we will look at later. At work, feelings are usually repressed because

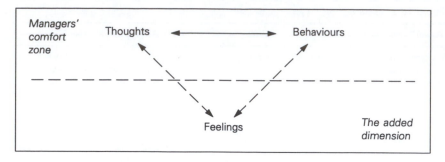

Figure 18.1   *Interrelationship of thought behaviours and feelings*

along with natural inhibition, many people consider it a sign of weakness to display emotion, especially in front of their manager. Yet, if a manager is skilled at establishing rapport, at mutual understanding and at creating an atmosphere of trust, it may well only take the most gentle of empathic responses to get beyond the surface problem to the real causes and concerns. It is this additional dimension that takes counselling skills beyond generic relationship skills and this is why their use can be so effective in helping both manager and employee to a deeper and clearer understanding of problems and situations.

Counselling Skills – 'Power Tools' for Efficiency and Performance

Managers can legitimately use counselling skills as a way of managing employees. In fact, counselling skills are a basis for good management in whatever context it occurs. The BAC *Code of Ethics and Practice for Counselling Skills* states 'what distinguishes the use of counselling skills' from counselling are 'the intentions of the user, which is to enhance the performance of their (the recipients') functional role' (1989: B.1.1). I believe that by developing his/her resources in the skills of counselling, a manager will be more able to lead his/her staff to better work performance.

The underlying psychology of this approach is not difficult to grasp. Put simply, it says that if people are treated as adults and not as children, if they are given the kind of non-judgemental support that enables them to sort things out by using their own resources, then they will grow in confidence and increase in ability to resolve future problems on their own. If a manager is able to respond non-defensively, to use the skills of rapport, empathic responding and clarification and to reflect and summarize, then he/she will enable each party to be better understood and thus to achieve clearer and more open two-way communication. In action, the process is visibly different from either imparting expertise or having a conversation because the manager will be listening for 80 per cent of the time and talking for only 20 per cent!

(Bond, 1993). Typically, an employee will experience this as unusual, but will be so pleasantly surprised not to be overwhelmed by the manager's views that she/he is likely to be highly motivated to think up and make changes of his/her own accord.

Counselling skills are powerful tools because by using them a manager is facilitating a person to explore, understand and take action to solve problems *without imposing a solution*. Changes which are needed for improved efficiency and performance happen more readily because the people who have to take action are the ones who have decided what to do and are self-motivated to do it. Responsibility for 'making it happen' shifts to them, with the manager there to support the process in pursuit of the organizational goal.

Surely this is what a manager wants? But, maybe not. It depends on the model of management that the manager espouses. Control freaks are certainly likely to say that, if employees are left to their own devices, or given too much rope, or allowed to make decisions, then either through lack of ability, apathy or possibly even vindictiveness, all hell will be let loose, for which they, the managers, are responsible. 'Give them an inch and they'll take a mile' is symptomatic of managers wedded to a controlling operational style, usefully termed 'macho-management' (Dutfield and Eling, 1990). But there is persuasive evidence to dispute this view. Semler writes of trying both ways. He tells how his Brasilian company Semco secured concrete commercial success and visible morale and job satisfaction improvements by relinquishing the control culture in favour of one built on support and autonomy.

> At Semco we did away with strictures that dictate the 'hows' and created fertile soil for differences. We gave people an opportunity to test, question and disagree. We let them determine their own training and their own futures. (Semler, 1994: 281)

Another example is computer giant ICL whose performance initiatives for managers aided its economic recovery. These required them to be both effective business managers *and* effective people managers (Incomes Data Services, 1992: 10–11). ICL's success confirms a balance between 'hard' business issues and 'soft' people issues and establishes a clear role for counselling skills within the manager's repertoire of competences. And Lane (1990) lists six key competences identified by the Business Institute of Management for high performance in managers (knowing yourself, managing yourself, communication, managing others, problem-solving, financial data). All but one – financial data – have a people orientation.

Finally, on the subject of business performance, managers may not make the connection between the use of counselling skills and successful selling. Precisely the same skills can be applied in this fiercely results-orientated environment. How do they help? A purchaser who feels secure that the salesperson understands his/her needs and concerns accurately, and who considers the product or service matches those needs and addresses these concerns, can justify making the purchase. Only if the salesperson has created rapport, listened attentively, supported the problem-solving process and not claimed ownership of the solution will this happen as well as it might. Sales coach and business guru Burch makes the point:

Sit with your customer . . . and steadily and thoroughly work yourself into an understanding of their situation. This requires a lot of gentle probing, sensitive questioning and active, understanding listening to absorb not only their aspirations and concerns but also any lurking anxieties, potential problems and underlying difficulties. (Burch, 1994: 248)

Such an approach as Burch suggests is greatly facilitated by being familiar and competent with the skills of counselling. However, while I hope to have de-mystified counselling skills and illustrated their value to line management in terms of employee care, performance, efficiency and problem-solving, there is a shrouded responsibility on line managers as to how they use them.

Counselling Skills Come with Concealed Ethical Responsibilities

Line managers in particular must understand that the unethical use of counselling skills can seriously damage their careers. As stressed earlier, the position for a line manager is unambiguous. He/she should never attempt to take the explicit role of counsellor because role conflict is inherent. But if a manager becomes even reasonably proficient at using counselling skills *the effect on the other person will be the same as if that manager was actually engaging in counselling*. For the recipient, the employee, the in-the-moment experience will be a strong match with that of professional counselling. This is the crux of the ethical issue. The argument is that employees who take their problems to their line manager and who are enabled to relax, who are made to feel they can really trust their manager and to feel secure that what goes on is confidential, are much more likely to overcome the reticence they would naturally have when speaking to their boss. This is exactly what both parties want in problem-solving, employee care and performance management, because real causes and concerns are uncovered. But there are paradoxes. For the line manager it is that the revelations may go too far, such that the manager hears things that create role conflict. For the employees, it is that they may later find themselves wondering about the wisdom of having been so open and how that might affect their future under that manager.

Carol, holder of a key managerial position, is a case where these paradoxes come to light:

Case Study

David, the department head, responds to Carol's request to discuss a new position advertised internally. Carol says she needs feedback about her abilities to support her application, fully aware that company policy requires the new department head to notify the existing one of the application. In session, David uses his counselling skills to put Carol at ease and successfully encourages open and honest discussion. Skilled in empathy, David becomes aware of how intensely Carol feels she needs more income. He feels inclined to support her despite it meaning the loss of a highly capable member of his own team. He reasons that it happens all the time and people need help to progress in their careers. But concern about her financial situation leads David to explore her aspirations. In the process Carol quietly discloses that she is resisting strong pressure from her partner to start a family. She explains that generating savings is her priority, but she fears she might have to succumb to the pressure and leave work at any time in the next two years.

David faces a dilemma. In effect, he has allowed the relationship to cross over from manager/employee to counsellor/client. Role conflicts now exist because Carol has disclosed a personal problem which creates consequences for David beyond those that he could have anticipated at the outset.

As trusted adviser, believing she could do the job and wanting to support her career, he feels he should encourage her application. But in the drive-for-results role he thinks it is a criminal waste to lose her from his team when the odds are she will depart the company completely in under two years. Better she should hang-on in his department and continue her excellent work. He wonders about offering a salary hike to keep her, but in his role of budget-holder he is worried how that would look to others and the unplanned expense.

As professional colleague to Carol's prospective boss, he is torn between keeping Carol's intentions confidential and forestalling the potential waste of company resouces in recruiting and training her, should she leave soon. As her team-leader, their working relationship is now compromised by their joint knowledge of the tenuous situation.

It does not matter what David decides to do, the unwelcome knowledge creates a risk to his credibility, the performance of his department and his relationship with his team. All measures of his job performance which impact on his career.

Almost all of these problems could have been avoided if David had explained to Carol at the outset the 'rules of engagement' or in counselling speak, the 'boundaries' of the session. The crucial boundary to make explicit *at the start* is that while the manager will do everything possible to help, there are limits to observe in what the employee or the manager should disclose. Specifically, if any disclosure is likely to affect the existing working relationship between them or the ability of either of them to act within their professional roles, then such disclosure should not be made. In a similar vein, the limits of confidentiality that are possible for the manager must be clearly stated.

Depth in the Training of Counselling Skills is Essential

Managers may resist the idea of upfront, explicit boundary-setting as I have presented it. They may argue that in doing so, employees will not open up. They may also argue that employees will always exercise caution over disclosures that might affect their position. These objections are valid but not ubiquitous. The case is that while some employees will remain prudent, many others will not. These others will, in effect, be lulled into a sense of security and will lose their natural caution. This is the power of counselling skills and why training in counselling skills must be thorough enough to do three things of unsurpassed importance:

1. Training must show managers how to deliver cautions around disclosure and confidentiality in a way that is both understood by, and acceptable to, employees in their charge.
2. Training must coach managers to be able to recognize the approach of the cross-over point where to continue the session would be unethical.
3. Training must enable managers to offer appropriate alternative courses of action at the cross-over point.

With good coaching, most managers will readily discover and develop ways of setting boundaries that are effective and suit their personal style. The issue of cross-over is not so easy. Ideally, during an interview both parties are sufficiently aware to know if the basis on which the helping started, that is, manager/employee is changing to one of counsellor/client. But the employee is most unlikely to be able to do this. Partly because he/she will be engrossed in the content and its associated emotions and partly because seeking help and advice renders one vulnerable in the relationship.

How fair is it to expect a person in this position to monitor what is happening and cry 'Stop! I don't want counselling'? It is neither fair nor realistic. It follows that the manager must take responsibility for being able to spot the cross-over point. This means being skilled enough to remain sufficiently detached from content to pay conscious attention to process, that is, what is going on emotionally for both of them and stay sensitive to the emergence of content which threatens to raise role conflict. The clues to imminent cross-over are:

*   Heightened emotions in the employee.
*   Heightened emotions in the manager.
*   Intrusion of personal agendas for the manager.

Emotional breakdown into personal issues, actual or pending, is the point at which it almost certainly becomes unethical for the line manager to continue using counselling skills. To continue becomes, in effect, an attempt at counselling. The manager must stop the session and take suitable action, which is generally to refer the employee to a source of impartial, professional counselling provision (IPM, 1992).

The intrusion of personal agendas means the point at which the employee's issues raise problems for the manager which start to take precedence over those of the employee. To continue to use counselling skills is unethical because the manager can no longer hold helping the employee as the primary role in session. In effect, the manager will become manipulative.

There is a further use of counselling skills which makes line managers manipulative from the start. Many managers and especially new managers, see their primary role as achieving results. They focus on task. When things go wrong it is because somebody is doing or not doing something which affects the completion of task. Thus their approach is not about wanting to solve the employee's problem, but to solve the problem that that person is causing them. If they use counselling skills to do it, the likelihood is that the person will open up and the manager will be guilty of manipulating the situation.

Conclusion

The values and beliefs that underpin professional counselling *are inseparable* from the use of counselling skills. The process is the same. It is the relationship which makes it counselling and, as we saw earlier, for line managers a counselling relationship is impossible.

The ethical use of counselling skills is both possible and desirable for line managers once they are trained, so long as they:

- 'Buy into' the basic values of counselling.
- Avoid manipulation by exercising self-discipline in choosing when to use them.
- Adhere to setting clear boundaries when they do.
- Observe the cross-over point into unethical practice.
- Have the facilities available and the skill to refer a person for further appropriate help.

Line managers must be aware that if counselling skills are to be accepted as credible tools by their subordinates, peers and superiors, the BAC *Code of Ethics and Practice for Counselling Skills* places the following expectations on their organization:

> It must provide a code of ethics and practice for users of counselling skills in their specific functional roles. (1989: C.1.1, 1.2)

> It must provide sufficient and ongoing training for counselling skills to be used appropriately. (1989: C.2.1, 2.3)

> It must enable the user to use the skills 'in a way which is consistent with good practice in the user's functional role'. (1989: D.1.1)

The availability of training courses in counselling skills is on the increase. It is incumbent on line managers in particular, because of their influential relationship with their subordinates, to ensure that their organizations choose courses which address these issues in depth. It is in the interests of all involved because conscientious line managers, who are skilled in this area and aware of their responsibilities, will empower their employees to achieve success for themselves, their managers and thus the organization.

References

Bond, T. (1993) *Standards and Ethics for Counselling in Action*. London: Sage.
British Association for Counselling (1989) *Code of Ethics and Practice for Counselling Skills*. Rugby: BAC.

British Association for Counselling (1992) *Code of Ethics and Practice for Counsellors*. Rugby: BAC.

Bull, A. (1994) 'How effective is counselling in the workplace?', *Evaluation of Counselling Selected References*: 5. Rugby: British Association for Counselling.

Burch, G. (1994) *Resistance is Useless*. London: Headline.

Carroll, M. (1995) 'The counsellor in organizational settings: some reflections', *Employee Counselling Today*, 7 (1): 23–9.

Culley, S. (1991) *Integrative Counselling Skills in Action*. London: Sage.

Dutfield, M. and Eling, C. (1990) *The Communicating Manager*. Shaftesbury: Element Books.

Egan, G. (1993) 'The Shadow Side', *Management Today*, September: 33–8.

Egan, G. (1994) *The Skilled Helper* (4th Edition). Monterey, CA: Brooks/Cole.

Honey, P. (1988) *Improve your People Skills*. London: Institute of Personnel Management.

Hughes, T. (1991) *Counselling for Managers*. London: Bacie.

Incomes Data Services (IDS) Ltd (1992) *Performance Management*. London: IDS Study 518.

Institute of Personnel Management (1992) *Statement on Counselling in the Workplace*. London: IPM.

Lane, David A. (1990) 'Counselling psychology in organizations', *The Psychologist*, 12: 540–4.

Megranahan, Michael (1989) *Counselling: A Practical Guide for Employers*. London: Institute of Personnel Management.

Murgatroyd, S. (1985) *Counselling and Helping*. Leicester: British Psychological Society.

Nelson-Jones, R. (1988) *Practical Counselling and Helping Skills*. London: Holt, Rhinehart and Winston.

Nelson-Jones, R. (1993a) *You Can Help: Introducing Lifeskills Helping*. London: Cassell.

Nelson-Jones, R. (1993b) *Training Manual for Counselling and Helping Skills*. London: Cassell.

Peters, T. (1993) *Liberation Management*. London: Pan Books.

Reddy, M. (1987) *The Manager's Guide to Counselling at Work*. London: Methuen.

Redman, W. (1995) *Counselling Your Staff*. London: Kogan Page.

Semler, R. (1994) *Maverick*. London: Arrow Business Books.

TDA (1994) *Counselling at Work Surveys 1993*. Brentford: TDA Consulting Ltd.

Thorne, B. (1992) 'Psychotherapy and counselling: the quest for difference', *Counselling*, 3 (4): 244–8.

19

Developing Training for Organizational Counselling

Eileen Pickard

Organizational counselling is an emergent application of counselling. Its identity is still unfolding and its roots are in a range of areas. Occupational psychologists engage in counselling which is often closely associated with career counselling. Business training involves elements of counselling which usually have an emphasis upon counselling skills. Counselling and psychotherapy themselves have contributed to counselling in organizations and the EAP movement has shaped organizational provision of these interventions.

What is both creative and problematic for those responsible for the development of training programmes in this field is the fact that counselling in organizations can mean many things. Sometimes, it is associated with career counselling. At other times it is viewed as a problem-solving intervention (Lane, 1990). Some organizations buy it in with an almost 'take-away' mentality; others try to embed it in the roles of human resource personnel or even managers (Nixon and Carroll, 1994). But this diversity is not, as yet, a confident one, rejoicing in the excitement of debate. It stems from the fact that we are still articulating the nature and purpose of counselling in organizational settings.

Exploration of the Organizational Context

A first task for any designer of a curriculum in an applied field is exploration of the context in which it is expressed because it is the context which shapes the nature and expression of the application. In the case of counselling in organizations, this exploration is in itself an influential one in that trainers, in the absence of clearly agreed philosophies and methods for the training of organizational counsellors, will inevitably become the creators of them. This initial exploration of the setting is a kind of detective task in which the curriculum designer gathers clues about the emergent role of the organizational counsellor. There are several questions which need to be answered. What do organizational counsellors do? What do organizations require of them? What is the nature of the organizational setting? And finally, what is the history that has created this setting and these needs?

McLeod comments upon the fact that there is a limited literature on counsellor training: 'Even the knowledge that tutors and trainers have gained through personal and professional experience is seldom written up for publication' (1993: 205). The situation in organizational counselling is more limited still, though there is an emergent literature on the use of counselling in organizations which provides some basis for the development of training programmes. Carroll (1995) has written on the complex role of workplace counsellors who may be required to work with related interventions such as mentoring, to manage the provision of counselling, to act as consultant and to provide career guidance. They may have some responsibility for training, change management or even marketing. Their mixed role engages them in a range of boundary and disposition shifts. It requires them to cope well with diverse activities and asks for an understanding of the organizational context within which these activities are to be interpreted and given meaning.

To the professional counsellor or psychotherapist with a training based upon the independent practitioner model, this mixed role can speak of boundary confusion or even unprofessionalism. To those engaged in the development of training for workplace-based National Vocational Qualifications (NVQs) in Counselling and related interventions such as Advice, Guidance and Psychotherapy it may be seen as an indication of the emergence of more creative and less traditional ways of working with counselling.

The Uncertain Role of the Organizational Counsellor

The uncertain role of the organizational counsellor can arise for several reasons. First, organizations are not always clear about their reasons for hiring a counsellor (Reddy, 1993). Purchasers of counselling provision may not always be clear about the philosophies and practices of the different practitioners who present their services. Highley and Cooper (1994), in a project funded by the Health and Safety Executive, explored reasons why organizations choose counselling. They include enabling employees to adapt to change and cope with high levels of organizational stress, providing support for staff and the desire to appear caring as an employer. However, whatever their awareness of their own needs, organizations have rarely influenced the nature of their own counselling provision. Their poor understanding of it and the externalizing and marginalizing of its provision has meant that counselling services and training have been designed, in the main, by those outside the organization. It is the trainers and the practitioners who are shaping this aspect of organizational development. Organizations themselves have yet to become active in the counselling training conversation. As a result, their culture and needs may not always be reflected in the provision of training and services.

Secondly, organizations often lack an integrated and coherent system of human resource provision and management within which counselling can find a place (McKenna and Beech, 1995). The philosophies and processes of employee support systems may not be well articulated and counselling may remain unrelated to them and marginalized. Tehrani (1995) recognizes this lack of coherent internal provision of employee support. Her organization, the

Post Office, is one of the few working towards 'an organizationally integrated approach to employee care' (Tehrani, 1994).

Thirdly, the fact that much workplace counselling is carried out by non-professionals (Reddy, 1993) who come to the task with various backgrounds, philosophies and practices tends to militate against the development and articulation of professionally agreed training systems. Where counselling is delivered by professionals, they may well belong to different professional bodies which have their own differences with regard to this emergent application of counselling. The Association of Counselling at Work (ACW), a Division of the British Association for Counselling (BAC) has just begun to articulate training requirements and, in the British Psychological Society (BPS), where organizational counselling is of interest to both the Division of Counselling Psychology and that of Occupational Psychology, there are no distinct recognition processes for the organizational counsellor. At present, therefore, the curriculum developer has little training guidance from professional bodies.

The Stages of Development of Organizational Counselling

The clues that we find about the history and current practices of counselling in organizations might be expressed in three main stages of development. They are provisional stages to be refined as we articulate our grasp of this application of counselling, but, for the moment, they enable us to begin to formulate the aims of a training programme for organizational counsellors (Table 19.1).

The first stage, *Counselling in organizations*, represents the most externalized approach to counselling provision. Counsellors may not be trained in the ways of the organization but will bring expertise in counselling itself. Their training will be based on the independent practitioner model in which the counsellor is a relatively free agent, selecting the philosophy, orientation, length of therapy and arrangement of location. There may be conflict between the objectives of the counsellor and those of the organization. The organization may be perceived as oppressing the client. This is a wholly external model of provision which is not integrated into the organization's philosophy and aims and whose practices derive from the freedoms of the independent practitioner model.

Stage two, *Counselling for organizations*, represents those services, both of individuals and of service systems such as EAPs, which strive to integrate counselling into organizational philosophy and practice. Counselling theory and practice is adapted in a pragmatic way. There is a parallel here with eclecticism in that practitioners adapt and select according to need, orchestrating their interventions into a working system (Dryden, 1992). This stage represents progress towards organizational counselling. However, it lacks conceptual and theoretical integration and because practitioners will be rooted in the independent practitioner model there may be conflict between the organizational and counselling cultures.

Table 19.1   *The stages of development of organizational counselling*

Counselling in organizations	Counselling for organizations	Organizational counselling
• Independent practitioner training • Ad hoc provision • Service marginalized	• Some knowledge of organizations • Pragmatic adaptations to suit organization • Some integration	• Integrated training • Provision designed for organization • Integration within and between systems

The third stage, *Organizational counselling*, might be viewed as an ideal type, towards which we are striving. It is integrated both conceptually and theoretically into organizational philosophy and practice. Here there is a parallel with integrative approaches to practice (Dryden, 1992). Both counselling theory and practice are transformed by their assimilation of organizational theory and practice and the outcome is an integrated system of employee support, leading to a new, higher level approach to the interpretation and practice of this application of counselling.

The range of organizational counselling is narrower than either that of counselling in organizations or counselling for organizations. In the main, it is concerned with issues and problems which are caused or exacerbated by the organization as well as those which affect organizational performance. It may not include the counselling of personal issues which have their roots outside organizational life, though organizations may decide that part of their policy of employee support is the provision of counselling for personal issues.

These three stages of development of organizational counselling are reflected in training programmes and in the experience of trainees. The degree to which programmes struggle with conceptual and theoretical integration varies. However, once curriculum planners take on board the search for conceptual and theoretical integration at organizational level, there is a need to explore what integration might mean at the more detailed level of organizational systems and sub-systems. This takes us back to the question of what organizational counsellors do and to the nature of the interventions with which they work.

Integration and Organizational Support Systems

The Advice, Guidance, Counselling and more recently, Psychotherapy Lead Body's continuum of employee support illustrates some of the ways in which counselling overlaps with other interventions such as advice and guidance. A consideration of the literature on employee support soon makes clear that counselling overlaps with a range of other interventions, such as coaching and mentoring. Further, all of these approaches claim to employ counselling skills. The NVQ Continuum (Figure 19.1) illustrates the overlaps of employee support interventions.

These observations require us to consider the nature and boundaries of the activities we have traditionally separated from counselling and the labels we

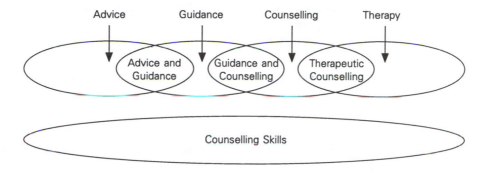

Figure 19.1   *The NVQ continuum, illustrating the development of employee support interventions (Janes, 1992)*

employ to demarcate them. A re-division of the boundaries of knowledge and practice might produce an approach to counselling that is better suited to organizational needs.

The Skills of Counselling and Related Workplace Interventions

Let us explore this by considering counselling skills. Training in counselling skills is popular in organizations. The objective is usually to enable people to be more effective in their people-handling jobs. The problems arise when individuals begin to equate counselling skills with professional counselling and to perceive themselves as counsellors. This is problematic for professional practice. It also blurs the identity of organizational counselling. As the Advice, Guidance, Counselling and Psychotherapy Lead Body indicated, what we have come to call counselling skills underpins a range of activities and goes by a range of labels. If we could agree to reserve the term counselling for professional counsellors and re-label counselling skills as 'people-handling skills', we would begin to recognize them as elements belonging to a range of activities but distinct from professional counselling (Pickard, 1994). This could be a first step from some of our present muddle to both a better demarcation and better integration of distinct but related interventions.

It is sometimes argued that the higher order skills of counselling, such as working with transference, belong properly to therapeutic counselling. However, as integration increases through creative practice, even these boundaries are crossed. O'Brien (1995) proposes a model of psychodynamic mentoring. O'Brien's work is interesting in itself. It is also another example of the creative integration of employee support interventions which is beginning to take place (Clarkson, 1995). What is becoming evident is that the ways in which we have come to construe interventions, their identities and their boundaries are changing. These changes are the result of reflective practice and creative integration, and have implications for the content and processes of training courses in organizational counselling.

Integrating Employee Support Interventions

McKenna and Beech (1995) suggest a number of ways in which counselling might be used with other interventions within an organizational context. They include enabling individuals to cope with organizational change and as a support to development appraisal. Earlier, McKenna (1994) also suggested that counselling could be used as part of people-centred organizational development. However, though workplace practices may integrate or couple different employee support interventions, there is little clear analysis of the nature of these integrations, their purpose and their effects. Training derived from good practice needs understandings of this kind. It is likely, for example, that mentoring and counselling have some process overlaps but their purposes and processes are distinct and different. The disciplinary interview differs markedly from most counselling relationships but might be supported by counselling and reward management might blend with cognitive behavioural approaches to counselling. But, as yet, our understanding of these possible relationships is hypothetical and the questions are rendered more complex by the fact that these different employee support systems are driven by different philosophies and processes. Untangling the web is a current training task. It gives trainees a sense of an emerging system and the opportunity to consider interventions relationally.

There are overlaps to be found between *counselling* and *mentoring*. Both are relational activities concerned with the potential of the person. Both draw upon counselling skills and each one can be driven by a range of philosophies and expressed in a range of practices. However, they remain distinct interventions. The purpose of mentoring is to transmit organizational values and practices, and in this it is essentially didactic. While it is a relational activity, there are usually status differences of company position and experience between the mentor and mentoree whereas in counselling there is likely to be more equality in the relationship. Mentoring focuses upon the individual in relation to the organization and upon the realization of the individual's personal potential or resolution of personal issues in relation to organizational needs. Mentoring requires learning, adjustment and even imitation on the part of the individual. Though organizational counselling is concerned with organizational issues, it places more emphasis upon the realization of personal potential and the resolution of personal issues for the sake of the individual than does mentoring. However, there will be times when the balance will shift and the two processes may appear to be indistinguishable. Finally, within organizations these two support systems might be located in different departments. Mentoring may belong to Human Resources and counselling to Welfare or Training. In practice, there may be no attempt to explore overlaps or to understand how they are processed by the individuals who experience them.

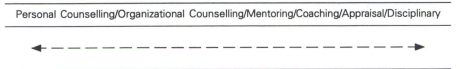

Personal Counselling/Organizational Counselling/Mentoring/Coaching/Appraisal/Disciplinary

Changing professional relationships from a boundaried, non-evaluative and personal one to an increasingly organizational and less personally supportive one.

Figure 19.2 *A relational continuum of employee support interventions*

Overlaps and distinctions exist between *organizational counselling* and *appraisal* and *development* systems as they do with other interventions such as *coaching*. As the continuum in Figure 19.2 indicates, the relational nature of the interventions varies from one end of the continuum to the other. These overlaps and relational differences have implications for both the knowledge aspect of a training programme and the supervision of the trainee's practice. However, there is a sense in which curriculum developers and researchers invent the ideas of systems and foster them in trainees. It is their reflections upon practice and research which underpin training programmes. In practice, there may be no system, no coherence and no sense of wholeness (Noon, 1992) either for the recipient or for those trainees who deliver the system.

Reflections on systems by curriculum developers influence the content of training programmes. It is the trainer's way of sending messages to organizations and a way of imposing values upon systems. However, it can also be a way of encouraging organizations to reflect upon their practices and to gain as much as they can from their resources. If, for example, elements of employee support are working in conflict or overlapping to a point where there is virtual repetition of a service, then there is resource wastage. Conceptualizing organizational provision is not just a task for curriculum designers. It is also of critical importance for organizational development.

Implications for the Curriculum

Jenkins makes the point that 'core elements of counsellor training are included by a rough consensus, and are then stretched and shaped according to many forces' (1995: 203). The curriculum for organizational counselling is the outcome of reflections upon organizations, their philosophies, structures and, in particular, their systems of employee support. It is also influenced by the experience of working with trainees who reflect their organizations. Like most curricula, there are three key aspects: content, structure and process. In all of these the integration of knowledge and experience is crucial to the formation and development of the identity of organizational counselling. In this section, two different kinds of training for the organizational counsellor are considered: the long course, which aims to contribute to the professional development of the counsellor, and shorter training programmes which intended to supplement longer-term training.

Curriculum Content

The organizational counsellor shares many of the training needs of the generic counsellor. For both, the aim is that of becoming a reflective practitioner who will engage in ongoing, personal professional development, appreciating that any training programme, however comprehensive, is a phase in an ongoing process (Skovholt and Ronnestad, 1995). Like the generic counsellor, the organizational counsellor's personal professional development can be expressed in a range of models (see, for example, Hogan, 1964; Grater, 1985; Hess, 1987). In their different ways, each of these models reflects the developmental stages of the emergent professional. Those involved in the training of organizational counsellors work with these same developmental stages but they are expressed and articulated within an organizational setting which colours both content and process aspects of organizational counselling training programmes.

Programmes for organizational counsellors need course elements which deal with the *organizational setting* itself so that its influences upon counselling processes and provision can be explored. The influences of counselling as an organizational change agent is the flip-side consideration. Trainees need time to reflect upon their own daily systems of work and to shift from the immediacy of pragmatism. The concept of the learning organization (Pedlar et al., 1988) implies reflection and awareness within which both personal and group development and creativity might be fostered. Trainees arriving from organizations which foster this learning context move more easily to the reflective tasks of counselling.

A trainee organizational counsellor needs to consider the issues involved in *establishing counselling practice* in organizations. Certainly, they go beyond those of the traditional counselling curriculum. Contracting is a more complex issue. It involves a three-cornered contract in which the organization must be understood and explored as client. The organizational counsellor has two clients, the organization and its employees. This situation raises a range of new boundary problems. Confidentiality, in particular, needs to be clearly articulated. Location of and access to the service require thoughtful planning. The organizational counsellor lacks many of the freedoms of the independent practitioner and has to learn what is an appropriate organizational constraint and what is a professional or ethical issue.

An analysis of *counselling and related workplace interventions* is central to the training of an organizational counsellor. Concerned as it is with the nature, dynamics, boundaries and interrelatedness of interventions, it is the conceptual melting pot for new understandings about employee support systems. Before trainees can think systems they need to understand their components. Those with backgrounds in generic counselling usually know little about mentoring, coaching or job search, while those trained in occupational contexts are likely to have a skills-based only approach to counselling. The delivery of the curriculum needs to be varied enough to take account of these differing needs.

Theory is a central component of all counsellor training because it gives meaning to practice. Here, this exploration of meaning needs to take place in relation to both organizational and counselling issues. For trainees with a resistance to theory and things abstract and a strong awareness of the immediate, the practical and the hands on, a meaningful starting point can be their own implicit theory. Exploration of their organization's values and assumptions and those of their own practice can lead to appreciation of the development of theory and prepare trainees for the task of evaluating major counselling theories and related practices. Because human resource contexts, from which many trainees come, are likely to be low on theoretical awareness and consistency (Noon, 1992), trainees may have poor knowledge of organizational theory.

Though organizational counsellors will, like the the generic counsellor, experience a range of familiar presenting issues and problems in their clients, for example, marital problems, depression and bereavement, organizations and workplaces do present particular *organizational issues* for which the trainee needs preparation. These include redundancy and survivor counselling, transitions and change, promotion and demotion and, in some cases, critical incidents. These are issues which are not normally included in generic counselling training and when they are the emphasis is more upon the needs of the individual than upon the individual in a particular setting. The organizational counsellor needs to understand the impact of these events upon the psyche of the organization itself and be able to work with the organization as client.

Finally, the organizational counsellor needs to be able to *manage the counselling provision* which includes the assessment of organizational need, provision and organizational philosophy, evaluation of provision and consulting within and on behalf of the organization. Generic counselling training rarely includes this preparation, which is essential for the organizational counsellor, because counselling provision, like any other provision, needs to be managed by those who understand its nature. It is this understanding which mediates the management of an essentially qualitative product in a setting likely to be characterized by quantitative management processes.

In both generic and organizational training programmes, the *skills* elements are central. For an organizational counsellor they are those people-handling skills that find expression in a range of workplace interventions. Often referred to as counselling skills, they will vary in use from intervention to intervention. The culmination of skills work is its blending with theory and organizational knowledge. As with the generic counsellor, the objective is an integrated personal style (Hill et al., 1981). The Myers–Briggs Type Indicator (MBTI), which is popular in organizations, can provide a focal point for this development. For the organizational counsellor the development of personal, therapeutic style involves a blend of organizational knowing and experience, personal theoretical preference and the development and use of self in the organizational setting.

As in mainstream counselling training, *supervised practice and personal development* are key elements of the organizational counsellor's training programme. In organizations, practice takes place in a range of interventions and raises new questions about the nature and identity of workplace interventions, about contracting, boundaries and confidentiality. Practice supervisors have to extend their knowledge beyond traditional counselling settings. They have, for example, to be able to work with the supervision of mentoring as well as counselling. They must also be able to understand the trainees' development in relation to the organizational setting as well as in relation to models and practices which have come to influence their own supervisory style. Most trainees will have experience of development work but it is likely to have been limited to short courses with an emphasis on professional rather than personal development, about which they may have anxieties and resistance.

As yet, there are few well-established programmes of training in organizational counselling but a consideration of existing ones indicates an emerging consensus over their content and an awareness of the need to integrate and shape relevant knowledge and experience into this growing application of counselling.

Curriculum Structure

When and how to start a training programme is a question for all curriculum planners, as is the task of integrating its components. Because the majority of trainees in organizational counselling are in practice of some kind, the practical, the hands-on, the desire for solutions is often uppermost. This requires trainers to structure programmes in ways that can recognize and meet this need but which, at the same time, will enable the trainee to move towards a more reflective stance. There is also a need to structure programmes in ways which integrate the structures, systems and practices of organizations with those of counselling to enable trainees to be aware of these conceptualizations. Further, every element needs to be related to every other element so that the identity of the total system and the influences within it can be explored. Human resource theory, for example, needs to be explored in relation to counselling theory and related to interventions, practices and personal development work driven by the two sets of theories. Mentoring and coaching need to find their place in skills work and supervision, as well as in the content dimension of the programme. In a sense, it is important to begin and to continue the programme 'with everything' and to reflect every element in every session in order to demonstrate the significance of integration (Table 19.2).

Processes of the Programme

Training for organizational counselling requires the same process aspects of programmes as do mainstream counselling programmes. Professional individuation (Skovholt and Ronnestad, 1995) is a significant goal but it needs articulation within an organizational setting. There are also additional factors

Table 19.2 *Every element of the two systems needs to be related to every other element*

Integration of	
Organizations	**Counselling**
• History, structures	• History, structures
• Philosophy, theory	• Philosophy, theory
• Interventions, e.g. mentoring, coaching	• Interventions, e.g., counselling, therapy
• Practice and supervision of organizational interventions such as mentoring, coaching	• Practice and supervision of counselling, therapy
• Personal/professional development	• Personal/professional development

of which we need to take account. In discussing *transitions*, Dryden and Throne indicate that 'self exploration leads to new inner discoveries and often sudden movement into unknown, psychological terrain' (1994: 4). Self-exploration has implications for both the explorer and for those with whom they are involved. When a trainee is sponsored by his/her organization, the trainer has responsibilities to the organization as well as to the individual trainee. Transitions can result in personal and professional changes which set the trainee at odds with the philosophy and practices of his/her sponsoring organization. The space and experience of the programme can become a kind of refuge between two cultures, that of the training world and that of the sponsoring organization.

In training for organizational counselling there is need for a period of *initial unlearning*, when organizational attitudes and expectations can be rested and new perspectives appreciated. Trainees in organizational counselling can arrive with attitudes and expectations which create a resistance to the processes of the programme. They work in worlds which are about speed, competititon, image, stress and job uncertainty. It can be difficult to adjust gear, to work with the uncertain and ambivalent, to wait upon what might seem to be unclear. The appreciation of spontaneity in training sessions can be difficult for those used to working to objectives on a printed programme rather than with the dynamic of the individual or group.

Trainees on organizational counselling programmes can show different *patterns and rates of development* from those on generic counselling programmes. Their organizational attitudes and experience can create resistance to developmental work. They may refuse to explore personal issues. Their expectations of developmental work may be of a professional rather than a personal kind. They may be unused to reflecting. Interviewing processes for admission to the programme may fail to convey the cultural shifts involved. They have to be experienced. It may take the major part of the course before the trainee is able to make and consolidate a shift, and then the trainer has to make decisions about deferral, ongoing support and development work for the individual.

Finally, *supervision for trainers* is essential. Because organizational counselling is still in process of being created, trainers have to work with the demands of inventiveness, uncertainty and creativity, and need ongoing supervision for the support of their actual training. They need a structure within which they can reflect with both trainees and colleagues upon the content and processes of the curriculum and an opportunity for peer supervision of their training.

Trainees and Trainers

Training is a very specific business. It has clear purposes, explicit targets and processes and a sense of efficiency about it. Usually, it is possible to measure performance outcomes or changes. Education is a quite different affair. It is about a leading out, an unfolding of the person. Its processes are often bound up with dimensions of human development that are difficult to control and measure. Its targets and processes may be less clear than those of training. The developing person can surprise the educator and defy the boundaries of measurement. Training and education engender very different cultures and attitudes in both trainees and trainers. For trainers used to designing programmes for counsellors, the training attitudes of those entering from organizations may be difficult to work with.

Trainees on long courses usually need to satisfy some form of admission process. Usually they will hold a first degree or acceptable equivalent. They will have some form of professional training and appropriate experience in a people-handling post. In brief, they will be well qualified and competent. The challenges they present lie in their organizational culture. The trainee from the organizational world is often at ease with brief training, training manuals and auditing rather than passing courses. Further, there is a willingness to interrupt training in the interest of company business or need. To face a trainer who will listen rather than tell, stay with a silence rather than fill it, and tolerate dissonance and open-endedness can be frustrating. Similarly, to face a trainee who is constantly seeking closure, who wishes to learn patience quickly and who will use the quiet times of a training day to fax and telephone is difficult for the trainer. Stereotypes these are, but they provide insights into the struggles that do exist in attempts to integrate the worlds of organization and of counselling into organizational counselling. At the start of programmes these differences might be perceived lightly and with amusement: on the one hand, the trainee, mobile phone at the ready and the jargon of downsizing, rightsizing and upskilling; on the other, the therapist, hearing and being present, with an apparent preoccupation with inner worlds and a naïvety about the business world. But these apparently superficial differences can herald deeper divisions that impact upon training.

Trainers sometimes speak of feeling de-skilled in the face of these trainees. Unreadiness for reflection can render tried and tested training tasks unhelpful, and resistance to personal development can be resented by trainers who might attack in return by asking if these trainees are 'real counsellors'. Skovholt and

Ronnestad (1995) speak of experiencing the discomfort of not feeling competent as a prerequisite for achieving professional identity. In the case of organizational counselling, it is a discomfort which can be experienced by both trainee and trainer as both training for organizational counselling and the supervision of that training seek their professional identity. Delivering an emergent curriculum calls for constant inventiveness and an openness to the trainee who reflects the needs of the organizational world in his/her attitudes and questioning. Proctor recalls her experience of having to 'devise and create, individually and collectively, structures, rituals and experiences' (1994: 53). This challenge of creating requires energy and strength of the part of the trainer.

Most trainees on programmes of organizational counselling are in posts which carry significant professional responsibility. Their previous training, professional development and work experience are strengths to be brought to the course and to be built into the training experience (Dryden and Feltham, 1994). Many are skilled trainers and presenters in their own fields and they have, as a consequence, high expectations of tutors. However excellent practitioners of counselling may be, not all make the most skilled presenters. The tasks are quite different ones. This can be a source of frustration to trainees and contribute to an unreadiness to listen. These same trainees may be highly competent and confident in their workplace. The contrasting vulnerability experienced in developmental work can create quite severe anxiety, as can little recent experience of developmental supervision, case studies, essays and papers.

There is a danger that trainees, excited by new insights and liberated from some well-contained personal denial in their personal lives, might wish to reject the organizational perspective. Trainers unfamiliar with organizations might be tempted to pull them towards new-found personal freedoms, forgetting that organizational counselling has an organizational purpose and that integration involves a harmony between the worlds of counselling and of organizations. Like Piaget's (1952) model of intelligence, it is when equilibrium is disrupted and when there is a striving for a new level of integration that growth takes place. The task of the trainer is to respect this disequilibrium and to hold the trainee during struggles to new levels of integration. It is also the task of the trainer to perceive and respect the organization as client and the language of empowerment must include the organization. Empowerment is not a process of setting employee against employer.

Assessment of Organizational Counsellors

Assessment of organizational counsellors needs to be rooted in the organizational tasks of employee support. Like the course itself, it needs to integrate the counselling and organizational aspects of organizational counselling. The methods used will be found on any counselling course: case studies, journals, papers, peer and self-evaluation. The difference is that those involved in the assessment processes need to be socialized into organizational counselling.

Generically trained examiners and external examiners may not always come to the task with an organizational perspective.

Examiners of organizational counselling courses are likely to experience the same culture clashes as the trainers but, unlike the trainers, they do not interact closely with the trainees. As a consequence, their own world-views are less challenged by organizational perspectives and their understanding of organizational counselling may lag behind that of the trainers. Ideally, generically trained examiners need some form of training or development work as a preparation for the examination of organizational work.

Short Courses for Organizational Counsellors

So far the focus has been on the long course. Organizational employees are usually more familiar with *short courses*. Unlike longer programmes, and particularly counselling programmes, they do not raise personal, and developmental dynamics to the same extent. Usually, they are not assessed. Attendance and participation are sufficient. They are often precise packages on particular or specialized areas and will come with attractive, supportive training materials. While there is nothing wrong with any of these factors in themselves, they can be poor preparation for organizational counselling courses which work with longer-term developmental dynamics and require more than attendance. Trainees whose main experience is of shorter training programmes can find it hard to accept developmental feedback, requirements to compensate for absences or the need to undertake further practice or personal development should their work fail to reach the required standard.

However, short courses are ideal ways of building upon a core training in organizational counselling. Trainees who have learned to work developmentally and who have a framework within which to understand organizational counselling are well placed to integrate the knowledge of shorter courses. Without this longer-term perspective there is the danger that trainees might end up collectors of facts and information rather than reflective, developing practitioners. Given that many trainees of organizational counselling seek part-time training, the ideal would be some professional agreements about what constitutes organizational counselling so that appropriate short courses could be orchestrated into part-time, modular training pathways.

NVQs and Organizational Counselling

Professional training is normally geared towards the requirements of existing national and professional standards. In their absence, or emergence, there has to be insightful anticipation. The development of NVQs in the areas of Advice, Guidance, Counselling and Psychotherapy, though surrounded by debate, has contributed significantly to the *identity* of organizational counselling. NVQs are rooted in the context of the workplace and they ignore or cross traditional professional boundaries, focusing upon competences which may be recognized or owned by more than one professional group. It is this crossing of traditional knowledge and professional boundaries which has been significant for the development of organizational counselling. Further, though the competence-based approach to interventions such as Advice, Guidance, Counselling and Psychotherapy has incited much criticism, it has brought counselling into the workplace and obliged those in the development of training in this field to struggle with the issues involved in defining and assessing these qualitative and overlapping interventions. The four awarding bodies – the City and Guilds, the Local Government Management Board with the Institute of Careers Guidance, the Open University Validation Service and the Scottish Vocational Education Council – all bring experience of occupational sectors. This experience will shape the development of organizational counselling.

The Role of Organizations in the Development of Counselling Training

In an ideal world organizational training and development would be generated and deliberated as a whole-organizational issue. It would be construed as an essential component of organizational development and a critical issue for the Board. The organization would map its training needs and would match services to these needs. Cultural and contextual factors would influence the selection of training, as would overall organizational objectives. The training selected would reflect the organization.

In practice, the selection of counselling and other employee development services can take place with little or no reference to the Board. There may be little attempt to match services to organizational culture. In some cases employee support services may be viewed as necessary but less important than the mechanistic aspects of organizational development.

This self-marginalization or distancing of organizations in both the use of and the training for counselling means that they have had very little direct influence upon the development of a product designed for their use. The take-away or send-out-for counselling attitude has also made organizations less able to support, receive back and reintegrate trainees who, through training in organizational counselling, have progressed beyond the insights and culture of their sponsoring organization.

There are a number of ways in which organizations can participate in the development of training for organizational counselling. First, the dialogue between curriculum developers and organizations needs to be developed. To some extent NVQ exercises have encouraged this dialogue. It is also important that organizations commit to training. Many can be generous in their funding of training but will not hesitate to withdraw participants for longer or shorter periods should they be needed for commercial opportunities. This disrupts training programmes, provides poor role modelling for the trainees and sets up conflicts among the parties involved.

Locating training in an organization as opposed to using external programmes can be valuable for both the organization and the development of
training. Training can become the focal point for organizational development
with counselling and related interventions working as developmental change
agents. When counselling is located in the training division of an organization,
it is likely to be concerned with upskilling, career or general training developments. Some of this provision will be in-house and some will be hired.
When counselling is located within the Human Resources division or when
this division works closely with training, it is well positioned to play a part as
an organizational change agent (McKenna, 1994). The human resource
context is an ideal one for the exploration of organizational counselling
because it takes account of both 'hard and soft problems' (McKenna and
Beech, 1995). In other words, it attempts to balance the mechanistic needs of
the organization with respect for and a fostering of human dispositions and
needs. In a well-coordinated organization such reflection could inform the
development of counselling training for organizations. However, this kind of
harmonious integration of organizational systems is based upon a clear and
explicit respect for employee and for training and development services which,
when well selected, can foster both individual and organizational potential.

Conclusion

Organizational counselling is an application of counselling designed to facilitate and support the development of individuals and their organizations. It is
rooted in the theory and practice of both counselling and organizations.
Orchestrating these two fields into a new, coherent application is a current
task and one which is informing and is informed by both practice and
training. The development of training is a creative task. It is the outcome of
the insights of those who reflect upon and interpret systems and practices. In
the case of organizational counselling there is a need for more collaboration
between organizations and training establishments on the development,
delivery and evaluation of organizational counselling. The Roehampton
Institute London TDA, BT and Post Office collaborative training ventures are
attempts to achieve this training partnership. The shared task of designing and
delivering training has led to new understandings of counselling and of the
organizational settings in which practitioners manage and deliver counselling
as part of a system of employee support.

References

Carroll, M. (1995) 'The counsellor in organizational settings: some reflections', *Employee
    Counselling Today*, 7 (1): 23–9.
Clarkson, P. (1995) *The Therapeutic Relationship*. London: Whurr.
Dryden, W. (1992) *Integrative and Eclective Therapy*. Milton Keynes: Open University Press.
Dryden, W. and Feltham, C. (1994) *Developing Counsellor Training*. London: Sage.

Dryden, W. and Thorne, B. (eds) (1994) *Training and Supervision for Counselling in Action.* London: Sage.

Grater, H.A. (1985) 'Stages in psychotherapy supervision: from therapy skills to skilled therapist', *Professional Psychology: Research and Practice*, 16: 605–10.

Hess, A.K. (1987) 'Psychotherapy supervision: stages, buber and a theory of relationship', *Professional Psychology: Theory, Research and Practice*, 18: 251–9.

Highley, J. and Cooper, C. (1994) 'An assessment of UK EAPs and workplace counselling programmes.' Project funded by the Health and Safety Executive.

Hill, C.E., Charles, D. and Reed, K.G. (1981) 'A longitudinal analysis of counseling skills during doctoral training in counseling psychology', *Journal of Counseling Psychology*, 28: 428–36.

Hogan, R.A. (1964) 'Issues and approaches in supervision', *Psychotherapy: Theory, Research and Practice*, 1: 139–41.

Janes, J. (1992) 'Advice Guidance and Counselling Lead Body Feasibility Study'. Welwyn, Herts: Julie Janes Associates.

Jenkins, P. (1995) 'Two models of counsellor training: becoming a person or becoming a skilled helper', *Counselling*, 6 (3): 203–6.

Lane, D. (1990) 'Counselling psychology in organizations', *The Psychologist*, 12: 540–4.

McKenna, E. (1994) *Business Psychology and Organizational Behaviour.* Hove: Lawrence Erlbaum.

McKenna, E. and Beech, N. (1995) *Essence of Human Resource Management.* London: Prentice-Hall.

McLeod, J. (1993) *An Introduction to Counselling.* Milton Keynes: Open University Press.

Nixon, J. and Carroll, M. (1994) 'Can a line manager also to be counsellor?' *Employee Counselling Today*, 6 (1): 10–15.

Noon, M. (1992) 'HRM, a map, model or theory?', in P. Blyton and P. Turnbull (eds), *Reassessing Human Resource Management.* London: Sage.

O'Brien, J. (1995) 'Mentoring as a change agency – a psychodynamic approach', *Counselling*, 6 (1): 51–4.

Pedlar, M., Boydell, R. and Burgoyne, J. (1988) *Learning Company Project.* Manpower Services Commission.

Piaget, J. (1952) *The Origins of Intelligence in Children.* New York: International University Press.

Pickard, E. (1994) 'Skills training: the beginning or end of counselling?', *Counselling at Work*, 6: 9.

Proctor, B. (1994) 'On being a trainer', in W. Dryden and B. Thorne (eds), *Training and Supervision for Counselling in Action.* London: Sage.

Reddy, M. (1993) *EAPs and Counselling Provision in UK Organizations: An ICAS Report and Policy Guide.* Milton Keynes: ICAS.

Skovholt, T. and Ronnestad, M. (1995) *The Evolving Professional Self.* Chichester: John Wiley.

Tehrani, N. (1994) 'Business dimensions to organizational counselling', *Counselling Psychology Quarterly*, 7 (3): 275–85.

Tehrani, N. (1995) 'The development of employee support: an evaluation', *Counselling Psychology Review*, 10 (3): 2–7.

20

Supervision for Counsellors in Organizations

Brigid Proctor

What is Counselling Supervision?

> Counselling supervision is a formal and mutually agreed arrangement for counsellors to discuss their work regularly with someone who is normally an experienced and competent counsellor and familiar with the process of counselling supervision. The task is to work together to ensure and develop the efficacy of the supervisee's practice . . . It should take account of the setting within which the supervisee practices . . . is intended to ensure that the needs of clients are being addressed and to monitor the effectiveness of . . . interventions. (BAC, 1995: 2.3)

This quotation from the British Association for Counselling (BAC) *Code of Ethics and Practice for Supervisors of Counsellors* gives a flavour of the task and spirit of what counsellors mean when they talk about supervision. In the world of work at large, the word has connotations of overseeing, controlling and managerial responsibility, so its use in the context of counselling is frequently misunderstood – and is mystifying to other established professionals. 'Surely once you are trained you should be able to practise independently?', they ask. At the same time, the concept of regular consultation with someone who has an understanding of work and setting, but is substantially able to be objective and independent, is an attractive one. When I was in New Zealand recently, I was asked on a number of occasions whether there is not a better word for the process which supervision comprises. Experienced counsellors found that they were increasingly being asked to offer such a service to doctors, business people, head teachers, etc., but that the word itself was a hindrance in 'marketing' the service. So, frequently, the words 'consultative supervision' may be used as a more congruent description, or 'non-managerial supervision' to distinguish the arrangement from the related tasks of managerial and training supervision.

In this chapter the word 'supervision', therefore, implies a consultative arrangement – 'a formal collaborative process'. It is an arrangement in which a professional counsellor *necessarily* engages regularly with a trusted and experienced colleague – necessarily, because adherence to a 'Code of Ethics' of a professional counselling or psychotherapy association requires that a practitioner makes and keeps to such a commitment: 'It is a breach of the ethical requirement for counsellors to practise without regular counselling supervision/consultative support' (BAC, 1992).

First, it is worth asking why there is this unusual, if not unique, requirement for professional workers who may be qualified, highly experienced and clearly competent and confident. At the same time, it will become clearer what the purposes of those supervision consultations are. Later in the chapter, I will address:

- The importance of a shared understanding about aims, objectives and boundaries of responsibilities between counsellor, supervisor and employer within an organization.
- Special considerations for
  - supervisors who supervise counsellors working in organizations;
  - counsellors who receive professional supervision as well as being accountable to a manager.
- The availability of different modes of supervision.
- The qualities needed for supervising and being supervised within organizations.

Origins – Apprenticeship Training

Historically, supervision of this sort has its origins in the Craft Apprenticeship model of training. This training model, an apprentice being supervised and scrutinized while gaining hands-on experience, remains quite common. In such a context, the supervisor, at best, combines the roles of trainer, manager, mentor and possibly tutor. This was the model adopted for psychotherapy training.

Where it differed from, say, a building apprenticeship, or even a training for a craft more concerned with people, like nursing, was that what was being supervised

- was not usually being *seen live*. The task of 'doing psychotherapy' was understood to be based on the quality and confidentiality of the relationship between therapist and client. The presence of a third party was considered to be intrusive and unhelpful for the task of therapy.
- was seldom concrete and practical. 'Doing it right' is something which is apparent for a building procedure, and for many nursing procedures. Psychotherapeutic work depended much more on 'getting *the relationship and communication* right' – a more elusive practice, which has only gradually become conceptualized.
- was a particularly personally engaging occupation. Both the nature of the relationship and the manner in which the client and his problematic issues were perceived were unique for each practitioner. To whatever extent perceptions and interpretations might be agreed upon by practitioner, supervisor and other trainees, etc., only *this* psychotherapy trainee was making *this* relationship with *this* client, based on *these* perceptions.

For all these reasons, training supervision came to be predominantly a forum in which 'two (or more) practitioner people talk together about a third person who is not usually present'. It was an opportunity for the trainee to talk *about* the client, to reflect on his *experience* of their work together, and to get *feedback* – the supervisor's view of the client and the client's problems; of how the trainee was working with the client; and of how he was relating with the client.

Process and Relationship

That last area of work required the supervisor to recognize if, for instance, the trainee appeared to be over-identified with his client's world-view and experience, so that he was not being usefully objective; or under-empathic and too clinically objective, so that the client did not feel safe or understood; or perhaps, that the trainee was feeling disapproving and judgemental without being aware of it, and the supervisor, at secondhand, could hear and sense the unspoken criticism. Was the trainee inadvertently reacting to the client with similar behaviour and emotions that the client somehow frequently seemed to elicit from acquaintances in the outside world? Or was the trainee perceiving and acting to the client 'as if' the client were a familiar person in the trainee's own network of relationships? Over time, and no doubt through the experience of supervising and being supervised, it became clear that working privately and intimately with one other troubled person, while maintaining respect, understanding, warmth and objectivity, can be a complex and confusing activity.

Depending on the skill and experience of the supervisor, the process of regular training supervision could be extremely rewarding. In that forum, trainees could learn how to work more effectively – the original training task. They could also become increasingly able to monitor what was happening for them and with their clients – at first within the reflective space of supervision, but later, as it was happening, within the therapy session.

Supervisory Responsibility

However, while that developmental opportunity was being offered, the supervisor was also required to exercise her managerial and supervisory responsibilities of monitoring. In helping the trainee talk about his work with a client, the supervisor would also be monitoring for what she heard, deciding whether to raise queries, give feedback, or question the wisdom or efficacy of interventions. At times, the supervisor might give directions where she deemed that the trainee, through ignorance or inability, was not working well with the client. This client–advocate role sprung from the supervisor having overall 'clinical responsibility'. As case manager, she was ultimately responsible for seeing that the client was receiving the expected help.

In addition, as guardian and gatekeeper of the psychotherapy profession, the training supervisor would be developing a sense of necessary standards and of ethical practice. Ideas about standards and ethics were also being collectively developed by supervisors, and other trainers, meeting and sharing ideas and impressions and writing about their deductions. So supervision became a major device for a young profession to gather information about effective, ineffective and harmful practice and to allow for the development of working hypotheses.

Hearing Distressing Stories

What also became apparent was the emotionally taxing nature of psycho-therapy. Psychotherapists (and, now, counsellors) become privy to a range of distressing, heart-warming, enraging life stories and experiences. None of these could be gossiped about – the traditional way of off-loading stories that have excited strong feelings or elicited curiosity. Cumulatively, this holding task becomes tiring, especially since psychotherapy and counselling practice entails 'engaged bystanding' rather than active intervention, and therefore denies practitioners the emotional release of 'doing something concrete to help'.

Formative, Normative, Restorative

So, together, trainees and supervisors were accomplishing a range of varied tasks. The supervisor was receiving, and the supervisee giving, access to a private interaction which was taking place off-scene. Through this story-sharing, the supervisee had an opportunity to think about what the client needed, and what he was doing with the client with increased objectivity; he was learning how to be a reflective practitioner. At the same time, he had an opportunity to learn about practice, not only from experience, but also from the feedback, information and modelling of his supervisor. These learnings could be called the *formative* task of training supervision.

In addition, the supervisor was undertaking a different level of learning – about the values and assumptions of his chosen profession, and about what should be judged as ethical, or unethical, practice in the light of those. Moreover, his acceptance into the 'guild' depended on him being monitored and tutored in this respect, and being seen to be ethically sound. This has been called the *normative* task of supervision.

The opportunity to discharge accumulated frustration or emotion, which may interfere with objectivity as well as sap energy and commitment, was the third task of supervision – a confidential, *restorative* forum. All three tasks – normative, formative and restorative – overlapped and contributed to each other's fulfilment. An alternative definition of supervision attempts to encap-sulate these complex tasks: 'Supervision is a working alliance between a supervisor and a counsellor. . . . The object of this alliance is to enable the counsellor to gain in ethical competence, confidence and creativity so as to give her best possible service to her client' (Inskipp and Proctor, 1993).

Ongoing Supervision

These needs for support and challenge do not go away with qualification. In this country, therefore, the tradition of continuing supervision after qualification was adopted by psychotherapists and was taken on by the related craft – now profession – of counselling. (Social case-work practitioners also adopted this practice; and youth workers, in some areas, were offered non-managerial supervision in addition to their managerial overseeing.) It is interesting to surmise why this is not the case in the USA, where *required* consultative supervision for counsellors ends at qualification. The difference may originally have resulted from the nature of the training in the two countries. The US training was usually full-time, leading to an academic qualification from within a university setting, and subsequently state registration. Trainings in the UK were usually part-time, more varied in standards, length and qualifications, and until the mid-1980s there was no registration or accreditation. Continuing standards depended on accountability to the profession by means of regular supervision.

Present Purposes

Maintaining it as a necessity now, in the wake of, for example, BAC accreditation and in the process of the establishment of a Register of Counsellors and Psychotherapists springs from several realizations. First, that counselling remains a private and intimate occupation which is very personally involving for the practitioner. This leads to the possibility of loss of objectivity and even opportunities for the exploitation of clients. Regular accountability through supervision cannot preclude charlatans practising, but it can ensure that practitioners with goodwill are being supported and challenged in their practice. Secondly, it is a rapidly evolving craft – new situations, like counselling in the workplace or in primary health care, call for fresh responses. Supervision ensures that at least one other person is helping the counsellor cover all the angles – best service to client, adherence to professional ethics and sensibility to the context of the service. Thirdly, many counsellors still practise independently, and often in relative isolation – supervision serves as ongoing professional development, and a reminder of the commitment to keeping up with new ideas and practice.

It would be true to say that supervision is something which almost all counsellors appreciate, having once experienced the opportunity of such regular consultations with a good supervisor. It is also a device which satisfies the professional need for accountability among colleagues, and credibility with clients and related professionals. In the way it is exercised, it is increasingly being a stimulator to the confidence and autonomy of practitioners, as opposed to being offered in an authoritarian and restrictive mode. It remains an additional way of feeding back into professional channels information about what works well and what does not. In organizational settings, where managers may not know how to monitor work to which they have no direct access, a trusted professional supervisor can be relied on to evaluate counsellor's performance and to feed back to the counsellor, and if necessary, the manager, any reservations about competence or suggestions for professional development.

Do Clients Benefit?

The one unknown area (due to the difficulties of researching such a question) is whether clients benefit from their counsellor's supervision. Supervisors and counsellors have a wealth of anecdotal and experiential evidence which suggests that they do. In the 1990s the craft of supervision has been receiving a great deal of attention. Some would now call it a profession in its own right, as opposed to an extension of the counselling profession (Carroll, 1996). Hopefully, as increasing agreement develops about the tasks and art of supervising, research can be done which will elucidate this crucial question.

Meanwhile, there is evidence of increasing awareness of its desirability. Counselling psychologists have adopted consultative supervision as an ongoing professional requirement; many clinical psychologists are asking for its adoption; there is now a Department of Health requirement of ongoing clinical supervision for all nurses. Bond (1993) suggests that there is an increasing interest in ongoing supervision for counsellors and psychotherapists in the USA. British visitors report that many US counselling agencies have now established ongoing supervision for practitioners. All these suggest that in practice, practitioners value regular consultation, and managers are beginning to appreciate its provision for counsellors in their employ.

Supervision in an Organizational Context

There will be at least three interested parties when a counsellor, who is employed within an organization, is receiving supervision – the counsellor, the counsellor's manager and the supervisor. The supervisor may be external to the organization or an internal employee. They will be interacting with each other with more or less awareness of the wider contexts within which the work is taking place (see Figure 20.1).

As Michael Carroll describes in Chapter 1 of this book, counsellors may be working in a wide variety of organizations. It is unrealistic to generalize about the relationship of consultative, professional supervision to organizational and managerial structures and processes. There are wide differences in culture

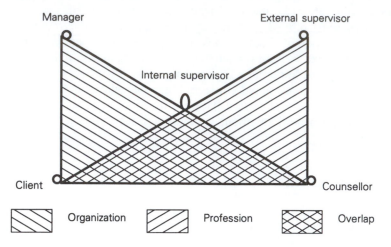

The *manager* is accountable to his/her line manager for quality of service and cost effectiveness.

The *internal supervisor* is accountable, within professional and agency or service Codes of Ethics and Practice, for professional practice of counsellor and self. He/she is also accountable to a professional association as client–advocate.

The *external supervisor* may or may not be accountable to the manager. He/she is accountable to a profession as client–advocate.

Figure 20.1   *Zones of accountability*

between, say, a voluntary counselling agency, using internal voluntary supervisors who have come up through its own counselling training and may still work as voluntary counsellors, and a private commercial organization which employs an external supervisor on a freelance basis to supervise two counsellors working in the Medical Centre. However, there are certain principles of good practice which extend to all organizational contexts. The difference in practice is the extent to which these principles have been understood and taken seriously. Also, to what extent responsibility for establishing the principles has been taken by the counsellor, the managment or the supervisor.

Inskipp and Proctor, in *Making the Most of Supervision* (1993), wrote the guidelines shown in Table 20.1. These were addressed to counsellors, and put the responsibility for establishing a clear working agreement between all parties to the contract on to the counsellor. In *Becoming a Supervisor* (1995), Inskipp and Proctor return to this and remind supervisors of their responsibility to address with counsellors or management (whichever seems most appropriate) the formalizing of appropriate lines of responsibility and communication between the three parties.

The guidelines in Table 20.1 hold good across the wide variety of organizational contexts. The BAC *Code of Ethics for Supervisors* (1995) has not been as explicit as this in its information to supervisors and counsellors. However, it does say:

Table 20.1 *Guidelines for counsellors on organizational accountability*
(Inskipp and Proctor, 1993)

The counsellor is employed by the organization to offer a professional service to clients, who may
be either

- organizational employees, or
- consumers (students, patients, etc.) or
- the public
  - in general, or
  - specific categories, i.e., young people, couples, people with specific difficulties, such as
    addictions, etc.

The counsellor is bound by a professional Code of Ethics.

The organization has a responsibility to the counsellor's clients. It also has a responsibility to
manage its employees and their work.

Good management practice suggests that all employees should have managerial supervision and
appraisal. In the case of a counsellor, such appraisal should be by a manager, or substitute, who is
capable of

- supporting and helping him/her or his/her work
- realistically appraising it
- recognizing and appreciating ethical dilemmas arising from it.

Such appraisal should be in accordance with a *Statement of Ethics and Practice* for the *Agency*
(for instance Relate) or *organizational department* (for instance, the Counselling Service), which
should include

- a statement of the agency/department's aims and philosophy of counselling
- a description of administrative practice, e.g. record-keeping
- an account of the management arrangements for the delivery of work, day to day and over
  time, e.g. case-load, distribution of cases, boundaries of work
- an account of arrangements for managerial *and non-managerial supervision*
- the relationship of these arrangements to appraisal.

3.3.6 Supervisors must ensure with a supervisee who works in an organization or
agency that the lines of accountability and responsibility are clearly defined:
supervisee/client; supervisor/supervisee; supervisor/client; organization/supervisor;
organization/supervisee; organization/client. There is a distinction between line
management and supervision.

3.3.7. Best practice is that the same person should not act as . . . line manager. . . .
where counselling supervisor is also line manager, the supervisee should have access
to independent counselling supervision.

3.3.8. Supervisors who become aware of a conflict between an obligation to a
supervisee and . . . employing agency must make explicit . . . the nature of loyalties
and responsibilities involved. (BAC, 1995)

Management Sympathy and Informedness

The two crucial dimensions when organizing supervision are management
sympathy and management informedness, both about counselling in general,
and about consultative supervision. The matrix in Figure 20.2 is a useful way

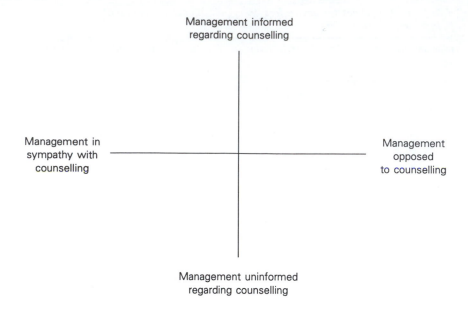

Figure 20.2   *The sympathy/management informedness matrix for counselling supervision*

for counsellors and supervisors to plot (in the scientific meaning of that word!) the working culture of the organization, if there are not already Statements of Ethics and Practice in place. This can enable them to diagnose what action is needed to ensure maximum feasible organizational support for the counsellor and counselling provision.

Given the wide range of organizations within which counsellors may be employed, and the variety of arrangements for managerial and consultative supervision, the relationship of each to the other will be particular. The following scenarios (none representing an actual situation but invented from known realities) may be helpful in showing the range of awareness and culture that can be encountered. Each could be placed on a different place on the matrix. This could indicate where effort could best be put, by counsellor and supervisor, in order to facilitate a culture for counselling. The scenarios also point to several considerations which need to be in the mind of some or all of the interested parties.

Case Study 1

Mary Jones is a student counsellor in a team of counsellors operating from the Student Service Centre of a university. She is managed by the Senior Counsellor, herself a practitioner, and has peer supervision, in a group of her colleagues, every fortnight. She has regular access to the Senior Counsellor in crisis situations, and meets with her four times a year for managerial supervision. In addition, she meets once every three weeks with an individual freelance supervisor – 'her' supervisor, chosen by her. The university pays for that supervision. Mary's manager does not want to 'vet' the supervisor, and is not required to do so by her line manager. There is no contract between Mary's freelance supervisor and the organization, nor does Mary's manager expect any feedback. She considers that part of her managerial responsibility is to check with the counsellor if her out-of-house supervision is meeting her needs.

In this situation, the manager understands and trusts both counsellor and supervision process. She has sufficient access to the counsellor's work, through managerial supervision and day-by-day contact, to be satisfied that she can support the counsellor in the case of a dispute, and support or challenge her in relation to her work and professional development. This arrangement works well. However, there might come a time when she was less sure about a counsellor's competence or ethical practice. If she had no information about the supervisor's suitability and no contract with him, she might not be able to trust the counsellor to raise issues in supervision; nor would she be able to raise the matter with the supervisor, with or, if absolutely necessary, without the counsellor's consent. Moreover, the supervisor would also have no agreed method for communicating his doubts, if the counsellor did not seem to be responding to his feedback or criticism.

Case Study 2

John Davies was asked to set up an employee counselling service within an NHS Trust. He had access to a steering committee, which had initiated the idea of the counselling service. Most of the members were keen on the idea, but had no experience of such services. He was given two days a week to offer and run the service. He had to fight for an office, funding, and the time and fees for supervision. His manager had no sympathy with the idea of the service and resented the steering committee's initiative. He sneered at John's 'need' for supervision, but once John had found a supervisor, he did not raise the matter again. The supervisor had no contact with the manager, but, with John's consent and approval, wrote to the steering committee, suggesting that she and John hold a six monthly review session, in addition to regular consultations. After each review they would write a report together to the committee about John's experience of his work and progress (as distinct from the annual statistical report which John provided for them).

In this instance both John and the supervisor felt the need for some formal contact between the organizational and professional 'worlds'. The job was tiring and the supervisor did not think it was the right time and place to engage in a conversation with the manager. The contact with the committee seemed the best hope for shoring up the support for John, the service and the clients to whom that service was offered.

Case Study 3

Ian Farquhar was a sole counsellor in a large commercial organization. He inherited a going service from a competent predecessor. He reported to the Personnel Manager, although he was allowed to be considerably autonomous. His manager asked him, on appointment, who his supervisor was, and what were her qualifications. The supervisor agreed to supply a CV, and the manager told Ian that he was going to consult with a friend in the counselling world about her suitability. Ian, mildly surprised, found himself both anxious and pleased. The CV passed muster and the supervisor was sent a contract of engagement, specifying when, how and what she was expected to feed back to the manager. At the same time she was invited to a meeting with Ian and manager. At this stage, saying that she was not prepared to be so engaged with management, nor to feed back, she bowed out. Ian arranged a meeting with the Personnel Manager, and asked him if, when he found another possible supervisor, they could meet as soon as the CV had been approved and together talk about lines of communication and limits of confidentiality. The manager agreed to this, and the second supervisor and Ian were able to agree with the manager a suitably satisfying contract.

This situation shows up a very understandable clash of 'cultural' expectations. The manager was actually, as far as counselling was concerned, a 'good guy' seeking to establish appropriate accountability. However, he did not see the need to be sensitive to a somewhat different professional culture. The first supervisor, unlike the one in the previous story, found herself acting in a reactive, as opposed to a proactive, situation. Ian, by his intervention with the manager, cleared the way for a climate in which each party could act freely to state their understanding and negotiate a mutually useful contract.

Case Study 4

An independent, commercial Employee Assistance Programme required its counsellors to have independent supervision for their cases, which would be self-funded. It provided a full-time case manager who was not a counsellor, with whom the counsellors could talk about any problematic issues that might have organizational implications. The organization also offered monthly group supervision, so that the team had some time for sharing its work with each other. The group supervisor was employed directly by the EAP. The case manager attended the supervision and a counsellor complained privately to the supervisor that the group did not feel safe enough to share some issues with the manager present. The supervisor told the counsellor that he must raise that directly with the manager. The supervisor had no further private communication with members of the group, nor did he ever hear if the matter were raised. The manager continued to attend the group. The supervisor decided to continue working, and to encourage members to speak as openly as possible. When the renewal of his contract was due he spoke with the manager about the implications of her attendance. She said that she was now too busy to keep attending.

In this instance, the supervisor regretted not having clarified the issue of the manager's attendance *before* contracting to work for the EAP. He did not regret having left the responsibility with group members to raise the issue with the manager. He found that many of the issues raised in the supervision were directly or indirectly concerned with agency policy. The presence of the manager meant that those issues could be raised and discussed in a forum where there was probably more reflective space than in an on-the-wing managerial supervision session. Although he raised the matter for discussion, he had decided that he would continue to supervise for the organization if the manager still thought it important to attend. The deciding factor for him was that each counsellor did have individual consultative supervision as well. Had the group been their only non-managerial supervision, he would have pointed out to the case manager what the BAC Code of Ethics said and, if she had not concurred, he would have refused to renew the contract.

Common Issues and Principles

From these examples, various principles and issues emerge. First, there is a need for clear contracts with organizations, so that each party can fulfil its responsibilities to clients, employer and professional Codes of Ethics. Secondly, a lack of understanding can arise when the needs for managerial and professional accountability clash. (This tension also occurs when members of other professions are employed by commercial organizations – dramas are built on the patient-centred doctor in the cash-greedy hospital, or the crooked lawyer who sells out to the Mafia.) Thirdly, counsellors require an amount of supervisory space of one sort or another, which usually compares favourably (or unfavourably, depending on your viewpoint) with the systematic support and challenge on offer to other workers in the organization. This can give rise to despising or envy by managers and peers.

Organizational Stage

The illustrations in the case studies above also suggest that organizations differ a great deal in the length of time they have employed counsellors, and in the sophistication of their systems for managing counselling work. As a rule of thumb, I suggest that it is useful for a counselling service to take time to discover what are the right channels and boundaries of communication between the different parties, within the Code of Ethics. Too embedded policies may end in wasted time, as in Case Study 2 (p. 351). However, as pointed out in Case Study 1, unless certain things are sorted out before the service gets bigger (and becomes less of a 'family firm'), policy may need to be made 'on the wing' and under stress. That is seldom satisfactory for anyone concerned. For instance, the senior counsellor of a rapidly expanding organization still relied on an 'open door' policy of management but had not established lines of communication with external supervisors. When a complaint was made about a counsellor by a client, the manager – a responsible and skilled man – felt foolish and recognized that clients, counsellor and the counselling service were all at risk. He had to make 'instant policy'.

Supervisor Clarity

In addition, supervisors have very different views of what they understand to be ethical (or desirable) when undertaking organizational supervision. The rule of thumb I would suggest here is that the supervisor consults carefully with the counsellor and/or manager before agreeing to supervise. (This applies not only to external supervisors, but also to those who are home-grown in an agency. It is easy to presume processes are in place, and to have blindspots about home territory.) If the supervisor has taken care to identify her own principles prior to the consultation, she will be in a better position to decide what she will and will not do. For instance, the managers of a counselling agency required their regular group supervisors to undertake the annual appraisal of each counsellor in their group. Boundaries of confidentiality and responsibility were ethically laid out for both supervision and appraisal. Some supervisors agreed to the contract. Others chose not to work for an agency that expected them to undertake managerial responsibilities.

What Should a Counsellor Look For?

In counselling agencies, counsellors may well have no choice of supervisor. In most other settings, they will have the opportunity to approach, or be allocated to, a supervisor whom they identify as suitable for them. Supervisors can vary in their theoretical orientation as a counsellor, in their area of client experience, in their organizational experience, in their supervisory style, and in fees, flexibility, mobility, etc. However, let us concentrate on the particular issue of a counsellor's needs when working in an organization.

In her research, C. Carroll (1994) has suggested how flexible, autonomous and multi-skilled many organizational counsellors need to be. This is probably particularly true of workplace counsellors. In that setting, supervisors may need to mirror that flexibility and autonomy. Michael Carroll (forthcoming) identifies the following supervisor tasks:

- Enabling supervisees to live and work within organizations.
- Helping supervisees control the flow (or release) of information within the organization.
- Helping supervisees to manage the counselling provision.
- Working with supervisees at the interface between the individual and the organization.

- Ensuring that supervisees look after themselves as a result of working within an organizational setting.

To this may be added:

- Helping a counsellor manage a team of counsellors and administrative staff.
- Supporting the supervisee with that part of the counselling provision which includes records, statistics, etc.

It is not essential that the supervisor be able to do all the tasks that are asked of the counsellor – one can facilitate others to work well in areas outside one's own expertise. However, it is essential to have sympathy with a counsellor taking on responsibility for more than individual client work. It is probably also essential that the supervisor be prepared to think about the difficulties and opportunities of working with, and within, complex and sometimes conflicting systems. Case Study 3 (p. 352) is a good example of this 'systems shrewdness'.

There are other issues which consistently arise in practice which relate directly to client welfare. Although not strictly speaking 'counselling', they are ethical dilemmas. For instance, it seems a common experience that however often counsellor and supervisor think that they have established, for all time, boundaries of confidentiality with managers and related professionals, fresh ethical teasers arise to try them. These are normative issues, and counsellors should have access to professional consultation when making these decisions.

There are other issues which a supervisor may need to pay attention to, if only because of the stress they place on the counsellor, or the counsellor's lack of knowledge about certain organizational or administrative matters. Examples of these are the carrying of dual roles (welfare officer/counsellor, for instance), designing feedback forms and statistical information, policies for when counselling demand is greater than counsellor time available (time-limited work, referral, supplementary services?). Supervisor and counsellor need to establish that clients' needs are to be given priority. They can then decide if it is suitable to deal with some of these additional issues in supervision time. They also need to clarify if the supervisor has the expertise needed to be the *formative* resource in these areas of work.

Alternatively, as part of the *restorative* task, the supervisor may find it necessary to confront a counsellor on meeting some of these needs for support and help elsewhere than in supervision. Could the organization pay for a separate consultancy for developing the service? Might work stresses be such that they are impinging on the counsellor's personal life? Could some counselling or psychotherapy be an added personal support at this time? Should the counsellor be firmer about holding to time boundaries, and confronting management about the limits of her personal and professional resources? In these cases, if the supervisor insists on, for example, spending at least half the supervision on the prime task of supervision of client work, he will be offering a model of prioritizing.

It is important, therefore, that a counsellor seeks a sufficiently flexible supervisor – boundaries set a lot more rigidly than those the counsellor has undertaken to work within will be added stressors. On the other hand, a supervisor who is over-engaged with the excitement and challenge of working in organizations may feed the counsellor's belief that he/she must respond to all challenges.

Perhaps a quotation from a workplace counsellor can illustrate this well:

> From the time I started setting up the service in my Local Authority until recently, I had a supervisor who told me that all she wanted to hear about were my clients. It certainly helped me give some reflective time to them – they seemed to be the easiest part of my work, and were not getting a lot of thought. I was so overwhelmed with organizational problems – I was starting a service from scratch, for which I had no models and I was having a lot of problems with my boss who was demanding bits of paper about it all, yesterday. However, I found myself dreading supervision, and resenting the time spent out of the workplace. I had a very rudimentary counselling training myself, and really thought that what I was offered by way of supervision was 'it'. After going to a conference about supervision, I realized that maybe other supervisors worked differently. I decided to contact and meet at least two, and to find out what they were prepared to offer. One seemed to know a lot about organizational counselling, but I felt that having supervision with him might be like having another demanding boss – he asked so many questions about the set-up and my way of working that I began to feel as if I was in an exam. The second person listened to me, helped me sort out what I wanted – the earth! – and then carefully negotiated what she was and was not prepared to offer. She said she wanted to preserve space for clients, but was happy, if she was satisfied that I was managing them all right, to take time in thinking through work crises. She suggested that I ask my boss for an extra hour's supervision a month to concentrate on strategic developments. She was insistent, too, that in each session we saved ten minutes for me to review my learning from the experiences I was having. That was a new idea for me. Since starting supervision with her, I have felt so much less stressed, and interestingly enough I am more, rather than less, aware of when my own issues may be affecting my counselling with clients.

Age and Stage – Counsellor

This experience is also a reminder that counsellors have differing needs at different stages of their experience and professional development. Once the service was up and running, a supervisor who gave attention wholly to clients could be refreshing and developmentally helpful (especially if some added consultancy for the service was provided). For another counsellor, with a well-established service, who had perhaps come to forget that there were other ways of doing things, an organizationally sophisticated supervisor might have been a breath of fresh air.

Modes of Supervision

It is usually easier to talk about individual supervision as the 'norm'. However, there are advantages for counsellors in organizations meeting with peers as well as supervisors. Inskipp and Proctor (1993) review the wealth of possibilities available to counsellors. They also offer a framework for systematically exploring varying needs for support, challenge and development. These might include letting off steam in confidence, or particular expertise – (organizational or specific client groups, for instance) – sharing work openly, getting new ideas, meeting like-minded practitioners, meeting counsellors who work differently, being sympathized with, being challenged. Meeting all these needs is an unrealistic remit for one supervisor, but it is possible to 'design' a supervision package which might meet many of them.

Examples of such 'packages' that I have come across include the following:

- *For a workplace counsellor* – supervision for two hours monthly with an external supervisor; a two-monthly, three-hour peer group with counsellors working in similar organizations.
- *For the senior counsellor of a Student Counselling Service* – a once-monthly one-hour individual supervision with a supervisor experienced in organizations; and a fortnightly, two-hour supervision group, led by a supervisor and consisting of four experienced counsellors from a wide variety of working contexts; facilitating an in-house supervision group fortnightly.
- *For two job share counsellors* – meeting for one and a half hours fortnightly for 'pair' supervision with an external supervisor, and meeting regularly on a weekly basis to review their work together.
- *For a very experienced counsellor working in a variety of organizational contexts* – a-one-and-a-half-hour session once every two months, with a 'long-distance' individual supervisor, alternated with one-hour telephone supervision twice a month with the same supervisor, and regular weekly 'pair peer' supervision locally.

The earlier case studies also suggest how counselling services can mix and match group, individual and managerial supervision.

Caveat

It is important, if a counsellor has organized such a mixed bag of supervision, that she takes responsibility for negotiating what work is taken where, and to what extent she expects the supervisor (peer or expert) to be the person to whom she is accountable. Without that clarity, peer supervisors, particularly, may lack permission to structure the sessions and to challenge. The BAC *Code of Ethics and Practice for Supervisors of Counsellors* devotes a special section (Section 5) to guidance on modes of supervision (BAC, 1995).

However, whatever age and stage the counsellor is at, and whatever mode(s) of supervison he employs, there are some basic principles of good supervision practice. A counsellor should expect the following from his supervisor:

- Respect and empathic understanding for himself and his clients.
- Respect for his working context.

- An ability to negotiate a clear working agreement which meets the need of employer, counsellor and clients.
- Respect for his model of working, and sufficient understanding of it to raise the right questions. (For instance, only time-limited counselling may be offered within the service, and the supervisor needs to be increasingly open to the opportunities and limitations of that way of working).
- An ability for forthrightness and authenticity, that is, to act steadfastly as an advocate for the clients and to engage intelligently with the counsellor in creating models of good practice in organizations.

Counselling in organizations is a developing practice. Counsellors are found increasingly in, for instance, the workplace and GP surgeries, both comparatively new counselling contexts. In addition, traditional counselling agencies and established services are operating in a new and stringent economic climate. Where the public sector still employs counsellors – schools, colleges, universities, health and social services – counsellors may have to demonstrate their worth in the 'internal market', or tender for the work. Counsellors need to be aware and increasingly skilled in working in this, for many of them, non-traditional culture. In addition, they need to hold true to what is unique and valuable in their own tradition. So, too, supervisors need to be attuned to the stress and the opportunities of this climate. They should keep in mind the way in which such settings allow additional people to have access to counselling at times of change, confusion or distress, people who might otherwise never think of going to a counsellor, but who can, often, benefit from quite brief work, and clients, too, who could not afford private counselling or psychotherapy. At the same time, supervisors need to be aware of the cost to counsellors of complex and pressurized work settings, and be prepared to support them in keeping professional faith with themselves and their clients.

What is needed of supervisors in this climate is only just being thought and talked about, conceptualized and researched. Together, supervisors and counsellors are researchers and conceptualizers. If their experience is to benefit clients, organizations and the counselling profession, they both need to find forums to share their experience with like-minded colleagues.

References

Bond, Tim (1993) *Standards and Ethics for Counselling in Action*. London: Sage.
British Association for Counselling (1992) *Code of Ethics for Counsellors*. Rugby: BAC.
British Association for Counselling (1995) *Code of Ethics and Practice for Supervisors of Counsellors*. Rugby: BAC.
Carroll, C. (1994) 'Building bridges: a study of employee counsellors in the private sector', MSc dissertation. City University, London.
Carroll, M. (1996) *Counselling Supervision: Theory, Skills and Practice*. London: Cassell.
Carroll, M. (1996) *Workplace Counselling: A Systematic Approach to Employee Care*. London: Sage.
Inskipp, Francesca and Proctor, Brigid (1993) *Making the Most of Supervision*. Twickenham: Cascade Publications.
Inskipp, Francesca and Proctor, Brigid (1995) *Becoming a Supervisor*. Twickenham: Cascade.

Index